THOSE WHO HOLD BASTOGNE

PETER SCHRIJVERS

THOSE WHO HOLD

BASTOGNE

The True Story of the Soldiers and Civilians Who
Fought in the Biggest Battle of the Bulge

YALE UNIVERSITY PRESS
NEW HAVEN AND LONDON

For information about this and other Yale University Press publications, please contact:

U.S. Office: sales.press@yale.edu   www.yalebooks.com
Europe Office: sales@yaleup.co.uk   www.yalebooks.co.uk

Typeset in Minion Pro by IDSUK (DataConnection) Ltd
Printed in the United States of America.

Library of Congress Cataloging-in-Publication Data

Schrijvers, Peter, 1963–
    Those who hold Bastogne: the true story of the Soldiers and Civilians
who fought in the biggest battle of the bulge / Peter Schrijvers.
    pages cm
Includes bibliographical references and index.
ISBN 978-0-300-17902-6 (alk. paper)
1. Ardennes, Battle of the, 1944–1945. I. Title.
D756.5.A7S34 2014
940.54′519348—dc23

                                                                2014006368

A catalogue record for this book is available from the British Library.

10 9 8 7 6 5 4 3 2 1

For Tom
That on occasion he may travel to Bastogne and remember his uncle

Thus, in the days of fables, after the floods and deluges, there came forth from the soil armed men who exterminated each other.

MONTESQUIEU
De l'esprit des lois

CONTENTS

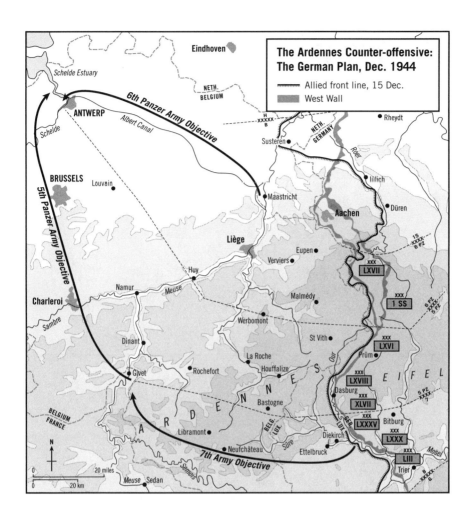

The Ardennes Counter-offensive:
The German Plan, Dec. 1944

Allied front line, 15 Dec.
West Wall

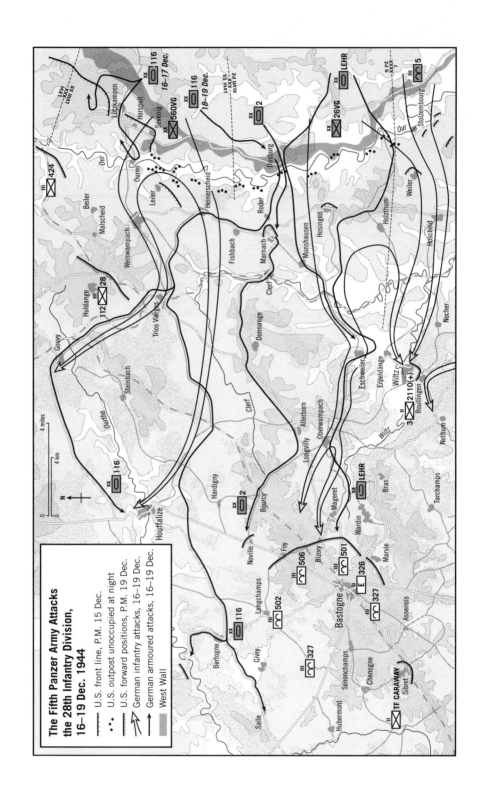

The Fifth Panzer Army Attacks
the 28th Infantry Division,
16–19 Dec. 1944

U.S. front line, P.M. 15 Dec.

U.S. outpost unoccupied at night

U.S. forward positions, P.M. 19 Dec.

German infantry attacks, 16–19 Dec.

German armoured attacks, 16–19 Dec.

West Wall

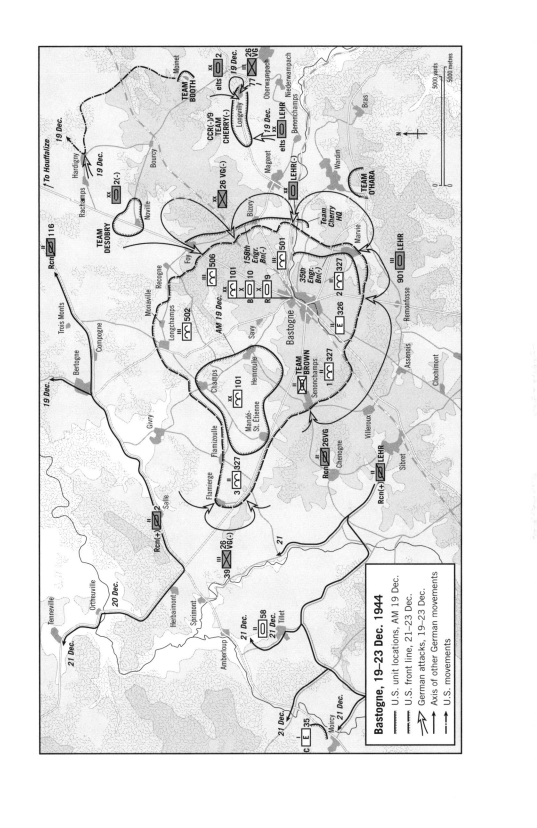

Bastogne, 19–23 Dec. 1944

Legend:
- U.S. unit locations, AM 19 Dec.
- U.S. front line, 21–23 Dec.
- German attacks, 21–23 Dec.
- Axis of other German movements
- U.S. movements

Place names and labels:
Moinet, TEAM BOOTH, To Houffalize, 19 Dec., Hardigny, Rachamps, Noville, Bourcy, 26 VG, Oberwampach, Niederwampach, Benonchamps, Longvilly, CCR(-)/9 TEAM CHERRY(-), LEHR, Mageret, LEHR(-), Bras, Wardin, TEAM O'HARA, TEAM DESOBRY, Bizory, Foy, Recogne, Monaville, Marvie, Team Cherry HQ, 501, 506, 158th Engr. Bn(-), 101, B 10, R 9, Saw, 35th Engr. Bn(-), 326, 327, 901 LEHR, Remonfosse, Longchamps, 502, AM 19 Dec., Bastogne, Assenois, Clochimont, Champs, 101, Hemroulle, Mandé-St. Etienne, TEAM BROWN, Senonchamps, 327, Villeroux, Givry, Compogne, Bertogne, Trois Monts, Flamizoulle, Flamierge, 327, Chenogne, 26VG, LEHR, Sibret, Salle, 2, 26 VG(-), 39, Ortheuville, Sprimont, Herbaimont, Amberloup, Tillet, 58, 35, Moircy, Tenneville

Dates on roads: 19 Dec., 20 Dec., 21 Dec.

N (compass, pointing up)

0 5000 yards
0 5000 metres

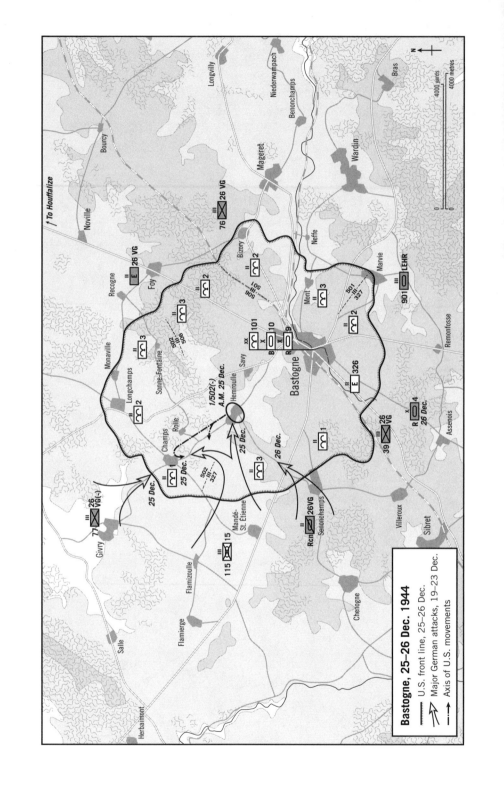

Bastogne, 25–26 Dec. 1944

U.S. front line, 25–26 Dec.
Major German attacks, 19–23 Dec.
Axis of U.S. movements

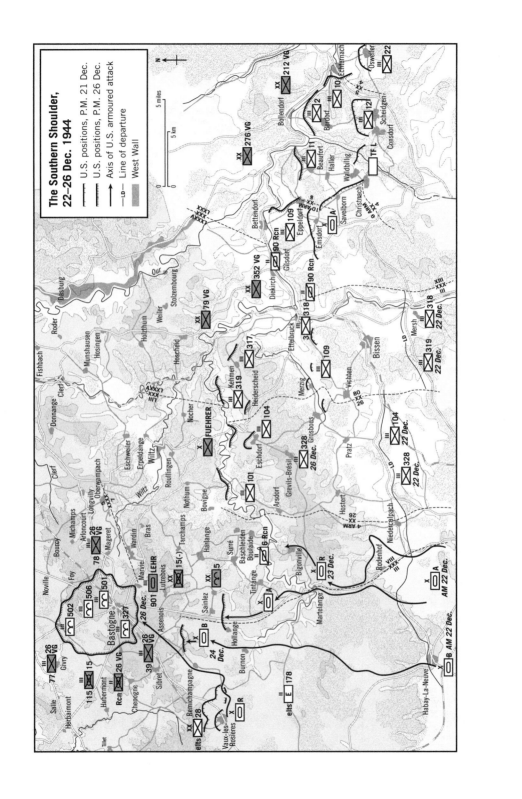

The Southern Shoulder, 22–26 Dec. 1944

U.S. positions, P.M. 21 Dec.
U.S. positions, P.M. 26 Dec.
Axis of U.S. armoured attack
—LD— Line of departure
West Wall

N

5 miles

5 km

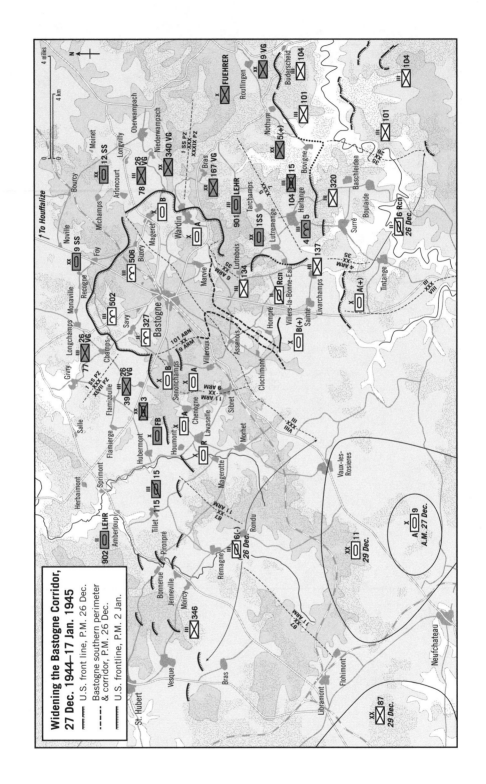

**Widening the Bastogne Corridor,
27 Dec. 1944–17 Jan. 1945**

U.S. front line, P.M. 26 Dec.

Bastogne southern perimeter
& corridor, P.M. 26 Dec.

U.S. frontline, P.M. 2 Jan.

4 miles

4 km

N

↑ To Houffalize

St. Hubert

Vesque

Bras

Moircy

Jenneville

Bonnerue

Pironpré

Remagne

Libramont

Flohimont

Neufchâteau

Vaux-les-
Rosières

Amberloup

Herbaimont

Spirmont

Hubermont

Flamierge

Salle

Givry

Longchamps

Monaville

Recogne

Foy

Noville

Bourcy

Michamps

Arloncourt

Longvilly

Moinet

Oberwampach

Niederwampach

Routlingen

Buderscheid

Nothum

Baschleiden

Boulaide

Surré

Tintange

Lvarchamps

Sainte

Hompré

Villers-la-Bonne-Eau

Lutremange

Lutrebos

Harlange

Bovigne

Tarchamps

Marvie

Wardin

Mageret

Bizory

Bastogne

Savy

Champs

Flamizoulle

Senonchamps

Villeroux

Chenogne

Lavaselle

Mortet

Sibret

Clochimont

Assenois

Magerotte

Rondu

Tillet

87
XX
11 ARM

87
XX
11 ARM

LEHR ▮▮ 902

▮▮ 115 15

III △ 346

6(−) 26 Dec.

XX 87 29 Dec.

A.M. 27 Dec. A ☐ 9 X

XX 11 29 Dec.

▮ 3 X ▮ A

FB ▮ A

X R

X O

X ☐ A

X ☐ B
101 ABN
9 ARM

III △ 327

III △ 502

III △ 506

9 SS XX

26 VG XX 77

39 XX 26 VG

LEHR III 901

1 SS XX

134 III

35 5
6 ARM

B(−) X ☐

A(+) ☐ X
4 ARM
VIII

137 III

4 5

320 III

15 III 104

167 VG XX

Bras

78 XX 26 VG

340 VG XX

12 SS XX

FUEHRER XX x

9 VG XX

104 III

101 III

101 III

104 III

16 Rcn 26 Dec.

Rcn ▮▮

1 SS PZ
XXXX
XLVII PZ

1 SS PZ
XXXX
XXXIX PZ

11 ARM
XX
9 ARM

INTRODUCTION

On January 12, 1945, the already legendary General George S. Patton wrote triumphantly in his diary, "I believe that the Bastogne operation is the biggest and best the Third Army has accomplished." "I hope," he went on, "the troops get the credit for their great work." At the time of writing it was becoming clear that at last the tide had been turned against the powerful German armies in the Ardennes salient. Bastogne, a small town tucked away in the densely forested southeastern corner of Belgium, was still playing a pivotal role in what the Americans would soon be calling the Battle of the Bulge.[1]

The Battle of the Bulge has been described as one of "the two most critical tests of the Army of the United States in World War II." The other one was, of course, D-Day and the Normandy campaign. Operation Overlord was an offensive campaign that aimed at gaining a foothold in Hitler's Fortress Europe. The campaign in the Ardennes, on the other hand, was very much a defensive one, a desperate attempt to halt the German armies as they tried to split the Western Front in two. Although British commanders and troops played important roles in the Ardennes, the operations against the salient were overwhelmingly American in nature; indeed, in terms of both manpower and geography, it was the largest single action of the American army in World War II.[2]

The German counteroffensive that began on December 16, 1944, was "a desperate affair that flowed from desperate circumstances." The Allies had captured Rome on the eve of D-Day in June 1944. The summer had seen Allied armies break out of Normandy and hurl themselves against the West Wall. The mighty Soviet armies had been steamrolling the Eastern Front and were already making deep inroads in Hungary and Poland. In early autumn, the Allied logistical lines had begun to feel the strain, causing the pressure on Nazi Germany to ease somewhat. But Hitler knew that, at the first sign of spring in 1945, the Allies would resume their unforgiving push and deal his Third Reich its deathblow.[3]

In mid-September 1944, Hitler surprised his generals with the momentous news that he had decided to launch a massive counterattack on the Western Front. The ambitious objectives of Operation Wacht am Rhein were to regain the strategic initiative, inflict a humiliating defeat, and force the American and British belligerents into a negotiated peace. As soon as that happened, Germany would be allowed to throw all its remaining force against its mortal Soviet enemy in the east. The Führer was convinced that the gamble was worth the risk. An ardent admirer of Frederick the Great, Hitler was well aware that the formidable coalition that had threatened to crush Prussia in the Seven Years' War had ultimately collapsed under the strains of war. He therefore designed his counteroffensive in such a manner that it would strike at the seam between the American military and the British–Canadian 21st Army Group in the Low Countries. German armies would smash through the Ardennes in Belgium and Luxembourg, cross the Meuse River, and finally capture Antwerp, the Allies' most vital port in Western Europe. If the plan succeeded, Hitler reasoned, it was certain to cause logistical nightmares and political recriminations that the American–British coalition on the Western Front might not survive.[4]

The Ardennes formed the obvious place for the Germans to launch their offensive. A rugged and densely forested region with few good roads, it was hardly an environment conducive to large-scale armored warfare. But that was, of course, exactly what would create surprise. In fact, the Germans had already mounted successful attacks through the Ardennes in 1914 and 1940. Moreover, intelligence had by now established that the Allies refused to believe that lightning could strike in the same place three times: in the autumn of 1944, the Ardennes formed an American sector where inexperienced "green" divisions trained and battered forces caught their breath.

The German build-up for the offensive began as soon as Hitler had made his decision. As early as the end of September, combat units were being siphoned off from the Western and Eastern Fronts for the daring strike through the Ardennes. That all this could happen without the Allies realizing German intentions constitutes one of the great intelligence failures of World War II. In part the explanation lies in strict German security measures. These included, among many others, the avoidance of radio traffic – a decision that made it impossible for the Allies to rely on the hugely successful

ULTRA decryptions of high-level military commands. Ultimately, however, the intelligence that was available was misread for the simple reason that the Allies refused to believe that the Germans by the end of 1944 were still capable of any offensive effort on the scale that they were soon to demonstrate.[5]

Surprise was total on the morning of December 16. Some 200,000 German troops smashed into the thin American lines with the support of 500 tanks and 1,900 artillery pieces and rocket launchers. On the first day of the offensive, the Germans enjoyed a three-to-one advantage in manpower, a two-to-one advantage in tanks, and general superiority in artillery. Even then it took some time for the Allied commanders to gauge the massive scale and ambition of the German offensive. By the third day, the width of the salient stood at 47 miles. On the tenth day, the Germans reached their deepest penetration, some 60 miles, before having their armored spearheads blunted within sight of the Meuse. After losing the initiative, the Germans continued to fight ferociously, drawing in ever more of the opponents' forces as the Blitzkrieg now became a war of attrition. All in all, Hitler committed some 410,000 men to the offensive, as well as 1,400 tanks and assault guns, 2,600 artillery pieces and rocket launchers, and just over 1,000 combat aircraft. By the time the enemy was pushed out of the bulge, General Dwight D. Eisenhower, the Supreme Allied Commander, had thrown almost 600,000 troops into the massive gap.[6]

"The odds were against it," one historian has remarked, "and the odds prevailed." Despite initial panic and Churchill calling on Stalin at the start of January to speed up the Soviet offensive to help relieve the pressure in the bulge, Patton early on read the German effort for what it was: the dying carp's "last flip" of the tail. In the midst of daunting two-front warfare and punishing air offensives, the German military build-up was remarkable. But Hitler had to scrape the bottom of the barrel to make it possible. There was, by contrast, no end to the number of barrels and crates and boxes that continued to arrive from the United States in response to the crisis. Unhampered by constant air war, displaying the efficiency that had made the country the economic envy of the world before the Great Depression, factories in the United States churned out the ammunition, trucks, tanks, and aircraft that the Germans could now no longer replace. America's industrial superiority was decisive in a battle that destroyed an estimated 800 tanks on either side. A week after the start of the offensive, the Americans had brought into position no fewer than 4,155 pieces of artillery; by January 3, they had fired a stupefying 1,255,000 artillery rounds. Equally important, American oil wells were providing crude in vast amounts at a time when the Germans had lost access to crucial oil reserves with the fall of Romania to the Soviets.[7]

By the same token, the Americans were finding it easier to mobilize replacements for casualties. By the start of 1945, German commanders had to make do with false promises. By mid-January 1945, Patton had received enough new soldiers to replace all the losses suffered in his Third Army, plus 6,000 more. These were critical advantages in the Battle of the Bulge, which ground down troops at horrendous rates: roughly 81,000 casualties (dead, wounded, captured, and missing) in American ranks, and an estimated 81,000 to 104,000 troops lost by the Germans.[8]

In the epic battle that unfolded in the Ardennes, it was by no means clear from the start that Bastogne was to play such a pivotal role. In one way, of course, the very fact that the biggest Battle of the Bulge ended up being fought for this town is a measure of German failure, given that Hitler's ultimate objectives were located on the far side of the Meuse River and not in the Ardennes. From day one, Bastogne, a valuable road junction in a forested area, was unmistakably a key objective, but only for von Lüttwitz's XLVII Panzer Corps. That corps was the southernmost of three in von Manteuffel's Fifth Panzer Army. Von Manteuffel's army was the center one of three attacking armies. It was, however, not the force that was to make the main effort. Hitler had entrusted responsibility for the decisive blow in the Ardennes to the northernmost force, the Sixth Panzer Army. This army was under the command of party faithful Sepp Dietrich and comprised a dozen divisions, four of which were elite Waffen SS panzer divisions. Dietrich's troops were to cross the Meuse between Huy and Liège, push on to Brussels, and then capture the ultimate prize of Antwerp. Although von Manteuffel was under orders to cross the Meuse at Namur with his Wehrmacht armor, his primary responsibility was to shield the Sixth Panzer Army as soon as it was across that river. In the southern part of the bulge, Brandenberger's Seventh Army, the weakest of the three armies, was to protect von Manteuffel's left flank.

But already in the first week of the offensive, the German game plan was derailed in dramatic fashion when it became clear that the formidable Sixth Panzer Army was not getting anywhere. American divisions were hurriedly siphoned off from the offensive against the Roer dams and massive artillery formations were soon helping to protect the northern shoulder along the Elsenborn Ridge. *Kampfgruppe* Peiper of the 1st SS Panzer Division did break through, reaching all the way to La Gleize and Stoumont. A little later, the 2nd SS Panzer Division managed to strike as far as Manhay. But these were isolated penetrations, and shortly after Christmas both had fizzled out completely.

The result was that the *Schwerpunkt* of the German attack shifted to the Fifth Panzer Army in the salient's center. That was particularly true when, on December 20, von Manteuffel's armored spearheads plunged into a gaping breach around Houffalize. Now, suddenly, two small towns and road junctions became vitally important for the outcome of the Battle of the Bulge: Bastogne and Saint Vith. For several days, American armor and infantry at Saint-Vith had valiantly fought off the onslaught with an eye to jamming the northern shoulder of von Manteuffel's breakthrough. But on December 21 the pressure finally became too much and the Americans were forced to abandon the town. In Bastogne, however, they held on against the odds. Parts of the 28th Infantry and 9th Armored Divisions had been sacrificed to delay the Germans long enough east of Bastogne in order to allow the 101st Airborne Division and various smaller units to slip into town before the Germans closed the net on December 21. All eyes were now on the Americans in Bastogne, because they alone remained in a position to continue to dam up and slow down von Manteuffel's forces along the southern shoulder of the breakthrough. Stubborn courage and determination made Bastogne's defenders hold out against four divisions – two elite panzer divisions, one Panzergrenadier division, and one Volksgrenadier division – long enough for Patton's juggernaut Third Army to reach them from the south on December 26.[9]

By that time, the German Ardennes offensive had reached its high-water mark. On December 23, the dismal ashen skies had cleared to a bright blue, allowing the tremendous power of Allied air superiority to be unleashed. Von Manteuffel's tank crews had come within sight of the Meuse at about the same time, but they never crossed the river. American and British armor blocked their way, and fighter-bombers finished them off. Saint-Vith paid a terrible price for its capture by the Germans: on December 25 and 26, more than 350 Allied bombers erased the town from the map to deny von Manteuffel's troops use of the Belgian road junction. As the initiative shifted back to the Allies at last, Bastogne became still more important to both sides. Hitler now wanted it captured to prevent Patton from using the road junction as a catapult from which to launch his Third Army deep into the salient. When that plan failed, too, Hitler ordered his troops to fight tooth and nail for the N15 highway leading north from Bastogne to Houffalize, the town where the Third Army had a rendezvous with the First Army, which began pushing down from the north early in January.[10]

German commanders understood that, even if the offensive was lost, they could at least grind down as many American troops as possible at Bastogne, while gradually and grudgingly pulling out of the bulge. In January's war of attrition, Bastogne became an even stronger magnet for troops. The Waffen SS was sent down from Dietrich's northern sector. Outfits from the German strategic reserve were rushed to the Belgian town. Advance spearhead units pulling out of the nose of the bulge formed dense armored shields north of the road junction. Patton responded in kind, sending in additional airborne, armored, and infantry divisions, some of them so green that they arrived straight from training camps in England. In support of the hard-pressed troops in and around Bastogne, Third Army artillery pounded the Germans with some 850,000 shells. The battle for Bastogne finally came to an end exactly one month after it had begun, when Patton's men linked up with First Army forces at Houffalize on January 16. By that time, the fight for the small Ardennes town of 4,000 inhabitants and seven roads had involved some 120,000 American soldiers and more than 130,000 German troops.[11]

*   *   *

On July 16, 1950, throngs of Belgians and Americans, among them many officials and reporters, gathered to witness the unveiling of the Mardasson Memorial. This is a massive tribute to the American soldiers who defended the Belgians against the return of the armies of Nazi Germany in December 1944 and January 1945. On a plateau hewn from Ardennes rock stands a towering structure in the shape of a five-pointed star. The monument is 39 feet high, and each of the star's arms pointing at the surrounding landscape is 102 feet long. In giant relief, the names of 48 American states are displayed in alphabetical order at the top of the inner and outer crown. On 90 supporting columns are listed all the American units that were involved in the Battle of the Bulge. Ten immense panels sum up the history of war in the Ardennes. On a memorial stone at the center of the star's circular atrium, an inscription in Latin states what is obvious: "The Belgian People Remember Their American Liberators."

The location of the Mardasson Memorial is Bastogne. It sits on a hill just northeast of the town where, on December 19, the Germans came so close to breaching the fragile American lines. It was soil from this corner of Bastogne that, on July 4, 1946, Belgian officials gently scooped into a carefully crafted box of ebony wood. The box was sealed and then lowered into a protective casing of malachite that carried the symbol of a smashed swastika. A Douglas DC-4 flew it from Brussels to New York via Newfoundland. In a solemn ceremony in Washington, D.C., the Belgian ambassador respectfully handed it over to President Harry Truman.[12]

Bastogne is an American and World War II icon. Yet in the rich literature on the Battle of the Bulge, no one has ever before attempted to devote a separate book to the battle for the Belgian town from December 16 all the way to its official end on January 16 – certainly not on the basis of American, German, and Belgian sources. This is the story of Bastogne's long winter of war. The story of the Americans, Germans, and Belgians who perished in the battle or emerged from it with their lives forever marked by the bitter experience.

CHAPTER 1

LIVES FOR TIME

"So Willie is in the Infantry!" Paul Yearout sounded both incredulous and apprehensive in the letter to his wife in Georgia. "I hope he doesn't have to come over here," he confided, "because this is a rough, rugged life, and I don't believe Willie could take it." "Sometimes," he confessed, "I begin to wonder about myself."

By now Paul Yearout knew a few things about life in the infantry. The university graduate was a lieutenant in the 110th Regiment of the 28th Infantry Division. Less than a month before, Pennsylvania's National Guard division, ominously known as "The Bloody Bucket" because of its distinctive red shoulder patch, had gone through the worst experience of the war so far. In November 1944, it had been sent into the dense Hürtgen Forest that shielded the German border south and east of Aachen. Hemmed in as they were by an experienced enemy dominating the high ground, the battle for soggy roads and decrepit villages had gone from bad to worse for the Americans. Some would later blame the disaster on the GIs' commanders, from the division level all the way up to the highest echelons. But the foot soldiers did not have the faintest idea of who was to blame for what they had been put through. All they knew was that, by the time they were withdrawn, the battle for the somber German forest had become "synonymous with futility in war" at a human cost that was staggering. One of their opponents in the ferocious battle, General Rudolf von Gersdorff, a veteran of combat on both the Western and the Eastern Front, claimed the fighting was "the heaviest I have ever witnessed." In a matter of weeks, two-thirds of Paul Yearout's regiment had been wiped out. Twelve hundred of his 3,200 comrades had ended up as battle casualties. Another 890 had fallen victim to trench foot, combat exhaustion, and sickness. "You are right about the missing link from

Nov. 12th to Nov. 21st," Paul continued in the letter to his wife Mimi. "I couldn't write during that time as I was in the thick of it up in the Hürtgen Forest. It was just plain Hell and I'll tell you about it some of these days."

In civilian life, the science graduate had been employed as a chemist by the DuPont Company, at its plant in Waynesboro, Virginia. Just months before the Japanese attack on Pearl Harbor and America's entry into World War II, it had transferred him to the Remington Arms branch in Missouri. Ordnance work was a vital part of the war effort on the home front. Still, in March 1943, married and the father of two small children, Paul had decided that his country needed him even more in the front lines overseas and had relinquished his military service deferment. It had been the start of a stressful nomadic life that had taken Paul and his family to training camps in Georgia and Texas, before abruptly whisking him off to war in Europe.

The wrenching experience in the Hürtgen Forest had left its mark on Lieutenant Yearout, as it had on all those lucky enough to survive the ordeal. The bespectacled officer tried to sound light-hearted in a message to his three-year-old son as he reached the end of his letter. "Tell Pete," he joked to his wife, "I had a good time yesterday chasing Jerries from Pillbox to Pillbox." But Mimi no doubt sensed the depth of his gloom when he made a clumsy attempt to put her mind at ease. "I'll be O.K.," he insisted, "and if I ever should get injured, it would probably be a break for me."

"I love you so much darling," Lieutenant Yearout wrote in closing, "and would give anything if this mess were all over and we could live normal lives again." The American managed to take at least some comfort from the fact that just recently colder weather had caused the ground to freeze a little. "Before long," he predicted, "tanks will be able to roll – then look out Jerry!!"

Lieutenant Yearout placed the long letter to his wife in an envelope and carefully sealed it on Friday night, December 15, 1944. Little did he know that, in a matter of hours, German tanks would be rolling through the front lines, making the normal lives that he and his comrades were dreaming of appear further away than at any other time during the war.[1]

1

Following the debacle in the Hürtgen Forest, the 28th Infantry Division, mauled and dispirited, had been withdrawn to allow veterans to rest and recover while replacements strengthened the badly depleted ranks. Lieutenant Yearout and his comrades had been sent to what was known to be a relatively quiet sector along the Luxembourg border with Germany. There they had come under the control of VIII Corps on November 20. The corps commander, General Troy Middleton, was operating his headquarters from the sleepy Belgian crossroads town of Bastogne, some 16 miles to their rear. Middleton was an affable, mild-mannered southerner. The fifth of nine children, the 55-year-old general had grown up on a 400-acre plantation in Copiah County, Mississippi. Now, stationed in the Belgian Ardennes in winter, he fondly remembered his Dixie upbringing: the sweltering summers, punctuated by the powerful sermons of Baptist preachers; the long days of hunting, catching catfish, and horseback riding; tables laden with cornbread, grits, collards, and black-eyed peas. The general, who looked more like a university professor with his round, thin-rimmed glasses, had been ordered to hold no less than 85 miles of the grim German West Wall with his corps. The area extended southward from the Losheim Gap, along a large stretch of the west bank of the Sûre and Moselle rivers. It left the Mississippian no other option than to spread his troops very thinly along this massive length of front.[2]

Where standard tactics prescribed the assignment of a front of 4–5 miles to a division, the 28th Infantry Division was told to settle down along a vast stretch of 28 miles. Their frontline terrain ran from Lützkampen in Germany, just north of the Luxembourg border, to an area south of the Luxembourg town of Vianden. This exceptional situation made any defense in depth impossible. General Dutch Cota was forced to place all his division's three infantry regiments in the front line, leaving only the most minimal of reserves at their backs, to offer support in case of an enemy attack in force. Even then it still proved impossible to build a continuous defensive line. Instead, troops were concentrated in village strong points that were connected by no more than roving patrols.[3]

The command post of the 110th Infantry Regiment to which Lieutenant Yearout belonged was set up in Clervaux, a Luxembourg town separated from the German West Wall and front line by no more than five miles. The regimental commander, 50-year-old Colonel Hurley Fuller, belonged in a category of his own. A Texan, he came from a broken home and, at the age of 20, had made the army his surrogate family. As a young lieutenant, he had seen action in the Argonne Forest during World War I. The horrors of trench warfare had left him permanently scarred. Moreover, his cantankerous manner and lack of political skills had made him few friends. When the regiment he commanded in the 2nd Infantry Division had become hopelessly stuck in the hedgerow country of Normandy in the summer of 1944, his commanders had relieved him on the spot. He owed his current job with the

110th Infantry to General Middleton. Middleton had known Fuller since World War I. He had placed the Texan at the head of the regiment when its regular commander was hospitalized with shrapnel wounds during the battle for the Hürtgen Forest.[4]

Now, in December 1944, Colonel Fuller had more reason than ever to feel frustrated and sullen. His regiment, placed at the center of the 28th Infantry Division's front, was made responsible for a full 10 miles of the 28 miles of front line. To make matters worse, of the three infantry regiments in the line, his had been selected to give up a full battalion that was to operate as a divisional reserve force. The 2nd Battalion, Lieutenant Yearout's outfit, had been taken out of the line and sent to the town of Donnange in the rear, just west of Clervaux. All that remained now were the 1st Battalion to cover the regiment's left flank and the 3rd Battalion to man the right flank. As was happening elsewhere in the division, each of Fuller's two battalions established a handful of village strong points. In Fuller's sector, these were perched on a ridge that ran parallel to the Clerf River somewhat farther to the west and the Our River that it overlooked immediately to the east. On the other side of the Our River loomed the West Wall, and behind it a German enemy that had, for some time now, remained uncharacteristically quiet. The American regiment's key strong points were those villages that were connected by a road running along the ridge. The road's impressive view, as well as its quality, remarkable in this densely forested area, had prompted American soldiers to dub it the Skyline Drive.[5]

On the other side of the West Wall, the spectacle of the Our River, and of the ridge and scenic road just beyond it, was causing few poetic stirrings among the Germans. They were all businesslike and were determined to keep their frantic activity hidden from American view. For several weeks now, they had steadily and secretly been building up a massive force in front of General Middleton's men. The Fifth Panzer Army, the middle one of three German armies poised to execute Hitler's counteroffensive in the West, dwarfed an American force that was of mere corps size and composed of troops that were either in desperate need of rest or dangerously raw. The reputation of the German army commander was just as massive. General von Manteuffel was so small and fragile-looking that his friends had come to nickname him "*Kleiner*" – "Little One." But his wiry frame harbored an iron will and a sharp intellect. Hasso Eccard von Manteuffel was born into one of the oldest noble families of Prussia. He had performed very impressively as commander of the elite Panzergrenadier Division "Grossdeutschland" on the

Eastern Front. So much so that the Führer had called him to Germany to promote him, not to corps commander, but to leader of the entire Fifth Panzer Army.[6]

The XLVII Panzer Corps formed the steel fist of von Manteuffel's army. It was designed to smash a hole through the weak defensive line of Fuller's 110th Infantry, capture the vital road center of Bastogne, 19 miles west of the German frontier, and then steal across the Meuse River upstream from Namur. The 26th Volksgrenadier Division brought up the infantrymen for the offensive. This seasoned division had participated in the invasion of France in 1940. Committed to the Eastern Front from the outset in 1941, it had been destroyed and rebuilt several times in the course of the Russian campaign. In September 1944, the badly mauled division had been pulled out of the Vistula front south of Warsaw, to be reorganized once again. Early in November, the infantrymen, under the command of Colonel Heinz Kokott, had been moved to the Eifel region, the German border area with Luxembourg. Here they were left impressed by the sight of large numbers of laborers from all over Europe and Russia hard at work strengthening the homeland's West Wall. Kokott's men, a force of more than 10,000, were soon reinforced with a backbone of two elite armored divisions, the 2nd Panzer Division and the Panzer Lehr Division, both of which had fought ferociously during the Normandy campaign. "During the days the Eifel roads were lifeless and deserted," one of Kokott's regimental officers noted, "and it was not until nightfall that obscure, cautious and silent movement set in." "Huge quantities of ammunition, all well-camouflaged," the German officer observed, "were dumped everywhere. Guns were placed in the forests and long columns of vehicles on the edges." By mid-December, a massive concentration of tanks "extended far back into the hinterland."

Even so, the Germans refused to be lulled into a false sense of security. The Volksgrenadiers, who had made their way from the Eastern Front to the West Wall in November, struggled to forget scenes of the horrific destruction wrought by Allied bombing raids in their homeland. On December 12, Colonel Kokott attended a final conference on the offensive at Hitler's head-quarters. He returned to his troops rattled by the image of a Führer "in poor health and physically in poor condition." Fritz Bayerlein, commander of the Panzer Lehr Division, was well aware that his outfit was nowhere near full readiness. He had seen his armored force virtually destroyed in Normandy and had been forced to abandon its rebuilding when ordered to join a coun-terattack against Patton's Third Army in the Saar region just recently. One of his tank battalions was missing, as it was still being reorganized far to the rear. Most of his replacement artillery pieces had arrived without the towing vehicles – the prime movers. One battalion of infantry had no mortars and very few machine guns. Bayerlein estimated that his division was down to 60 percent of standard troop strength, 60 percent of artillery, 40 percent of tanks and tank destroyers, and 40 percent of other weapons.

At the same time, German troops took much courage from the quality and experience of the senior and junior officers who were to join them in the front lines. Not just von Manteuffel, but von Lüttwitz too, the commander of the XLVII Corps, was a dyed-in-the-wool professional soldier. Fritz Bayerlein, who had served under legendary commanders like Guderian and Rommel, brimmed with confidence and charisma. Kokott worried about the uneven quality of the replacement NCOs, but he was confident about his officers. "The regimental and battalion commanders," he noted, "as well as the company commanders were those officers who had proven themselves time and again during the Russian Campaign and who knew their stuff." Kokott also took heart from the fact that, although many of his infantry replacements were drawn from navy and air force personnel and lacked combat experience, he had seen for himself that they were "fresh, healthy young men of great willingness." Bayerlein, too, conceded that "despite inadequate equipment and practically uninterrupted combat," his armored force of almost 13,000 men demonstrated an "aggressive spirit." "Attack," he commented smugly, "suits the German troops better than defense." By mid-December, with each GI in the 110th Infantry's sector facing ten enemy soldiers poised for the attack, the odds were decidedly in Germany's favor.[7]

The Americans of the 110th Infantry thought of their thinly held front line more as a ghost sector than a quiet sector. They were stationed in the less densely populated northern area of the Grand Duchy of Luxembourg. Known to locals as the Oesling, the region was one of deep valleys, forested hills, and windswept castle ruins, which bore testimony to the long and turbulent history of a region wedged between armed European rivals. The atmosphere was made even more eerie by the almost total absence of civilians in towns and villages along the sector's front line: as the Allied offensive had come to a halt in front of the West Wall early in the autumn of 1944, the Americans had ordered them to evacuate, together with many thousands of other Luxembourgers inhabiting the forward settlements along the Our, Sûre, and Moselle rivers.[8]

Exceptions were made only for a very few civilians with special passes, who were allowed to tend crops during certain hours. Lieutenant Thomas

Myers was pleasantly surprised one day when at last he caught sight of three Luxembourgers in a field while on patrol with I Company in the village of Weiler. It had been no longer than three months since he had been rushed to Europe from New York on board a ship carrying some ten thousand replacements. In that brief time, he had first served as a replacement with the 5th Armored Division at the Siegfried Line near Aachen. Shortly after, he had been assigned as a permanent replacement with the 28th Infantry Division during the battle for the Hürtgen Forest. These had been jarring experiences, and the lieutenant ached for his wife and two-year-old daughter back home. He and his men halted to check the passes of the young man and his two sisters. Lieutenant Myers was happy to strike up a conversation with people not wearing a uniform for a change. But the language barrier made any meaningful exchange of thoughts difficult. The Americans made up for it by generously handing out army ration chocolate bars – D bars – and chewing gum. Lieutenant Myers was intrigued when the elder girl walked away, beckoning him to follow her to a corner of the field. The young woman invited him to sit down. She took a thick sandwich of homemade bread and bacon from a lunch basket. Then she joined him on the ground, handed him a large piece of the sandwich, and encouraged him to tell her more about his family and life in America. The lieutenant never forgot the woman's kind gesture.[9]

Nights in the 110th Infantry's sector were still lonelier. They left ample time for veterans to relive bad memories and for replacements to dream of how they might react to their baptism of fire. They also, however, caused old hands and newcomers alike to focus on any sounds drifting in from the German lines across the river that seemed even slightly suspect. However cautiously and silently the Germans went about their business, tense GIs reported the distinct sounds of people moving about in the chill December nights, of horses whinnying, and engines humming. Darkness was also when patrols were most likely to take prisoners and when would-be deserters seized their opportunity. Back in the regiment's Headquarters Company in Clervaux, a sergeant interrogating prisoners with the help of an interpreter was alerted by a significant shift in the Germans' demeanor. "They were very smug and very confident," he noted, "so we sort of sensed something was in the air." Quite a few deserters were sending out even clearer warnings. GIs in a foxhole near Hosingen told a German soldier who had just fled to their lines to sit down on a tree stump. "He could talk good English," one of the men of K Company remembered. "He said he was a school teacher. He was about twenty-five, thirty, years old. He had had enough. He said he was gonna get the hell out of it. He said there was gonna be a big push before Christmas." The GIs handed the deserter over to their company commander and never heard any more about it. Reports on all this did move through the chain of command, and all the way up to the desks of intelligence officers at the highest levels. But the weather was too bad for aerial reconnaissance to establish a clear picture of any serious threat that might be brewing. More importantly, there existed a firmly entrenched conviction at all levels of command that the battered Germans now lacked the capacity and audacity to launch a major offensive in this rugged area. As a result, fragments filtering in from the front lines were regarded as just part of an avalanche of white noise, and far from sufficient to warrant any major alert.[10]

2

As Lieutenant Yearout sealed the envelope with the letter to his wife and children and tried to catch some sleep on the evening of Friday, December 15, nervous tension on the ghost front was mounting rapidly among guards in the forward foxholes. First they thought it strange that, unlike most previous nights, none of the enemy's flares were being fired over no man's land, leaving the stygian darkness intact. Then suddenly, in the middle of the night, their positions became bathed in a bright glare, as the enemy reflected searchlight beams off low-hanging clouds. GIs stared at the glare with open mouths as the dead silence sent chills running down their spines. Before long, some insisted they could hear humming noises in the distance, as if from vehicles on the move or machines at work. Even then, however, the guards failed to detect any movement as the German lines remained shrouded in the cold, black night.[11]

At 0530 on Saturday, December 16, puzzled observers called in from the water tower in Hosingen to report that in the German lines they were spotting "countless pinpoints of light." The GIs were still clarifying their observation when shells came crashing down all around them. The American observers had, in fact, just witnessed the flashes from the initial barrage that set in motion the massive German counteroffensive in the Ardennes. For the next half hour, 554 artillery pieces from von Lüttwitz's XLVII Panzer Corps mercilessly raked the front and rear lines of the 28th Infantry Division. "The *Nebelwerfers* howl like wild animals," a proud soldier of the 26th Volksgrenadier Division noted in his diary, "the thunder of the explosions resembles that of carpet bombing." The division's commander, a veteran of the Eastern Front, was equally impressed by the effect of the opening barrage. "Along the enemy front," wrote Heinz Kokott, "the clouds turned red with the flames of burning farm buildings."[12]

The element of surprise had a devastating effect in the American ranks. In Bourscheid, several miles to the rear, Corporal Clifford Iwig had come off guard duty in the 687th Field Artillery, a support battalion for the 110th Infantry, just in time to watch the cooks prepare breakfast. Minutes later, the first shell hit. The initial thought that flooded the corporal's mind was "one of the cooks' stoves blew up." It did not take long, however, for reality to sink in among troops up front at the Our River. Guards in foxholes were flabbergasted to see large groups of German infantrymen emerge from forests and gullies almost as soon as the shelling died down. They did not know that as early as 0300 that night, engineers in rubber boats had ferried assault companies and heavy infantry weapons across the river. These advance forces had stealthily infiltrated under cover of darkness to form a line of departure virtually touching the American garrison points. As early as 0615, barely 15 minutes after the churning barrage lifted, word reached the 110th Infantry headquarters at Clervaux that enemy troops were slicing through American lines.[13]

As dawn broke, more and more German soldiers flooded the American lines on the heels of the forward assault teams. "The initial pockets of resistance were stormed and overrun with assault rifles and cold steel," the commander of the 26th Volksgrenadier Division noted with grim satisfaction. "After a short period of time, the forward enemy line was torn open at many points along a broad front." Speed was of the essence in the German plan. Orders were to bypass and isolate American strong points and to continue moving west. The message had been drilled into troops at all levels that the first crucial objective in this sector was Bastogne and that this major crossroads had to be captured without delay. Von Lüttwitz, the hard-driving commander of the XLVII Panzer Corps, much admired for his daring and dash, had warned divisional commanders that, if they failed to take Bastogne, "it will always remain an ulcer on our lines of communication." "The corridor towards the West," Panzer Lehr's commander summed up the situation, "was too narrow without Bastogne." That is why, on the eve of the offensive, he had received clear orders, Bayerlein said, for "the sudden capture of Bastogne by a coup-de-main."[14]

As Horst Helmus moved up to the front with his anti-tank battalion at dawn, they too were told that, although the ultimate goal of the offensive was Antwerp, the first objective of the 26th Volksgrenadier Division was Bastogne. Helmus came from Gummersbach, near Cologne, and had just turned 18. He had never been in battle before, but he was caught up in the almost electric atmosphere of pride and confidence. At last, after long and humiliating months of having been on the run, German soldiers were able to strike back at their pursuers. And this time they were convinced they had the capacity to strike back hard. Their troop concentration was massive, their corridor narrow, the enemy lines thin and without any significant reserves. For veterans of the Eastern Front, moreover, the fact that the opponent was American was also reassuring. We felt, said one of them, "safe and superior." "I am so excited that I feel wound up," Horst Helmus scribbled in his diary as they pushed off. "The same goes for my comrades." Was this, he mused, "1940 or 1944?"[15]

For the Americans of the 110th Infantry, the predawn shock was followed by a day of mayhem. On the regiment's right flank, where the 3rd Battalion was dug in, Hosingen was soon bearing the brunt of the attack by Kokott's Volksgrenadiers. Defended by no more than the men of K Company and a small unit of engineers, the village, located on the Skyline Drive, overlooked two of the four main roads running east to west in the regiment's sector. At first the Volksgrenadiers were content to push past Hosingen, leaving the village "in the eye of the hurricane." From high up in the church tower, Captain William Jarrett, commander of the engineers, looked on in disbelief as Germans swarmed across the Skyline Drive on foot and on bicycles, horses pulling their artillery caissons. A map taken from a captured German officer soon revealed that Bastogne was their immediate objective. A runner was dispatched to report this to Colonel Fuller in Clervaux. He failed to break through the enemy lines, however. German troops were found to be massing west of Hosingen already, and the runner barely made it back to the village alive.

Observers in the church steeple and water tower began to call down mortar fire to try and slow the German advance. Ineffectual as these attempts were, they sufficed to remind the enemy that bypassed strong points would continue to be a thorn in the side. As the Americans strengthened the perimeter around the village, two German companies launched a frontal assault, coming down a gentle slope in the east. Mortars, machine guns, and rifles furiously fired salvos at the easy targets. "We slaughtered the shit out of 'em," one GI remarked dryly.

In the afternoon, however, the Germans completed a bridge over the Our at Gemünd that could carry heavy armor. By dusk, Mark IV tanks were joining the Volksgrenadiers in the battle for Hosingen. A handful of Sherman tanks, rushed to the village from the 28th Infantry Division's meager reserves, proved no match for the superior German vehicles. Artillery battalions in the division's rear were under so much pressure themselves that they could lay down only limited supporting fire. Still, the infantry and engineers in Hosingen stood fast. "The German infantry tried to enter the town but we were firing point-blank with all our weapons plus some anti-tank guns we had placed on the road into town," recalled Sergeant John Forsell. "We did a lot of damage."[16]

Frustration steadily mounted among the Germans. Enemy harassing fire had made it impossible to continue ignoring Hosingen as planned. Now unexpected resistance from the small force was delaying its capture. The enemy, Heinz Kokott grudgingly acknowledged, was "tough, stubborn, and death disdaining." More troops were rushed to the scene as darkness deepened. They brought flamethrowers and self-propelled guns to blast the Americans from the village. Kokott realized that the desperate fight of the Americans in his sector was more for time than for space. He also knew at the end of the first day that his timetable was in tatters, as his troops were nowhere near the east bank of the Clerf River, where they should have been.[17]

To the north of Hosingen, Colonel Meinrad von Lauchert learned a similar lesson that day, as his 2nd Panzer Division of nearly 13,000 men tore into the left flank of the 110th Infantry. His elite armored unit had fought the Allies tooth and nail all the way from Normandy to the German frontier. It had been rebuilt with quality replacement personnel, as well as the newest models of Panther tanks. But his troops, too, had to await the arrival of heavy armor until a sturdy bridge was completed at Dasburg in the afternoon. Until then, Panzergrenadiers who had been ferried across the Our in rubber boats before dawn were to clear the way. Marnach, a village on the main road from Dasburg to Clervaux and Bastogne, could not be allowed to form an obstacle to the arrival of the armor.

Marnach was held by no more than B Company and a tank destroyer platoon. Alerted by the ferocious predawn barrage, seasoned veterans had quickly herded heavily armed troops into foxholes on the village's outskirts to stave off the attack they were sure would follow. Their instinct had been right. As daylight filtered through and the mist lifted, hundreds of Panzergrenadiers were spotted emerging from the woods. The American defenders opened up with all the firepower available to them. Moreover, they managed to get artillery battalions in their rear to rain down shells on the German attackers in the open fields. The result was carnage that turned the stomach. "They just kept coming," a sergeant from Milwaukee said, "one wave after the other." "It was," he lamented, "one of the saddest things I'd ever experienced in my life."

By evening, however, there remained little room for pity in and around Marnach. The badly mauled grenadiers, whose losses included the regimental commander, welcomed the arrival of their division's sleek Panther tanks with a sigh of relief. The new models were equipped with infrared sighting devices and had just rolled off assembly lines in factories near Breslau. Americans and Germans girded themselves for a night battle. Incendiary shells soon had more than a dozen houses blazing like torches. The church tower was blown to bits. Repeated direct hits pounded the stately presbytery into rubble. GIs were driven from their hiding places as Panzergrenadiers pushed their way into the village. Shortly after midnight, Colonel Fuller from Clervaux ordered an infantry platoon and a handful of tanks to try and reach the men at Marnach. But as soon as they approached the village's edge, the small force was driven back by the combined fire of small arms, Panzerfausts, and Panthers. Even then, however, GIs remained holed up in Marnach, fighting the Germans house to house, buying their side more valuable time.[18]

At dawn on the second day of the German offensive, von Manteuffel had reason to feel worried. Seven divisions, totaling 110,000 troops, had smashed into the thin lines of the 28th Infantry Division. But those troops that German General Baptist Kniess had considered to be of "mediocre" quality were now found to be derailing the tight time schedule. In the sector of the 110th Infantry, von Lüttwitz's crucial armored spearheads had been delayed. Von Manteuffel had hoped to be in control of Bastogne by noon on the second day. Now, as dawn turned to day on Sunday, December 17, Panzer Lehr had not even reached the Clerf River, while the 2nd Panzer Division had still to capture the town of Clervaux on the road to Bastogne.[19]

General Middleton, commander of the VIII Corps, could not realistically expect Colonel Fuller's men to continue to delay the German onslaught for much longer. In accordance with established doctrine, most of the available Allied reserves were being sent to hold the shoulders of the salient and prevent the bulge from widening. This meant that the 28th Infantry Division, which was being torn to pieces in the middle of the gap, could not immediately expect significant reinforcements. Still, Middleton desperately needed more time. To prevent enemy armor from catapulting itself onto the plains to the west, it was of paramount importance to deny the Germans use of the main roads running through the dense forests of the rugged Ardennes. The 28th Infantry Division, and the 110th Regiment in particular, had the misfortune of straddling the terrain in front of Bastogne, one of the key road junctions in Middleton's VIII Corps sector. It was clear that the Allied higher command would have to rush additional forces to Bastogne if the town was to be held. It was also clear, however, that the most likely candidates for this operation were the two airborne divisions that were resting and refitting at Rheims in the wake of Operation Market Garden. It would take them time to get ready and move from France to Belgium. The conclusion was hard and cruel: the lives of the men of the Bloody Bucket, veteran and green alike, would have to be sacrificed to buy time. Even before dawn on the second day of the German offensive, the orders coming down from Middleton's head-quarters were unequivocal: "hold at all costs."[20]

By now there was little else that the men from K Company and their comrade engineers inside Hosingen could do: they were an island in a sea of German gray. They were out of range of the supporting artillery, and they waited in vain for reinforcements of any kind. As the enemy tightened the noose, tanks, artillery, machine guns, and snipers raked the village. Even in these conditions, however, the Americans managed to stave off several attacks in the course of the morning. Early that afternoon, the Germans launched a concerted effort to dislodge the GIs, with elements from the 26th Volksgrenadier Division, Panzer Lehr, and even the 2nd Panzer Division joining in. The battle raged for hours. The hard-pressed Americans gradu-ally fell back to the command post in the village's southern part. They fought for every house, spraying the streets from windows, setting booby traps, then quickly exiting through the back door. By nightfall rifle ammunition was so scarce that many GIs were fighting back with no more than hand grenades. Finally, past midnight, the 3rd Battalion commander contacted Captain Feiker to tell him to get out. "We can't get out," came the reply. "But these Krauts are going to pay a stiff price if they try to get in." Half an hour later, the radio went dead.[21]

Also on Sunday, enough men of B Company appeared to be continuing resistance inside Marnach, on the left flank, to warrant a new and more concerted attempt to send in reinforcements. Two American infantry compa-nies that tried to break through from the west were instantly beaten back. A platoon from the 707th Tank Battalion was all that managed to reach the village's southern edge, but then it too was blasted back. From Fischbach, just north of Marnach, D Company of the 707th Tank Battalion descended the hill towards the besieged village. The crews of the light M5 Stuart tanks were engaged in what amounted to a suicide mission against the fearsome Panthers of the veteran 2nd Panzer Division. The lead tank immediately went up in a ball of fire. Then, as the entire column stalled, the Germans methodically took out one American tank after another. In less than ten minutes, nothing much remained of D Company. As the Germans led the surviving crewmen away, Lieutenant Orville Nicholas tried to get closer to the burnt and lifeless body of a platoon member in a ditch. His captors forced him back into line with their rifle butts.[22]

Meanwhile, an exhausted Ed Uzemack, in a former life a student at Northwestern University and a Chicago newspaper reporter, kept up the fight inside Marnach. Peering through his cracked spectacles, he zigzagged his way to dwindling remnants of B Company in desperate need of the ammo bandoliers he was carrying. He plopped down next to a machine-gun team inside the shell of a house. In a nearby room lay the crumpled body of a dead comrade. Outside could be heard the terrible moaning of a wounded German. A GI crawled up to the soldier and let off a few bursts. The moaning abruptly stopped. Numb, Private Uzemack prayed for help that would never come.[23]

With the defenses at Marnach crumbling at last, the 2nd Panzer Division hurriedly turned its attention to Clervaux, a town barely two miles further west, where Colonel Fuller had installed the 110th Infantry's headquarters. The Luxembourg town lay nestled in the deep, narrow basin of the Clerf River. Fuller and his men were determined to deny the Germans use of its two key bridges for as long as they could. But that was not going to be easy. Fuller had limited forces at his disposal in Clervaux. Small reserves had arrived, only to march through town as reinforcements for defenses further east. Moreover, the situation inside Clervaux was chaotic: long-range artillery had been pounding it since the first day of the offensive. A couple of German forward observers had slipped into town unnoticed and were now directing the shelling with increasing precision.[24]

Unlike the civilians in villages close to the Our River and the West Wall, the inhabitants of Clervaux and surroundings had not been evacuated and were giving the Americans serious headaches. In Urspelt, a hamlet just outside Clervaux, GIs prohibited villagers from moving about outside their homes. But German shells had ruptured the mains water supply, and farmers disobeyed the order and risked their lives hauling water for their cattle from public sources in the square. Accurate shelling had driven most of Clervaux's population of 2,000 into their cellars. The surprise had been so total that flight for most was made impossible.[25]

The Luxembourgers were paralyzed with fear. The Germans had occupied their tiny country in May 1940, destroying its independence with the stroke of a pen, and declaring it an integral part of the Third Reich. For four years the Nazis had worked hard to Germanize the Luxembourgers. They had prohibited the use of Letzeburgesch, the duchy's native language, and all French-sounding place names had been converted into German. Luxembourg resistance to Nazi occupation had grown steadily since 1940. But it had exploded in 1942, when the Germans began conscripting the young for labor in the Reich and service in the Wehrmacht. Some 6,000 young men had dodged conscription or later deserted from their units. They had either gone into hiding in Belgium or disappeared in Luxembourg with the help of underground networks. Many had become active members of the resistance. All of them faced harsh punishment under German reoccupation. Now, on Sunday, civilians in Clervaux clung to the Americans, desperate to know what was happening and what they should be doing.[26]

Those in the American garrison wished they knew the answers to these questions. Dotted with hotels, picturesque Clervaux had been serving as a rest and recreation center for troops from all over the 28th Infantry Division's sector. On Saturday, on the orders of Colonel Fuller, some 300 of them, armed with no more than rifles, had been hastily rounded up and assigned to a makeshift force guarding the entry into Clervaux from the Marnach road. They were unnerved at the sight of countless wounded streaming back, on foot and on litters in vehicles, from the failed attempts to break through to Marnach.

Soon after, the lightly armed defenders were overrun by Mark IV tanks and half-tracks packed with Panzergrenadiers, as these rumbled down the Marnach road from the heights to the east. The attackers hurled themselves against the sanatorium on the southern edge of Clervaux. A handful of tanks from the 707th Tank Battalion, Colonel Fuller's armored reserve, were rushed to the scene to prevent a breakthrough. A ferocious battle erupted on the road near the sanatorium. Some 150 townspeople had flocked to the building as soon as the first shells had started falling on Saturday. Now Panzergrenadiers sprayed the windows with machine-gun fire and lobbed grenades through cellar vents. The Luxembourgers held their breath as doors were kicked in. Heavy boots stamped through the upstairs rooms. Then abruptly the noise over their heads ceased. As the acrid smoke cleared outside, the smoldering and twisted wrecks of four German and three American tanks could be seen littering the road.[27]

Another platoon of five Sherman tanks was sent in. It arrived with the permission of General Middleton and belonged to the 9th Armored Division's Combat Command Reserve, a regiment-sized force that had taken up position to the rear of the 110th Infantry west of Clervaux, to help shield Bastogne. More and more of the massive force of the 2nd Panzer Division – some 130 tanks and armored assault guns – now stood perched on the heights overlooking Clervaux. They clinically took out one Sherman tank after another, until wrecks clogged the narrow road near the ancient castle overlooking the south bridge. "We're surrounded and can't get out," radioed Sergeant Donald Fink from his tank to the commander of Combat Command Reserve. "They're closing in, and we're fighting like hell. Guess this is it." A few blocks further up the road, in his command post in the Claravallis Hotel near the north bridge, Colonel Fuller, puffing on his pipe, knew the end was near. He made a plea for reinforcements, but was told over the radio that none were available for Clervaux. Combat Command Reserve was now more urgently needed to guard the immediate approaches to Bastogne.[28]

As darkness fell on Sunday, a Panther fired 75mm shells at point-blank range into the first floor of the Claravallis Hotel. Colonel Fuller and his staff were forced to flee out a back exit. By Monday morning, German troops were in control of all of Clervaux – except for its twelfth-century fortress, where about a hundred men from the 110th Infantry's Headquarters Company manned the walls and turrets. In the dungeons, German POWs and scores of civilians anxiously awaited their fate. From behind the apertures, American snipers picked off enemy soldiers at will. Only armored vehicles could cross the Clerf River with impunity.

Infuriated, German soldiers forced civilians out of their homes and ordered them to collect the dead and bury them. They then started shelling the castle's roof with white phosphorus, so that liquid fire ran from the moss-covered slates. Thousands of tiny flames dripped from the fortress walls, searing the earthen moat. The ancient beams caught fire and the drafty buildings sucked in smoke. The civilians panicked, children screamed, and mothers ran through the courtyard not knowing where to hide. Shortly after noon, a fortress window swung open. An American slid a long pole through the opening. At the end of it dangled a limp white flag. Clervaux was German again. Within hours the Gestapo was combing through the Luxembourg town. It soon arrested two people, one of them a deserter. Both men were sent to Buchenwald.[29]

<h2 style="text-align:center">3</h2>

As the 112th Infantry veered away towards the north, and the 109th Infantry peeled off southwards under heavy enemy pressure, there was no longer any protection on Colonel Fuller's flanks. On Monday, December 18, German forces steamrolled the 28th Infantry Division's middle regiment as they lurched towards Bastogne in an effort to make up for lost time. What still remained of the 110th Infantry was captured or scattered to the four winds.

More and more men of the 110th Infantry began to slog their way east as prisoners of the Germans. Shortly after dawn on Monday, Captain Feiker in Hosingen waved a white flag and walked to the German lines to negotiate the surrender of his surrounded force. Before leaving, he ordered his men to destroy all the remaining equipment. Trucks and jeeps had their tires slashed and engine parts ripped out. Some vehicles were set on fire. Field ranges were destroyed and documents burned. GIs smashed their rifles and threw away the bolts. Those who could reach the kitchen were issued packaged K rations and D bars until the supplies ran out. When Captain Feiker returned with the Germans, 8 officers and 300 men were formed into a column amidst the rubble and were marched out of town.[30]

All over the 110th Infantry's sector, relations between prisoners and captors were tense. Captain Jarrett of the Hosingen garrison had wrapped his dentures in a handkerchief and placed them in his pocket. The Germans frisked the officer and took everything from him, including his teeth. Teenage soldiers descended on Private Ed Uzemack and fellow survivors of B Company in Marnach. They subjected the Americans to rough strip searches, taking "watches, money, cigarettes, anything they could get their hands on." Before being marched to the rear, POWs were made to dig graves for the large number of German dead – around 300 in and around Hosingen alone. Across the entire sector, American prisoners buried an estimated 2,000 soldiers from three different German divisions.[31]

The trek to prison camps in Germany was long and painful. German soldiers who marched past Vincent Speziale and his captured comrades jeered that they would be in Paris by Christmas. "They will push us back all the way to Normandy," Speziale thought bitterly. Robert Probach and some 300 other men from the 110th were made to march for three days with barely any rest. Only on the second day did they receive food, when guards herded them into a large field and threw 30 loaves into the crowd. On the third day, the GIs finally boarded a dirty cattle train in a station east of Trier.[32]

Sergeant Robert Miller from the regiment's Headquarters Company had failed to escape from the Claravallis Hotel in Clervaux in time. He was sent east with another group. "There began," he recalled, "the most terrible 8 days I ever want to live." They walked for five days, each step taking Sergeant Miller farther away from his home in Altoona, Pennsylvania, and his fiancée

Polly. On the sixth day they were jammed into a boxcar. Before pulling out of the station, each prisoner received a thin slice of black bread and a meager portion of horsemeat, their first food since capture.[33]

The drafty cattle wagons were like freezers, and frostbite ravaged hands and feet on the long ride. Allied aircraft strafed and bombed the trains as they slowly wound their way through Germany. One such attack killed 8 POWs and wounded another 38 on Sergeant Miller's train. "The dead," Robert Probach said of his German transport, "traveled with us until we arrived at the prison camp."[34]

There were also those, however, who managed to evade capture, often slipping away just moments before the Germans overwhelmed their strong points. They wandered around in groups of various sizes, groping their way west, hoping to link up with larger formations as soon as possible. Their ordeal was just as harrowing as that of the prisoners heading east. Chester Kuzminski and five other men from I Company hit the ground when a German flare lit up the night. They had just escaped the German onslaught at Weiler, a village a few miles south of Hosingen. The GIs burrowed into a field and held their breath. Then suddenly a stick grenade sailed into their midst. One of the Americans pounced on it and hurled it back. A wail and horrible moaning followed the resulting explosion. Two GIs rushed over to the writhing shape and silenced it. The group of six made it back all the way to Clervaux, only to be caught up in the fighting there. This was followed by yet another close escape. "We got on the hood of the jeep," Private Kuzminski recalled, "three of us hanging on, a red-headed officer held my belt so I wouldn't fall off." The jeep got hit and crashed. The Germans took a badly wounded Kuzminski to an aid station crammed with casualties in much pain. "I don't want to remember any more," Kuzminski wrote much later. "It brings back memories and I cry about the killing."[35]

As the resistance in and around Clervaux collapsed, GIs scrambled to get west of the Clerf River as soon as possible. Five men from the 2nd Battalion's Headquarters Company clasped hands as they descended the river bank. The current was swift and icy water washed over their shoulders and heads. Bob Pocklington, a farm boy from Illinois and the eldest of seven brothers, watched the far shore get closer. But then the chain was broken and Siegel, a headquarters clerk from Pennsylvania, was swept away thrashing and hollering. Pocklington did not hesitate for a second. He went after Siegel and clung onto him, even though he seemed to weigh a ton. The two men made it to the other side. "My fingers," Pocklington recalled, "were sticking to the rifle. I could not even unbutton my pants and I needed to urinate; finally I had to just let it go – the warmth felt good."[36]

For a brief time, Colonel Fuller and some of the others who had fled the Claravallis Hotel tried to improvise a semblance of resistance near Donnange, west of Clervaux on the road to Bastogne. But on Monday, the Germans cornered them in a patch of woodland. Fuller received a blow to the head and a wound to the stomach from a bayonet. The Texan's humiliation was complete when a German soldier pistol-whipped him for whispering some advice to his fellow prisoners.[37]

There was painful irony in the fact that it had been the men from the 28th Infantry Division who, just months earlier, had liberated Bastogne to the acclaim of euphoric crowds lining the streets. Charles McWhorter, a soldier from the 110th Infantry's E Company, vividly remembered that, as they had moved through the Belgian town in September, impoverished civilians could be seen stripping the boots off three Germans who had been killed by mortar fire. Now, as the tide turned against them once again, Private McWhorter and his comrades felt for the civilians fleeing their homes between the Clerf River and Bastogne. In Lullange, a village just west of Donnange on the road to Bastogne, people had hastily packed on Sunday evening. But American troops, accompanied by the village priest, had gone around dissuading people from leaving in the dark, in which they could be mistaken for the enemy. As soon as dawn came on Monday, however, the petrified villagers stirred themselves into action. Horse-drawn carts, loaded with boxes and baskets, rolled out of sight. Still more people followed on bicycles and on foot. Mothers pushing baby carriages tried to keep up with the rest. Farmers released their animals from the stables. A man on a motorcycle was appointed to chase the village herd westward. That same day, many more refugees spilled onto the roads from villages in the path of the 2nd Panzer Division and of Panzer Lehr to the south.[38]

If it was safer for civilian refugees to travel during the day, American soldiers trying to evade capture could only move about during darkness. Lieutenant John Maher was part of a large group of some 200 men trying to reach American lines. He and his comrades were the remnants of a force that had managed to hold the Germans at bay in Munshausen, just southwest of Marnach. On Sunday, they had fought house to house, barricading the village streets with overturned trucks, before making their escape and crossing the Clerf River in the face of overwhelming odds. At dawn, they withdrew deep into the forest, dried out their socks, and tried to get some rest. As soon as night fell, they pushed on again. "Because the weather had been overcast, visibility was zero in the darkness," noted Lieutenant Maher, "and each man kept one hand on the rifle belt of the man ahead."[39]

For another group west of the river, matters were further complicated by the presence of a high-ranking officer with a serious knee injury. Lieutenant Colonel Ross Henbest, commander of the 2nd Battalion, 110th Infantry, told his men to give him a rifle and a canteen of water and to leave him behind at a crossroads. Sergeant Bill Korte, in civilian life a police officer from Washington, Pennsylvania, bluntly refused to obey. "Hell no, Colonel," he barked, "we all go together or we don't go."

And so, men in groups small and large, able-bodied and wounded, inched closer to Bastogne. They dug up turnips, beets, and potatoes, devouring them raw. Luxembourg and Belgian farmers fed them apples and bread, as well as valuable information on German whereabouts. During the daytime, GIs listened to the metallic, screeching sound of tanks rumbling by. Night after night, they resumed their trek, shell-shocked and groggy. Some men cracked and had to be subdued with force. Trench coats were shredded on barbed-wire fences, and soldiers discarded their heavy overshoes, knowing that this would expose them to trench foot, but refusing to fall behind. "Our feet," one GI recalled, "were in such pitiful condition that we could hardly hobble along by this time."[40]

The 110th Infantry, General Middleton insisted immediately after the war, "put up very stiff resistance for three days." Although it had eventually been "overrun by the attack," the Mississippian nevertheless commended the Pennsylvanian regiment for "a splendid job." The outfit had, in the words of one observer, thrown "a series of monkey wrenches" in the "well-oiled machinery" of von Manteuffel's Fifth Panzer Army by delaying von Lüttwitz's XLVII Panzer Corps. In doing so, the regiment had bought Middleton's VIII Corps and the Supreme Headquarters of the Allied Expeditionary Forces vital time to harness reinforcements for the defense of Bastogne. But the price had been extremely high. By the time the remnants of the 110th Infantry began reaching the American lines anchored on Bastogne, the recently rebuilt regiment of more than 3,200 officers and men had been reduced to under 600 soldiers. One of the survivors was Paul Yearout, the lieutenant and father of two children who, in a letter to his wife Mimi just hours before the German counterattack, had expressed the hope that soon they would be living "normal lives."[41]

CHAPTER 2

LOCKING SHIELDS

On the morning of Monday, December 18, with the 110th Infantry savaged and torn to pieces, the approaches to Bastogne lay wide open for the German armor and infantry. Still, General Middleton in VIII Corps headquarters in Bastogne kept his cool. He carefully studied maps, as well as the messages that kept filtering in via radio and telephone. Just moments before, higher headquarters had informed him that the 82nd and 101st Airborne Divisions were already on their way to the Ardennes front, and that at least one of those was destined for Bastogne. Middleton now knew that if he could somehow slow down the German juggernaut for another 24 hours, he would have an experienced and hardened force of at least 11,000 paratroopers at his disposal for the defense of Bastogne. The Mississippian reasoned that the arrival of such a crack unit might suffice to deny the Germans use of the vital Belgian crossroads. He was well aware that this could help knock the wind out of the dangerous enemy offensive in the Ardennes.[1]

At Eisenhower's Supreme Allied Headquarters, the bigger picture was already showing that the main effort by Sepp Dietrich's Sixth Panzer Army in the north was being slowed to some extent. Although *Kampfgruppe* Peiper, a powerful combat force of the 1st SS Panzer Division, had succeeded with a dangerous penetration, stubborn resistance by the men of Major General Gerow's V Corps had derailed the timetable of most of the other armored divisions of the Waffen SS. Potentially, however, this meant that Middleton's sector might only gain in importance in the next few days, should it become clear that the *Schwerpunkt* was shifting to von Manteuffel's Wehrmacht. There were early indications that this was the case. Like von Lüttwitz on the left, Walter Lucht, commander of the LXVI Corps in von Manteuffel's army, was being delayed on the right. But in the center of the

Fifth Panzer Army, armored divisions were picking up speed as a massive gap beckoned from Bastogne to beyond Gouvy, a small town northeast of Houffalize.

Middleton grimly assessed the reserve forces still available to him to delay the Germans east of Bastogne for another day. His most powerful corps reserve was Combat Command R of the 9th Armored Division. Even this, however, was no more than a regiment-sized force that had already suffered some losses in attempts to shore up the 110th Infantry at key points. Beyond that, there remained no more than two combat engineer battalions and one armored artillery battalion. Given the stubbornly overcast weather, no help was to be expected anytime soon from the powerful Allied air forces.

Middleton carefully weighed up all the information and decided that, despite the desperate picture, there was a fighting chance that his men could hold on to the crucial Belgian crossroads. He came to that conclusion because he knew that yet another force was on its way to Bastogne and was scheduled to arrive possibly even before dusk that same day. As early as on the evening of the first day of the offensive, General Bradley, commander of the 12th Army Group, had ordered General Patton, commander of the Third Army, to release the 10th Armored Division from a rest area in France for support on the southern flank of the VIII Corps near Luxembourg City. Middleton, judging the situation at Bastogne to be critical, had just urged Combat Command B to split off from the division and hurry all the way up to the threatened Belgian town. If these tank crews managed to arrive in time to link up with his 9th Armored Division reserve late on Monday, they might just buy enough time for the paratroopers to arrive next.[2]

Amidst all the hurried calculations and reasoned gambles that Monday morning, one thing stood out clearly and starkly: Middleton's pitiful corps reserve would, like the 110th Infantry, be asked to pay a heavy price to keep Bastogne safe.

1

By midnight on Sunday, Colonel Duke Gilbreth, in charge of the 9th Armored Division's Combat Command R, had hastily set up two roadblocks on the N12, the main road leading into Bastogne from Clervaux to the northeast. The northern roadblock, led by Captain Lawrence Rose, stood at Antoniushof, a junction near the village of Lullange. Three miles to the southwest, Lieutenant Colonel Ralph Harper was in control of a task force at Allerborn that blocked another N12 crossroads, this one no more than nine miles from Bastogne. Combined, Task Forces Rose and Harper consisted of 30 tanks and a little more than 1,500 men. They were the last major force standing between Bastogne and multiple German divisions. The Battle of the Bulge was their very first action in the war.[3]

The Antoniushof junction near Lullange was on a desolate, windswept plain, broken only by a few patches of forest. As night began to lift with its excruciating wintry slowness, tense tank crews and infantrymen peered ahead, scanning the horizon. They did not have to wait long to detect movement. At dawn, figures in field gray could be seen weaving in and out of a copse. These were reconnaissance elements of the 2nd Panzer Division, and almost immediately they began probing the American roadblock. Support from howitzers of the nearby 73rd Armored Field Artillery helped keep the Germans at bay for several hours. By noon, however, the impatient veteran division was bringing its full force to bear against Task Force Rose. White phosphorus engulfed the American positions in flames, tanks blasted the infantry from their foxholes, and smoke screens allowed the German infantry to creep up from three sides. At 1405, Colonel Gilbreth, from his command post in Longvilly, just northeast of Bastogne, put in a phone call to VIII Corps headquarters and asked for permission to have Task Force Rose "fight their way out." For General Middleton, who now expected the 10th Armored Division's Combat Command B to arrive at any moment, each minute gained was of crucial importance. He denied the request. Barely half an hour later, the Germans overran and silenced the American position near Lullange.[4]

The men of Task Force Harper at the N12 junction near Allerborn knew what was coming their way. For several hours they had listened in alarm to the sharp noise of battle just miles away. Now the sudden silence was even more nerve-wracking. Advance elements of von Lauchert's armored division began harassing the Americans in late afternoon. Darkness fell soon after, and it was as if the enemy had been waiting for this to launch the decisive push. The night tactic unnerved the American defenders, perhaps because the enemy tanks had the advantage of infrared sighting devices. German Mark IVs and Panthers set American tanks and half-tracks alight, mowing down anyone spotted moving amidst the dancing flames. Panzergrenadiers swiftly infiltrated the American ranks, and the confusion of the inexperienced troops quickly turned into full-blown panic. Task Force Harper disintegrated in no time. One Sherman tank tried to draw a bead on a Panther, but could not move its turret because too many soldiers were clinging to the armored vehicle for dear life. Lieutenant Colonel Harper, the task force commander, was killed trying to escape the inferno in a half-track, and that signaled the end of organized resistance. Crews scrambled out of their tanks and joined armored infantrymen in a headlong rush for safety in the darkness.[5]

The collapse of Task Force Harper would have left the N12 to Bastogne wide open, had it not been for one further obstacle. In and around nearby Allerborn, a small and most unlikely force was still holding out. It was made up of remnants of the 110th Infantry Regiment that a certain Colonel Seely had been gathering throughout the day.

Ted Seely had been the regiment's commander before Hurley Fuller. He had just been released from hospital and had rushed back to his unit. With Colonel Fuller on the run at Clervaux on Sunday, division had promptly put him back in command. The leadership and composure of Seely and several junior staff officers had rallied stragglers and convinced them to stay put. There were 260 of them. One was Paul Yearout, the Hürtgen veteran and father of two who, just three nights earlier, had told his wife in a letter that he did not mind getting wounded because it would at least give him the break he so longed for.

Brave as Lieutenant Yearout and his comrades were, there was not much they could throw in the way of the crack 2nd Panzer Division that evening. They possessed not a single armored vehicle, and not even so much as a bazooka for protection. As a wave of German tanks slammed into the small band, Colonel Seely quickly realized that it was utterly futile to continue resistance. He gave the order to abandon positions and fall back towards Bastogne. In their command post in a solid, two-story stone house, Seely and his small staff rushed to put on coats and pack away documents. But they were too late. German tanks rocked the building with shells as the colonel and his men tried to find a safe way out. Some of the officers had been with Colonel Fuller at Clervaux. It was the scene from the Claravallis Hotel all over again. But this time the Americans did not even make it out the door. Somewhat to the puzzlement of the Germans, Colonel Seely was the second commander of the 110th Infantry they captured that day. Many of the troops in the foxholes around the command post did manage to slip away in the darkness, including Paul Yearout, who had avoided getting wounded.[6]

Sergeant Bill Korte belonged to a separate group of stragglers from the 110th Infantry who were trying to make their way back to Bastogne that night. He and his comrades had taken turns carrying Lieutenant Colonel Ross Henbest on their backs. They had struggled to get the commander of the 2nd Battalion, his knee badly injured, to safety. But now they at last entered American lines in what turned out to be Longvilly, the first Belgian village just over the border from Luxembourg, less than six miles northeast of Bastogne. As they dropped their injured battalion commander off at the nearest aid station, the infantrymen were immediately assigned to one of the village's defensive outposts.

Sergeant Korte and his men learned that the Americans in Longvilly belonged to the command post of the 9th Armored Division's Combat Command R. The place was in a state of utter confusion. Gilbreth and his staff pored over the situation map in the kitchen of a large house across the street from the church. Clerks, mechanics, and cooks were armed and in foxholes surrounding the village. The atmosphere grew tenser by the minute, as disheveled stragglers from the 28th Infantry Division continued to pour in and mauled remnants from Combat Command R's own task forces began to filter back. Colonel Gilbreth knew that both his roadblock task forces had been overrun. All that now remained of Combat Command R was his command post at Longvilly and a small task force that had taken up position on the heights overlooking the stretch of the N12 that ran from Allerborn to Longvilly. The latter force was Task Force Booth. But Lieutenant Colonel Robert Booth had now lost all radio and telephone contact with Gilbreth's command post. Some of Combat Command R's roadblock survivors reached Booth's lines "real shook up." There were faint sounds of battle that seemed to come even from behind the task force. Booth sent runners to Longvilly in hope of reestablishing contact, but they never reached the command post. Neither did they make it back to the task force. All that Gilbreth and Booth could do in their isolated positions was stand fast and prepare for the worst.[7]

There was nothing more that the combat engineers could do either. Positioned to the back of Gilbreth's command post and Task Force Booth, they literally formed Bastogne's last line of defense. That line was razor thin. On Sunday evening, key points along a chain running from Foy in the northeast all the way to Marvie in the southeast had been manned by no more than the 600 soldiers from the 35th Engineer Combat Battalion. These men had demonstrated excellent unit cohesion in the European campaign thus far. They were a hardened bunch, undaunted by the winter weather of the Ardennes. All this was the result of their previous war experience: they had spent a year and a half in the harsh environment of British Columbia and the Yukon Territory, where they had worked in near isolation on the construction of a military highway connecting the United States with Alaska, in a bid to stave off the Japanese threat from the Pacific.

Still, when daylight came on Monday, the engineers of the 35th were only too happy to greet the arrival of another 600 men from the 158th Engineer Combat Battalion. They were loaded down with close to a thousand anti-tank mines. But more importantly, they brought with them 14 tanks and tank destroyers, all scrounged from ordnance repair shops and manned by ordnance mechanics. The reinforcements immediately took over the 35th's left flank from Foy to Neffe. Throughout the day, both battalions worked feverishly to create a string of minefields and strengthen roadblocks. By Monday evening, engineers armed with machine guns and bazookas had taken up their posts in sight of Bastogne's eastern gates. They, like the men of the 9th Armored Division's Combat Command R, were well aware that they had been assigned what amounted to a suicide mission.[8]

2

On Monday, tension among the 4,000-plus inhabitants inside the town of Bastogne was building, too. The previous two days, the civilian population had remained fairly calm. The Bastognards had failed to comprehend the severity of the situation, and they had found it impossible to imagine that anything could threaten the might of the American military that they had been witness to since the liberation three months previously.

On Saturday, it had been business as usual in the shops. Girls at the boarding school of the Institute of Notre Dame had quietly passed the day embroidering handkerchiefs for the GIs to send to their families in America as Christmas gifts. That night, the distinct rumble of explosions had drifted in from the east. On Sunday, GIs had started scrutinizing the documents of anybody entering Bastogne on foot or by tram. Late in the afternoon, the power lines had been cut. People had lit candles and flocked to church to get more. American Civil Affairs authorities had announced a curfew to begin at 1800 that evening.

On Monday morning, the supply of water was cut off and the rumble of battle in the east intensified. Still, the stern principal of the Seminary, the town's boarding school for boys, decided to go ahead with Christmas exams, as if nothing was wrong. Other schools proceeded with their routine, too. It did not last long. By noon, large numbers of haggard refugees were streaming into town with tales of horror and destruction just miles away. Panic spread like wildfire now. Exams were broken off and classes cancelled. Distraught parents came to fetch their children. Eight-year-old Michel Mazay knew Monsieur Mayeresse, the schoolteacher with the dark-rimmed glasses, as a grave and imposing man. But now the teacher returned to his class with news that left him visibly shaken. "Children, school is out," he announced in a tremulous voice, "go home immediately, the Germans are at the gates of Bastogne." As they filed out the door, a pale Monsieur Mayeresse clasped the hands of his pupils one by one.[9]

At no time did the American authorities order a general evacuation of Bastogne. They realized that the swift and orderly removal of so many people was impossible in the circumstances, especially because there was a lack of sufficient transportation. Still, by noon on Monday, people had begun leaving of their own accord. Their numbers swelled rapidly when, in mid-afternoon, the first German shell shook the town and debris rained down. Young people and able-bodied men went first. They hopped on their bikes with small bundles across their backs. Some had been part of the resistance against the Nazi regime and they feared reprisals. All had vivid memories of Belgians being sent to Germany as forced laborers during a brutal occupation that had lasted more than four years. In a matter of hours, the mood turned dark and fearful. All over town, Bastognards could be seen removing Belgian and Allied flags that for months had hung proudly from windowsills. Six-year-old Roland Delperdange saw haggard American troops shuffle through town from the east late on Monday afternoon. Many were wounded and bandaged up. Some "held on to each other," others "used rifles as crutches." It was, the Belgian recalled many decades later, "very hard to watch."[10]

The scenes of civilian commotion in the streets outside their headquarters and the news of how defenses to the east were rapidly melting away caused General Middleton and his staff to track the progress of the reinforcements with mounting anxiety. Even before daybreak on Monday, Combat Command B had broken away from the 10th Armored Division in Luxembourg City, as ordered by Middleton. Patton's men had fought hard in the Lorraine campaign and had helped capture Metz. On the eve of the German counter-offensive, they had been stationed in a rest area near Rémeling in France. They had been taking it easy, replacing equipment, and training replacements.

It was in Rémeling that Private Don Addor had received a Christmas package from his home on Geranium Street in Washington, D.C. Among the cookies and cakes had been a sprig of evergreen with a red ribbon in a big bow. He had attached it to the front of his half-track. But the welcome lull had been cut short abruptly. By noon on Monday, Private Addor's half-track was part of the mechanized force racing through the streets of Luxembourg and Belgian towns. A chill wind drove rain and snow flurries into their faces. "Mud was everywhere," Don Addor noted. "It had fallen off the tires and tracks of the vehicles in front of us so that there was at least a foot of it on top of the road's hard surface. All of these vehicles plowing through this mud sent up a fine spray until every part of us was covered with mud." Don Addor and his comrades had no idea of where exactly they were heading. But during brief halts along the road, increasingly worried civilians accosted them with news of a massive German breakthrough.[11]

On Sunday night, the announcement to pack up and get ready for battle had come as a still greater shock for the men of the 101st Airborne Division in Mourmelon-le-Grand. They had been stationed at a French army barracks in the Champagne region since their arrival there from the Netherlands at the end of November. After almost two months in the front lines against an overwhelming German force in Operation Market Garden, the paratroopers were physically and mentally exhausted. They, together with the men from the 82nd Airborne Division, were now part of the European theater's strategic reserve. The paratroopers generally assumed that they would not be sent into battle again until the arrival of spring, when they would probably be asked to jump into Germany on the far side of the Rhine. That left plenty of time for much-needed rest, recuperation, and refitting.

The French army compound was not far from Rheims, and paratroopers were given passes to the cathedral city, as well as to Paris. At the barracks in Mourmelon, there were regular movie sessions for relaxation and endless games of baseball, basketball, and football to help the men get back into shape and forget the worst of what they had seen in Normandy and Holland. But the gray weather and cold barracks had dampened spirits. Trench mouth and scabies stubbornly refused to heal. Minds were even more difficult to mend. Mourmelon lay on the plain just north of the Marne River, and the sight of trenches and craters dating back to the Great War was a depressing reminder of why the American soldiers were really there. "The realization," one paratrooper wrote to his parents, "that there is no escape, that we shall jump on Germany, then ride transport straight to the Pacific for the battle in China, does not leave much room for optimism." It was widely known in the 101st Airborne Division that in the past two weeks at least three men had committed suicide, one of them a high-ranking officer.[12]

The news on the night of Sunday, December 17, that they were urgently needed in the front lines had caught the paratroopers completely off guard. At dawn on Monday, the Mourmelon barracks was a hive of activity and confusion. Special trains were on their way from Paris, with comrades rounded up by the military police (MPs) in bars, brothels, and Red Cross clubs. Officers scoured hospital wards in Rheims to encourage any patients who thought they were fit enough to join the fight. Soldiers locked up for misbehaving were released from regimental guardhouses.

The 463rd Parachute Field Artillery was at Mourmelon, even though it did not belong to the 101st Airborne Division. A veteran outfit that had seen much action in Italy and southern France, this battalion had just arrived. It had not even had time to unload its trucks, and now it suddenly found itself attached to the 101st and ready to move out again.

But at least it had most of its equipment ready and available, whereas the men of the 101st had handed in much of theirs for repairs or replacement. They could now be seen scrambling for anything – from weapons to shovels, helmets, and boots. Many paratroopers had not yet drawn their full complement of winter clothing. After one last hot meal around noon, the soldiers were told to pack as many K rations as possible. Next, the division's four regiments started lining up for departure. Chaplains held an improvised service, and soldiers and commanders knelt to say prayers. No one had any clear idea of where they were heading. But the airborne men soon realized how serious the situation was when sergeants began reading the Articles of War, with an emphasis on desertion and cowardice in the face of the enemy and the heavy punishment these would bring.

Some 380 trucks arrived with large trailers attached. These were open topped, the sidewalls wood-slatted. The men were made to press together so tightly that there was no room even to sit. As the drivers – many of them African-American – gunned their trucks through French villages and towns, veterans learned the names of replacements. These men had received no more than basic training and were desperate for tips on how to survive. Rain, sleet, and wind that cut to the bone made the men shiver uncontrollably. Rest stops were few and far between, so soldiers used helmets and five-gallon cans to relieve themselves, tossing the foul-smelling contents into the streets. MPs at crossroads pointed the way for the ten-mile-long convoy, urging the drivers on with rapid motions of their forearms. Darkness fell long before the trucks reached the Belgian border, and the paratroopers were flabbergasted to learn that the drivers were under orders not to dim the lights, despite the threat of air raids.[13]

At around 1600, Colonel William Roberts was the first of the reinforcement commanders to arrive at VIII Corps headquarters. The command post was housed in a Belgian army barracks of solid brick buildings in the northern part of Bastogne. Roberts had served with General Middleton in World War I, and the two men knew each other well. Middleton greeted the commander of the 10th Armored Division's Combat Command B with an expression of exhaustion and strain etched on his face. But he briefed Roberts in his calm southern manner, jabbed his finger at a map on the wall, and instructed him to split his force into three teams as soon as it arrived. The remaining defenses, Middleton warned, were now "badly cut up." Roberts was to rush his teams to the three most critical villages on the main roads leading into Bastogne in an arc stretching from northeast to southeast. The most critical by far was Longvilly, on the N12 coming in from almost due east. There Colonel Gilbreth's command post of the 9th Armored Division's Combat Command R was expecting the deathblow at any moment. Roberts was an experienced armor commander. He was steeped in the doctrine of concentrated power, and hated being told to divide his force and parcel it out. But he had no choice. He had to trust the senior commander's instinct. He stepped into his jeep and drove back to meet the leading column of his troops.[14]

Shortly after Colonel Roberts's arrival, a pleased General Middleton was shaking hands with Brigadier General Anthony McAuliffe. McAuliffe, too, had gone ahead of his troops to reconnoiter the situation. He had been told that the 101st Airborne was to go to Werbomont for action on the northern flank of the bulge. But he had decided to halt at Bastogne to see what VIII Corps headquarters could tell him. To his surprise, Middleton immediately informed him that his division was to defend Bastogne.

Until a few weeks earlier, McAuliffe had been the division's artillery commander. But then General Maxwell Taylor, the regular commander of the 101st Airborne, had been called to the United States to attend to official business in the capital. And, some time after that, Taylor's deputy, Brigadier General Gerald Higgins, had been flown to England with five other senior officers from the division to discuss lessons learned from Operation Market Garden. So now, suddenly, the 46-year-old McAuliffe, who hailed from Washington, D.C., found himself in overall command of 12,000 or so troops – troops who were badly needed to help stem the tide in one of the most serious crises of the war in Europe.[15]

McAuliffe was a man of few words and sparse humor. His hair was raven black, parted in the middle, and slicked back. He was not a tall man, and he lacked the flamboyance of commanders like Patton. But the general was known for his physical stamina, and had impressed his men by volunteering to parachute into Normandy without having received any formal training.

He was also the kind of person who, in the words of one who knew him well, "did not get fussed up over trivialities." These were qualities that were to serve him well in the days ahead at Bastogne.[16]

McAuliffe and Middleton carefully studied the maps and the positions of the armor and the engineers to the east that the paratroopers were to reinforce the following morning. It was dark now, and the first elements of the airborne force were not expected to arrive before 2100. Meanwhile, however, the tanks and half-tracks of Combat Command B were rolling into town. There was some tension when Colonel Roberts refused to relinquish his armor to the authority of the airborne commander, but Middleton resolved the issue by allowing them to keep separate commands, so long as they agreed to cooperate closely.[17]

Colonel Roberts immediately organized the first column of his mechanized force into a separate team under the command of Lieutenant Colonel Henry Cherry. Team Cherry roared out of Bastogne east on the N12. The men of the 10th Armored Division were under orders to hurry and establish contact with the little that remained of Combat Command R of the 9th Armored Division. When Lieutenant Colonel Cherry finally strode into his command post that evening, Colonel Gilbreth responded with a palpable sense of relief. "You couldn't look any better to me if you were Jesus Christ himself!" he exclaimed. Guffaws and backslapping broke some of the tension and gloom of the day.[18]

As two more of his armored teams took up defensive positions that evening – one in Noville in the northeast and the other in Wardin to the southeast – Colonel Roberts had his staff set up headquarters in Hôtel Lebrun, a two-story brick building on the rue de Marche, just off Bastogne's main square. At about the same time, General Middleton and his VIII Corps headquarters received direct orders from the First Army to leave town that night, while they still could. They were to relocate to Neufchâteau, 17 miles to the southwest, to oversee the defense of Bastogne from a safer distance.[19]

As the staff and service troops of VIII Corps headquarters readied themselves to move out of Bastogne, the paratroopers of the 101st began to arrive. General McAuliffe had taken Lieutenant Colonel Kinnard to the area just west of Bastogne to decide on an assembly point. Harry Kinnard was the division's plans and operations officer, and the commander's right-hand man. Born into an army family in Dallas, Texas, the 29-year-old was proud of his military background and Scottish roots. The young staff officer was "delicately handsome" and well liked. The two men decided to direct the estimated 12,000 troops to Mande-Saint-Étienne, some four miles west of

Bastogne. They set up a temporary command post for the division in the hamlet's schoolhouse.[20]

The first of the four regiments to complete the 107-mile trip from Mourmelon was the 501st Parachute Infantry. Troops continued to pour in on trucks throughout the night. The men were cautioned to treat their arrival as a combat situation. The second regiment to arrive was the 506th Parachute Infantry. Among them was Private Donald Burgett from Detroit, Michigan. He was only 19, had recovered from severe wounds in Normandy just in time for the jump into Holland, and now tried to get the circulation in his legs going again as he jumped from the truck with a grimace. "We moved down the road in complete silence," he recalled. "The only sounds were those of our creaking harnesses; the light metallic clanking of machine guns, mortars, base plates, and bazookas being shifted on shoulders."[21]

Next came the 502nd Parachute Infantry, and finally the 327th Glider Infantry Regiment, with the 463rd Parachute Field Artillery Battalion in tow. It was the order in which they would be sent into battle the next day. Thanks to the desperate efforts by the men of the 28th Infantry Division and the 9th Armored Division's Combat Command R, the American reinforcements had won the race for Bastogne. It remained to be seen how long they could hold on to the crucial Ardennes crossroads.

3

On Monday night, McAuliffe ordered Julian Ewell to have the 501st Parachute Infantry ready before dawn, march to Longvilly, make contact with the armor there, and feel out the enemy. He was convinced that Colonel Ewell was the right man for the job. Born in Oklahoma, the skinny regimental commander had "a slouching gait and a mountaineer drawl." "Julian," Lieutenant Colonel Kinnard once remarked, "acts like he was born on a battlefield." Like Kinnard, Ewell was only 29 and had earned the respect of his men in Normandy and Holland.[22]

Some of the last elements of the 101st Airborne were still arriving on Tuesday morning, as the men from Ewell's 1st Battalion scrambled to their feet at Mande-Saint-Étienne. They moved out at 0600, while it was still pitch dark. Chill rain was falling sporadically. In the fields around them, para-troopers were dug in "like a bunch of gophers." Some had poured gasoline into puddles and set it alight to get warm. Ewell's men walked into Bastogne from the west, and then out of town again through its eastern gate. In a little while, they were on the road to Longvilly in the foggy countryside. They formed the spearhead of the 101st Airborne and had no clear idea of what awaited them.[23]

The paratroopers did not know that on, Monday night, the 9th Armored Division's Combat Command R in Longvilly had been spared by the decision of the 2nd Panzer Division not to continue along the N12 to Bastogne. General von Lauchert's veteran outfit had been ordered to veer to the north of Bastogne, skirt the town, plunge into the gap that extended all the way to Gouvy, and push on towards the Meuse River and beyond. Ewell and his men were also in the dark about a new threat that had emerged instead. Just before midnight on Monday, Fritz Bayerlein's Panzer Lehr, the armored division that was operating on von Lauchert's left, had managed to slip a *Kampfgruppe* into Mageret, a village in the rear of the American blocking position on the N12 in Longvilly. That meant that it had cut off Gilbreth's armor in Longvilly, as well as the main force of Team Cherry strung out along the road from Mageret to Longvilly. It also meant that at dawn on Tuesday, Bayerlein's troops stood poised to push from Mageret into Neffe – one of the last hamlets between Panzer Lehr and Bastogne and the first hamlet to come into view of Ewell's 1st Battalion as they pushed out of the town. Ewell's paratroopers were about to be hit by the steel fist of the German offensive.

The advance guard had heard the racket of battle just east of Bastogne as soon as they headed out of Mande-Saint-Étienne. They did not know that it was the sound of the 158th Engineer Combat Battalion at Neffe desperately trying to slow down the advance of Bayerlein's *Kampfgruppe*. The engineers knew that they formed the last thin line of resistance between the Germans and Bastogne, and this knowledge inspired several of them to acts of extreme courage. Lieutenant William Cochran crawled through intense small-arms fire to help direct the fire of the few supporting American tanks. Loyd Parcel, a "red-headed farm youth" from Centerville, Iowa, moved close enough to two machine-gun crews to eliminate each of them with hand grenades. These actions earned the Pennsylvanian officer and the Iowan private a Silver Star apiece.[24]

Private Bernard Michin from Rhode Island waited at the Neffe roadblock with a bazooka. He allowed the first German tank to come as close as ten yards to make sure he would take it out. The explosion seared his face, blinding him. As he rolled into a ditch in excruciating pain, he heard a nearby machine gun open up on his comrades. Guided by the sound only, he tossed a hand grenade at the German crew and silenced it. Private Michin managed to make it back to his lines and was later awarded the Distinguished Service Cross, one of the highest military honors in America.

By the time Ewell's 1st Battalion approached Neffe, the fighting had died down and only the staccato of small-arms fire could be heard. The engineers had suffered at least 30 casualties at and around the roadblock. But Bayerlein's men, too, had suffered heavy losses. They kicked in the door of the Joseph farm in Neffe and barked at the inhabitants to make room for their wounded. They supported a comrade with a bullet in his leg and another with a gash in his arm. They carried in a third soldier who had a broken nose, part of his hand torn off, and a foot missing. With the Germans all over his farm, 49-year-old Jules Joseph used the lull in the battle to slip outside. As he nervously tried to bury some incriminating papers, the Belgian farmer was caught by a burst of machine-gun fire. One bullet tore into his thigh; another shattered his elbow. It took some time for German soldiers to stumble across the crumpled body. They dragged Jules Joseph back to the farm and placed him on the floor between the wounded soldiers. Medics gestured to his wife and children that he had lost too much blood to be saved.[25]

Ewell's men were now close enough to Neffe to see the first farms. B Company led the way. Ahead of them the road curved round to the right. Two jeeps were dispatched to find out where the enemy was, but as soon as the first jeep turned the corner, all hell broke loose. The second jeep came screaming back in reverse, as German machine guns riddled the first with bullets. Its driver, Chuck Tyler from Cincinnati, was killed instantly. In the front seat next to him, Tony Benedetto from Chicago also died, his bulky radio set still strapped to his back. They were among the first paratroopers to be killed in the battle for Bastogne. John Moore, who had been sitting on ammunition boxes in the rear of the jeep, was badly wounded, but he managed to extricate himself from the wreckage and make his way back to the line, where a medic immediately gave him a heavy dose of morphine. The 101st Airborne had just clashed with Panzer Lehr.

The rifle companies immediately went into defensive positions, digging in on both sides of the road. German tanks now entered the fray and soldiers yelled for bazookamen to come forward. Wayne Calloway was one of them. He was 21 and had married his high-school sweetheart just prior to going overseas. The Oregonian had jumped at the Dutch town of Heeswijk on September 17. His M1 rifle was still at Mourmelon for repair after the Market Garden ordeal, and he had been given a bazooka instead. Stanley Kaminski joined Calloway as he was carrying the bazooka's ammunition. Kaminski was from Buffalo, New York, and had joined the battalion as a replacement in Mourmelon. Both men ran forward into the fog. They disappeared and were never seen alive again.[26]

As both sides rushed more troops forward, the battle at Bastogne's eastern gate turned furious. For some paratroopers, the clash at Neffe came too soon after the harrowing experiences of Normandy and Holland. In one of B Company's foxholes, Sergeant George Adomitis threw all caution to the wind, showed himself, and was soon screaming that he was hit. "I was told," a comrade later recalled, "that Adomitis's mind had taken all the combat it could and that he stood up to end it all."[27]

Others immediately displayed the kind of courage shown by the engineers on the same spot just hours earlier. Word came that a few hundred yards down the road a paratrooper lay seriously wounded in a culvert near the railroad track. Medic Leon Jedziniak from A Company was a replacement, and this was his very first combat action. But he figured he could reach the wounded man and thought it was worth the risk. Francis Sampson, a Catholic chaplain with a shaved head and the strength of a bear, crawled alongside the medic. One soldier who rose to point out the casualty's exact location was hit in the arm by a sniper. Sampson and Jedziniak rolled into a ditch and inched forward on their bellies. Some distance away an enemy tank stood disabled, though a German continued to man its machine gun, raking the road at periodic intervals. This did not stop Father Sampson from hearing the wounded man's confession and anointing him. Next, Leon Jedziniak gathered his strength and dragged the nearly lifeless body all the way back to his lines under constant fire.[28]

That same morning, Lieutenant Colonel Henry Cherry was pacing his command post in an elegant château just outside Neffe. His armored force was stuck on the stretch of the N12 between Longvilly and German-held Mageret. Worse, the troops and tanks of Team Cherry were getting hopelessly entangled with the column of Gilbreth's Combat Command R, which was now attempting to retreat from Longvilly along the same road. Vehicles of all kinds clogged the N12 as elements of two armored divisions mingled with stragglers from the 28th Infantry Division. They soon formed an enormous traffic jam in a perfect German trap.

The enemy showed no mercy. Arriving from the north, Panzer Lehr, supported by some armor from the 2nd Panzer Division, descended on the low-lying road. Simultaneously, the 26th Volksgrenadier Division struck the N12 from the southern shoulder. What followed was, in the words of a soldier from the 110th Infantry, "a turkey shoot." Machine guns methodically raked the exposed troops, while mortars and artillery churned the road, setting vehicles on fire. Mark IVs and Panthers sought out Shermans, shredding their inferior armor. Stocks of ammunition were sent skyward in big balls of fire. Fog swirled and mixed with the acrid smoke.[29]

The cornered Americans fought back with desperate courage. Crews on the self-propelled howitzers of the 8th Armored Field Artillery somehow managed to maneuver their vehicles into position amidst the mayhem and debris. Soldiers of the 482nd Anti-aircraft Artillery Battalion aimed their formidable quadruple guns directly at the Germans and fired until the barrels glowed red. Mess Sergeant Charles Sklenar and the other cooks of the anti-aircraft battalion joined in, shooting at the enemy for the first time in their army careers.[30]

On the N12 just west of Longvilly, Saint Michael's grotto formed a surreal spectacle for men at war. The Catholic shrine was made up of a cross, an altar, and candles behind a metal grate. Opposite the shrine, statues of saints, their arms outstretched, looked down from a rocky ridge on the suffering in the road. Nearby, Lieutenant Carl Moot of Team Cherry's 2nd Tank Battalion set about killing with clinical precision. In the distance he spotted a wave of Germans swarming down from a hilltop. Several were armed with Panzerfausts, and it was clear that the Shermans were about to become a target. As the American tanks opened fire, Lieutenant Moot radioed back the coordinates of the hillside to an artillery position on the outskirts of Bastogne. The barrage that followed cut down most of the attackers, and the Shermans' machine guns finished off the few Germans who made it to the road.[31]

But the exposed Americans suffered many more casualties. Sergeant Wayne Wickert was among them. He was a squad leader in the 55th Armored Engineer Battalion that formed part of Team Cherry. The sergeant had jumped out of his truck, sprinted to the side of the road, and taken up position at the base of an evergreen tree. He stared up the steep hill to make sure no Germans were coming down through the dense forest on that side. Then suddenly a shell coming in from the other side of the road overshot one of the vehicles. The explosion pulverized the tree Wickert was crouching under. When the sergeant regained consciousness some time later, he thought he had fallen asleep on guard duty. He slowly opened his eyes. The fog was lifting and he was looking up through tall trees. With one arm he pushed himself up to a sitting position. To his right he could see his rifle some 20 or 30 feet away, by the stump of the tree he had been hiding behind. He felt no pain, but his left arm was cold and clammy and twitched uncontrollably. Jagged bone poked through the ripped sleeve at the elbow. Wickert could not get to his feet so he just sat there. A medic came running up and gave him some sulfa pills. He said he had run out of morphine and quickly moved on.

Out of nowhere, two men of his squad appeared. They grabbed him by the shoulder straps and started running. Wickert's buttocks bounced along the ground. The men dragged him through a puddle, and icy water ran through his pants. The cold made him more alert again. Back on the road, his comrades put him on his feet and told him to seek help. Vehicles stood bumper to bumper and the road was a roaring inferno. Blood seeped from his left sleeve, but the sergeant managed to reach an aid station, where he was patched up and put in an ambulance with three other stretcher cases.

The vehicle tried to find a way out, but it was hit by machine-gun fire, swerved and hit a tree. The driver lay slumped over the steering wheel and wheezing through the bullet holes in his chest. Then the motor caught fire. A medic managed to get the patients out. He dragged them to the woods, covered them with blankets, and hid them under brush. It was late afternoon when Wickert's stretcher was loaded onto a jeep. He arrived at an aid station just in time to hear the radio crackle orders for the medical personnel to with-draw. They were to leave everything behind except the most valuable drugs and equipment. Sergeant Wickert was loaded onto another jeep. This time he arrived at a field hospital far enough to the rear to be safe. He stayed conscious just long enough to witness the cleaning of a soldier's horribly damaged face and the amputation of a neighbor's leg. Then everything went black.[32]

Team Cherry lost 175 officers and men between Longvilly and Mageret – a quarter of its total strength. The Germans destroyed 17 tanks and as many half-tracks. Much of the rest of the equipment had to be abandoned. It could have been much worse had rearguard elements not managed to stave off troops from the 26th Volksgrenadier Division at Longvilly for as long as they did. Some of Gilbreth's men held out at the village until noon. Lieutenant Edward Hyduke from Team Cherry denied the Germans direct access to the N12 from Longvilly into the afternoon. This junior officer from Detroit, the son of Polish immigrants, did so with only a handful of men, earning himself a Silver Star.[33]

At the other end of the embattled stretch of the N12, Cherry's men and Ewell's paratroopers were hurling themselves against Mageret. They were trying to push the Germans out of the village to enable the trapped Americans to break out and reach Bastogne. But repeated efforts to dislodge Bayerlein's men proved futile.

Futile, too, were the attempts of two Belgian teenagers to get away from Mageret. At their boarding school in Bastogne, Paul Goosse and Alphonse Dominique had packed a heavy suitcase each on Monday afternoon, said goodbye, and walked out of town. They had spent the night at Mageret with relatives, only to wake up surrounded by the enemy. Bayerlein's troops stamped through the village's houses, grabbing anything they could lay their hands on: bacon, medicines, even shoes. Fooled by a lull in the fighting, the boys seized their suitcases and tried to make their way to Bourcy, where their parents lived. But machine-gun fire forced Paul into a ditch. The boy tried to see where Alphonse was, but angry bullets continued to kick up dirt, forcing him to keep his head down. He yelled for Alphonse to follow him, crawled along the ditch, and disappeared into the woods. Eventually, American soldiers intercepted the boy, questioned him, and drove him back to Bastogne. The body of Alphonse, riddled with bullets, would be found more than a month later beside two suitcases in a ditch.[34]

Throughout the day, soldiers like Sergeant Wickert managed to escape the inferno on the N12 via back roads and fields north and south of Mageret. They reached the airborne lines as more of the 501st paratroopers were arriving just east of Bastogne. Ewell's men were now finding it hard to cut their way through the town from Mande-Saint-Étienne. Refugees and worn-out stragglers from the 28th Infantry Division were clogging the roads. The paratroopers were happy to take arms and ammunition from the retreating infantrymen. The 2nd Battalion pushed on to Bizory, while the 3rd Battalion managed to reach Mont, where it was surprised to find a small band of soldiers firmly dug in. These were men from the 35th Engineer Combat Battalion, the battalion from Alaska that had taken up lonely positions on Sunday evening and had stuck together ever since. "Just when things looked the worst and we were strung out across a pasture in skirmish line," one of the hugely relieved engineers said, "the 101st Airborne Division came over the hill from Bastogne."[35]

Mess Sergeant Sklenar was no less happy to be surrounded by paratroopers. He and other cooks of the 482nd Anti-aircraft Artillery had somehow managed to fight their way out of the German trap east of Mageret. Now they were manning a kitchen truck that was parked in Bastogne's town square. They cooked for the airborne men who were streaming by until they ran out of stocks. Then they took a dozen smoked hams from a town store and sliced those up for the paratroopers. "I asked one guy what he was going to do without a rifle," recalled Charles Sklenar. "He said he would take one off a dead Kraut."[36]

4

As the paratroopers of Ewell's 3rd Battalion shook hands with the Alaskan engineers at Mont, I Company received orders to push on to Wardin, the next village just to the southeast. They were to cover the battalion's right flank. More importantly, they were to link up with Team O'Hara, another of the combat teams of the 10th Armored Division sent out the previous night to form a roadblock. After a mile or so, the road sloped down, and I Company caught sight of a dozen farms clustered around a church and a small stream. All seemed tranquil as the 140 paratroopers set up positions and sent out patrols. But they had just entered another perfect trap.

They had been unable to locate Team O'Hara, which was nearby but failed to communicate with the airborne troops. It was Middleton's earlier decision not to place Colonel Roberts's teams under the direct control of General McAuliffe that was largely to blame for this situation. But to make matters worse, I Company's radio connection with 3rd Battalion went dead in Wardin (possibly because of the surrounding dense forest). Meanwhile, as soon as Bayerlein learned of American troops on the move to Wardin, the veteran commander interpreted this as a flanking threat to Panzer Lehr and immediately dispatched a reconnaissance battalion to the village. This German force was many times stronger than the American company and had the support of seven tanks.

It was early afternoon when the German force smashed into Wardin from several directions. The paratroopers had no armored vehicles of any kind, and they could not radio back to Bastogne to have artillery fire brought down. The men had to fend for themselves. Their firepower consisted of nothing but rifles, machine guns, and a couple of bazookas. From his command post in a house in the western part of the village, Captain Claude Wallace desperately tried to keep his company organized. Experienced platoon sergeants like Robert Houston ran from squad to squad barking instructions. Sergeant Houston had earned the Distinguished Service Cross in Normandy, where, at great personal risk, he had destroyed an enemy gun that was pinning down his men. He now watched his comrades run even greater risks trying to take out tanks with bazookas. One team saw its burst barely scratch the heavy armor of a tank's sloping front. They quickly moved to the side of the tank and fired another round from just a few yards, finally disabling the monster. The German crew were mown down as they scrambled from the vehicle. Another tank came up and pushed the wreck off the road. Sergeant Calderan held his breath as he saw a soldier from another platoon crawl forward and fire his tube from up close. The explosion made the bazookaman tumble backwards. He crawled back onto his feet and roared, "I got it! I got it!"

More Germans streamed into the village, using the tanks as cover. Houses and barns were set on fire, and smoke filled the streets. Platoon radios crackled with pleas for help. For some the strain became too much. In the Belgrange farm, villagers witnessed paratroopers get into an argument as some threw down their arms and made to surrender. An officer drew a pistol and forced them to pick up their weapons.

Others decided to make a brave last stand all on their own. Private Wilbrod Gauthier placed himself in the middle of Wardin's main street. He stood facing a tank, a bazooka balanced on his shoulder. He squeezed off a round and scored a direct hit on the German menace. In response, a machine gun on another tank rattled off an angry volley and the paratrooper slumped to the ground.

The Germans were taking Wardin house by house. They closed in on the command post. A tank shell drilled through the wall and killed a sergeant inside. Darkness had fallen some time before. Captain Wallace went on the company radio and ordered the platoons to save themselves. He slipped out and tried to reach the stream, but was mowed down, together with one of his lieutenants. Villagers watched the Germans capture two paratroopers at the Grandjean farm and club them into submission with their rifle butts. But others did get away. One was Robert Houston. Despite the pain in his knee (an old injury from Normandy that was playing up), he stumbled through the village's tiny stream until he reached the forest. Of the 140 men who marched into Wardin early on Tuesday afternoon, 57 never made it back again.

When the fury of battle finally died down that night, many of Wardin's houses and barns were in ruins or ablaze. In some of the smaller streets villagers found dead paratroopers bunched together where they had run into machine-gun fire. The rock-solid cellars of the Ardennes farms had kept most villagers safe, but there were also civilians among the corpses. One farmer had been killed trying to rescue his harvest from a burning barn. And a shell had killed Margareta Schank when she was trying to escape from the cellar of a blazing farm. Margareta was 22 and had fled all the way from Luxembourg to escape the returning Germans. Fellow refugees buried the girl beside a road. A week later, when the snow came down and the front had moved still closer to Bastogne, they dug up her body and wrapped it in a shroud. An ox pulled the sledge that took her home.[37]

By nightfall on Tuesday, Colonel Ewell was satisfied that his spearhead 501st Parachute Infantry had done all it could to test the enemy's strength east of Bastogne. His losses in Wardin in particular convinced him that the time had come to switch from offense to defense. He now had his regiment dig in deep on the outskirts of Bastogne, along a line from just north of Bizory all the way to the Wiltz road north of Marvie.

Stubborn resistance from the airborne arrivals and the desperate rear-guard action of armored elements east of Mageret had caused Bayerlein and the Volksgrenadiers to lose the race for the crucial Ardennes crossroads. "Bastogne," Bayerlein realized that night, "appeared to be defended by very good troops." A German *coup de main* was now out of the question. The battle for the Belgian town was shaping up to be a long slog.[38]

5

On Tuesday, none of the American troops defending Bastogne were in a more exposed position than Team Desobry. Late on Monday evening, the armored force had arrived in Noville as another of Colonel Roberts's three blocking positions. The crossroads village was located slightly northeast of Bastogne, and straddled the N15, which ran straight into town from Houffalize. That made the road as important as the N12. Tall and lean, Major William Desobry was only 26, but he had proven a capable commander and had achieved rapid promotion. As he assessed the situation at dawn on Tuesday, Desobry was well aware that his troops were in a vulnerable spot. Almost five miles separated Noville from Bastogne. On low ground, with ridges overlooking it from the north and the east, the village was hard to defend. Ominously, some time before dawn the constant stream of American stragglers from a variety of infantry and armored units had suddenly dried up. Now the sound of roaring motors and metallic clanking could be heard ever more distinctly from several directions. "Oh brother!" Major Desobry murmured to himself. "There is really something out there!"[39]

Desobry had no way of knowing that what was bearing down on his force of barely 400 men was the full weight of the 2nd Panzer Division. Neither did he know that von Lauchert's crack force had been ordered to bypass Bastogne and smash its way westward. There was some irony in Major Desobry's situation. The fierce fighting his troops were about to be drawn into would be not so much a battle to keep Bastogne safe, but a battle that would slow down one of the offensive's major thrusts to the Meuse River. Regardless of the bigger picture, Major Desobry's instructions were very clear: under no circumstances was he to fall back on Bastogne without specific orders to do so.[40]

Not long after dawn, a terrific racket erupted about a mile northeast of Noville. The 10th Armored Division men were unaware that they were listening to the destruction of the last task force of the 9th Armored Division.

Task Force Booth, surrounded north of Longvilly since Monday night, had decided to break out in hope of reaching American lines. As they pulled back in the direction of Noville, they had the bad luck to stumble straight into the path of the 2nd Panzer Division. The task force never stood a chance. Its commander had been badly injured even before the engagement started, his leg mangled when he got caught under a half-track as he was shouting orders up and down the column. Now, trapped on a road between high banks, light American tanks and half-tracks were picked off one after the other by massive German Panthers. Those who survived the slaughter scrambled from their vehicles. Together with his buddy from Chicago, Corporal Ray Stoker, a New Englander, crawled into a pile of hay. Despite his wounded leg, Lieutenant Colonel Booth managed to reach a barn and hide, but he was soon captured. Many more troops were flushed from a nearby wood and taken prisoner. Major Eugene Watts, the task force operations officer from South Carolina, hid out until dark with dozens of others. He then organized the men into small groups and told them to head south for Bastogne. Watts later estimated that of the task force's 300 to 350 men, only 100 to 125 ever made it to the Belgian town.[41]

With Task Force Booth smashed, the 2nd Panzer Division quickly turned its full attention to Noville. Desobry's men gasped as the thick fog briefly lifted around 1000, long enough to reveal a massive concentration of German armor to the north.

Just days before, the Americans had been resting in France and looking forward to a relaxing Christmas. Private Boyd Etters had used the time to ask the home front to send him canned fruit, cakes, and "anything that is eatable." But the 22-year-old had also let slip in letters that his time on the Lorraine front had "seemed like a year," and that this was when "my nerves began to hop around." "About all I can say," the Pennsylvanian had concluded in a letter from the rest area, "is that I hope it doesn't last much longer, it is really a terrific ordeal." Now, peering out at German tanks coming in "at full steam," Boyd Etters realized that the ordeal had only just begun.[42]

It took desperate and ferocious fighting to halt several armored probes before noon. Some enemy tanks and infantry actually managed to get into Noville. But with the help of a platoon of tank destroyers, the village held – against all odds and at a high price. As their morning offensive faded, the Germans started up a merciless barrage from the surrounding ridges. The casualty numbers steadily mounted. Captain Jack Prior did what he could for the wounded streaming into his makeshift aid station, a former café. He was fresh from medical school at the University of Vermont and had arrived as a replacement for the regular battalion surgeon, who had been evacuated with pneumonia. Now he found himself practicing medicine on his belly as explosions shattered the windows and red-hot shrapnel zinged through the spacious tavern room. They had run out of stretchers and were organizing patients into rows on the floor.

Major Desobry worried that his dwindling force might soon be overrun. The road leading out of Noville to the south and into Bastogne had not yet been cut. Desobry placed a phone call to his commander at Hôtel Lebrun, asking for permission to withdraw. Colonel Roberts replied that he would have to use his own judgment, but that he should know that a battalion of paratroopers was on its way to strengthen his team.[43]

This unexpected good news at once convinced Major Desobry to stay put in Noville. The battalion he was promised belonged to the 506th Parachute Infantry. Colonel Robert Sink's regiment was under orders to anchor its defenses on the heights just south of Foy, a hamlet on the N15 just below Noville. The 1st Battalion now was to be the regiment's advance outpost in support of Team Desobry of the 10th Armored Division. It would take some time for the paratroopers to arrive: they were still struggling to push their way through the jammed streets of Bastogne and would have to cover the five miles to Noville on foot. But Major Desobry wasted no time. He sent his intelligence officer to Bastogne in a jeep to pick up the airborne commander. Lieutenant Colonel James LaPrade made it to Noville just before noon. He was about as tall as Desobry and, noted the armored commander, "very confident." He agreed with Desobry that their next step should be an attack on the German positions on the surrounding ridges.[44]

As the men of the 1st Battalion headed in the direction of the N15, civilians stood on Bastogne's sidewalks with pots of coffee and kettles of soup, determined to get some hot liquid into the American soldiers. Little did the paratroopers know that what awaited them somewhere down the road was a direct assault on a veteran armored division.[45]

The battalion was still not fully armed: some men carried no more than a trench knife, and most were lacking ammunition. Not far from Foy, supply officers from the 10th Armored Division had positioned themselves in the middle of the road with several vehicles. These were loaded with ammunition hastily scrounged from Combat Command B's supply trains. Troopers grabbed bandoliers, bazooka rounds, and mortar grenades as they marched past.[46]

The rumble in Noville intensified, creating the sensation, Private Burgett noted, of "walking into a thunderstorm up ahead." The troopers spread out even more now. They crouched closer to the ditches, scanning the forests on both sides of the road. There were thin patches of snow, and men scooped some into their mouths to moisten parched throats.[47]

Inside Noville, there was barely time to brief the paratroopers as they made ready to head off towards the ridges. Private James Simms was new to combat. Before the war the 25-year-old had been an Alabama high-school teacher and football coach. Now he was teamed up with a bazookaman as an assistant gunner. He watched a lieutenant nervously pace back and forth. "Man," he heard the officer mutter, "this is going to be a bastard." "My anxiety level," Simms remembered, "tightened up like a banjo string."[48]

At 1430, LaPrade's battalion rose and stormed in the direction of the ridges. They never stood much chance against an entire division looking down on them from the heights. A terrifying barrage plowed the fields, explosions and shrapnel scything men down. The barrage was followed almost immediately by an attack with the dreaded Mark IV and Mark V tanks. The few remaining Shermans and tank destroyers from Team Desobry desperately attempted to provide support. But all the devastated airborne force could do now was try and fall back in an orderly fashion, resisting every step of the way. Those lucky enough to make it back to Noville would be scarred for life by the horrific scenes they witnessed that afternoon. Private Steve Polander, concussed by an explosion, stumbled into a barn. Inside, a fellow soldier sat on a block of wood. "His skull on the upper right side," the trooper registered vaguely, "has been totally torn off by a huge chunk of shrapnel. His brains are showing. The medic kneels, dabbing his skull." Another soldier, Donald Burgett, the private from Detroit, watched one of the replacements scream for a medic, "his guts trailing in the dirt behind him." They tackled him to the ground, spread his guts on a raincoat, washed the dirt off with water from a canteen, and forced the entrails back into his belly. Then they quickly bound him up, dragged him into a ditch, and moved on, praying a medic would locate him in time.[49]

Some tanks managed to push their way into Noville under cover of darkness. Private Addor had long since abandoned his half-track with the festive Christmas decoration of evergreen and red ribbon. He was now part of a bazooka team with Team Desobry, and he spotted an enemy tank so close that he "could have spit on it if my mouth had not gone dry all of a sudden." He was instantly knocked over by a loud blast. When he came to, he looked up at the long barrel of an American tank destroyer that had fired at the enemy tank over his head. A lieutenant was standing over him, trying to tell him something. "I could not hear anything at all," Don Addor recalled, "but a tremendous ringing and roaring."[50]

As small groups of defenders kept throwing back enemy intruders, General McAuliffe in Bastogne realized that the Noville force was close to being overrun. He picked up the phone and placed a call to General Middleton in Neufchâteau. He requested to have the men fall back to the main line of resistance at Foy. "No," the corps commander replied tersely, "if we are to hold on to Bastogne, you cannot keep falling back." LaPrade and Desobry now had no option but to discuss how to strengthen the Noville perimeter as best they could for the night. They bent over a map on a table inside the schoolhouse headquarters. Two shells slammed into the building in rapid succession. Soldiers rushed to the scene. They grabbed Lieutenant Colonel LaPrade's legs and dragged his dead body into the street. Major Desobry sat slumped amidst the rubble. His face was caked with dust. There was a gaping wound in the back of his head, and one of his eyes dangled from a badly smashed socket.[51]

William Desobry was spirited into a jeep and rushed to Bastogne for medical treatment. The defenders of Noville dug in, knowing that the night would be even more terrifying with their trusted commanders gone. In a basement that served as an American prison pen, paratrooper James Simms reflected on his life as a high-school teacher in Alabama. It all seemed so far away now. "A German prisoner told me," he recalled, "that he could really fight if he had about three or four good shots of booze just before a battle. I believed him."[52]

6

As the rumble of battle drifted in from the east and from Noville on Tuesday, the tension inside Bastogne rose by the hour. In mid-morning, General McAuliffe decided to have divisional headquarters moved from the assembly area at Mande-Saint-Étienne to the town itself. The obvious location was the Belgian military compound that had housed General Middleton and his VIII Corps staff. The Heintz barracks lay in the northern part of Bastogne, near the cemetery, and about a quarter of a mile away from the central market square. The 101st Airborne's staff decided against taking over the two-story main structure that corps personnel had just vacated. Judging it too obvious a target for shelling or for an attack penetrating the town, they settled for one of half a dozen modest buildings ranged along the north side of the central courtyard. By noon the place was bustling with action. A switchboard was installed and connected with the corps telephone lines that radiated across town. Crude cardboard signs on doors indicated the various parts of the nerve center, the most important of which were the War Room and the Operations Room. Awaiting orders, runners and liaison officers hung around in the courtyard, smoking and stamping their feet. Near the buildings, where there was a wide gateway in the compound wall, a tank destroyer squatted menacingly.[53]

As the day wore on, shells started landing in town with greater regularity, telling the shaken Bastognards that the Germans were now in sight of their town. For a long time, Joss Heintz, the 19-year-old son of the town's pharmacist on the rue du Vivier, stood scrubbing the façade of their home. In the delirious days of September, they had splashed "thank you" slogans across it, welcoming the American liberators in fat letters. Now Joss cursed under his breath as the paint refused to come off. A deafening explosion made him abandon his work abruptly. He jumped on his bicycle and joined the waves of civilians and American stragglers heading out of town. Joss did not stop pedaling until he reached Remoiville, a village more than six miles southwest of Bastogne. The chaotic scenes on the road reminded refugees of the exodus in May 1940, the first time Nazi Germany had invaded Belgium.[54]

Fearful as they were of war and the Nazis, many Bastognards decided it was already too late to try and outrun the German troops. Ida Nicolays was one of them. She had turned 20 the day the Germans launched their counteroffensive. Her brothers, former members of the resistance, had already fled. But their mother was suffering from pneumonia and was in no fit state to travel. Even on Monday, they had continued to repair watches in the family's jewelry store. Now, late on Tuesday afternoon, as the shelling increased, Ida decided it was time to hang up the "closed" sign. She and her sister went upstairs and began dragging mattresses to the basement. There would be no customers for a very long time.[55]

That evening, Phil Burge and a comrade returned from a visit to McAuliffe's command post. They belonged to the headquarters of an engineer battalion in Colonel Roberts's armored command in Bastogne and had been discussing the tight supply situation. As they passed the Catholic church, Phil's comrade insisted they pay a visit "so that he could make peace with his maker." When they pushed open the heavy doors, the sound of prayer came gushing out. The church, Phil Burge recalled, "was crowded with civilians."[56]

As darkness tightened its grip, more shells began to rock Bastogne. The sound of explosions could be heard all the way to the 326th Airborne Medical Company, a tent camp at an important crossroads near Sprimont, eight miles northwest of the town. The surgical hospital was the highest medical echelon in the division. It was to take care of the serious cases after these had received treatment in the battalion and regimental aid stations. The 326th had been one of the last units to leave Mourmelon on Monday. Medical stocks were still in disarray after Operation Market Garden and, when the unexpected call had come to move out again, personnel had rushed to sterilize equipment and get more of everything, sending trucks all the way back to Rheims. The company had only arrived at Mande-Saint-Étienne mid-morning on Tuesday. By noon, after "feverish setup activity," the hospital facility was up and running. And by early afternoon, ambulances and trucks were bringing in the first patients.

The medical staff knew they were in an exposed position. Their canvas tents dotted a meadow near a major road junction in flat terrain, devoid of buildings. During daylight, refugees streamed by, desperate to get away from the enemy. "The looks on their faces," one medic noted, "will be ever in my memory." In mid-afternoon, a worried Captain Willis McKee had traveled to Bastogne to ask permission to set up the hospital inside the town. McKee was an experienced surgeon who had seen combat with the 101st in Normandy and Holland. He was allowed to express his concerns to McAuliffe himself, but the general had dismissed them. "Go on back, Captain," he had said, "you'll be all right."[57]

Now, late in the evening, there was no more time to worry. The hospital was being flooded with severe casualties brought in from aid stations closer to the front, where they had received only preliminary treatment. Some had suffered horrific burns and arrived covered in soothing ointments. Others had had limbs torn off and were unloaded from trucks with plasma bags on their bellies. Almost all had been given heavy doses of morphine to dull the pain. The doctors and medics barely registered the drone of approaching vehicles as they worked frantically to save lives. But they were flat on the floor in seconds when mayhem erupted and bullets ripped up the canvas tents. Patients screamed as doctors tried to lower them onto the ground. Medical vehicles were set ablaze, and the horn of one of them got stuck and blared away eerily. Lieutenant Herb Viertel had just arrived at the hospital from Noville, where he had suffered wounds in a mortar attack. He had been awaiting his turn for treatment and had still not been unloaded from the medical vehicle. He lived through the whole agonizing experience on a stretcher inside the ambulance. Another medical convoy came down from Noville and headed straight into the battle zone. Machine guns opened up on the vehicles, instantly killing the litter cases carried by the first jeep.[58]

The 326th Airborne Medical Company had fallen foul of German recon-naissance elements of the 116th Panzer Division. It, together with von Lauchert's 2nd Panzer Division, was feeling its way north of Bastogne in the race to the Meuse River. Both divisions were plunging through the huge gap that was opening up in front of von Manteuffel's Fifth Panzer Army. When the shooting abated, medical personnel and their patients were told they were now all prisoners. They were loaded into their own vehicles, together with as much of the sought-after American medical supplies as the Germans could gather. One of the prisoners was veteran surgeon Willis McKee, who had tried to persuade General McAuliffe to assign them a safer location inside Bastogne. Another was Major Desobry, the armored commander who had been badly wounded in Noville earlier in the evening. He had been anesthetized and operated on just before the Germans hit the hospital. When he came to in an ambulance, the major in his dazed state briefly thought that the German voices around him were a good sign, as his men were apparently capturing many of the enemy. The ambulance driver soon set him straight, making it clear that it was he who had been taken prisoner.[59]

Several dozen medical personnel evaded capture and started to make their way to the surrounding woods. Edward O'Brien joined them. O'Brien belonged to Ewell's 501st Parachute Infantry and was a medic in the regimental aid station inside Bastogne. He had arrived at the hospital area just before the German attack, bringing more patients, as well as urgent requests for additional blankets, plasma, and morphine. Now he was crawling on his belly, a trench knife in his fist. At each suspicious sound he pretended to be dead, like "an old possum back in Missouri." O'Brien managed to get back to Bastogne the following day. The mood inside his regiment's aid station was glum. News of the fate of the division's hospital had preceded him. It was a serious blow to all. More than 140 doctors, nurses, and other medical personnel had been captured. Evacuation of the seriously wounded was now all but impossible. Large amounts of medical supplies had been lost. The Americans now also knew that the Germans were cutting them off much more quickly than they had imagined. There was much suffering to come. And there would be too little morphine to ease all the pain.[60]

CHAPTER 3

LOCKING HORNS

On Wednesday, December 20, word of the loss of the 101st Airborne's field hospital came as a big blow to the men in Bastogne. And there was more bad news: the forecasts indicated that, although the weather in the Ardennes appeared to be changing, there was little hope of any real improvement before Friday, at the earliest. When told during the morning briefing at First Army headquarters that there would yet again be "no air activity" that day, General Courtney Hodges "shook his head in resignation." At all levels it was understood that the massive superiority of the Allied air forces would be crucial in turning the tide. As soon as the scale of the German offensive had become clear, the Supreme Headquarters of the Allied Expeditionary Force had begun readying large numbers of fighter-bombers, as well as medium and heavy bombers, for the counterattack. Now, however, for the fifth day in a row, menacing clouds and dense fog forced all aircraft to remain idle. "Today," First Army headquarters complained, "the ceiling was completely on the ground." General Middleton at VIII Corps headquarters in Neufchâteau shared their frustration as he monitored the critical situation in Bastogne. "Talk about the fog of war," he recalled. "Why, you couldn't get even a Cub plane up."[1]

Even through the fog of war, however, the bigger picture in the Ardennes could be discerned at Eisenhower's headquarters. In front of Luxembourg City, the Americans were holding the southern shoulder of the breakthrough, forcing the Seventh Army on the defensive there. Divisions from the First Army were being siphoned off to shore up the American blocking position on the northern shoulder. But although this meant that the Sixth Panzer Army was stonewalled at Elsenborn Ridge, *Kampfgruppe* Peiper had pushed forward as deep as La Gleize and Stoumont. Worse, overcast skies prevented Allied air forces from blunting von Manteuffel's armored spearheads in the center of the salient as the 2nd and 116th Panzer Divisions slipped in between Saint-Vith and Bastogne. These two towns and road junctions would now be crucial in stemming the advance of the Fifth Panzer Army to the Meuse River. Late on Tuesday, a large part of the trapped American 106th Infantry Division had surrendered in front of Saint-Vith, leaving only the 7th Armored Division and the remnants of other outfits for a desperate defense of the town. With no more than a lightly armed airborne force the core of its shield, the situation at Bastogne appeared just as bleak.

Inside the town, however, General McAuliffe was determined to remain focused on the positives. Two days earlier, an air controller from the Ninth Air Force had slipped into town and set up a radio communications center. As soon as the skies cleared, it would take just a few words to bring down death and destruction on enemy targets closing in on Bastogne. Meanwhile, McAuliffe took still more comfort from the fact that additional firepower had arrived that could be put to use without delay. During the night, elements of the 705th Tank Destroyer Battalion had been rushed to the town's perimeter. The tank destroyers – a force commanded by Lieutenant Colonel Clifford Templeton – had arrived late on Tuesday evening. They had left the German town of Kohlscheid more than 24 hours earlier and traveled 60 miles south to Bastogne. Fleeing GIs and civilians had cost them precious time on the roads, and on several occasions Templeton's men had had to beat back attacks by roving units sent out in advance of the enemy's main force. The crews were exhausted when they finally arrived in Bastogne, but they were not allowed any rest. Their fast and highly maneuverable M18 Hellcats were a godsend, particularly as they were equipped with the new, long-barreled 76mm guns that were a serious match for most of the German tanks. That is why, at dawn on Wednesday, Templeton's red-eyed men found themselves among the paratroopers and tank crews peering at enemy lines from Noville and from Bastogne's eastern gates.[2]

An artilleryman first and foremost, McAuliffe was especially pleased to be adding to the growing firepower of the artillery battalions at his disposal. His own division artillery had arrived intact, and the battalions had quickly taken up concentrated positions in support of each of the four airborne regiments. An airborne landing generally involved a substantial element of dispersion and damage, so this was an unusually advantageous position for the paratroop force to be in. Still, most of the 101st Airborne's guns were lighter than those of a standard division, and their range significantly shorter. This was partly offset, however, by the presence of the 420th Armored Field Artillery, the guns organic to Colonel Roberts's Combat

Command B. To this force had been added the 755th Armored Field Artillery, a unit that, like Templeton's tank destroyers, had been rushed to Bastogne from Germany and had arrived on Tuesday.[3]

By a stroke of good luck, Bastogne's firepower had been further augmented by the arrival of a battalion of African-American gunners. Originally attached to the 28th Infantry Division, the 969th Field Artillery had been ordered to pull back when it became clear that the infantry troops were disintegrating. The battalion had drifted back and forth until it was pulled into the slowly forming defenses around Bastogne. The three field battalions, all equipped with heavy 155mm pieces, had coalesced near the village of Senonchamps, just west of Bastogne. McAuliffe was well aware that the range of their guns was sufficient to allow devastating firepower to be brought down around the entire sweep of the perimeter. Dark and forbidding as the skies over Bastogne might look, the American airborne commander and artilleryman felt he was ready to lock horns with the Germans.[4]

1

An incident at dawn on Wednesday made Captain Richard Winters question whether his men were ready to withstand what the Germans might soon be throwing at them. He was the executive officer of the 506th Parachute Infantry's 2nd Battalion. The day before, his men had hurriedly dug in on the edge of a forest overlooking fields southeast of Foy. On their left, they tied in with the 3rd Battalion, whose troops were anchored on Foy, the last village before Bastogne on the N15 from Noville. The two battalions formed the main line of resistance northeast of Bastogne. But with the men of the 1st Battalion fighting for their lives in Noville, some 2,500 yards further north, the main line was stretched precariously thin.

Suddenly, as Captain Winters was contemplating all this in the cool air outside his headquarters, he froze as a German soldier casually stepped out from between some trees and walked to the middle of a clearing. Two GIs instantly shouldered their rifles, but the captain gestured that they should hold their fire. The German took off his long overcoat, dropped his trousers, and relieved himself. As soon as he was done, Captain Winters mustered his best German and yelled 'Kommen Sie hier!' When the Americans searched the bewildered soldier, they found no more than a few photographs and a piece of stale black bread. If one unarmed soldier could penetrate as far as battalion headquarters, Captain Winters asked himself, what would a full-blown attack do to their line?[5]

Faced by the firepower of the entire 2nd Panzer Division for a second day, the American paratroopers and tank crews inside Noville already knew the answer to that question. The night had brought a quick change of leadership and some most welcome reinforcements. Major Charles Hustead had replaced the badly wounded Desobry as commander of the 10th Armored Division's team. Meanwhile Major Robert Harwick had been on leave in Paris when his airborne division moved out to the Ardennes. He had arrived in Noville just in time to learn that the 1st Battalion's commander was dead and that he was to take over without delay. The reinforcements consisted of three platoons from the newly arrived 705th Tank Destroyer Battalion, with each platoon consisting of four M18 Hellcats.[6]

The arrival of the tank destroyers was the only good thing to happen to the troops in Noville on Wednesday. When dawn came, the Americans had already been enduring a vicious pounding for several hours. The village was ablaze and crumbling, and the men's nerves were in tatters. They had barely slept since leaving France on Monday. There was not much to eat, and thirst made swallowing difficult for many. As daylight struggled to pierce the heavy mist, Noville's defenders knew that an all-out attack was imminent and that worse was to come. "How is it at home?" Major Harwick wondered. "I'm glad they don't know the spot I am in."[7]

Von Lauchert's superiors were getting impatient with the delay his 2nd Panzer Division was experiencing in breaking through to the Meuse. The armored commander received orders to take Noville "under any circumstances, as fast as possible." When, around mid-morning, the German attack finally came, Private Donald Burgett saw the fog lift just enough to reveal "a swarm of enemy tanks." There was little to be done, other than to allow the Panthers to steamroll over their foxholes and to wait for the enemy infantry to arrive in their wake. For Zygmunt Chmielewski, one of Burgett's paratroop buddies, these long, tense moments proved too much. He jumped to his feet, stumbled after a tank, and emptied his carbine at the steel hull in a futile attempt to stop it. Enraged, he pleaded with his comrades to come to his aid as shells exploded all around him. But he encountered only blank stares, so he slumped back to his foxhole. "When he returned to us," said Burgett, "we could see tears streaming down his face."[8]

As von Lauchert's tanks lumbered towards Noville, the agile M18 Hellcats sprang into action. Corporal Colby Ricker and Private Ellie McManus worked their tank destroyer like mad. They had been together since training in the United States, and they slipped into a deadly routine even amidst the thundering chaos. They forgot all about the exposed position they were in as

McManus, a South Carolinian, swiftly reloaded the gun each time Corporal Ricker blasted away at a target. They had taken out no fewer than five tanks when a shell hit their own vehicle. Both men were wounded and later received a Bronze Star for their actions.[9]

Inside the village, a paratroop sergeant was pointing a bazooka out of a basement window. Private Simms pulled the safety pin from a round, placed it in the sergeant's tube, and wired it up. "So many German tanks moved toward Noville," the high-school teacher from Alabama recalled, "that the ground actually trembled." They watched as one massive tank rumbled over a series of mines in the street, exploded them all, and simply kept going. A lieutenant stumbled into the basement with a radio and began yelling instructions. Shells screamed in, rocking the building, but the tank hugged the outside wall, before moving out of sight unscathed.

As the dust settled in the small basement room, two wounded soldiers were brought in. One was a boy whose eyeball was "hanging down on his cheek in a bloody mess." The other was Sergeant Morris. A jagged piece of shell fragment had ripped into his back. It had passed straight through him and now sat lodged against the taut skin of his abdomen. A medic jabbed both men with a shot of morphine. The sergeant was soon unconscious, "pale and waxy-looking as a corpse." "I sat down against the wall," Private Simms later recalled, "and tried to figure out how civilized people could ever get themselves into such a mess."[10]

As Hellcat crews and bazooka teams hunted down tanks in and around Noville, the paratroopers climbed out of their foxholes to halt the waves of Panzergrenadiers. Brave forward observers from the 321st Glider Field Artillery rained down 105mm shells on the enemy infantry. To the frustration of von Lauchert and his superiors, by noon the Americans had somehow managed to halt yet another fierce attack. Majors Harwick and Hustead realized, however, that the reprieve would be a short one. They had all but run out of armor-piercing shells, and the light howitzers of the glider artillery could stop infantry, but not tanks. The heavy artillery that was concentrated southwest of Bastogne could not reach as far as outlying Noville. Most worrisome, the casualties were now so numerous that the aid stations could no longer absorb them. Even some of the switchboard operators and clerks from the command post had been sent to strengthen the frontline companies. Airborne Major Harwick, the overall commander of the forces at Noville, understood that the time had come to withdraw or be annihilated in the next attack. He had a soldier jump into a jeep and race to Bastogne to relay that urgent message. Not long after noon, the radio of the artillery observers in Noville crackled with news that the defenders were to pull out as soon as possible.[11]

That was easier said than done. Von Lauchert's 304th Panzergrenadier Regiment had now bypassed Noville and slammed into the thin lines that Captain Winters had earlier been so concerned about. The 3rd Battalion on Dick Winters' left had been pushed out of Foy and forced onto the high ground south of it. The N15 from Noville to Bastogne was straight as an arrow, and the area to its left and right was flat and bare. As if that did not make the road enough of a death trap, Foy straddled this sole escape route and was now in the hands of the Germans. McAuliffe and his team quickly improvised an emergency plan: there was no other choice but to have the 3rd Battalion retake Foy. Major Harwick's force was to pull out of Noville as soon as they heard the noise of battle at Foy. They were to take a leap of faith, praying that their paratroop brethren to the south would have cleared the way by the time their badly mauled force approached.[12]

Amidst continued shelling, Noville became a hive of nervous activity. Majors Harwick and Hustead moved back and forth between the troops, snapping orders to ensure the exodus was as smooth as possible. Noville's main road was sealed off with wrecked vehicles in order to slow down enemy pursuit. Mines, 81mm mortar shells, and all other heavy ordnance were assembled at the base of the church tower, which had somehow remained standing. The explosives were wired up for detonation, to prevent the enemy getting hold of them. It was also hoped that the church tower would collapse in the explosion and block the main road. A detailed escape plan was hurriedly hammered out: many of the paratroopers were to descend on Bastogne on foot and make their way through the fields left and right of the N15; meanwhile a convoy of the surviving vehicles was to snake its way southward on the N15 in some semblance of order. At its head would be a Greyhound scout car, some half-tracks, and five tanks. Immediately behind these would be the vehicles carrying the wounded. Next would come the bulk of the half-tracks and other vehicles. And a platoon of Hellcat tank destroyers was to bring up the rear.[13]

Captain Jack Prior did not think the plan would work for his patients. The young physician from Vermont had seen his aid station in the café fill to overflowing. He estimated that at least 50 men were so badly wounded they would have to be carried. But there were nowhere near enough stretchers. He decided there was no option open to him but to remain behind with his patients and be made a prisoner of war. But his first sergeant refused to accept this. He barked at his men to take as many doors as possible off their hinges. Captain Prior watched the sergeant and his medics carefully strap the men onto the makeshift litters and carry them in the direction of the convoy. Chauffeurs, armed paratroopers and infantrymen, walking wounded, and litters were hastily assigned to each vehicle. The body of Lieutenant Colonel James LaPrade was loaded onto a vehicle for burial in Bastogne. James Simms and some of his comrades hurried to a tank with Sergeant Morris on a stretcher. They quickly lashed stretcher and patient to the back of the tank and ran off to take their places in a half-track. Private Simms watched the tank's heavy-caliber machine gun fire bursts down the street and straight over the sergeant's head every few minutes. The sound was deafening, but did not appear to bother the comatose sergeant.[14]

At 1315, the signal was given for the foot soldiers to push off. Some ten minutes later, the vehicles started rolling on the N15 to Bastogne. Donald Burgett and some fellow paratroopers clung to the deck of one of the tank destroyers, the last of the vehicles to pull out of Noville. Their assignment was not only to protect the rear, but also to make sure that the explosives at the church blew up. If the charges did not detonate, the men had been told that they would have to go back and set them off themselves. The paratroopers heaved a collective sigh of relief when, after some anxious minutes, "one hell of an explosion" made the church tower collapse onto the village's main road. One of the last Americans to escape from Noville was Lieutenant Milton Frank from the 10th Armored Division's engineer unit. Despite intense shelling, he had stayed behind until the very last minute to ensure the ammunition's detonation. Just one of countless examples of bravery shown at Noville, this earned the lieutenant from Illinois a Silver Star.[15]

Many more acts of courage would be required that afternoon. For a while, it looked as if the men might actually reach Bastogne without too much bloodshed. The fog was so dense again that it made vehicles and men on the flat stretch all but invisible. Although the men from Noville did not know it, ahead of them the 3rd Battalion was successfully pushing the Germans out of their roadblock at Foy. As the half-track he was in rolled on at a leisurely pace, James Simms made small talk with a German prisoner, who told him he was 17. One of several enemy prisoners in the convoy, he had been shot in the leg and seemed glad that for him the war was almost over. Without warning, a GI in the half-track suddenly leaned over, grabbed the boy's arm, and tried to wrestle his watch from him. "Leave the damn boy alone," snarled Simms. The GI backed off without protest.[16]

Hope of any miraculous escape vanished in a flash, when, at around 1400, an enemy force of tanks and infantry slammed into the left flank of the convoy, just as it approached Foy. "Words cannot describe what took place," a tormented soldier from the 10th Armored Division later wrote to his parents. Roaring blasts engulfed the leading tanks, forcing them to a dead stop. Don Addor was in one of the half-tracks immediately behind the Shermans. "The fog up front," he noted, "turned bright orange."[17]

Private Delmer Hildoer was sitting on the floor of a tank turret, behind the driver, when the gun shield was hit twice in rapid succession. The Pennsylvanian had manned the tank's machine gun throughout the battle for Noville. But now he was being transported as a casualty: during the German attack early in the morning, a direct hit on his tank had peppered his hands with shrapnel, and a little later another explosion had ripped off his right ear. The morphine now made him feel like he was drunk. But that did not stop him from clambering from the disabled tank in record time, even though his right leg, too, was now shredded with shell shards. The tank caught fire. One of the crew was shot in the face as he tried to get away from the blaze. He slumped back into the hatch. The men dived after him and pulled him out. Private Hildoer crawled away from where the gunfire was coming and disappeared into the dense fog that hung over the fields west of the N15.[18]

All along the convoy, soldiers were exiting their vehicles and making themselves invisible. From a ditch, Don Addor watched the hellish scene in disbelief. "Dead were lying all around on the road and in the ditches. Some were hanging out of their vehicles; killed before they could get out and seek cover. Our trucks and half-tracks were either burning or had been torn to shreds." Addor saw a medic at work on a soldier whose arm had been blown off. Seconds later, the medic was himself hit and crying out for help. A fellow medic tried to come to his rescue, but was shot in the chest in the middle of the road.

Private Addor hurriedly calculated his chances, jumped up, and dashed into the swirling mist that clung to a nearby pasture. He had not gone very far before he heard a whooshing sound and was lifted into the air. When he came to, he was lying on his back. He felt no pain and saw no blood. He sat up and reached for the small of his back. About an inch from his spine, a mortar shard poked through his skin and uniform. In a reflex action, he looked around for his rifle, getting to his feet to pick it up. A burst from a machine gun ripped through the fog and several bullets tore into his right leg. One splintered his shinbone; another severed an artery. Warm blood spurted onto the moist grass, and the ferrous tang pricked his nostrils.

Wounded twice in the blink of an eye, for some moments Private Addor thought he was going to die in a cow pasture, far from his home on Geranium

Street in Washington, D.C. Then, when the initial shock passed, he sat up again, fumbled with his webbed belt, and managed to apply a tourniquet that stopped the bleeding. He crawled to his rifle, wiped off the mud, and cradled it in his arms. As the din of battle gradually subsided, he sat waiting in the fog, lonelier than he had ever been. A while later, he heard a vehicle come to a halt nearby and dimly made out the shape of an American jeep. Two soldiers jumped out, bent over a dead body, and removed the dog tags. Don Addor alerted them with a feeble cry, and the GIs carefully loaded him into the back of their jeep.

As they tried to get past one of the convoy's disabled lead tanks, they heard moaning. The GIs stopped, went over to the tank, and returned with a soldier who had suffered a wound to his forehead. Don Addor believed he could see the man's brain. The soldier was placed on the hood. Each bump on the way to the American lines made him howl with pain.[19]

By dusk, more survivors of the German ambush were groping their way towards the American lines. James Simms' half-track was one of the vehicles plowing across the fields northwest of Foy. They halted just long enough to help medics dislodge a jeep that had become buried up to its axle in mud. As they climbed back into the half-track, Private Simms caught sight of a dead paratrooper. He lay face down on the ground, the Alabaman noted, almost as if he was "on a bed taking a nap." James Simms kept staring at the dead American as they pulled away. "I imagined," he said, "that his family would be discussing the last letter they had received from him, without realizing that he was already dead."[20]

Colonel Sink, the commander of the 506th Parachute Infantry, was up front to welcome the survivors from Noville. Robert Sink was the only original commander of any of the 101st Airborne's four regiments to have emerged from Normandy and Holland unscathed. He was not the kind of man to allow emotions to bubble to the surface. But as the gaunt and ragged soldiers filed past – unshaven, mud-caked, bandaged – the colonel could be seen in the middle of the road, "shaking hands with the men and slapping them on the back in greeting."[21]

A relatively small team of tank crews and airborne troops had managed to hold up von Lauchert's veteran armored outfit for two long days. In doing so, they had destroyed at least a dozen tanks and inflicted between 500 and 800 casualties, significantly weakening the division in its race to the Meuse. But the Americans had paid a high price, too: approximately half of Team Desobry's 400 officers and men had been killed or wounded. The armored unit left behind a few dozen tanks, tank destroyers, and half-tracks, and many other vehicles. Of the 473 paratroopers who, shortly after noon on Tuesday, had marched into Noville to Team Desobry's rescue, 212 were casualties by dusk on Wednesday.[22]

2

On the same day that troops were pulled back from the exposed position in Noville and integrated into the main line of resistance, paratroopers at the eastern gates of Bastogne braced themselves for what they knew would be long and decisive hours. They *were* the main line of resistance: if they failed to hold, Bastogne would be lost. Von Lüttwitz was well aware of that, of course. At the same time, however, he lamented that even now he was still not able to launch a massive, concentrated attack on Bastogne from the east with his XLVII Panzer Corps. Only two of the 26th Volksgrenadier Division's four regiments were in place. At least one infantry regiment, much of the artillery, and the bulk of the division's trains had failed to catch up with Panzer Lehr's armored spearheads. Meanwhile, temperatures remained mild for December, and, with fields wet and muddy, Bayerlein's tanks were forced to continue to operate on narrow, churned-up roads.[23]

Even on Tuesday, the Germans had hit the lines at Bizory, just northwest of Mageret, hard enough for the paratroopers to rename the village "Misery." In the thick of it that day, a runner from company headquarters had made his way to Bill Hayes, one of six men in a 60mm mortar squad, to tell him that the mortar squad leader in 3rd Platoon had been lost and that he had to take over. Hayes had barely arrived at the platoon when the runner returned to say that the mortar squad leader from 1st Platoon had been wounded and that he was more urgently needed there. Now, before dawn on Wednesday, as the men of Julian Ewell's 2nd Battalion were told that a large infantry force was heading their way with the support of tanks, an exhausted and tense Bill Hayes readied his squad once again. On their farm, an equally tense Monsieur and Madame Nisen decided it was time for their two small children to be taken to safety. They bundled them up against the morning cold, drove them off in a cart, and organized a place for them in the shelter beneath Bastogne's Franciscan church. Then they hurried back to Bizory to weather the storm and look after their animals.[24]

By the time the Nisens returned, American Hellcats were already engaged in fierce duels with German armor. Impressed paratroopers watched them fire rapid volleys, then, in quick maneuvers to evade counterfire, spin their tracks in reverse to hurl mud far in front. The platoon from the 705th Tank Destroyer Battalion had arrived just in time during the night and was now taking out target after target. That took some of the sting out of the attack, just as McAuliffe decided it was time to put his artillery battalions to the test. A concentrated barrage of airborne and heavier supporting guns was laid down on the enemy infantry and sustained for about 20 minutes. Staff members in General McAuliffe's command post bunched together by the phone, eager for reports on the impact. They soon learned that from their foxholes Ewell's men had seen the Germans in the fields "fall in unbelievable numbers." Someone turned to McAuliffe: "Julian says you took care of the sonsabitches real, real good, General." There was jubilation in the Operations Room. McAuliffe welcomed Colonel Sherburne, the acting commander of artillery, into the small room. "Let your people know I appreciate it, Tom," he said to the colonel.[25]

The storm over Bizory blew over in two hours. Ewell's 2nd Battalion suffered few if any casualties. The prisoners they took that morning were either wounded or shell-shocked. They were revealed to be from the 2nd Battalion of Kokott's 78th Volksgrenadier Regiment. The unit had been decimated. Von Lüttwitz fumed at the disastrous results of yet another piecemeal attack. The Nisens now felt confident enough about the strength of the airborne defenses to attempt to collect their children inside Bastogne. This time, however, American sentries, ever suspicious of infiltrators, refused to let them through. The distraught farmers were to sit out the siege in the paratroop front lines, separated from their children by two very long miles.[26]

In mid-morning on Wednesday, an advance guard of Bayerlein's 901st Panzergrenadier Regiment began probing the American perimeter at Marvie. A tiny village barely a mile southeast of Bastogne, Marvie looked down on the N34, a major road leading into town from Wiltz. The attackers consisted of no more than an infantry company, supported by four tanks and a self-propelled gun. But the Germans soon sensed they had discovered a weak spot in the American defenses. Marvie lay just outside Ewell's strong 501st Parachute Infantry sector. At dawn, the area had been defended by no more than a single company of airborne engineers. One of them was Leo LeBlanc, a private from Maine with Canadian roots who spoke French. As he sat in his lone foxhole, the engineer took comfort from the fact that, on his way through Bastogne the previous day, he had scribbled his home address on a scrap of paper and asked a Belgian couple to hold onto it and contact his parents should he fail to return from the front. Private LeBlanc had been much relieved to see reinforcements arrive at Marvie shortly after dawn. The previous night, McAuliffe, sensing that the engineers' position was too exposed, had urged the 2nd Battalion of the 327th Glider Infantry to hurry to Marvie from its assembly area at Mande-Saint-Étienne.[27]

Panzer Lehr's attack came just as the glidermen were relieving the engineers, and it caught the Americans off balance. The men of the 2nd Battalion had arrived without maps of the area they were supposed to defend, and in the dense fog they had to grope their way to their positions with the help of the engineers. The initial German blow instantly caused havoc, and almost immediately left one of the company commanders a casualty. Minutes later, soldiers came running to seek urgent help from medics for the battalion commander, who had been badly wounded when a shell slammed into his headquarters.

The German tanks inched closer. One fired point-blank into the house of Ernest Annet, killing him and his six-year-old daughter Marie. Five American tanks were in Marvie to give the paratroopers support. They were part of nearby Team O'Hara, one of the three blocking teams sent out by the 10th Armored Division's Combat Command B on Monday night. But they were light tanks, and their 37mm guns proved so ineffective against the German Mark IVs that they were soon beating a retreat. The paratroopers were now left exposed in their foxholes.[28]

Private Frank Denison had never been one to feel much fear. His father was from Los Angeles, but he had insisted his wife give birth to their son in San Antonio because he believed "you weren't a real man if you weren't born in Texas." Now a replacement whose name the private did not know suddenly keeled over in the foxhole next to him. Denison saw that the man had suffered a serious head wound. He grabbed him under the armpits and, in full view of the attacking Germans, labored to get him up the hill to an aid station. "I was never so scared in my life," he later admitted.[29]

The Panzergrenadiers were pushing their way into Marvie at the worst possible moment for McAuliffe and his staff, who at that time were still busy deliberating what to do with the forces that looked set to be overrun in Noville, to the northeast. But just then, from a hill near Marvie, the more powerful Sherman tanks from Team O'Hara zeroed in on the German armor and brought it to a standstill. A wild melee ensued, as paratroopers cleared farm after farm of the enemy, killing some 30 Panzergrenadiers and capturing 20 more. Feeling as frustrated as Kokott to the north, Bayerlein decided to let Marvie be for now. In the lull that followed, the airborne men called for the village priest. They told him they wanted all the villagers out of Marvie without delay. Scores of civilians hurriedly loaded food and blankets onto carts. Fearful and exhausted, they set off in different directions, one group stumbling southward through the German lines, another making its way into Bastogne.[30]

As soon as news came that the attack on Marvie was blunted, McAuliffe readied himself for a visit to Middleton in Neufchâteau. The Noville force at that time was fighting its way towards Bastogne, and there was nothing more McAuliffe could do for them, other than hope and pray. Earlier that morning, Middleton had called McAuliffe to tell him he was now the overall commander of all Bastogne's forces: the decision on Monday to let McAuliffe and Colonel Roberts of the 10th Armored Division have separate commands had proved unsustainable. A lack of communication between the forces had cost the paratroopers dearly at Wardin on Tuesday. And the extrication of the mixed force of airborne men and armor at Noville had again shown the urgent need for a unified command. Combat Command B's headquarters was to remain at Hôtel Lebrun, but Colonel Roberts himself now immediately joined the 101st Airborne's headquarters in the northern part of town to serve as the advisor on armor. Roberts stayed in close communication with his staff at Hôtel Lebrun, mostly by field telephone, but on occasion also by means of messengers and radio.[31]

It was just before dusk when McAuliffe's staff car raced along the 17-mile stretch of road southwest to Neufchâteau. Middleton was happy to see the airborne commander again. Both were keenly aware that this was to be their last face-to-face meeting before the Germans closed the ring around Bastogne. There was only little time for McAuliffe to digest much information, but he did so phlegmatically, with his trademark inscrutable face.

Earlier that day, the Supreme Commander, General Eisenhower, had decided to transfer control of the American forces north of the German bulge to British Field Marshal Montgomery's 21st Army Group. Among other things, this meant that General Omar Bradley's 12th Army Group, south of the salient, had to relinquish command over Hodges' entire First Army, apart from Middleton's VIII Corps. Bradley remained in control of Patton's Third Army, however, and he now shifted operational control of Middleton's VIII Corps from Hodges to Patton.

Eisenhower's decision had left Bradley angry and frustrated. But the only thing that mattered to McAuliffe was to learn what it was that General Patton intended to do. Middleton had spoken with George Patton in person at a meeting in Arlon that morning. Patton had halted the Third Army's offensive against the West Wall in Lorraine. At a tense conference in Verdun the previous day, he had made Eisenhower and other top brass gasp with his announcement that he could start wheeling his massive army around within an hour of the order being given. Now Middleton had just learned that one armored division and two infantry divisions from the Third Army had already begun their race to the Ardennes. Patton had claimed at Verdun that these divisions could be ready to begin their assault in the direction of Bastogne on Thursday, December 21. More than any other Allied commander, the aggressive general fully appreciated the value of the Belgian town as a springboard for an American counteroffensive from the south that would help cut off the salient and trap the German troops inside.[32]

After the hurried evening briefing, Middleton shook hands with the Bastogne commander. "Now, Tony," he grinned, "don't get yourself surrounded." McAuliffe's chauffeur gunned the staff car and managed to reach Bastogne safely again under cover of darkness. McAuliffe had no way of knowing that night that most of the 4th Armored Division's 2,600 vehicles had assembled as far north as Arlon in record time. An astonishing 4,500 vehicles had also already brought up the bulk of Patton's 26th and 80th Infantry Divisions. But McAuliffe did not feel he needed to know the operational details. Patton's driving force and boldness were legendary. And his massive Third Army was known to be as mobile as it was powerful. If Patton had told Middleton that he could be on the way to Bastogne with his troops as early as Thursday, McAuliffe and his men would move heaven and earth to hold on until they finally arrived.[33]

McAuliffe barely had time to analyze the news from Neufchâteau with his staff. Shortly before 1900, phone calls from Ewell's 501st Parachute Infantry set the 101st Airborne's Operations Room abuzz with messages of yet more serious trouble brewing, this time from the direction of Neffe. Enemy shelling rapidly swelled in intensity, cutting most of the telephone lines between Ewell's regiment and Bastogne's general staff. When the barrage suddenly lifted, radio communications signaled that a large infantry force was advancing from Neffe with the support of tanks and self-propelled guns.

The attack was part of a larger push ordered by an increasingly impatient von Lüttwitz and executed by Bayerlein's entire 902nd Panzergrenadier Regiment. The Americans could not guess the full scope of the attack. But Neffe lay alongside the N12 from Longvilly, and McAuliffe was determined to prevent any armor from smashing into Bastogne's eastern gate along this major road. For the second time that Wednesday, all available artillery battalions hurriedly zeroed in on a threatened sector of the eastern perimeter. Before long, they were bringing down "a terrible explosive curtain." The barrage laid waste to Neffe. In the terrain in front of the 1st Battalion, three enemy tanks were set alight in seconds. Silhouetted against the orange flames, the attacking soldiers never stood a chance. Machine guns opened up all along the 1st Battalion's line, greedily mowing down wave after wave of foot soldiers.[34]

Even while the German thrust from Neffe was being smashed, more Panzergrenadiers from Bayerlein's 902nd Regiment were throwing themselves against Ewell's 3rd Battalion at the nearby hamlet of Mont. Here, as at so many other key points that day, crews from Templeton's 705th Tank Destroyer Battalion gave the defenders a decisive edge. They immediately engaged enemy tanks and self-propelled guns, furiously firing away at muzzle blasts in the distance. When that failed to silence the armor, they sent up flares over the valley. The glaring light instantly exposed not only the armor, but also the vulnerable lines of infantry heading towards the paratroop positions. What followed was slaughter on a scale that, even half a century later, American veterans found it difficult to talk about.

The combined firepower of the 3rd Battalion's machine guns flailed the Germans. Barbed-wire fences crisscrossing the fields slowed down the attackers, making them even easier targets. The tank destroyers' heavy-caliber machine guns joined in the murderous frenzy, each blasting off 2,000 rounds in a matter of minutes. By the time the fighting finally died down that night, bodies lay entangled in the wire and strewn along the fences. Some of the German dead stood upright, their bulky winter clothing caught on razor-sharp wire.[35]

One of the farms ablaze in Neffe was that of Madame Joseph. On Tuesday morning, her husband had been caught in the crossfire while trying to make incriminating documents disappear. The body of Jules Joseph had been laid out on a mattress in the living room. Madame Joseph plunged into the sea of flames and dragged her husband's corpse from the sagging building. The mother and her two children spent the night in the garden, protected against the cold by some humid straw and the warmth of their four dogs. They were to spend the next two weeks in one of their stables, surviving on water from a well, milk from a few cows, and some oatmeal rescued from the fire.[36]

In a building of the gendarmerie in the southwestern part of Bastogne that Wednesday night, Lieutenant Allen was keeping very busy. The son of an antiquarian bookseller from Philadelphia, George Allen had an excellent knowledge of German. He was part of a unit of the 101st Airborne that took care of the interrogation of captured soldiers. The previous day he had been sent to the gendarmerie to oversee the day-to-day operations of the prison pen that MPs were setting up. The first prisoners of war had begun to arrive on Wednesday afternoon. By nightfall, their number had increased to more than 150. They were organized according to their regiments, battalions, and companies. Interrogations had already revealed that this was no longer the German army of 1940. Many had been sent into battle in units that were understrength and poorly equipped. Some soldiers claimed they had not eaten for three days.

Allen went to check on a prisoner brought in on a makeshift stretcher. One of his arms had been torn off at the elbow joint, and he had lost much blood. The lieutenant shook his head. The man should have been taken to an aid station. But for some reason, perhaps the onset of night, he had been dropped off at the prison cage. Now, as he knelt over him, Allen could hear the German whisper for something to eat. Allen put his arm under the man's head and crumbled some crackers into his mouth. He asked the prisoner if he cared for a cigarette. The man nodded weakly. The lieutenant lit one for him and placed it between his lips. The wounded German, Allen recalled, "feebly breathed the smoke in several times." Then he "exhaled and died in my arms before he could finish the cigarette." It was the American lieutenant's third night in Bastogne and he broke down in tears.[37]

That same night, soldiers of Kokott's 26th Volksgrenadier Division were stealthily penetrating a wooded area northeast of Bastogne. They made their way along the railroad track from Bourcy that entered the town not far from the compound where McAuliffe had his headquarters. In theory, the track formed the seam between Sink's 506th Parachute Infantry and Ewell's 501st to its south. But both regiments had been so involved in repulsing attacks in their sectors that the matter of closely tying in their flanks had been neglected. German patrols had relayed this as early as Wednesday evening, and in the course of the night more troops were sent into the gap. American patrols soon clashed with the infiltrators, alerting the men of the 506th and 501st to the fact that the enemy was slipping in behind their lines. Several companies from both regiments were sent in to seal the enemy pocket. They discovered that the infiltration was much more significant than had first been assumed. The order came down to have reinforcements sent in to help eliminate the pocket without delay.[38]

Just before dawn on Thursday, Major Harwick could hardly believe what he was hearing. Two of his companies were to be rushed to the woods along the railroad track between the 506th and the 501st. His paratroopers were the survivors of Noville. They had barely had enough time to sleep off some of the extreme exhaustion in haylofts near Foy. Groggy and filthy, the soldiers pulled themselves together to face the enemy once again. They arrived at the infiltrated area in an unforgiving mood, memories of suffering and loss too fresh in their minds.

The sweeping of the woods lasted throughout the morning. The German infantrymen were trapped and called down artillery fire for support. Private Michael Caprara saw a buddy cut down by one such burst. "I asked him where he was hit," said Caprara, "and the only response I got was a gurgling sound." As the tree bursts claimed further casualties, the men from Noville grew more enraged. By noon, over 230 of the enemy had been killed or captured. Those Germans who came out of the woods as prisoners considered themselves extremely lucky. So reluctant had the men of the 506th been to spare lives that regimental headquarters had felt it necessary to put phone calls through to the companies, ordering them to bring in prisoners for information gathering. A historian who interviewed paratroopers soon after the battle characterized the action as "rat hunting."[39]

3

Kokott's battalion-strength infiltration along the Bourcy–Bastogne railroad on Wednesday night was the last gasp of the offensive against the eastern perimeter. Two days earlier, the Germans had lost the race for Bastogne to the Americans – above all to the paratroopers. "Of all the fine accomplishments of the 501st," McAuliffe later said of their first action on Tuesday, "north of Carentan, in the Veghel area, and at other places, I think the attack east from Bastogne was the greatest." The American defenses had been consolidating ever since. Piecemeal attack after piecemeal attack had fizzled out, and the rapid blow against the Belgian town that the Germans had hoped for had failed to materialize.[40]

After much delay, Kokott's infantry division and the armored divisions of von Lauchert and Bayerlein had now at last assembled their full strength in full view of Bastogne. But the repeated attacks on the town's defenses had been whittling down their forces. More importantly, much valuable time had been lost in trying to capture the crossroads. An impatient Hitler was ordering his generals to keep their eyes on the main objective and get their forces across the Meuse and onto the roads to Antwerp. Increasingly, much of that pressure bore down on General von Manteuffel.

Hitler had intended the Sixth Panzer Army, the northernmost of the three attacking armies, to be the most powerful juggernaut. But American troops, supported by massive artillery power, were derailing the ambitious plans of Sepp Dietrich and his fearsome Waffen SS. The unexpected development now forced the *Schwerpunkt* of the offensive to shift to the Wehrmacht's Fifth Panzer Army in the center. This made Bastogne's road network even more important for von Manteuffel. But, ironically, it also allowed him less time to capture the town.[41]

The solution to the dilemma was a compromise. Both Panzer Lehr and the 2nd Panzer Division were to swing around Bastogne and make crossing the Meuse their top priority. Kokott's 26th Volksgrenadier Division was to remain behind, encircle the town, and begin probing for weak spots away from the eastern perimeter. More than anything else, it was this compromise approach to the siege that was to allow the American defenders enough breathing space to survive, even as the Germans wrapped themselves around their prey more tightly. "It was," Bayerlein observed immediately after the war, "one of the greatest mistakes that Bastogne, on failure of the coup, was not immediately captured by a concentrated attack of all our forces. If this had been done, it would certainly have fallen."[42]

Despite their reservations, the commanders were quick to obey orders. Late on Wednesday afternoon, Kokott had instructed Major Kunkel to take a reconnaissance group of between 600 and 800 men, supported by tanks, and to swing around Bastogne's south. On Thursday, Volksgrenadiers from the newly arrived 39th Fusilier Regiment were following in their tracks. Colonel Kokott experienced a deep sense of pride as he welcomed "these decent, morally clean frontline soldiers." He knew they all "shared their love for their country and the same sense of duty." The colonel only wished his troops would demonstrate greater calm on the roads and more discipline in traffic. But he blamed this impetuousness on "the campaign in the limitless vastness of the Russian countryside, where since the fall of 1941 all feeling for space and time had gradually died within the troops." Heinz Kokott was also aware that a considerable number of their vehicles were simply unfit for frontline duty. In fact, most of his men were encircling Bastogne on foot. And much of their equipment was in wagons drawn by the division's 5,000 horses, some of them of the small but tough Russian breed.[43]

In hamlets and villages south of Bastogne, farmers were helpless as Kokott's men seized more horses and all the fodder they could find. The Volksgrenadiers were hungry and set up improvised abattoirs, where they butchered hogs and cows, leaving nothing for the Belgians. Elements of Panzer Lehr followed on the heels of *Kampfgruppe* Kunkel. But Bayerlein admitted that his men, too, lacked supplies and that they were spurred on in part by "the hope of booty."[44]

In a letter to his parents in Hilchenbach, a town east of Cologne, Fritz Engelbert, a Panzer Lehr corporal, said they had had a hard time these past days and had suffered heavy losses. "Our Lieutenant Neubert was killed," he noted ruefully, "and this has saddened us." But he cheered up when he described the American treasure they had just captured in a Belgian village: chocolate, cookies, flashlights, uniforms, shoes, and even a postal bag full of presents. "We felt," he said, "as if Christmas had already arrived."[45]

Compared with the stiff resistance on the eastern perimeter, the push south of the town felt like cutting though butter with a warm knife. Losses were few, and by dawn on Thursday Kokott's motorized *Kampfgruppe* Kunkel found itself at Sibret, a village four miles southwest of Bastogne. Here, however, the Americans did resist. Sibret was where General Dutch Cota had set up the command post of what remained of his unfortunate 28th Infantry Division. Some 200 stragglers from a variety of units tried to halt Major Kunkel's men. One of the Americans was Sergeant Bill Korte from the 110th Infantry. For several nights after the destruction of his unit, he had helped carry his injured battalion commander all the way to Longvilly, only to be thrown into the desperate defense of that village east of Bastogne. Now, on the sixth day of ceaseless fleeing and fighting, he was told to help hold yet another Bastogne outpost. But the situation was as desperate at Sibret as it had been at Longvilly. Sergeant Korte was dismayed to see dozens of exhausted stragglers break and run. There was a particularly frightening incident when one American in his position "went berserk." The soldier started screaming, grabbed a hand grenade, and pulled the pin. An officer wrestled him to the ground. He carefully squeezed the man's hand until he was able to ease the grenade into a ration can that prevented the trigger handle from popping up.[46]

As Sibret's defenders melted away and General Cota hurriedly moved his command post further south, two battalions of VIII Corps artillery north and west of Sibret tried to blast *Kampfgruppe* Kunkel out of the village again. They did so just as a group of villagers in the home of the Henkards thought it safe to come up from the cellar to snatch something to eat. A shell came through the roof and exploded in the kitchen. Five people were left dead on the floor, one of them a two-year-old boy. A sixth victim lay in a pool of blood, her arms shredded by shrapnel. Villagers carried the woman to a nearby store, where a civilian doctor and a German surgeon worked side by side to save her life. They took the decision to amputate her right arm, but were happy to be able to repair the other one.[47]

As Kunkel's men pushed on, the GIs of one of Middleton's corps artillery battalions panicked and fled, leaving behind a few dozen valuable guns and much ammunition. The atmosphere grew tense in McAuliffe's command post as the *Kampfgruppe* drew close to Senonchamps. This was where the heavy artillery battalions were stationed that had recently proved so crucial in halting the attacks on Bizory and Neffe. Artilleryman McAuliffe realized better than anyone else that the loss of these battalions would weaken Bastogne's defenses considerably. But a scratch force under the command of a determined Lieutenant Colonel Browne decided to protect the artillery with their lives. An anti-aircraft artillery battalion joined the fight with the murderous quadruple guns that GIs called "meat choppers." When the guns turned on Kunkel's men, the attack was stopped dead in its tracks. Sighs of relief could be heard in McAuliffe's Operations Room.[48]

Panzer Lehr's advance guard had followed *Kampfgruppe* Kunkel through Sibret, and by late Thursday had managed to push as far west as Tillet. Kunkel's troops concluded the day with the capture of Chenogne, a village just northwest of Sibret. Fearing reprisals, the inhabitants hastily removed everything that the American troops had left behind on their farms. They burned maps, ripped out phone cables, and made binoculars vanish. The last of Chenogne's young men grabbed their bicycles and slipped away on the roads to the west. Nineteen-year-old Marie-Louise Incoul watched the Germans take over the village. They put a rifle to her father's back and told him to check out the upstairs rooms and hayloft to see if any Americans were hiding. "We were," the woman recalled much later, "overcome with despair." The Germans in Chenogne took whatever they needed, including all the bed sheets they could find. In the course of the day, the weather had changed abruptly and a cold front had moved in over the Ardennes. Temperatures continued to drop and the ground began to freeze. But the skies remained overcast and the fields and forests were now dusted with a thin layer of fresh snow.[49]

As Kokott's Volksgrenadiers and Bayerlein's tank crews cut off Bastogne to the south, the first Fallschirmjäger also began to make their appearance in the area. Some of these German paratroopers had, in fact, helped *Kampfgruppe*

Kunkel take Sibret. They belonged to Colonel Ludwig Heilmann's 5th Parachute Division, which was part of Brandenberger's Seventh Army, the southernmost of the three attacking armies in the Ardennes. General Brandenberger's troops were mostly meant to be a shielding force against the inevitable American counterattack from the south. The 5th Parachute Division, which had been held up by American resistance at Wiltz, was now developing a screening position south of Bastogne. The division was a sizeable force of some 16,000 men, but it had only recently been rebuilt after a bad mauling in Normandy. The few remaining veterans showed the strain; meanwhile many of the troops lacked combat experience. Moreover, Colonel Heilmann and several of the regimental commanders were new to the division. Despite their unit's weaknesses, the Fallschirmjäger were told to keep fanning out to the west and south of Bastogne. Then they were to dig in deep and wait for whatever it was that Patton's Third Army would be sending their way to try and rescue the Belgian town.[50]

In Sainlez, a village south of Bastogne on the road to Arlon, a German paratrooper entered the kitchen of one of the farms. He found himself face to face with a woman and her two small children. He asked her where the father was. The woman told him that he had been a prisoner of war in Germany for more than four years now. The soldier looked sad and hung his head. Then he reached into his pocket and handed some candy to the children. The next day he walked into a nearby pasture and shot himself.[51]

North of Bastogne, it took the 2nd Panzer Division somewhat longer to shake loose from Noville and turn westward. On Wednesday, an exasperated Meinrad von Lauchert asked for permission to chase the withdrawing Americans and smash into Bastogne along the N15. But his superiors told the colonel in no uncertain terms to disengage from Noville and resume his advance towards the main target. A reconnaissance battalion began heading for the Meuse late on Wednesday. The rest of the division had to wait for fuel to be brought up from the rear and for maintenance units to repair dozens of badly damaged vehicles. By Thursday, the 2nd Panzer Division was at last getting up steam again. It soon stretched out all along Bastogne's northern perimeter.[52]

The noise of the armored column made the Americans of the 502nd Parachute Infantry very nervous. Major Hatch, the regiment's operations officer, was overseeing the move of his troops into defensive positions in the northwest sector. The dense fog made visual observation all but impossible, but the troops suffered the unsettling experience of hearing "German tanks and trucks going around us almost bumper to bumper." "With limited ammo," Jim Hatch noted, "all we could do was bite our finger nails."[53]

For the civilian population northeast of Bastogne, the return of the Germans was a traumatic experience. As the battle for Noville raged and more and more troops of the 2nd Panzer Division became concentrated in the area, they ordered the Belgians to make daily contributions of meat, potatoes, eggs, and preserves from rapidly dwindling stocks. The troops rounded up the men and made them dig graves for their fallen comrades from dawn to dusk. All in all, however, von Lauchert's men treated the villagers as humanely as was possible in a combat zone. Ten-year-old Guy Maquet later remembered one of the soldiers playing games with him on the family farm in Bourcy, and even lending a hand making candles. The German had claimed that he was only 16 years old, and he had especially enjoyed reminiscing about his two older brothers, both of whom had been killed in Russia.[54]

But in the wake of the frontline troops came a much more insidious danger. The nightmare of life in a police state returned to the Ardennes, with the arrival of a panoply of security forces under direct orders from Berlin. Incredibly, even in the fluid situation of the combat zone, agents instantly began the work of clinically and meticulously weeding out all enemies of *Führer* and *Reich*. Even on Wednesday, the agents of a Gestapo unit were asking the inhabitants of Bourcy for the names of those involved in the resistance. Their work was expected to be much easier now than during the first occupation. For in the months after liberation, members of the Belgian underground had proudly revealed their identities. They had been fêted, and photos of the brave men and women had appeared in patriotic newspapers. Still, the answers in Bourcy remained evasive. Angry at the shoulder shrugs, the Gestapo began a systematic search of the homes.

In the cellar of the Rolands, they uncovered an American flag. It had been stitched together from pieces of dyed cloth to welcome the liberators in September. The Germans dragged Marcel Roland to an interrogation room in the village. People heard the 47-year-old scream as the agents beat him up. Then the Gestapo took the Belgian outside again, his face bruised and his clothes bloody. They led him to a muddy area near the gendarmerie. There they finished the job, smashing the man's skull with hammers and clubs.

There was much more terror in Noville the next day. Even as the ruins smoldered and the tail of the 2nd Panzer Division could still be seen, the Gestapo made its entrance from Bourcy. They arrested some 20 men who had just returned from the surrounding woods or come up from the cellars now that the battle appeared to be over at last. One was Auguste Lutgen, the village teacher. Almost without interruption, and with little food or water, he had spent two days and nights in the school basement, seated on a chair, trying to keep his two young sons calm on his lap. He was now taken to a building for interrogation, along with the others. The Gestapo agents spent a long time firing questions at them about the resistance. Then they marched the men to Noville's main road and forced them to scoop up rubble and mud with their bare hands. When they were satisfied that the Belgians had suffered enough humiliation, they told five of the younger men to stand apart from the others. They motioned the village priest to join them. Then they eyed the 45-year-old schoolteacher and barked at him to do the same. Their hands behind their heads, Auguste Lutgen and the six other villagers were led away. Minutes later, shots rang out from behind the ruins of a café. Only after the Gestapo had left did the villagers dare to verify their worst suspicions. They identified the bodies of Auguste Lutgen and the other men, all of them lightly dusted with snow and each with a bullet hole in the neck.[55]

4

As the German menace closed in on Bastogne, Americans and Belgians inside the town tried to make the best of a very bad situation. Some civilians waited until the last minute before deciding that it would be better to flee. Among them were four priests who taught at the Seminary. On Wednesday, after much agonizing, they packed some belongings and quickly shepherded the school's remaining 40 pupils westward. They dropped the youngest off at a château in Isle-la-Hesse, a sturdy building still within the American perimeter. The rest of the group struck out along the N4 leading northwest to Marche. Exploding shells repeatedly forced them to hit the ground. Some time later, the refugees again split up. One group managed to cross the Ourthe River, eventually making it all the way to Bande on the N4. Four days later, on Christmas Eve, three of the older pupils from Bastogne's Seminary and 29 villagers would lie dead in the basement of a burnt-out house in Bande. An official investigation after the war showed that they had fallen victim to a special commando of the *Sicherheitsdienst*, the security service of the SS. They had rounded up all the men aged between 17 and 32, tortured them to find out more about the resistance in the area, and then led them away to be executed with a shot to the back of the head.[56]

American soldiers, too, took enormous risks as they darted in and out of
Bastogne on the hunt for supplies to improve the logistical situation before
the trap closed. In the command post of the 101st Airborne, Lieutenant
Colonel Carl Kohls was "near collapse from fatigue." He was in charge of the
supply situation and had been in crisis mode ever since the hurried departure from Mourmelon. His eyes "inflamed and swollen," he was continuously
scanning reports and adding up figures. Food was not yet the most urgent
problem: the paratroopers had stuffed their pockets with K rations before
leaving France; the division had trucked in some additional food; and to this
had been added stocks left behind by Middleton's VIII Corps. Kohls had also
requisitioned flour and sugar from civilian warehouses. Just as importantly,
the autumn's crops had been harvested, and in Bastogne's basements were
piles of potatoes, beets, turnips, and onions to last through the winter. On
shelves in most cellars also stood jars of preserves, ranging from greens to
sour cherries and sweet plums.[57]

Of more immediate concern to Kohls and McAuliffe was the supply of
ammunition. The artillery battalions inside Bastogne and southwest of the
town were proving crucial in halting German attacks. But the massive
barrages were rapidly depleting the limited stocks. By Wednesday, the
supporting glider artillery battalion of Colonel Ewell's hard-pressed 501st
Parachute Infantry was running out of shells. The field battalion was using
snub-nosed 105mm howitzers and needed special ammunition for these
short-barreled guns. One party had already been sent out to find the necessary M3 shells, but it had apparently been captured. On Wednesday morning,
five more trucks and trailers slipped out of Bastogne. The supply party
managed to reach Neufchâteau, only to discover that there was none of the
specialized ammunition there. The drivers slowly made their way to Saint-
Hubert, where they were finally able to pick up 1,500 rounds. By the time the
GIs tried to get back to Bastogne, however, it was dark and the fire from
enemy small arms and tanks was intensifying. After many detours along
roads that American engineers were systematically blocking off by felling
trees, the trucks and their precious cargo finally made it back to the Belgian
town.[58]

Other supply parties went in search of gasoline. It was desperately needed
for the tanks and tank destroyers that were plugging breaches on the perimeter and for the portable generators that provided command posts and
aid stations with electricity. Joseph Gambino, a corporal in the airborne
division's signal company, somehow managed to evade German raiding
parties long enough to fill up all the five-gallon cans in his truck. But by the

time he headed back to the perimeter of the 327th Glider Infantry late on Wednesday, the Germans were fast closing the net. "Step on the gas," the glider troops called out to him, "and don't stop for anything else."[59]

It was the fate of the wounded, however, that was uppermost in the minds of troops and commanders inside Bastogne. The capture of the airborne division's field hospital meant that the bulk of the medical supplies for the town's defenders was lost just when the wounded started flooding in. In the wake of the withdrawal from Noville, Captain Jack Prior was caring for some 150 patients in Combat Command B's aid station in the rue de Neufchâteau. It was decided that the aid station of Ewell's 501st Parachute Infantry was now to serve as the new central collecting point for the entire airborne division. The hospital was housed in the chapel of the Seminary, the town's school for boys. Medics had already been ordered to remove all the pews to make more room. From a village just west of Sibret, VIII Corps sent one platoon of the 429th Medical Collecting Company to Bastogne to help evacuate the worst casualties. But there was only so much that five ambulances and two weapons carriers could do to transport wounded men safely to the rear.[60]

Father Sampson moved between the expanding rows of casualties on the chapel's floor, offering help wherever he could. One paratrooper, a medic recalled, was brought in "raving mad." Although he did not have any wounds, the man was "hysterical." Father Sampson helped the medic hold the soldier down so that he could be sedated. But even while the medicine was taking effect, the chaplain from Iowa was being called "every foul name that was in the book." "The good father continued to restrain the man," the medic noted, "he'd heard all the words before." Alerted by such scenes and the warnings that they were quickly running out of medicines and other supplies, on Wednesday Father Sampson told Corporal Adams, his driver, to take him to the area where the field hospital had been overrun the previous day. The Catholic chaplain was hoping to bring back whatever they could salvage. The corporal managed to drive the jeep all the way to the site west of Bastogne. Then suddenly they ran into an enemy reconnaissance vehicle and a large group of German soldiers. For Father Sampson and his chauffeur, the war was over. "Stop the jeep, Adams," the chaplain said. "I'm sorry I got you into this mess."[61]

More and more of those inside Bastogne, soldiers and civilians, were falling victim to intensified shelling on Wednesday. Shortly after noon, a shell exploded next to the cellar window of a wing of the Institute of Notre Dame, the town's school for girls. American medics rushed to the scene and carried away a badly wounded Sister Céline. For Sister Emmanuel, however, there could be no help. A shell fragment had pierced her chest and the convent's mother superior was dead within minutes. The loss caused panic among the pupils and teachers in the shelter, and news of the fatality spread across town like wildfire.[62]

Just before midnight, another shell hit a home and exploded with enormous force. Madame Mahnen groped around in the dark and the suffocating dust, only to find her husband, two daughters, and a grandchild dead. Jacqueline, her other granddaughter, lay amidst the rubble, still alive, but with one arm severed. The grandmother picked the girl up off the floor and stumbled to a nearby house. But the four-year-old bled to death in her arms before she got there. Maddened by the loss, Madame Mahnen had only one thought left: to get out of Bastogne. Somehow the woman broke out of the American perimeter and then managed to cut through the encircling German forces. She did not stop walking until her bleeding feet caused her to collapse at a farm in Malmaison, some eight miles south of the besieged town.[63]

Madame Mahnen was probably the last civilian to escape from Bastogne before the enemy closed the trap. She fled along the highway to Arlon, a vital artery that the Germans had already severed much earlier in the day. On Wednesday night, the road from Neufchâteau in the southwest was also in German hands. On Thursday it was still possible for the Americans to move in and out of Bastogne along the roads to the west. But these were extremely dangerous, as the raid against the airborne division hospital had shown as early as Tuesday. Still, Colonel Roberts managed to have Combat Command B's supply trains slip out of town at the eleventh hour. He ordered Captain Warren Schulze, the commander of the service company, to round up his men and have them drive some 150 empty supply vehicles to safety immediately, without any protection from armor or troops. Threatened by German raiders on all sides, the long and winding convoy somehow probed its way to Tillet in the west, and from there to VIII Corps headquarters. "The only thing I can say," noted a relieved supply sergeant, "was the Good Lord was with us."[64]

The men from the service company did not make it back to Bastogne to help with the defense, however. The same was true of several others on Thursday. A supply party sent out by Colonel Roberts that day to go in search of still more of the urgently needed 105mm shells was never heard of again.[65]

One of those who did not get back to Bastogne that day from another supply run was Lieutenant Yearout. In the week since he had last written to his wife Mimi, Paul Yearout had seen his fair share of the German offensive. The science graduate and father of two had survived the destruction of the 110th Infantry, the last stand at Allerborn, and a trek to Bastogne of several nights, during which time he and some other stragglers had had no more than a single candy bar between them to eat. Now, in the relative safety of Neufchâteau, he was relieved to be able to write to his wife once again. "Have been pretty busy," the officer apologized meekly.[66]

Don Addor, the private from Washington who had been seriously wounded during the escape from Noville on Wednesday, was one of the last soldiers to get out of Bastogne that day. He did so in an ambulance of the 429th Medical Collecting Company. In no time, the evacuation chain had him on his way to a hospital in Paris, and from there to one in England. It failed to save his right leg, but it did save his life. Much grimmer would be the fate of the badly wounded still stuck in Bastogne when, late on Thursday, the ambulances were cut off, too.[67]

Meanwhile on Thursday the shelling was becoming ever more intense. It was reported to McAuliffe's headquarters that explosions had caused about a hundred cuts in telephone wires in the previous 24 hours. There was a terrific roar when a shell blew up mines and bazooka rounds stockpiled in a depot of the airborne engineer battalion. Another shell hit the prisoner-of-war cage in the town's southwest, sparing all the captured Germans, but killing two American guards. It became obvious now that the central command post would have to go underground. A hurried move was organized from the flimsy barracks to the cellar of a two-story brick building in the five-acre compound. The basement was grimy and smelled of the coal that was stored at one end. But three cramped rooms on either side of a small corridor offered just enough space for the various offices of the commanding officers. A portable generator in the courtyard lit the bare bulbs. More importantly, the metal joists made the ceiling strong. The general staff was reminded of how crucial this was when, later that day, a huge explosion shook the cellar. Word soon reached the occupants of the Operations Room that the shell had hit one of the nearby barracks, killing two soldiers and wounding four others.[68]

More shells rocked the Institute of Notre Dame. In the convent's cellars, terrified civilians clung to each other, some hiding their heads beneath blankets with each new explosion. GIs advised them to form teams with shovels and pickaxes to dig their way out of the rubble in case the ceiling or walls collapsed. "My friends," a priest addressed the crowd in the basement on Thursday evening, "the Americans do not hide the danger. The Germans can enter the town any moment now. Let's make certain not a single light can be seen."[69]

CHAPTER 4

TRAPPED

Although late in coming, on the night of Thursday, December 21, von Manteuffel's Fifth Panzer Army reported two pieces of good news. First of all, after days of stubborn resistance from American forces, Saint-Vith had fallen at last. With this key obstacle out of the way on the right flank, all attention turned to Bastogne, the only remaining thorn in the side of von Manteuffel's force and now the *Schwerpunkt* of the Ardennes offensive.

But on the Fifth Panzer Army's left flank, too, the situation appeared promising. The Germans had first hammered McAuliffe's linear defense east of Bastogne into a semicircular barrier. They now caused it to stretch even thinner, morphing it into a full-blown perimeter defense. To the east, German troops were dug in as close as two miles from the town square. To the west, they were actively probing American lines that were still bulging out up to six miles from the small Belgian town. For all practical purposes, Bastogne was surrounded.[1]

On Friday, GIs and civilians were discovering that there was no longer any way out of the town. An effort by Ewell's 501st Parachute Infantry to repeat the successful escape of Combat Command B's supply convoys a day earlier ended in disaster when the baggage train ran into the enemy near Sibret, causing the regiment to lose at least 15 trucks. If even the paratroopers could not break out on December 22, surely the chances of success for Madeleine Barthelemi were even slimmer.[2]

Heavily pregnant and totally exhausted, the young woman felt as though she was going to suffocate in the cramped basement of her neighbors. A few days earlier, her husband and brother, fearing German reprisals, had fled in the company of other young men. The shelling of Bastogne now convinced Madeleine that she, too, would do better to seek shelter elsewhere.

Accompanied by her parents-in-law, a cousin, and two dogs, Madeleine hurried away from Bastogne along the road to Neufchâteau. All their belongings were strapped onto a single bicycle. They managed to walk no more than three miles in a southwesterly direction before German machine guns opened up. The Belgians flattened themselves against the snow and then stumbled back in the direction of Bastogne, finally halting at Isle-le-Pré, a hamlet not even two miles from town. There Madeleine and her companions found refuge in a farm cellar. The young woman pressed in among the crowd, her few remaining possessions limited to some spare clothes and a bottle of eau de Cologne to dab on her face.[3]

More and more civilians that Friday were finding out that any attempt to get away from Bastogne was inevitably blocked in one of the villages or hamlets just inside the American perimeter. And since these were the very places where combat troops had dug in, it was quickly becoming clear that they threatened to be even worse deathtraps. Most of the German activity on Friday was west of Bastogne, where Americans of the 327th Glider Infantry were badly exposed, as their positions poked out of the perimeter like a fat thumb. It was in this dangerous sector that the flight from Bastogne came to an abrupt halt for the Meurisses and their eight-year-old son, André. Driven from Hemroulle by machine-gun fire and from Champs by shelling, the Meurisses eventually ended up in the crowded cellar of a farm in Mande-Saint-Étienne.[4]

But here, in the hamlet where the 101st Airborne had assembled on the morning of December 19, Sergeant Robert Bowen and his platoon from C Company now became involved in a furious fight. It appeared that German troops had slipped in behind A Company, thrown up a roadblock with farm vehicles, and cut it off from Bastogne. The battalion commander ordered the roadblock to be removed at all costs. Supported by a single tank, the sergeant from Maryland led the assault. The German Volksgrenadiers were no match for the tank's cannon and machine guns, and the glider troops quickly picked off those who tried to get away from the Sherman. Eighteen bodies "littered the snow in bloody heaps," and more than thirty Germans were taken prisoner. Many of them were very young. One captured soldier was brought in "with a gaping wound from knee to hip." He was "a kid of 17," noted Sergeant Bowen, "and scared to death."[5]

André Meurisse felt even more frightened. In the farm cellar, the boy had listened to bursts of fire and bloodcurdling screams. At one point, two Americans had rushed into the cellar. They were "out of breath," André observed, and "sweating profusely from fright and fatigue." When the battle finally died down, the owner of the farm where the refugees were hiding silently made his way to the barn to milk his cows. Children and adults gratefully dipped cups into buckets filled to the brim with frothy cream, and then settled down for a rest. They had a shock when two German soldiers barged in armed with Schmeisser submachine guns. The men appeared dazed and might have been drunk. One of them unbuttoned his trousers and proceeded to urinate in each of the pails with leftover milk. Then both slipped away again.[6]

As the noose around Bastogne tightened, General Middleton and his VIII Corps staff were settling in on the ground floor of a girls' school. The previous night, they had judged it prudent to pull back even further from Bastogne. They had packed up their papers and equipment and withdrawn to Florenville, a Belgian town some 11 miles southwest of Neufchâteau. A corps radio-link vehicle had made it into Bastogne just before the road to Neufchâteau was cut. A distant crackle of voices was to keep them informed about the fate of General McAuliffe and his besieged troops.[7]

1

Bastogne was a small town with an estimated population of slightly over 4,000 at the time of its liberation in September 1944. In the Middle Ages, it had been fortified with towers and walls, but these had been demolished by French invaders in the seventeenth century. The road junction was located on a slightly elevated plateau, however, and this provided the American defenders with a fairly good view of the surrounding area – mostly rolling hills and fields, interspersed with dense tracts of woodland. It was an advantage, too, that Bastogne lay at the heart of concentric circles of villages and hamlets. These formed ideal defensive anchors because of the ancient sturdy farms and cellars, built from materials dug from local quarries.[8]

Now that they were cut off entirely, no one knew for certain exactly how many able-bodied defenders were holed up in the town and surrounding farmsteads. Fred MacKenzie, a reporter for the *Buffalo Evening News* who spent the siege inside General McAuliffe's command post, claimed that American strength was estimated at no more than 15,000. The spine of this force was, of course, the 101st Airborne Division, an elite and veteran outfit of which, by the time the trap was closed, five battalions had suffered significant casualties. Even though Colonel Roberts's force was badly mauled already, 10th Armored Division's Combat Command B continued to form another key element of Bastogne's defenses. Its 420th Armored Field Artillery, and six other artillery battalions from various sources, combined with the airborne division's field pieces to provide the defenders with significant firepower. A further crucial role lay in store for the 705th Tank Destroyer Battalion in a fight against an enemy renowned and feared for the quality of its panzer weapon.[9]

Like the 110th Infantry of the 28th Division, the 9th Armored Division's Combat Command R had disintegrated in stubborn attempts to delay the enemy east of Bastogne. But so many men from these and a variety of smaller units were filing past on the town's road network that Colonel Roberts decided to have the stragglers collected and reorganized into a reserve force. Named Team SNAFU (after an army slang expression – Situation Normal: All Fucked Up), it was estimated by Colonel Roberts at one point to be made up of between 700 and 800 men. These were infantrymen without rifles and tank crews without vehicles, plus cooks and office personnel. Many were suffering from battle fatigue. Still, after a brief rest and some hot food, most were deemed fit enough to man task forces desperately needed to help plug potential breaches.[10]

Several days of battling the Germans at Bastogne's eastern gates had gone a long way towards molding the various components of the American defenses into an oiled machine. Rivalries and suspicions between the different branches quickly melted away. "There were," commented one airborne officer, "no strangers in Bastogne during the siege." Now stationed in the 101st Airborne's underground command post, Colonel Roberts described the officers there as "the best and keenest staff I've ever seen." He was particularly satisfied to find that General McAuliffe "listened to reason," usually taking on board advice he gave him with regards to the paratroopers' use of his precious armor. At the same time, Colonel Roberts was not afraid to admit that, in matters of defense, Colonel Templeton's tank destroyers "taught me and my tanks a lesson." As had been amply demonstrated on previous days, the combined arms response was further facilitated by the fact that General Taylor's replacement as commander of the 101st Airborne happened to be the division's experienced artillery chief.[11]

An airborne division was smaller than a standard infantry division. But the 101st Airborne benefited from the fact that it was organized into four regiments, rather than the three of its infantry counterpart, for this now allowed it to box in Bastogne solidly on four sides. Also, backed up by 40 medium tanks, tank destroyers with 76mm guns, and heavy 155mm howitzers, the 101st Airborne now packed more of a punch than at any time in Normandy or Holland. The high-quality signals equipment of the attached armor and artillery units also facilitated fast communication with McAuliffe's headquarters. Moreover, Bastogne's roads served as "the spokes of a wheel," allowing relatively quick movement of mobile reserve forces to the sectors of all four airborne regiments.[12]

On Friday, December 22, two of these regiments were densely packed together where the Germans had been doing most damage in previous days: the 506th in the northeast – west and east of Foy and the road to Noville – and the 501st on its right, stretched out to just south of Neffe. While the 502nd Parachute Infantry defended Bastogne's northern sector, however, the 327th Glider Infantry ended up covering both the southern and the western approaches to the town. This left its three battalions spread so thin that frontline support had to be provided by the airborne division's 326th Engineer Battalion at the Neufchâteau road and by the 10th Armored Division's 420th Artillery Battalion near Senonchamps.

The numbers of the Americans inside the Bastogne perimeter were swelled by thousands of people that soldiers prefer not to have around in battle: civilians. Many Bastognards had fled, most of them young males afraid of their fate under renewed occupation. But others had decided to stay, their ranks swelled by exhausted refugees from as far away as the Grand Duchy of Luxembourg. The traumatic memory of the chaos and dangers of the exodus during the German invasion of May 1940 was still vivid. Moreover, American Civil Affairs authorities in Bastogne never issued formal orders telling the population to pack up and leave. One reason was that it was the task of Allied Civil Affairs during the German counteroffensive to prevent panic movements from east to west in the direction of the Meuse River. The first priority for Civil Affairs was to assist military commanders in keeping roads clear for the movement of troops and supplies. By the time the Germans completed their encirclement of Bastogne on Thursday, an estimated 3,000 civilians had disappeared underground across town. Still more people were hiding in the farms of surrounding hamlets, determined not to abandon their precious livestock.[13]

Fearing reprisals for having cooperated with the Allied authorities, Bastogne's mayor and most of the town officials had fled before the Germans, leaving a civilian power vacuum. Almost immediately, however, the American authorities found 50-year-old Léon Jacqmin willing to serve as mayor during the siege. A respected businessman and veteran of the Great War, Monsieur Jacqmin knew how to take charge, and without delay he set out to address the most pressing issues. The acting mayor appointed auxiliary policemen to help enforce order; he helped organize care for the sick and elderly; and he made sure there was a system in place for the transport and burial of the dead. He also urged volunteers to comb the town in search of food stocks: they turned up, among other things, seven tons of flour, two tons of tinned biscuits, significant quantities of vegetable oil and margarine, and even some decent stocks of canned salmon. The Seminary became the central location for the storage and distribution of foodstuffs and it was transformed into a bakery. Meanwhile, butchers were told to set up shop in the rue du Vivier and prepare meat from hog and cow carcasses stored in the nearby abattoir.[14]

After a night of frightful shelling, civilians on Friday were trying to get their underground shelters as organized as possible. Some had withdrawn to their own cellars, dragging mattresses down the stairs, stocking up on candles and petrol lamps, and trying to get small wood and coal stoves working. Others had joined neighbors in what were believed to be sturdier constructions, at times packing together up to 30 or 40 people in the basement of a single home. In some streets, holes were made in the walls between cellars so that people could move from one house to the next without having to expose themselves to shellfire. Two of the town's physicians, Dr. Govaerts and Dr. Heintz, ran a huge risk darting from one underground community to another. So did priests like the young Louis Dethienne, who had arrived in Bastogne just two months earlier and now insisted on spreading news and words of encouragement to his isolated flocks.[15]

Religious leaders also played an important role because close to a third of the remaining civilians in this intensely Catholic town were seeking safety and company in the spacious and solid underground shelters of their institutions. The Franciscan sisters had evacuated their home for the elderly and had carefully moved them on stretchers into the Seminary's cellars. The Récollets took care of 100 civilians in the vaulted cellars of their seventeenth-century monastery. The Franciscan fathers herded at least 120 Bastognards and refugees into the hideaway beneath their church. The largest shelter by far, however, was that provided by the Institute of the Sisters of Notre Dame. Here some 600 people, including 100 of the boarding school's girls who had failed to be reunited with their parents, packed the underground rooms and corridors.[16]

In one of the Institute of Notre Dame's cellar compartments, Maria Gillet on Friday watched conditions deteriorate. She was not one of the pupils, but was a young woman training to be a teacher. In the past days, more and more of the town's frightened inhabitants had pressed in upon them, so that now most of the institute's teachers and girls were seated on rows of chairs in a cramped space lit by a single candle. The previous day and night, shell blasts had rocked the building, shattering all the windows, ripping doors from their hinges, and shaking dust from the ceiling as if through a sieve. To protect themselves against the icy drafts, the girls had placed mattresses against the broken windows and wrapped their bodies in coats and blankets. "We sit covered up like that . . . awaiting what?" pondered Maria. "Death quite simply, if it so pleases God."[17]

It was left to Colonel Curtis Renfro of the 327th Glider Infantry to liaise with the civilian authorities. He was charged more specifically with reassuring the population and trying to prevent needless casualties. Throughout the siege, the American colonel was to perform these crucial duties with such "calm" and "good judgment" that it earned him a Silver Star.[18]

There were tensions nevertheless. Colonel Kohls, the airborne supply officer, took over all stocks left behind by VIII Corps, but he also seized flour, sugar, jam, and margarine from civilian warehouses, beating Monsieur Jacqmin's volunteers to it. American requisitioning inside the Bastogne perimeter was to be a constant reminder of the fragile line between coopera- tion and competition where food was concerned.

The most serious problems were caused, however, by stubborn American suspicions that the precision shelling of Bastogne was the result of intelli- gence relayed to the enemy from within. The situation was made worse by the fact that countless refugees had become mixed up with locals, including some from neighboring Luxembourg who spoke a dialect strongly resembling German. MPs repeatedly entered crowded cellars in search of suspected radio equipment. At gunpoint, dozens of people were taken to Combat Command B's headquarters at Hôtel Lebrun, where they were interrogated for many hours before being released. One of them was a man who had been out in the streets with a suspicious bag. After some tense hours, the man finally managed to convince his interrogators that he was Dr. Govaerts, and that he had been doing his rounds to help patients. In the basement of a home on the route de Marche, people pleaded with MPs not to arrest a man they knew to have joined them from the nearby hamlet of Mont. The testy MPs finally relented. But on their way out, they warned the civilians that they would be executed if it was later discovered that the man had disappeared.[19]

All in all, however, the dominant mood in Bastogne was one of strong solidarity in the face of terrible hardship and danger. A special group of civilian volunteers was formed, for example, to offer services to the

Americans. Many of them were no more than boys, but they itched to lend a hand and knew little fear. They proudly called themselves "the vagabonds," and troops gladly called on them to scout on the perimeter's edge, unload ambulances, and assist in aid stations. Most Bastognards helped the cause more simply by means of quiet determination and less conspicuous acts of solidarity.[20]

Corporal Heyman was a reconnaissance section leader in Team Cherry's tank force. His men happened to be billeted in the home of Bastogne's acting mayor. Monsieur Jacqmin's cellar was known to be particularly solid and, as a result, it was already providing shelter for several families. Even then, however, Mike Heyman was impressed by the "grace and dignity" with which men, women, and children accepted the soldiers' arrival. "The rapport," he observed, "was immediate and seamless." Schedules were spontaneously agreed upon to facilitate use of the kitchen and washrooms upstairs. GIs shared their rations; the families insisted that the Americans taste "local goodies." Soldiers and civilians tried their best to have intelligible conversations. They even managed to have "a bit of quiet fun in the evenings." Heyman's men quickly grew fond of the Bastognards. "Those of us who had nighttime duties," the corporal noted, "would assume the risk of sleeping on the upper floors, to minimize disturbance and to alleviate congestion."[21]

Taking stock of the situation on Friday, the Germans were fairly optimistic that Bastogne was ripe for the taking. Judging from a letter written by a lieutenant that day, troop morale remained high. "Always advancing and smashing everything," the officer told his wife. "The snow must turn red with American blood. Victory was never as close as it is now." Field Marshal von Rundstedt, commander of the German forces on the Western Front, was convinced the time had come for Bastogne to be crushed. The road junction was urgently needed to help support von Manteuffel's Fifth Panzer Army, as his force was now spearheading the drive for the Meuse and Antwerp. Von Manteuffel, in turn, put pressure on his subordinate von Lüttwitz. XLVII Panzer Corps commander von Lüttwitz had just had a visit from General Erich Brandenberger, who had assured him that the Seventh Army, and the 5th Parachute Division in particular, were steadily strengthening their shield south of Bastogne. This meant that, for the time being, von Lüttwitz could focus on Bastogne without looking over his shoulder to see where Patton's Third Army was.

At the same time, however, von Lüttwitz was well aware that the force he had at his disposal to "crush" Bastogne was not a very strong one. The Führer himself had made clear that the armored divisions of his XLVII Panzer Corps were to head for the Meuse and leave Bastogne behind. The result was that now only a single regiment of Panzer Lehr remained near Marvie, southeast of Bastogne. The main effort would have to be made by the 26th Volksgrenadier Division; but Kokott's troops had already been dealt heavy blows east of Bastogne. Two divisions were said to be on the way as reinforcements. For the moment, however, they were nowhere to be seen.[22]

Von Lüttwitz felt he was not yet ready for an all-out assault. He was loath also to squander more troops in piecemeal attacks. That may have been why he decided to engage in a round of bluff without consulting von Manteuffel. With the help of a translator from Vienna, his staff hastily put together a surrender ultimatum in German and English, to be delivered to "the U.S.A. Commander of the encircled town of Bastogne." The message put pressure on the surrounded defenders by threatening to have German artillery "annihilate the U.S.A. troops." They warned that this would result in serious civilian losses, too, and at the last minute decided to add to the message that this "would not correspond with the well-known American humanity."

A major delivered the message to Bayerlein's Panzer Lehr headquarters. The translator from Vienna did not make it there in time. Bayerlein therefore ordered Lieutenant Henke from his operations staff to accompany the major. Bayerlein knew that Hellmuth Henke had been in the import business and was fluent in English. When the two officers arrived in the sector of the 901st Panzergrenadier Regiment near Marvie, its commander, Paul von Hauser, a seasoned veteran decorated with the Iron Cross, joked that if enemy soldiers ever handed him a similar message, he would "immediately place them against a wall."

Not exactly reassured by this, Lieutenant Henke and the major were driven to the front line at a point where it was cut by the road from Arlon. Just before noon, they took off their pistols and put them in the vehicle. A nearby mortar platoon was drawing American fire, and it took the officers some time to convince the gunners to silence their weapons and give up two enlisted men to strengthen the delegation. Preceded by the two soldiers waving white flags, the officers crossed no man's land in a "tense dead silence." Then, suddenly, American airborne troops rose from foxholes near a farm. Lieutenant Henke explained to the Americans that they carried a message for Bastogne's commander. Both officers were blindfolded and driven away. After a short distance, they were ordered out of the jeep. An officer told them he would take their written message to the town commander, and the German officers were left standing in the cold. The wait, Hellmuth

Henke recalled, lasted "an incredibly long time." Unable to see, but acutely aware of being gazed at by enemy soldiers, "our courage began to fail us." All that Henke and the major could do was remain silent, avoid any movement, and take in the sounds of battle all around them.

What the German officers did not know was that General McAuliffe was asleep when the message arrived at his underground headquarters. He had been up and about for several days and nights now, and his staff had insisted he take a daytime nap while they took care of minor emergencies. They wanted him rested for the next real crisis. It took McAuliffe's staff some time to understand that the message was serious, and that the Germans were really trying to convince the elite unit to surrender. When they finally woke their commander to explain the situation, a dazed and incredulous McAuliffe mumbled, "Aw, nuts!" Minutes later, when McAuliffe seemed unsure about how to word his rejection of the ultimatum, one of his staff officers suggested that "Nuts!" might sum it up best.

Lieutenant Henke was relieved to hear a vehicle approach. Americans quickly spirited the Germans back into a jeep. "We had the impression," observed Henke, "that the Americans were less polite now." After an abrupt halt, the Germans were made to clamber from the vehicle. They were nudged along for a small distance, and then told they could remove their blindfolds. An American officer handed them McAuliffe's written reply. Lieutenant Henke asked him if he could disclose the nature of the content, as they had been granted authority to negotiate some aspects of the surrender on the spot. The answer was, the American replied, "Nuts!" Lieutenant Henke was so puzzled by the reply that he simply repeated the word. "It means," the officer clarified, "go to hell." Lieutenant Henke turned to the major to explain. "We should go," the major snapped.

Bastogne's commander rejected the surrender ultimatum "with remarkable brevity," Kokott commented dryly when corps headquarters notified him of the answer. Von Manteuffel on his part was furious when he received word that von Lüttwitz had allowed the Americans to make such a fool of them all.[23]

News of McAuliffe's refusal to surrender spread like wildfire. The Germans threatened to annihilate Bastogne in response, and soldiers and civilians across town began preparing for the worst. In the cellars of the Institute of Notre Dame, rumor had it that the Germans were already on their way and that they would be committing atrocities. The men wanted to flee, but had nowhere to go. Two priests announced that they were willing to present themselves as hostages to have the lives of the others spared. "Those words," Maria Gillet remarked, "caused a dead silence." Then she and the others fell to praying "like they had never done before."[24]

There were many "grim faces" also in the 101st Airborne's underground command post. Fearing that the Germans were about to "level the town," an officer of the 463rd Parachute Field Artillery who happened to arrive at the headquarters shortly after the ultimatum was rejected, instantly rushed back to have his men prepare for the onslaught. George Koskimaki, a headquarters radio messenger who had been keeping a detailed journal, assembled his notes, ready to have them destroyed before Bastogne was overrun. The men of F Company of the 327th Glider Infantry were convinced that the Germans were about to descend on their positions and "wipe us out." They were the ones who had given the German delegation its frosty reception earlier that day. "We got all the extra ammo we could find," one of the glidermen recalled, and "dug some extra holes."[25]

But the defenders waited in vain that day for German retribution. Von Lüttwitz had known all along that, because of transport shortages and clogged roads, the troops surrounding Bastogne did not possess sufficient firepower to shell the town into submission. That was why von Manteuffel was so angry at the news of the rejected ultimatum: there could now be neither a massive barrage in response nor a hastily prepared all-out assault. As the American defenders gradually relaxed again, however, serious trouble was brewing at Senonchamps, the location just west of Bastogne where much of the strength of the vital artillery battalions was concentrated. As had happened the day before, Kokott's *Kampfgruppe* Kunkel hammered away at these positions in assault after assault. By evening, General McAuliffe was forced to shore up defenses at Senonchamps, siphoning off one company from the 327th Glider Infantry's already thin line. A hundred men from Team SNAFU were also sent to help plug the hole. They arrived thoroughly shaken: a mortar shell had just exploded inside Colonel Gilbreth's half-track, killing most of the crew. The colonel, a survivor of the 9th Armored Division's exploits east of Bastogne, had been rushed to an aid station with a bad case of shell shock.[26]

Later that evening, McAuliffe and his staff were relieved to learn that their artillery concentration had again escaped serious harm. Some of the officers engaged in murmured conversation in the cellar cubicle that served as Colonel Templeton's command room. The colonel was a lively character, and newspaperman Fred MacKenzie joined in, glad to be distracted from the day's tension. With barely any warning, an explosion of "terrific force" shook the basement, rattling objects in the corridor and rooms. Moments later, word came that four soldiers had been killed in an upstairs room of the Heintz barracks, one of them a young, red-haired captain of the division's artillery, well liked by McAuliffe. Fred MacKenzie went out to have a look at the damage: the walls "bulged from the force of the explosion," the steel frames of the windows were "bent outward." Metal shards from the high-explosive shell had pierced the plaster walls and wooden furniture. Blankets in the room were "filled with blood," and a soldier sweeping the floor could be seen picking up "a bit of skull with its patch of hair." Fred MacKenzie returned to the command post cellar pale and shaken. The reporter for the *Buffalo Evening News* was finding it increasingly difficult to order his thoughts and commit them to paper.[27]

2

In Bastogne that night, the exhausted Americans were well aware that the worst was yet to come. But then, as day broke on Saturday, the fog dispersed, the clouds parted, and the skies turned to a blue so bright that soldiers thought they were witnessing a miracle. Americans of every rank instantly knew what this meant: the awesome power of the Allied air forces was about to be unleashed over the German salient. "General Bradley, like everyone else," a top aide of the 12th Army Group commander exulted in his diary, "was ebullient." "It was," Private Donald Burgett recalled of that day in his foxhole, "like a storybook fantasy."[28]

As the cold winds of a Russian high-pressure system chased the Atlantic clouds away, aircraft were already on their way from England to Bastogne with two teams of pathfinders. These specialists, one officer and nine enlisted men to a team, were trained to guide transports to drop zones. No time was being lost because, two days earlier, the 101st Airborne had sent an urgent request for aerial resupply. Artillery shells and medical equipment were top priorities. On Friday, colored panels had been laid out to mark drop spots, and recovery crews with trucks had been stationed nearby, ready to pick up supplies. By evening, however, it had become clear that they were waiting in vain. That night, observed Fred MacKenzie, Colonel Kohls, the supply officer, had looked "doleful" and "in constant misery."[29]

Now, however, shortly after 0900 on Saturday, Colonel Kohls' spirits soared. Two Douglas C-47 Skytrains could be seen flying in low with an escort of fighters that had joined them over France. Lieutenant Colonel Joel Crouch from Riverside, California, was piloting the lead Skytrain. He weaved the aircraft through tracer fire and flak bursts. Then the green light came on. Ten pathfinders jumped and opened their chutes over Bastogne.

Sergeant Jake McNiece was one of them, and he felt ready for the challenge. Part Choctaw, the second youngest of ten children, Jake's parents had been sharecroppers in Oklahoma. The Great Depression had left the McNieces even worse off, forcing them into a migrant life of cutting broom-corn all over Oklahoma and picking cotton in Texas. The 25-year-old sergeant landed in Bastogne with the same boots he had been wearing in Normandy and Holland. He had filled the holes in his soles with pasteboard. Jake McNiece and the others set off orange smoke grenades to signal to the second plane that they were in a safe location. Ten more pathfinders descended almost on top of them.

Both teams quickly established contact with airborne headquarters to learn the preferred location of the drop zone. Then they went to work. They unpacked smoke pots and laid out fluorescent orange panels and directional beacons. They set up high-tech CRN-4 radio sets in three locations, one on a brick pile, the others on nearby knolls. They raised the long antennas and began transmitting.[30]

While the pathfinders inside Bastogne were establishing contact with the IX Troop Carrier Command in England, Marie du Bus de Warnaffe watched her château in Roumont, a village several miles northwest of the American perimeter, being hurriedly transformed into a staff center. Earlier in the day, a junior officer had turned up to announce the imminent arrival of General and Baron Heinrich von Lüttwitz. The young orderly, a Sudeten German, was extremely polite, disarmingly charming and, the Belgian viscountess noted approvingly, he spoke French "to a divine perfection." Inhabitants from Roumont were commandeered to clean up the dirt left behind by enlisted troops, drag comfortable *fauteuils* into makeshift offices, and put fresh sheets on the beds.

Shortly after, there was a great commotion in the courtyard. A heavy-set von Lüttwitz was helped out of his car. The monocled general briefly addressed the viscountess and had his aide translate his sincere apologies for the unfortunate inconveniences of war. Then he lowered himself into a plush *fauteuil*, grabbed one of the many newly installed telephones, and started barking orders. His elite 2nd Panzer Division, the formidable force that the Americans had delayed at Noville, was now no more than four miles from the Meuse and poised to cross the river. This encouraging development made Bastogne's road network to the rear more important than ever.

Yesterday's surrender ultimatum had been a debacle. It was time now for determined action. All day long, von Lüttwitz would be working the phones to help coordinate a three-pronged offensive against Bastogne.[31]

Around noon, the first hammer blow fell on the thumb-like salient sticking six miles out of the perimeter west of Bastogne, along the main road to Marche. The salient was held by the 327th Glider Regiment's 3rd Battalion. At its extreme tip, in the village of Flamierge, sat Sergeant Robert Bowen and the men from C Company. They were to bear the full brunt of an attack involving Kokott's 39th Fusilier Regiment and more than a dozen lethal tanks.[32]

A biting wind whipped up snow "like ocean foam." Kokott's troops, experienced veterans from the Russian campaign, wore snow capes and their armor had been painted white. Within minutes, Sergeant Bowen's men were called to the aid of a nearby platoon that was in danger of being overrun. A lone Sherman had already been knocked out. Calls for artillery support remained largely unanswered because of a desperate shortage of shells. When Bowen's platoon arrived, there were wounded men everywhere, "some of them screaming in delirious agony." A medic risked his life to crawl closer to three of them under intense fire. He quickly looked them over, but found the men too badly mutilated to risk dragging them back. Among the dead, Sergeant Bowen recognized a private from Massachusetts who had been "the platoon clown" and had often made the men laugh with his imitations of Disney characters.

The presence of a single tank destroyer, commanded by a stout blond sergeant from Milwaukee, did much to help Bowen's men resist. At one point, Bowen spotted a bazooka lashed to the side of a half-track. He grabbed the weapon and a pouch of rocket grenades, loaded the tube, and blasted away at a tank that was targeting his comrades in their foxholes. The projectile grazed the turret without exploding. Another Panther scored a direct hit on the command post, almost tearing the shoulder off the platoon leader inside. Without support from heavy weapons, the American platoons were being chopped to pieces. But their company commander bellowed that they were under orders to hold. German tanks ramped up the pressure. Bowen watched a huge fir tree disintegrate in a single explosion. "Then," the sergeant recalled, "the world seemed to blow up around me." When he came to, several men lay around him in crumpled heaps. Shrapnel had pierced Bowen's upper body, and a big piece sat lodged in the bone of his right wrist. Medics carried him to the basement of an aid station.

The Germans were closing in. Civilians in the basement wailed hysterically by the dim light of candles. Sergeant Bowen took a .38 Smith and

Wesson from his shoulder holster and put it in his lap. Then he changed his mind and hid the pistol beneath some straw. Kokott's men barged in. They ordered the walking wounded into the farm's courtyard. The Germans took their watches, wallets, and rings. Some were furious about *Kameraden* they had just lost and began calling the Americans names. For a brief moment, Sergeant Bowen regretted having disposed of his pistol. Then the tension abated again, and the sergeant and his fellow glidermen were loaded onto trucks as prisoners of war. Later that day, Colonel Ray Allen, commander of the 3rd Battalion, decided to have his men abandon the salient and link up with the core perimeter at Mande-Saint-Étienne, just a few miles west of Bastogne. "This is our last withdrawal," a grim colonel told his staff. "Live or die, this is it."[33]

As Allen's men began falling back, the pressure also increased just south of the thumb, in Senonchamps, where McAuliffe's heavy artillery was concentrated. *Kampfgruppe* Kunkel had been trying to smash this vital position for several days now. Their failure to do so was, in large part, due to the exceptional leadership shown by Lieutenant Colonel Barry Browne, commander of the 420th Field Artillery, which was part of Roberts's armored force. An amalgam of piecemeal reinforcements had been sent to Browne's aid: tanks and infantry from what was left of the 9th Armored Division's Combat Command R, stragglers from Team SNAFU, and a company of glider infantry. When Major Watts of Combat Command R arrived in the area with still more troops, he found foxholes littered with the corpses of an entire airborne platoon, wiped out by shells that had exploded in nearby trees. The barrages that followed, Watts said, were "about the heaviest I saw during the war." Even then, however, Browne managed to hold his ragtag army together and made them resist fiercely. The colonel continually moved among his troops in the front line, directing fire from an exposed position in a half-ton truck. At one point, Browne personally led five tanks and two squads of infantry in a counterattack that cost the Germans dearly and earned him a Distinguished Service Cross.[34]

Some of the heavy corps artillery that Task Force Browne was trying to protect stood assembled in Isle-la-Hesse, just east of Senonchamps. Lieutenant Colonel Hubert Barnes and his staff had made themselves as comfortable as possible in the thick-walled château of the Greindls. On paper, they were in charge of a field artillery group of one white and two African-American battalions. But the white gunners had fled under pressure at Chenogne on Thursday, and one of the African-American units had been badly mauled. All they had left now was the 969th Field Artillery, an experienced battalion of black gunners who had taken part in the Normandy campaign and the siege of Brest. These gunners manned powerful 155mm howitzers, and they were providing both Task Force Browne and various elements of the 101st Airborne across the perimeter with vital support. Still, the officers at the château were tense. Their stocks of 155mm shells were running dangerously low, and it was clear that the enemy was steadily closing in on their valuable pieces.[35]

Baroness Greindl read the tense faces of the Americans and knew that the situation was bad. Her thoughts went out to her 12 children. Only the youngest ones had remained behind, and they were now hiding in one of the château's cellars. She was also concerned about the fate of the young boys from Bastogne's boarding school, whom clergymen had placed in her care a few days before. As if all that was not enough, she worried about her husband, something she had been doing since August 1944. Baron René Greindl, a civil engineer and former governor of the Belgian province of Luxembourg, had been active in the resistance. The 46-year-old had been arrested just weeks before American troops liberated Bastogne in September. The last news she had of him was that he was being held in a prison in Cologne.[36]

Madame Greindl had no way of knowing that Saturday that her husband was about to be transported from Cologne to the notorious concentration camp at Buchenwald, and that in another two months he would be dead. At the same time, however, Belgians all around Bastogne were finding that, in the wake of German troops, Nazi security forces were resuming their round-ups. They had already brought terror to the villages of Bourcy and Noville to the northeast of Bastogne. Now they descended on Givry, a village just northwest of McAuliffe's besieged troops and not far from where von Lüttwitz had his comfortable château headquarters. Gestapo agents arrested eight men and boys. They questioned them about the resistance and administered savage beatings to ensure they got answers. Then they released four suspects and loaded the others onto a truck that sped off to an unknown destination. It would take three months for a farmer in a nearby village to discover the bodies of the executed prisoners. All four lay in shallow graves, their hands tied together. The youngest was 17.[37]

Saturday, December 23, was a surreal day of horror, punctuated by elation. Even as soldiers and civilians were dying just west of Bastogne, Americans and Belgians inside the town were cheering. Just before noon, a wave of sluggish aircraft was spotted heading towards Bastogne from the west. Lieutenant

Colonel William Parkhill, commander of the 441st Troop Carrier Group, was one of 21 pilots who had taken off from an airbase at Dreux, just southwest of Paris. Their C-47s carried almost 70,000 pounds of ammunition, more than 15,000 pounds of rations, and 800 pounds of medical supplies. The flying weather was excellent. "You could see," observed Parkhill, "for a hundred miles in all directions." There were no enemy aircraft in the skies. Below, enemy armor and other vehicles jammed the roads "bumper to bumper." At first, the Germans ran away from the roads, mistaking the Skytrain transports for fighter-bombers. Then they hurried back and opened up with all the anti-aircraft weapons at their disposal. One of the C-47s towards the rear of the formation was hit and went down. The others homed in on the pathfinders' signals. These directed them to a drop zone squeezed in between Madame Greindl's château and the town center. The pilots dropped most of their loads on target and banked away as the flak bursts increased rapidly.[38]

It was just the first of several successful supply runs that Saturday. Early in the morning, men of the 490th Quartermaster Unit in England had worked feverishly to get a much larger cargo ready. In wave after wave that afternoon, a total of 241 Douglas C-47 transports flew in all the way from Chalgrove airfield in Oxfordshire. "Bastogne," one airborne officer wrote, "vibrated with the thunder of American engines." Countless bundles floated down, their parachutes dyed various colors, each one indicating a different category of supplies. Some Skytrains came in so low that the besieged villagers could see the faces of airmen who were kicking bundles out of windswept doorways. The C-47s of the IX Troop Carrier Command dropped some 192 tons of ammunition, 12 tons of gasoline, and 35 tons of provisions and medical supplies.[39]

Although this time around, the C-47s approached from the south and were protected by more than 80 P-47 Thunderbolts, enemy flak brought down seven more aircraft. Captain Paul Dahl of Los Angeles was flying one of the doomed planes. He was only moments away from the drop zone when two simultaneous flak bursts riddled the transport. Dahl was wounded, and so were his copilot, a lieutenant from Chicago, and his navigator, Lieutenant Zeno Rose from Virginia. Large parts of the instrument panels were "sheared away." Still, Captain Dahl somehow managed to hold the plane steady, find the target, and release the supplies. Then, as he turned to get away, another explosion hit them "flush in the nose." There was a fire. Smoke filled the cockpit and Dahl ordered his crew to bail out. The radio operator and the crew chief failed to escape in time. They crashed with the burning plane.[40]

Despite such horrific scenes, the joy of those below could not be disguised. Worried soldiers had been confiding to Monique Guiot that they were fast running out of supplies. "They thought," the girl noted, "that it was all over for them and us." But now the 14-year-old was electrified to see the Americans so buoyed up: "We were all jumping up and down, we were all dancing, we were all hugging." What gave morale a huge boost was not just the arrival of desperately needed supplies, but the knowledge that they had not been forgotten by the outside world. "After a week cut off from everybody else, hidden back in the woods," said a paratrooper who had been on the perimeter's northeast, "we'd lost any sense of context, that we were part of something bigger than just staying alive." The Americans, one Bastognard noted, suddenly were "happy like big children."[41]

But so were the Belgians. Ten-year-old Paul Remiche ran after his father as he rushed to the fields where the bundles were coming down, ignoring the danger of shellfire. A proud Paul watched his father work side by side with the Americans, as they tried to get as many of the supplies onto trucks as fast as possible. When, later that afternoon, word spread in the Institute of Notre Dame that a crew member from one of the downed C-47s had been brought to their shelter, civilians gave him "a triumphal welcome," chanting "*Vive les Américains*" over and over again.[42]

Meanwhile, supplies were rapidly being distributed to where they were needed most. Freezing soldiers stripped the packaging off the bundles for their own use. Canvas bags were cut into pieces to be wrapped around feet; silk parachutes were turned into sleeping bags; thick padding made its way to foxholes and aid stations as floor insulation. It was ammunition, however, that troops were looking for most urgently among the supplies. For by now, each of the 101st Airborne's four artillery battalions possessed stocks of less than 200 shells. The previous day, orders had come down to begin rationing ammunition. McAuliffe had quipped to his artillery commander to hold fire "until you see the whites of their eyes." But no one was laughing in the front lines. In the sector of the 506th Parachute Infantry, for example, the men of E Company in Captain Winters' battalion were virtually out of ammunition. The single artillery piece covering the road into Bastogne from Noville had three rounds left, and orders were to use these for anti-tank purposes only. Other than that, there were an estimated "six rounds per mortar, one bandolier for each rifleman, and one box of machine-gun ammo per gun."[43]

The reality was, however, that the supplies trickling in on Saturday were like drops on a hot plate. Commanders warned troops that ammunition would have to remain strictly rationed. Badly discouraged by the limited medical supplies brought in by recovery teams, officers in charge of Bastogne's aid stations were reaching breaking point. In an empty warehouse, care for the ambulatory cases was left to Captain Samuel Feiler. A dentist, the officer could barely keep up with the hundreds of men pouring in to be treated for wounds, barking coughs, and high fevers. In the aid station for the badly wounded from 10th Armored Division's Combat Command B, Captain Prior was much worse off. His patients had first been assembled in a garage, but the place had been impossible to heat and soon had proved too small. Amidst the shelling, the patients had carefully been moved to the basement of the Sarma, a three-story local store on the rue de Neufchâteau. There were at least a hundred serious cases on stretchers and mattresses. Jack Prior had virtually no instruments to work with, a rapidly dwindling supply of plasma, and only small quantities of hydrogen peroxide and sulfa powder with which to disinfect wounds. "Patients with head wounds or injuries to the chest or abdomen were awaiting a slow death," Dr. Prior noted ruefully, "because they could not be operated on."[44]

Morale at the Sarma hospital improved a little when two young Belgian women offered their services as nurses. One of them was 30-year-old Renée Lemaire. She worked at a major hospital in Brussels, and it was in the capital that she had met her fiancé, Joseph. A Jew, he had been arrested by the Gestapo in February 1944 and had not been heard of since. Renée had returned to Bastogne just before the start of the German offensive to be with her parents, who owned a hardware store near the town's market place. The other nurse, Augusta Chiwy, was still in her early twenties. A black girl who worked at the university hospital in Louvain, she too had returned to Bastogne to celebrate Christmas. The illegitimate daughter of a Congolese woman and a Belgian veterinarian, as a child she had been sent to her uncle in Bastogne to be educated. The girl had had a hard time fighting prejudice among white people, who ruled her native land as a colony. Now she was impressed to see black American soldiers in uniform and armed. Although a few white GIs refused to be treated by a black nurse, most of Dr. Prior's patients were exceedingly grateful to have both women by their side.[45]

There were many more seriously wounded soldiers in the chapel of the Seminary, the boys' boarding school. Initially the aid station of the 501st Parachute Regiment, the place had rapidly been transformed into the central airborne hospital after the capture of the division's 326th Medical Company. On Saturday, it was estimated that the chapel harbored some 250 patients. The atmosphere inside was stifling. Operations were being improvised in a space behind the altar. By the yellow light of gas lamps, Major Carrel, the regimental surgeon, and medic Ed O'Brien were preparing to amputate a leg poisoned by gangrene below the knee. The soldier reacted violently to the news. With much difficulty, sodium pentothal was used to sedate him. The stretcher was placed on two large medical chests, and the procedure was performed with no more than a saw and two trench knives heated over a squad cooker. "I don't know which was worse," said O'Brien, "the smell of burning flesh or the sound of bone being sawed." In the midst of such frenetic activity, wounded enemy soldiers were being brought in, too, placing an added burden on exhausted medical staff. One of the Germans, O'Brien saw, came in with multiple wounds in his belly. All O'Brien could do was "try to push the intestines back into the abdominal cavity and apply a wet compress." A visiting paratrooper was sickened by the smell and sounds inside the chapel hospital. He recognized one of his buddies among the patients. "He was delirious from shell shock," the horrified private noted, "and every minute or two would sit up and start yelling that someone was stealing his boots." In the Seminary's walled courtyard, corpses lay stacked up under frozen canvas covers.[46]

For several days now, patients had been diverted from the choked chapel to newly improvised hospitals across town. One had been set up in the riding hall of the Heintz barracks, the same compound where McAuliffe and his staff sat hidden away in their underground command post. When Captain Prior paid a quick visit to this hospital to see if any supplies could perhaps be spared, he was shocked by the scene before him: some 600 patients on stretchers and blankets spread out across sawdust and dirt. So bad was the medical situation that on Saturday the girls in the Institute of Notre Dame were told to clear part of their underground corridor for American casualties. Their legs badly swollen from sitting still on chairs day and night with little to drink, the girls pressed together even more tightly. But the horrific scenes on the other side of the corridor kept them from complaining. Maria Gillet caught a glimpse of one of the soldiers brought in on a stretcher. "Where his legs had been," she scribbled in her journal, "I can see only a shapeless mass of crushed flesh . . . blood spills onto the floor." "My thoughts go to his faraway mother," shuddered Maria. "Why, Lord, do people hate each other like this?"[47]

The pilots of the P-47 Thunderbolts had no time for such thoughts. As soon as the supply planes they were escorting had dropped their supplies and headed home, they turned their attention to the enemy below. Loaded with up to 2,500 pounds of bombs and rockets, and armed with eight wing-mounted Browning .50 caliber machine guns spewing armor-piercing rounds, more than 80 fighter-bombers began providing McAuliffe's troops with much-needed additional firepower that Saturday afternoon.

All around Bastogne, staff of the 10th Armored Division's Combat Command B noted, "there were more enemy targets to shoot at than they could take care of." Working frantically, Captain James Parker proved vital in coordinating the Thunderbolts' lethal work. A Ninth Air Force air controller, the Californian had slipped into Bastogne five days earlier. He had set up air–ground radio equipment in a tank borrowed from Colonel Roberts's Combat Command B, installed the vehicle on the parade ground of the Heintz barracks, and impatiently waited for the skies to clear. Now that they had at last, information on enemy targets was pouring in by field phone from McAuliffe's nearby headquarters and from regimental command posts all around the perimeter. Captain Parker had seen combat as a fighter pilot in the Pacific and Europe, and knew how to talk with airmen. One of the men assisting him in the precision work of rapidly relaying target locations was Lieutenant George Woldt. Employed by an insurance company in Manhattan in peacetime, Woldt had been trained in air–ground liaison duties for the 101st Airborne, and had been in the thick of it in Normandy and Holland. So efficient was this team of air controllers that Thunderbolts could be seen swooping down on German targets within minutes of ground troops requesting assistance. "Attacks," an impressed McAuliffe observed, "were made on targets within 400 yards of our infantry lines."[48]

The Thunderbolts in search of prey over Bastogne belonged to four fighter groups from General Otto Weyland's XIX Tactical Air Command. Making heavy use of fragmentation bombs and napalm, the damage they wrought on Saturday was massive. The 362nd Fighter Group, whose pilots proudly called themselves "Mogin's Maulers," in 107 sorties claimed 12 tanks and 84 motor transport vehicles.[49]

But it was the pilots of Colonel Anthony Grosetta's 406th Fighter Group who were determined to outdo all the others. They were stationed in Mourmelon and had earlier befriended the paratroopers there, swapping liquor for German pistols and other souvenirs. They had watched them scramble onto trucks and head out for an unknown destination on Monday. Now, during a briefing early in the morning, they had been told that the airborne men and former neighbors were among the troops surrounded in Bastogne. In the slush and icy wind, men worked "their tails off" (as one of the ground personnel put it) to arm the Thunderbolts of the 406th to the teeth. One of the unit's pilots was Lieutenant Howard Park. The name of his aircraft was "Big Ass Bird II" and there was a good reason for the roman numeral. His previous machine had been damaged by ground fire in August and had then been completely wrecked by Messerschmitts in September. On both occasions, Lieutenant Park had been wounded. But now he was back in action with his second Thunderbolt and, like his comrades, itching for a fight. Tracers and flak bursts forced Park to slip and skid across Bastogne's perimeter. Nevertheless, time and again the experienced pilot managed to dive at the enemy at dizzying speed, make targets go up in smoke and flames, and then safely bank away again. North of Bastogne, Park and his fellow pilots roamed as far as Houffalize in search of tanks. At the end of the day, the 406th claimed to have destroyed 11 tanks, as well as 97 other motorized vehicles, 20 horse-drawn vehicles, and 24 gun positions. On Bastogne's northern perimeter, Major Jim Hatch and the men of the 502nd Parachute Infantry watched the P-47s in awe. "Morale," he said, "went up 300 percent."[50]

But as the smoke rose from villages and hamlets all around the perimeter – "almost as if the fog was closing in again" – civilians soon found that air strikes were more dangerous than any artillery barrage. The Meurisses and their eight-year-old son André had survived unscathed the fighting and shellfire on the western perimeter and were now sheltering at a farm in Mande-Saint-Étienne. But when panicked Germans had cried "*Jabos!*" (fighter-bombers) and Thunderbolt attacks had made the farm tremble, the Meurisses and other refugees had dashed to a nearby vaulted stable just moments before the main house caved in. Now André was complaining about a slight pain in his shoulder. A worried Monsieur Meurisse peeled off André's many layers of clothing to reveal a small wound caused by a jagged piece of shrapnel. André's father knew that, if left untreated, infection would soon set in. He begged a medic to try and get their son to an aid station in town. The American agreed reluctantly. But since the trip to Bastogne was going to be extremely dangerous, he refused to allow André's mother to join them. That evening, the boy, just one of many wounded civilians taxing medical staff even more, was operated on successfully. But his anguished mother had no way of knowing this and would remain in the dark about the fate of her son and husband inside Bastogne for several weeks.[51]

There was a reason why the Americans were strict about preventing civilians from moving about inside the perimeter. By late afternoon, von Lüttwitz from his château in Roumont had directed two of the three assaults he had planned for Saturday. The violent air attacks of the past few hours, however, had forced him to postpone the third blow and to wait for darkness to fall.

American intelligence, helped by Thunderbolts flying reconnaissance missions over the perimeter before heading home, was suggesting a build-up near Marvie.

On Wednesday, this small village, barely a mile southeast of Bastogne, was where Bayerlein's Panzergrenadiers had come close to rupturing the perimeter. The 2nd Battalion of the 327th Glider Infantry had been rushed in that day and, with the support of Team O'Hara's tank crews, had finally managed to halt the assailants. Both American forces remained dug in at Marvie. But the glidermen in particular were spread dangerously thin, as Colonel Joseph Harper's three battalions were covering almost half the perimeter, from Marvie all the way to Hemroulle, northwest of Bastogne. Meanwhile, the opposing force had remained the same: Panzer Lehr's powerful 901st Regiment, the only element of the veteran armored division to have stayed behind to help Kokott's infantrymen capture Bastogne.

As darkness fell that Saturday, an increasingly intense artillery barrage was churning the front line in and around Marvie. Then, at 1845, Bayerlein's Panzergrenadiers launched a fierce attack with the support of at least two tank companies. Almost immediately, an engineer platoon and some hundred airborne men from G Company found themselves cut off on Hill 500, just south of Marvie. Colonel Harper placed a phone call to the command post on the hill. "We are continuing to fight them back," a lieutenant told the regimental commander as he glimpsed tanks through a window, "but it looks like they have us." Three minutes later the line went dead.[52]

Almost all the men on Hill 500 were killed or captured. Buoyed by the success, Paul von Hauser, the 901st Regiment's experienced commander, was exhorting his men to keep up the momentum. On the nearby N34, the main road into Bastogne from Wiltz, Colonel O'Hara's tank force was now coming under heavy pressure, too. Dug in near a couple of farmhouses beside the road were soldiers from the 54th Armored Infantry. Elturino Loiacono was one of them. The 19-year-old had been born in Washington, D.C. But because his parents, Anastasio and Carmela, had clung to their native language after emigrating from the Italian town of Troia, Elturino was still not always comfortable speaking English. Now he and three other GIs held their breath as they saw German tanks approach their foxholes. They sat draped in Belgian bed sheets for camouflage. When a soldier on Elturino's right fired a bazooka at the lead Panther, the tanks responded furiously. Within seconds, an explosion caused a piece of shrapnel to bury itself in Elturino's eye. Clasping his hands to his face, he fell to the bottom of his foxhole. Tanks were churning the area around him and the thought that his comrades were being buried alive caused him anguish. An only child, Elturino (named after one of Troia's patron saints) thought of his parents and how the news of his death would break their hearts. In a flash, he remembered what the nuns at school had always told them: if they wanted the help of Jesus, they should ask His mother to intercede on their behalf. Elturino hid beneath the sheet and offered up prayer after prayer to the Blessed Virgin. He was interrupted when German soldiers approached his foxhole. They jumped in and prodded his apparently lifeless body. Then they started kicking dirt into the hole. Elturino gasped for air. After what seemed like an eternity, the Germans stopped and turned back. Elturino pushed away the dirt. He resumed his prayers until he passed out.[53]

Backed up by Shermans, Team O'Hara's armored infantry managed to hold the line near the Wiltz road as evening turned to night. But the Germans were now hammering away at Marvie, as tanks had already pushed into the southern part of the village and were setting houses alight with white phosphorus. This meant that the perimeter had been breached and that, at less than a mile from the market square, Bayerlein's formidable Panthers were threatening the very heart of Bastogne. A wan-faced Colonel Kinnard grabbed the phone and placed an urgent call to Middleton's VIII Corps in Florenville. "In regard to our situation," the Texan reported tensely, "it is getting pretty sticky around here."[54]

There was no other choice now but to throw everything into the breach. Rapidly depleting their already low stocks, artillery battalions at Senonchamps began spewing fire in the direction of Marvie. Reinforcements were scraped together all over Bastogne to help back up the glidermen of the 2nd Battalion. Some tanks were siphoned off from nearby Team O'Hara to prevent the Germans from bursting out of Marvie. The remaining half of the 10th Armored Division's Team Cherry was also rushed to Marvie. But this meant that Bastogne had no more reserve force left to counter a simultaneous attack elsewhere. It forced a reluctant McAuliffe to call back from Senonchamps a force that had been sent there earlier in the day to help protect the hard-pressed and vital artillery. Smaller groups were arriving in Marvie too, among them one platoon from Ewell's 501st Regiment in the eastern sector and two batteries from the 81st Anti-aircraft Battalion.[55]

That night, Americans fought with fierce desperation to hold onto Marvie's northern edge and prevent the Germans from pouring into Bastogne. Lieutenant Thomas Niland, a 2nd Battalion intelligence officer, rallied command post personnel, clerks, and cooks, and had them take up key defensive positions. Continually exposed to heavy tank and small-arms fire, the junior officer also took upon himself the command of two of Team O'Hara's Shermans, weapons that were absolutely crucial in the battle against the Panzergrenadiers.[56]

Even though he was in danger of being overrun near the command post, Private Harry Bliss stayed put with his machine gun, fired salvo after salvo into the attackers, and then, when his ammunition ran out, killed the last surviving German with the toss of a hand grenade. Norman Osterberg, a 19-year-old from Headquarters Company, grabbed his bazooka and single-handedly confronted several tanks that had broken through. Though under intense direct fire, the Pennsylvanian refused to budge, repeatedly driving away Panthers that approached to within ten yards of his position. By the time he was wounded, the citation for the Distinguished Service Cross later read, Private Osterberg had been engaged in "fierce action" for about three hours. It was such death-defying stubbornness that helped gain time for reinforcements to arrive and join the battle. When dawn broke on Sunday, the Americans were still in possession of Marvie's northern edge. Once again, McAuliffe's forces had managed to block the way into Bastogne at the last minute. Although Fritz Bayerlein's troops continued to cling to houses in the village's southern outskirts, the battle for Marvie was over.[57]

That morning, too, Elturino Loiacono woke up in his foxhole next to the Wiltz road. With his one good eye, he could make out the wreck of a German tank near the rubble of one of the farmhouses. He crawled to a building somewhat further to the rear. American voices yelled at him to halt. He told them not to shoot and gave his name. When the GIs showed themselves, it turned out they were the comrades he thought had died in their foxholes. The men were even more surprised to discover that Elturino was still alive. When he came closer to greet the young kid with the strong Italian accent, Elturino's sergeant, who was miserable with a bad cold, broke down in tears.[58]

3

On Sunday, December 24, the pressure on McAuliffe's troops eased some-what. As soon as it had become clear the previous night that the attack on Marvie was running out of steam, von Manteuffel himself had paid a visit to Colonel Kokott's command post. The Americans in Bastogne were hampering logistical support of the armored spearheads of his Fifth Panzer Army that were now in sight of the Meuse. More worrisome, if Patton's vanguard managed to link up with the defenders, the road network would help the

Third Army claw deeper into the German salient. The town, an impatient von Manteuffel emphasized, "must be taken at all costs."

The pressure on the German general had mounted that day with news of the destruction of *Kampfgruppe* Peiper at La Gleize, news that signaled the end of any significant offensive role for Dietrich's Waffen SS in the northern salient. Von Manteuffel had already consulted with von Lüttwitz in Roumont, and they had come to the decision that the *coup de grâce* at Bastogne would have to be dealt on Christmas Day. Kokott had been happy to hear that this time his Volksgrenadiers could expect reinforcements in the form of the 15th Panzergrenadier Division. Though not fully refitted, it was a powerful force that had fought tough battles in North Africa, Sicily, southern Italy, Aachen, and the Vosges Mountains. The scholarly looking Kokott had suggested attacking Bastogne's defenders in what he now regarded as their softest spot: the northwestern sector around Champs, where an overextended battalion of the 327th Glider Infantry on its right was showing a weak seam with the 502nd Parachute Infantry. His commanders had agreed with his judgment. For the Germans, Christmas Eve was to be a day of poring over maps, regrouping, and getting troops ready for the decisive blow.[59]

In the early hours of Sunday, many of the staff in the 101st Airborne's headquarters were fast asleep after an exhausting day of staving off one attack after another. Most were bedded down in the small cubicles on either side of the cellar corridor. Some lay sprawled on blankets spread over the coal at the end of the central passage. Just before dawn, however, the command post again turned into a hive of activity. Colonel Kinnard, the division's operations officer, was at the center of the day's activity. Events of the previous day had left him seriously worried, and so he set about giving Bastogne's defenses a thorough overhaul. There would be a fresh German challenge soon, he knew; and, when it came, he wanted the troops to be better prepared. Given the dwindling forces at his disposal, there was, of course, only so much that he could do. The Texan's first step was to tighten the perimeter. At Marvie the Germans had already made this happen anyway, and the glidermen were now digging in deep just north of the devastated village. Glider troops had already pulled out of the salient at Flamierge, too, but they were now told to fall back still further to just behind Mande-Saint-Étienne.[60]

The most significant decision was to have troops at Senonchamps abandon the sector they had defended so fiercely for four days. Events on Sunday showed that the time had come, as continued German pounding disabled three tanks and fatally wounded Colonel Barry Browne, the much admired team commander. In Isle-la-Hesse, a concerned Baroness Greindl watched more artillery take up positions in the area just west of her château. The day before, she and her American guests had toasted the arrival of supplies with a glass of port. Now, nervous officers were peering out of her windows with binoculars, and a soldier in the attic was scanning the horizon with a periscope. Four Shermans stood in the courtyard, their motors growling, guns aimed in the direction of Senonchamps. In one of the larger rooms, black soldiers of the 969th Field Artillery were hastily setting up an aid station.[61]

With the perimeter reined in to about 16 miles of front line all around town, Kinnard's next move was to turn the four airborne regiments into combined arms teams. Tanks and tank destroyers were parceled out to each regiment, so that, rather than wait for armored reinforcements to arrive from the town center, they could strike immediately and in closer cooperation with the foot soldiers. Even then, however, a breakthrough might occur and would have to be countered with a reserve force. Although this proved hard to scrape together, it was eventually made up of Team SNAFU and 14 battered medium and light tanks from Colonel Roberts's Combat Command B.

Kinnard completed his overhaul with the creation of an interior guard for the defense of Bastogne's nerve center. Forty soldiers and four tank destroyers from Templeton's unit, joined by more men from Team SNAFU, were ordered to take up positions around McAuliffe's cellar headquarters.[62]

For those living underground in the town's civilian shelters, the redrawing of operational maps meant little. By the wan light of candles and petrol lamps, people huddled together under blankets in search of some warmth. The air they breathed was growing thick and putrid. Although there was no critical shortage of food yet, stocks in the cellars were running low. The rations of bread, meat, and canned food that were being doled out at the Seminary were meager, and shelling made it dangerous to try and get there. Many, especially children, had fallen ill with bronchitis and pneumonia; gastrointestinal disease was rampant. The town's remaining doctors did what they could to help, but American requisitioning of medical supplies made their job even more difficult. Medics had picked Dr. Govaerts's cabinet clean, leaving him only his gynecological instruments. Fortunately so, for he was soon called to a dank cellar, where he was needed to help save a woman from a bad hemorrhage. The elderly were least able to withstand the pressures of the underground existence. Brought down from the nursing home to the Seminary's basement, some lost their mind in the gloomy cavern and had to be restrained; others lay still on their mattresses and died almost unnoticed.[63]

In the cellars of the Institute of Notre Dame, the atmosphere was growing more claustrophobic by the hour. Some 600 people sat packed together. And the space available shrank steadily as more and more American wounded were brought down. Conditions were appalling: dust, shaken from the ceiling by explosions, blackened faces and clothing; buckets had been distributed to serve as toilets; sheets from the upstairs rooms were ripped to pieces and handed out as sanitary napkins. Parents could not change nappies regularly enough, and babies, their bottoms encrusted in excrement, howled in agony. People suffered from lice and scabies. The stench made it difficult to eat what little food was being distributed. Louise Lamotte, one of the girls on the chairs in the corridor, remembered that throughout the siege, as well as an occasional bowl of soup, they received two cooked potatoes for lunch, and another one for dinner.[64]

And yet, somehow the communities in their suffocating shelters managed to hold together. In the Institute of Notre Dame, Norbert Nicolay, the town photographer and a veteran of the Great War, revealed himself to be a born leader. He moved tirelessly among the refugees, booming directives through the cellars, and on several occasions intervening to quell panic. Each day without fail he went above ground to gather news and assess the situation. Many others simply did their bit by refusing to have their spirits broken by fear and hardship. Time and again, the boarding-school girls in their corridor fell silent as medics carried away soldiers who had died of their wounds. Yet, in between, they hummed jazz tunes and sang songs they had picked up from the Americans, determined to keep up their morale and that of the pallid wounded stretched out nearby.[65]

For the soldiers in the front lines, the absence of a major German assault on Christmas Eve did not do much to lessen the hardship. Airborne veterans from the Normandy and Holland campaigns had been in poor shape even before they were rushed to the Ardennes. "By the time we got into Bastogne," one paratrooper acknowledged, "we were all flaky to start with." The unrelenting pressure of the past week had taken a further toll of veterans and replacements alike. In the 506th Parachute Infantry, Private Donald Burgett's A Company, which had fought hard at Noville and near Foy, had suffered nearly 75 percent casualties and was down to 50 men. Thinned ranks meant that guard and patrol duties came around more often, putting even more strain on already exhausted men.[66]

Freezing temperatures made it almost impossible to sleep anyway. "They feel the cold even more than we," a German soldier facing the 501st Parachute Infantry wrote to his wife, "for they are lying in their holes without having been issued winter clothes." The 101st Airborne estimated that only half of their men were wearing overshoes. Countless paratroopers had arrived in Bastogne from Mourmelon without so much as an overcoat or gloves. They sat shivering in their foxholes, field jackets lined with newspapers, feet swaddled in burlap sacks, heads wrapped in towels. They filled their dugouts with anything that could provide insulation: canvas, cardboard, pine boughs. Many were suffering from respiratory ailments. So loud was the coughing of a 3rd Battalion soldier at night that the men in the 2nd Battalion, on the other side of the Noville road, feared he would give away their position. It was estimated that in the 2nd Battalion a third of all non-battle casualties resulted from trench foot and frostbite. Eugene Roe, one of the battalion's medics, made a point of collecting the morphine vials from the dead. That way he ensured that soldiers in the front line had sufficient quantities to help them fight the pain from feet swollen to a dark purple.[67]

There was never enough water to quench the thirst that came from constant tension and exertion. The little snow that had fallen could not be melted, as any fire would risk giving away their positions; meanwhile streams were polluted with white phosphorus and corpses. After the first couple of days, K rations were dwindling fast. Hungry paratroopers scoured farms for potatoes, beets, onions, eggs, or some milk. But their needs were always in competition with those of the Belgian men, women, and children packed together in the farm cellars and stables. And the search for provisions in a battle zone was never without risk. Two men from G Company in the 502nd Parachute Infantry alerted an outpost to their plan to find food and, under cover of darkness, crawled to a farmhouse in no man's land. On their way back, they became lost and wandered into a neighboring sector. An American machine gun opened up. Dawn revealed the foragers' bodies, and soldiers were sent out to retrieve them. "As we watched them being placed onto a jeep," recalled Private John Fitzgerald, "we could see some potatoes rolling from their pockets onto the ground."[68]

"Morale was always good," said Captain Winters of his experience in the 506th Parachute Infantry. "The low point was Bastogne." Life within the town's perimeter, the 2nd Battalion's executive officer noted, "defied description." More than had ever been the case in Normandy or Holland, Winters maintained, paratroopers were now suffering from combat fatigue. Catching a second shift of guard duty in pitch darkness, James Simms, the Alabama high-school teacher who had emerged unscathed from the battle for Noville, suddenly sensed he was about to crack. He simply could no longer endure the prospect of endless hours of freezing cold and nothingness. "Eventually," he recalled, "I found myself thinking about my M1 rifle. A click of the safety and a tug of the trigger and my suffering could be over."[69]

Simms straightened himself out that night. But others could no longer do that by themselves. Joseph Liebgott had been a barber in San Francisco before the war. He had been awarded a Bronze Star as a machine gunner in Normandy, and had fought bravely in Holland, where he had been wounded. But in Bastogne, observed Captain Winters, "stress began to catch up with 'The Barber.'" Liebgott, at 30 one of the oldest men in his company, was becoming a danger to himself and others. Winters first pulled him back to the battalion command post to have him serve as a runner. When that failed to do the trick, he had the German-born paratrooper transferred to division headquarters as a translator.[70]

Meanwhile, steadily and insidiously, enemy fire further thinned the ranks, even at times when the front was said to be quiet. Patrols ran into ambushes. Shells exploded in trees, showering jagged shards and splinters into foxholes. An occasional mortar round or machine-gun burst took men by surprise. German snipers infested the woods all around the perimeter and had an easy task picking off Americans who had arrived without snow capes. In Longchamps, just north of Bastogne, in the sector of the 502nd Parachute Infantry, 12-year-old Henri Spoiden never knew what killed the sergeant who had taken a liking to his sister. His family had befriended the paratrooper during the brief moments when he stole time to thaw out in their farmhouse. Then one day the sergeant seemed hesitant about returning to his platoon. He said goodbye to the Spoidens, gave Henri's sister a scarf, and stroked the dog for a good long time. All Henri knew was that for three days his family waited for the American to come back, until finally some of his comrades told them that he, too, was dead.[71]

The American troops could draw some comfort from the fact that the enemy was increasingly seen to be in poor shape as well. Men from E Company in Captain Winters' sector looked on in amazement when, in broad daylight, an ambulance crawled up the road to where they were dug in on the forest's edge. The vehicle came to a stop and the Americans trained their weapons on it as the doors slowly opened. "Out came a German soldier," recalled Californian Buck Compton. "He had no gun, so none of us made a move. Then came out another and another. They stood with their hands up, surrendering. This was a surprise. We had all thought we were the ones surrounded."

In ones and twos, and in groups small and large, more and more prisoners were led into town for interrogation. "G-2 interpreters," wrote reporter Fred MacKenzie, "examined letters, photographs, and other personal effects piled in a corner of the War Room." The material was taken from the dead as well as the captured. After interrogation, the prisoners were sent to the enclosure in the town's southwest. As their numbers swelled, Lieutenant George Allen grew worried about how to feed them. It was clear that, with American troops going hungry in the front lines, none of the rations dropped by the C-47s were intended for German POWs. The Philadelphian had no choice but to search pantries and cellars in nearby houses. He uncovered potatoes, apples, oatmeal, turnips, and sizeable amounts of sugar beets. All this he had prisoners mix in large laundry vats and cook into a gruel that was then passed around in buckets once or twice a day.[72]

The captured Germans were grateful for the soggy meals. Each day it was becoming clearer that this was no longer the superior enemy from the start of the war, when newsreels in American movie theaters had shown one Nazi victory after another. Some German infantry units in the Ardennes were now more reliant on horses than their counterparts had been in 1918. Many of the vehicles in Kokott's division were in such bad repair that they had to be abandoned. The poor Ardennes roads, and the ice and snow, were all making the arrival of sufficient quantities of ammunition, gasoline, and food even more difficult. The ration of bread, a staple of the German soldier's diet, had already been cut because not enough flour was getting through.[73]

Nothing made the supply situation more difficult for the Germans than the Allied air forces, which, as Bradley's top aide noted on Christmas Eve, were ripping into the enemy "savagely." On December 24, beautiful flying weather allowed the Allies to deploy more aircraft than on any other day in the Ardennes campaign. Bombers continued their campaign of interdiction west of the Rhine, dropping more than 1,500 tons of explosives on rail centers and bridges. Fighter-bombers from at least three different squadrons pounced on the enemy around Bastogne. They strafed troops, blew up tanks and trucks, and at one point bombed an ammunition dump in a wood near Bourcy, causing a terrific explosion. From dawn to dusk, radio chatter picked up by Captain Parker's special tank echoed around the headquarters courtyard. "Planes," observed Fred MacKenzie, "sped above at bewilderingly low altitudes, wheeling and diving in numbers that sometimes seemed to fill the sky." German troops had lived in fear of the fighter-bombers – *Jabos* as they called them – since D-Day. They had cost Bayerlein's Panzer Lehr 5 tanks, 84 half-tracks and self-propelled guns, and 130 trucks even before the division managed to reach the Normandy battlefield. Much like the German Stukas in 1940, just the sound of diving Thunderbolts now had Bayerlein's and Kokott's soldiers scrambling from vehicles and getting clear of the roads. German POWs readily admitted that the Allied fighter-bombers were hugely demoralizing, and that machine-gun strafing and rocket attacks in particular were extremely frightening.[74]

At times they could be just as scary for the Americans and Belgians. At 1340 on Sunday, six P-47s swooped down on Marvie, where Germans remained holed up on the village's southern edge. Although glidermen to the north of Marvie sat dug in behind orange panels, six 500-pound bombs struck their positions. Colonel Harper, the regimental commander, happened to be inspecting the lines and was himself taken by surprise. He made it to a foxhole just in time to watch the American aircraft turn back, fly in low over the rooftops, and strafe the streets. In pursuit of targets between Noville and Foy, P-47s were bombing so close to the airborne lines that McAuliffe's head-quarters placed a frantic call demanding that the mission be aborted instantly.[75]

The order to do so came too late for farmers in German-held Cobru, where napalm had set several farms ablaze. Sixteen villagers had been hiding in one of these. Neighbors tried to rescue them, but by the time they reached those trapped inside, six people from four different families were dead. Only one of the ten survivors, a ten-month-old baby, was unharmed. All the others were badly wounded, most of them horribly burnt. They would remain without proper care for almost three weeks, and were forced to watch ten-year-old Charlotte Genon die from her burns. By nightfall on December 24, houses and barns all around Bastogne's 16-mile perimeter were on fire, raining down sparks that ate holes in the clothing of soldiers and civilians alike.[76]

Frustrated by the ceaseless air attacks that were killing their comrades and preventing supplies from getting through, it was all too easy for German soldiers to vent their rage on civilians, making their lives even more miserable. In Bertogne, northwest of the perimeter, they butchered the hogs at the Bleret farm, threw the carcasses onto the kitchen table, and ordered the farmer's daughters to clean them. To the southwest, in Morhet, German troops were in such a pitiful state that they barked at the village men to assemble, and then told the dumbfounded Belgians to take off and hand over their shoes. In the village of Michamps, northeast of Bastogne, enemy troops descended on the farm of the Girs family, and in the courtyard proceeded to smash all their glassware, crockery, and china. Only when there was nothing left to destroy did the soldiers at last calm down.[77]

More C-47s, meanwhile, were lifting the spirits of the besieged inside their shrinking island. If medical supplies, food, and clothing remained a serious problem, stocks of ammunition were now running dangerously low as a result of the heavy shelling the previous night in support of Marvie's defenders. The airborne batteries were down to ten rounds per gun. The 420th Armored Field Artillery was rationed to just five rounds per mission. And the black gunners of the 969th Field Artillery's 155mm howitzers at Isle-la-Hesse were under orders to fire no more than 40 rounds in total during the entire day. In less than four hours on Christmas Eve, 161 C-47s dropped 1,446 bundles and parapacks over Bastogne, a total of almost 320,000 pounds of critical supplies. So desperate for ammunition were McAuliffe's men that *Stars and Stripes* sent one of its reporters along with a C-47 crew to cover the delivery of such a vital cargo. Newspaperman Richard Wilbur gritted his teeth as the pilot, Major Thomas Ricketts from Richmond, Virginia, closed in on Bastogne with his highly explosive load. "A gale of winter wind blew into the ship," observed Wilbur, as crew chief Kenneth Cade of Kansas City threw open the cargo doors. Bracing himself, the corporal shoved bundles of rifle ammunition over the edge, at the same time as six parapacks, slung under the Skytrain and loaded with 75mm shells, were cut loose.[78]

Even while the much-needed relief was trickling in from the air, McAuliffe and his staff were anxiously trying to find out more about the progress the Third Army was making. They all knew that only Patton and his men could save them from disaster. But time was running out, and it was becoming increasingly clear that stubborn German resistance south of Bastogne was taking the steam out of Patton's spearheads. "We'd get their progress from time to time," noted Colonel Roberts, "and that arrow on the map moved slowly."[79]

As early as mid-morning on Friday, McAuliffe's headquarters had received a message from the 4th Armored Division, assuring them that help was on the way. On Saturday, someone in the Heintz barracks aid station had announced that Patton was just miles away, and the news had brought applause and whistles among those of the 600 wounded not too weak to take notice. That same evening, however, as the Germans threatened to break through at Marvie, there had still been no sign of the 4th Armored Division, prompting Colonel Kinnard to place a call to VIII Corps headquarters with the urgent message that "They must keep coming." Now, however, on Sunday afternoon, relief seemed to be truly close, as VIII Corps relayed a message from General Patton himself: "Xmas Eve present coming up. Hold on."[80]

That evening, Bastogne's senior officers made sure to spread a Christmas message to their troops, in an effort to boost morale. Colonel Roberts told the men from Combat Command B that, together with their "superb team mates of the 101st Airborne Division," they were "making history." McAuliffe wished his troops a Merry Christmas, and then added: "What's merry about all this, you ask?" He went on to emphasize that, by holding onto Bastogne, they were assuring "the success of the Allied armies," and in doing so were "giving our country and our loved ones at home a worthy Christmas present." Around 1900, more than a hundred headquarters personnel gathered in a large building in the Heintz compound for a Christmas service. Candles in improvised tin fixtures along the walls cast a dim light. The service was brief. So was the chaplain's sermon. "Do not plan," he counseled, "for God's plan will prevail."[81]

No one understood this better that evening than the soldiers in the perimeter's foxholes. In Captain Winters' sector, the men from a mortar platoon had cut down a small spruce tree and decorated it with shell casings, ration cans, and metal chaff thrown out by American transport planes to confound enemy radar. Christmas Eve made memories of home and the fear of never making it back again especially hard to bear. In G Company's command post in the 327th Glider Infantry sector, Lieutenant Regenburg sat down with a soldier who had just been brought in by his platoon leader. The young private had been on guard duty and the isolation had been too much for him. "We ended up," said Al Regenburg, "splitting a couple ounces of cognac. I showed him pictures of my wife and baby. He showed me pictures of his wife and baby." When the private left again, both men were feeling much better.[82]

Back in town, in the Seminary's chapel, Colonel Ewell dropped by the crowded aid station to chat for a few minutes. Medics had covered the shattered stained-glass windows with canvas tarpaulins, but snow continued to drift in through the cracks. A group of soldiers and officers from the 501st Parachute Infantry quietly filed in and bunched together to form a choir. The gas lamps hissed and gusts of wind shook the tarpaulins. As the men struck up their first carol, the patients who had been dozing looked up. Some softly joined in the singing, their breath frosting in the air. Others hid their faces and could be seen wiping their eyes with their sleeves.[83]

In her château in Roumont, Marie du Bus de Warnaffe looked on as more than 20 villagers bustled about in her large kitchen. They had been commandeered to help peel several hundred pounds of potatoes, so that von Lüttwitz and his large staff would have a decent Christmas meal the following day. A flustered German cook was slaving over the stoves and ordering the Belgians about. Each time he looked away, the villagers took aim and scornfully spat in one of his simmering pots and pans.[84]

CHAPTER 5

THE SKIN OF THEIR TEETH

As von Lüttwitz put the finishing touches to the plan for Christmas Day, Americans and Belgians inside Bastogne were waiting for the next blow to fall. Intelligence showed a significant enemy build-up to the northwest, and McAuliffe's staff realized full well that dawn would bring serious trouble. But the next blow came much sooner than anyone had expected, and it struck Bastogne quite literally like a bolt from the blue.

The Luftwaffe, its backbone broken, played only a minor role in the Ardennes offensive. At around 2030 on Christmas Eve, however, an unfamiliar drone could suddenly be heard approaching Bastogne. The sound was that of Junkers 88s, twin-engine bombers from *Lehrgeschwader* 1 and *Kampfgeschwader* 66. Magnesium flares descended, bathing the town in blinding light. The flares were followed almost immediately by piercing shrieks, as sticks of bombs hurtled towards the illuminated target. Some of the first explosions rocked McAuliffe's headquarters. The noise was "petrifying," recalled Fred MacKenzie. Men crouched down along the walls of the cellar corridor, "drawing their physical parts into tight knots." A senior officer edged out of the Operations Room. "His voice hushed, seeming far away," the newspaperman noted, "he breathed, 'Steady men. Keep calm. Don't crowd.'"[1]

The bombs plowed a path through town. Soldiers from Team SNAFU saw the walls of a brick building they were hiding in "buckle and fold like a piece of flexible tin." In a neighbor's cellar packed with close to 30 people, six-year-old Roland Delperdange was violently tossed about on his mattress. So dense was the dust thrown out by the shaken concrete and coal that his horrified mother failed to locate him even with a flashlight in her hand. There was mass panic in the bowels of the Institute of Notre Dame, where hundreds of people were hurled against each other in pitch darkness. People could be heard screaming, praying, calling out the names of loved ones. "To be waiting for death to come," thought Maria Gillet, as she huddled in the girls' corridor, "is much more frightening than death itself."[2]

In Combat Command B's aid station in the rue de Neufchâteau, many of the seriously wounded were no longer waiting for death to come. Their doctor, Captain Jack Prior, was taking a break in a nearby building just when the Junkers 88s came over. He and a few other soldiers were having a glass of champagne to celebrate Christmas Eve, and the physician from Vermont had asked Augusta Chiwy, the black nurse from the Congo, to join them. "The explosion," the young woman recalled, "knocked everyone to the ground and for a few minutes it was chaos." It took the medical personnel a while to realize that it was not they who had been hit, but the aid station. Dust-caked and coughing, they stumbled into the street. "The sight that I saw there," said Augusta Chiwy, "was terrible." A direct hit on the Sarma store had made the three-story building collapse on top of the hundred or more wounded soldiers inside. Flames were shooting up from the structure's interior, "like the fires in a blast furnace." Soldiers were organizing a bucket brigade, but the German Junkers returned and began strafing the rue de Neufchâteau. The Americans fought back with carbines.[3]

In the basement of Sarma, Captain Geiger had survived the explosion. He had suffered shrapnel wounds in the battle for Noville, but was now trying to help those less fortunate. The patients' mattresses were ablaze and giving off an acrid smoke. "One boy was pinned down by a beam on his leg," recalled Gordon Geiger. "Someone found a saw and began to cut at the beam to free him. The boy was saying, 'Shoot me! Please shoot me!' " The GIs refused to give up and managed to get the soldier out in time. But more than two dozen patients were left behind in the mountain of rubble. Their charred and mutilated corpses could not be recovered until the fire died down days later. Among the bodies was that of 30-year-old Belgian nurse Renée Lemaire.[4]

That evening, a concerned McAuliffe was on the phone with General Middleton. "The finest Christmas present the 101st could get," he insisted, "would be a relief tomorrow." From his headquarters in Florenville, the mild-mannered southerner replied, "I know, boy. I know."[5]

1

Just before midnight, one of Kokott's Volksgrenadiers sat down to scribble a letter to his wife. He was terribly homesick and tried to picture how his two small children had spent Christmas Eve. "I haven't sent you anything in a long time," he apologized to his wife. "May God grant that I'll be able to make up to you one day for everything that you have missed." The German was quick to point out, however, that in the present circumstances they were the fortunate ones, since "many families of boys in our company" had recently suffered a fate that was "hard and cruel." Then he sent his family all his love and signed off: "It's eleven now, God knows what terrible things tomorrow may bring."[6]

As the Volksgrenadier was writing these words, McAuliffe was being driven to Savy in a jeep. The hamlet lay just northwest of his command post, and the general wanted to celebrate midnight mass there with the men of the 321st Glider Field Artillery. He was not sure what tomorrow would bring either. But word had it that the rumble of tanks had been drifting in all evening from the vicinity of nearby Champs. If the enemy were to attack on Christmas Day, the blow was almost certain to come from the northwest, making the artillerymen and other troops in this sector the very last line of defense.[7]

After a brief service at Savy, McAuliffe withdrew to his underground cubicle for some much-needed rest. He had slept barely a couple of hours when another wave of Junkers 88s made a run over Bastogne. The second raid took place around 0300 and left more parts of the small town in ruins and disarray. A direct hit on the headquarters of Team Cherry's reserve force killed four junior officers, and there were several casualties among the black artillerymen in positions around Isle-la-Hesse. A brief scare erupted when 600 Germans began to run wild in the POW enclosure. Afraid of their own bombs more than anything else, calm was restored when the American guards allowed them to seek safety in the buildings' basements and joined them there.[8]

Many buildings on the market square and on several of Bastogne's main streets were ablaze. Three civilians lay dead in the rubble. The Lepere home collapsed onto the cellar and the family escaped asphyxiation only by hacking a way into the neighbor's basement with pickaxes. Hundreds of civilians added to the chaos, as they now abandoned their cellars in search of safety in the center's packed collective shelters or in hamlets close to the perimeter. Some had lost their minds: one woman could be seen tearing at her coat's fur collar as she screamed that an animal was biting her throat.[9]

As panic gripped the town, the concentrated artillery from Kokott's 26th Volksgrenadier Division opened up on the perimeter's northwest, just minutes after the second wave of Junkers 88s had disappeared. The bombing raids had been meant to soften up the target for what Kokott's superiors now considered to be the decisive blow against Bastogne. Colonel Kokott himself, however, had serious doubts about the outcome. The Luftwaffe's lukewarm effort had done little to weaken the American perimeter. And Kokott felt disappointed, even deceived, by the promise of support from the 15th Panzergrenadier Division. Instead of the entire division, he had been given only one regiment, and these reinforcements had arrived late in the evening, giving them barely any chance to engage in reconnaissance and get ready for the predawn battle.[10]

When the barrage lifted after about 15 minutes, Kokott's own 77th Grenadier Regiment took the lead in an assault on Champs. An entire battalion of men in white capes hurled itself against the small village that straddled a secondary road leading into Bastogne from the northwest. As soon as the battalion of Volksgrenadiers had taken Champs, another was to leapfrog onto the road to Bastogne and link up with the Panzergrenadiers biding their time just to the south. In the path of Kokott's men stood no more than a single company: A Company of the 502nd Parachute Infantry's 1st Battalion. There were too few paratroopers to prevent the Germans from blasting their way into Champs. But the Americans were determined to deny the enemy total control of the village. The battle went on for hours, as A Company put up a fight for each street, supported by two of Colonel Templeton's tank destroyers that were aiming point blank at infantry holed up in buildings. All that time, Corporal Fowler continued to fire away at the Germans from a central position: "We could hear the Germans hollering as the bullets hit them." As airborne machine guns fell silent one after the other, soldiers rallied to Willis Fowler's position, feeding his weapon with more ammunition, even as the barrel turned blazing hot.[11]

Corporal Fowler was later awarded a Silver Star for his role in the battle for Champs. But even as Kokott's men were being slowed down at the village itself, *Kampfgruppe* Maucke slammed into the area between Champs and the highway to Marche, just south of the village. Made up of Colonel Wolfgang Maucke's 115th Panzergrenadier Regiment, two battalions of self-propelled artillery and 18 tanks, the *Kampfgruppe*, although much less than had been promised to Kokott, was nevertheless a powerful force. Like other veteran glidermen in the forward positions, Private Harold Hansen and his comrade flattened themselves against the bottom of their foxhole as a whitewashed German tank passed over them. The steel monster, Hansen noted, "destroyed my M1 and our bazooka. My buddy's helmet got smashed."[12]

With the armor's exhaust fumes still thick in the air, the thin line of Americans rose up from their dugouts to confront the foot soldiers, several of whom were armed with flamethrowers. The glidermen's courageous resistance did nothing, however, to prevent *Kampfgruppe* Maucke's tanks from widening the dangerous hole they had just blown in McAuliffe's perimeter. Within minutes, Maucke's armor split up into two groups: 7 tanks swung northwards to Champs; the remaining 11 veered off to the east and headed straight for the center of Bastogne. By now daylight was breaking and the men at Champs could see the enemy descending on them from a hill to the south. Skilled tank destroyer crews and alert forward artillery observers stopped the Panzergrenadiers cold. The Americans, Kokott noted, put up "a desperate defense" and "consumed quantities of ammunition as had previously not been experienced there."[13]

But some elements of Maucke's armor managed to bypass Champs. By dawn, they were threatening the hamlet of Rolley and the château that served as the 502nd Parachute Infantry's headquarters. Regimental commander Steve Chappuis was so taciturn and reserved that fellow officers jokingly called him "Silent Steve." But the colonel from Louisiana had earned the trust of his men and was not one to be easily rattled. Captain James Stone was told to collect cooks, clerks, drivers, and orderlies to have them form a defensive screen. Walking wounded came up to join their ranks, and there was a mad scramble for bazookas. Inside the regimental aid station in the château's stables, a medical officer gave a rifle to a wounded man on a stretcher "to calm him." Then he set fire to medical reports to prevent the enemy from learning "how many men we had lost." But the Panzergrenadiers were stopped in front of Rolley, too. At least one soldier from Captain Stone's scratch force earned a Silver Star for heroism as a bazookaman. "I could hear," a corporal recalled, "some of the enemy wounded screaming in burning tanks." Private Leonard Swartz, the 502nd's mailman, watched those who piled out of the tanks being mowed down. "It was," he shuddered, "just red blood in the white snow."[14]

Strengthened by more men from the 502nd Parachute Infantry's 1st Battalion, the survivors from A Company in Champs now threw themselves against the Volksgrenadiers who were still holding out. "The fighting that followed," said Major John Hanlon, the 1st Battalion commander, "was the most vicious I ever knew." Germans were flushed from homes, barns, woodpiles, haystacks, and the church steeple. Close to a hundred Germans lay dead in streets and farm courtyards. Sergeant Merlano reported in with 80 prisoners. Tempers were running so high among the paratroopers that

Captain Swanson, A Company's commander, wrote down how many prisoners there were, to ensure that they all made it to Bastogne's prison pen alive.[15]

Even as Champs held, Hemroulle was in danger of being overrun by the other tanks of *Kampfgruppe* Maucke. If that happened, Bastogne would be lost. Hemroulle was a tiny hamlet barely a mile northwest of the town's market square. It was the last obstacle on the secondary road that led from Champs into the northern outskirts of Bastogne, where the 101st Airborne had its headquarters. The mood inside McAuliffe's underground command post turned grim. "The danger of being overrun," recalled reporter Fred MacKenzie, "was close at hand." Headquarters personnel were arming and checking the condition of their weapons. Corporal David Bernay, a member of the intelligence staff who had been decorated for heroism as a bazookaman in Normandy, was told "to round up any bazookas he could find."[16]

On the outskirts of Hemroulle, Lieutenant Colonel Allen, commander of the 327th Glider Infantry's 3rd Battalion, was on the phone with Colonel Harper, the regimental commander. Ray Allen was a small, wiry man, but he was known for his energy and resourcefulness, and his men thought him "a hell of a good soldier." Now, however, the battalion commander was yelling at his boss that tanks could be seen just 150 yards away, and that they were firing straight at his command post. Allen and two of his staff officers slipped out of the building and, under a hail of small-arms fire, managed to disappear into a wooded section unharmed. Sensing that the tide was turning, German POWs in the compound in Bastogne's southwestern corner sought to put Lieutenant George Allen's mind at ease. Since he had been kind enough to provide them with food, they said, they would ask their comrades to treat him well when he was captured.[17]

The situation became even more desperate when Kokott's *Kampfgruppe* Kunkel entered the fray from Senonchamps, just southwest of Hemroulle, in support of Maucke's tanks and Panzergrenadiers. In his château in Roumont, von Lüttwitz was on the phone to exhort his troops. Orders had come down all the way from Hitler to have Bastogne captured on Christmas Day, and von Lüttwitz feared that Patton's spearheads might roll into town first. But Bastogne's defenders were very much aware that this was shaping up to be the decisive moment of the siege. Although Colonel Allen had been made to flee his headquarters, his glidermen were still in position, and reinforcements were pouring in from the sector of the 502nd Parachute Infantry. The Americans were putting up resistance that Kokott described as "fanatical." In deadly games of cat and mouse, M18 Hellcats were hunting down Mark IV tanks, putting several out of action with salvos fired into their more vulnerable rears. As *Kampfgruppe* Kunkel brushed past their positions at Isle-la-Hesse, black artillerymen hurriedly drained fuel from their vehicles to keep four Shermans in the vicinity mobile. As a last resort, McAuliffe ordered more and more tanks from his central reserve into the gap.[18]

Meanwhile, the men from the 463rd Parachute Field Artillery in Hemroulle were getting ready for the fight of their lives. They did not belong to the 101st Airborne Division, but had gained significant battle experience in the Italian campaign and southern France. Their weapons, 75mm pack howitzers, were designed for indirect fire with high explosives. Now, however, they were told to stop the 27-ton tanks that were coming straight at them. Preparations unfolded at a frantic pace. Gun pits were dug deeper to get the howitzer barrels depressed enough for direct fire. There was a limited stock of armor-piercing shells, and they were taken from their wooden crates, together with large numbers of incendiary rounds. The artillerymen grabbed rifles, and a machine-gun section was set up to defend the field pieces. The men piled up the barracks bags with their personal belongings and stood ready to set them on fire. Inside the 463rd's command post, all classified documents were destroyed, as was the M-209 cryptographic machine.[19]

But when the 463rd's gunners let loose at the tanks and Panzergrenadiers from close range, they wrought havoc on the unsuspecting Germans. Armor-piercing shells took out several Mark IVs. White phosphorus set men and armor on fire. Trying to escape the flames, one tank crew member got his foot snagged on something near the turret. The German, wrote Corporal James Evans, "burned to a crisp hanging upside down on the right side of the tank." The 463rd's machine-gun teams mowed down infantry and those who managed to escape from the tanks. The firing was so furious that at times teams had to call a quick halt to replace barrels that had become too hot. Corporal Nicholas Bellezza recalled that his buddy was in such a rush that he forgot to use his asbestos gloves and burned his hands on the barrel.[20]

By mid-morning, the German assault had ground to a halt and troops were reforming. In Roumont, it appeared that von Lüttwitz was still optimistic, as he made time to hand out Christmas gifts to Belgian children – American K rations that had mistakenly been parachuted into German lines the day before. Fog had kept Allied fighter-bombers at bay during the early hours of Christmas Day. But now the skies began to clear again, and any German optimism about the success of the Ardennes counteroffensive quickly withered. In the northern part of the salient, B-26s arrived over Saint-Vith, a road junction comparable to Bastogne, but captured by von Manteuffel's troops on December 21. The American bombers released more than 130 tons of explosives, turning the town into what was called a "chokepoint." Meanwhile, barely four miles from the Meuse River, the tip of the German salient, formed by von Lauchert's 2nd Panzer Division, was being bludgeoned by American and British armor, also with massive support from the air.[21]

Sergeant Bowen from the 327th Glider Infantry had a chance to observe at close range how scared the Germans were of the *Jabos* all over the bulge. He and many of his comrades had been taken prisoner at Flamierge. For two days now, their guards had been herding them in the direction of Germany. They had been forced to spend a night in a barn, the floor "ankle deep in wet, urine-soaked straw and cow manure." The Americans, many of them wounded, were cold, hungry, and exhausted. Some of the guards made the weak prisoners carry their bulky rucksacks. It was proving difficult to get out of the salient, largely because of the relentless attacks by P-47s, which at one point had shot up a German field hospital where Sergeant Bowen was receiving treatment. On the roads, Belgian refugees "wandered about like lost children." POWs were made to drag wrecked German vehicles and muti-lated corpses into ditches. Each time they heard the sound of Thunderbolts, Germans and Americans "scattered like pins in a bowling alley." One attack caught their column by surprise. When the strafing stopped, a German guard lay in a pool of blood alongside Sergeant Bonner, one of the medics in Sergeant Bowen's unit.[22]

By early afternoon, P-47s from two fighter groups were again plastering German troops all around Bastogne's perimeter. The 406th Fighter Group was ordered to concentrate on enemy troops to the town's northwest. It was feared that they were reassembling for a new blow in a sector where American troops were now close to breaking point. The fighter-bombers turned the area into a killing field, lashing out at anything that moved. Within hours, they were claiming 156 German vehicles destroyed, as well as 21 half-tracks and 16 tanks. The attack on an enemy concentration at Rouette – one of many in the area – lasted no more than 15 minutes. Scorching napalm set the hamlet's farmhouses ablaze. The fire spread so rapidly that the Belgians were unable to save anything – not even their cattle, which burned alive in the stables, together with the German horses. When Lydie Gaspard tried to flee, slugs from an aircraft cannon mowed her down. Villagers rushed the 23-year-old woman to a nearby aid station in a blanket drenched in blood. The German surgeon took one look and shook his head. But collateral damage was a price the Allies were willing to accept.[23]

The air forces left the ranks of the Panzergrenadiers so devastated that a new attack that same day was out of the question. By dusk, all staff members in Wolfgang Maucke's 1st Battalion, for example, were either dead or wounded, leaving overall command in the inexperienced hands of a young lieutenant from one of the rifle companies.[24]

By that time, too, the Americans had sealed the perimeter again. The men from the 502nd Parachute Infantry had even retaken the high ground west of Champs, vital for observing the enemy. They had done so with the help of Lieutenant Robinson. A forward observer with Major Hanlon's men, Jim Robinson had lived through one of the worst days of his life and had relished calling down an orgy of death and destruction from his 377th Parachute Field Artillery. When he made his way to the hill to see the effects of the barrage for himself, the dead lay bunched together and blood flowed in the grooves of the frozen earth. The lieutenant searched the bodies for decorations and other souvenirs. In the haversack of one of the dead he found cookies that appeared to have been sent by the German's family for Christmas. The officer nibbled at them as he took in the carnage. In a field nearby, a paratrooper was examining the corpse of a German tank crew member lying face down in the snow. His curiosity satisfied, the American planted his foot on the man's head. Then he asked a comrade to take his picture and to make sure the tank could be seen in the background.[25]

Christmas Day was not a good one for McAuliffe's men. At dawn, the Germans had been a hair's breadth away from victory in Bastogne. Clear skies over the Ardennes had allowed fighter-bombers to muscle their way in, but poor weather over England was preventing C-47s from dropping more supplies. Still worse, despite emphatic promises the previous day, it was becoming clear that there was to be no Christmas present from Patton. "They have stood off overwhelming enemy strength," an officer in Bradley's headquarters noted admiringly, "clinging stubbornly to their positions like a wagon train in the pioneer days of the west." But in the American headquarters inside Bastogne, the mood was growing desperate. In his radio communications with VIII Corps in Florenville, the square-jawed Colonel Paul Danahy, the 101st Airborne's intelligence officer, sounded angry and frustrated, at one point blurting out that the men of the 4th Armored Division were "a bunch of sissies" who were taking "a lot too long to get to them." "We have been let down," an exasperated McAuliffe bluntly told General Middleton in a call later that evening.[26]

Through a vent in the underground shelter at the Institute of Notre Dame, one of the boarding-school girls on Christmas Day fixed her gaze on a soldier on the sidewalk. The American knelt, his rifle in one hand and a rosary in the other. He closed his eyes and prayed. Then he got up and hurried to where the rumble of battle could be heard. For the unarmed civilians inside Bastogne's perimeter, there remained nothing to do but pray, as they, too, were getting more desperate by the hour. Some 50 people had fled their cellars after the Luftwaffe strikes and headed towards Baroness Greindl's château in Isle-la-Hesse. But they had run into some of the fiercest fighting that day and, after spending frightful hours in the château's cellars, were herded back into town by American troops under cover of darkness. The Bastognards returned to find the situation in the town out of control. Several sections of the market square and nearby streets were ablaze, and the fire was spreading. In the already packed Institute of Notre Dame, the number of refugees had now risen to 800, and the thick smoke that drifted in from the street was making people gag.[27]

Still, in Isle-le-Pré that evening, Madeleine Barthelemi was hoping she could reach the beleaguered town as soon as possible. Three days previously, the heavily pregnant woman had fled Bastogne with her parents-in-law, a cousin, and two dogs to find shelter in a cellar of the hamlet just inside the American perimeter to Bastogne's south. Now, Frank Menard, a Cajun from Lafayette, Louisiana, was carrying her to his jeep. Earlier that day, during a brief visit to the kitchen, a shell had exploded and shrapnel had ripped into Madeleine's foot, leaving white tendons visible among the lacerations. The young woman had lost a lot of blood and Private Menard had decided that she needed to see a doctor in one of the aid stations in town. The American climbed behind the wheel and made the sign of the cross. Then he gunned the engine and ran the gauntlet of enemy shelling all the way to the Heintz barracks north of town, where doctors that night managed to save Madeleine's foot. "It was the only time in the war," Frank Menard later claimed, "when I was truly brave."[28]

Airmen were displaying more acts of bravery as they tried against the odds to get aid to Bastogne's defenders. Due to bad cloud cover over England on Christmas Day, no aid could be sent in the form of C-47 supplies. Still, shortly after midday, Captain Rufus Woody of the 31st Photo Squadron was bringing his P-38 Lightning down to no more than a hundred feet over Bastogne. As soon as he spotted the smoke signal, he jettisoned a small container. Inside was information that McAuliffe's headquarters had been clamoring for incessantly: highly detailed maps of Bastogne and surroundings, as well as 150 very recent aerial photos of the entire area. Together they made it possible for the artillerymen to make the limited number of shells count.[29]

From the 101st Airborne's command post, another request had climbed all the way up to Bradley's 12th Army Group headquarters on Christmas Eve: they urgently needed more surgeons to be flown in to help treat the most serious casualties. "My God," a colonel on Bradley's staff had gasped, "where will they get the volunteers?" On Christmas Day, however, two volunteers did step forward, and by the afternoon they were readying themselves at a fighter airstrip in Luxembourg. One was pilot Ancel Taflinger, an air liaison officer at Third Army headquarters, who had suggested using a Stinson L-1 Vigilant for the dangerous mission. The two-seat observation plane was light and slow, but it had a large wing surface and was capable of taking off and landing within a very short space. The other volunteer was Major Howard Serrel from Greenwich, Connecticut. He had studied medicine at Cornell University and was specialized in treating abdominal wounds. He carefully stowed his surgical kits, as well as a precious cargo of penicillin.

The L-1 took off just after dark. It climbed to 6,000 feet and, accompanied by a couple of fighter planes, headed straight for the besieged town. Flak bursts greeted the volunteers as soon as they approached Bastogne. But the Vigilant came through unharmed and Lieutenant Taflinger "dived down steeply" the very moment he saw the signals indicating the location: a small strip within the perimeter built for artillery liaison planes. As soon as the aircraft touched down, a jeep from the 101st Airborne raced over to pick up the surgeon. Lieutenant Taflinger immediately took off for the return trip, rising "almost vertically above Bastogne." He again survived the flak and, with a radio that had broken down and no more fighter escort at his side, managed the lone trip back to Luxembourg in pitch darkness. In Bastogne, Major Serrel set to work without delay. He would work nonstop for the next 36 hours, performing 15 operations in a row. Both the pilot and the surgeon were awarded the Silver Star for their bravery.[30]

2

The day after Christmas, it was becoming clear to the Allies, from the Supreme Commander, General Eisenhower, all the way down to corps commander Troy Middleton, that the German spearheads would not succeed in crossing the Meuse River, let alone in reaching Antwerp. Von Lauchert's 2nd Panzer Division was being mauled by Allied armor and air strikes in view of the river. Fritz Bayerlein's Panzer Lehr tried to get through to von

Lauchert's force, but failed. When von Lüttwitz ordered Bayerlein to fall back to Rochefort, the retreat of Panzer Lehr was the clearest evidence yet of the failure of Hitler's gamble. Allied bombers were now also pounding La Roche and other towns in the Ourthe Valley to prevent any more supplies from getting through to the stalled spearheads. So overwhelming was the power of the fighter-bombers all over the salient, reported the Fifth Panzer Army's artillery commander, that even "motorcycles could only get through by going from cover to cover."[31]

To the extent that the bigger picture was even known to McAuliffe and his staff, it offered little immediate consolation. The ranks of Bastogne's defenders were growing thinner by the day, and the troops still manning the foxholes were utterly exhausted. Fires continued to rage in the town center. American engineers blew up a building to create a firebreak and prevent the blaze from reaching the Institute of Notre Dame. When that did not help, soldiers, nuns, and refugees formed bucket brigades, keeping the flames at bay with water drawn from the convent's cisterns. To make matters worse, shortly after dawn on Tuesday, December 26, a small assault group of Volksgrenadiers, supported by tank destroyers, again penetrated the perimeter from the west and again managed to get as far as Hemroulle.[32]

Kokott's men were thrown back once more, but at the expense of some of the last artillery rounds. McAuliffe knew that to the south of Bastogne Patton's 4th Armored Division was now very close – its clashes with the Germans could literally be heard. But he also knew that his men had virtually nothing left to defend themselves with, and that from now on, hours would feel like days. Fred MacKenzie watched General McAuliffe as he stretched his legs in the courtyard of the Heintz barracks, crossed the road that ran past the gates, and strode towards the nearby cemetery. German prisoners were digging more graves with pickaxes and shovels. The general halted and gazed at the mound of earth that marked Colonel LaPrade's grave. McAuliffe was, the newspaperman noted, "surrendering a little to the weariness," and suddenly appeared "much older."[33]

Before disappearing again into the dank cellar that was his command post, McAuliffe lingered a few minutes near where Captain James Parker and his team were relaying messages to the fighter-bombers. The skies this morning, they had been told, were clear all the way to England. That meant that Allied air forces would be helping out with everything from firepower to supplies. That was "a godsend," Colonel Roberts remarked, for he estimated the effect of air operations to be "equivalent to the work of 2 or 3 divisions." McAuliffe agreed: until Patton's men arrived, air support was, now more than ever, to play a vital role in keeping Bastogne's defenders going.[34]

For the fourth day in a row, Captain Parker was on the radio in his tank, ceaselessly calling for strikes against targets all around Bastogne's perimeter. "The missions were on a rotating basis, like a conveyer belt," recalled Howard Park, the pilot of "Big Ass Bird II." So long and exhausting were the days in the skies over Bastogne, said Lieutenant Park, that they turned into "a blur in my memory." Claims for the P-47 pilots of the 406th Fighter Group on Tuesday amounted to 32 armored vehicles and 75 motor transport vehicles. Captain Warren Lenhart led a flight of the 406th against a bridge at Bertogne, northwest of Bastogne. They took it out, Captain Parker said admiringly, "against all the flak the Germans could throw up at them" and then called for another target.[35]

That same day, Thunderbolts of the 362nd Fighter Group went in search of targets as far away as Donnange, northeast of Bastogne, and destroyed 50 motor transport vehicles with bombs, and another 40 with machine guns. In their next mission, they attacked half-tracks, armor, and 75mm anti-tank guns south of Bastogne.[36]

In Senonchamps, Horst Helmus, one of Kokott's 75mm gunners, joined fellow Volksgrenadiers and Belgian villagers in a mad rush to one of the village's cowsheds. Farmhouse after farmhouse went up in flames, and streets were strafed mercilessly. "The Jabo attacks," wrote the 18-year-old from near Cologne in his diary, "are driving us insane." They were also leaving the Germans enraged and vengeful. When American officers of the 327th Glider Infantry on the southern perimeter tried to negotiate the evacuation through enemy lines of some of their most seriously wounded, the Volksgrenadiers angrily rejected the proposal.[37]

In one of their fiercest strikes that Tuesday, P-47s of the 362nd Fighter Group pounded villages and hamlets just northeast of the American peri-meter. They made liberal use of incendiaries like napalm and white phos-phorus. Sensing the heat, the Marons in Arloncourt burst from their cellar. Flames singed Madame Maron's hair and burned her daughter's hands. Monsieur Maron tried in vain to rescue his horses from a blazing stable. The Marons and other villagers fled to Oubourcy, only to find that this village had been razed to the ground by napalm the previous day. They joined the villagers in one of the few stables still standing, bringing the total there to more than 90 people. All along Bastogne's perimeter, hundreds of civilians were now cast adrift just outside the American lines. Many decided that the only place to escape the wrath of the Thunderbolts was in the icy forests. Some would stay hidden away there for the next three weeks, catching hares for food and eventually even eating their horses.[38]

With the weather clear over England on Tuesday, December 26, and with McAuliffe's men short of everything, the Allies set in motion the biggest airlift of the siege. Protected by yet another fighter group, some 269 C-47s dropped 169 tons of supplies over Bastogne. This contained, among many other things, ammunition for the African-American gunners of the 969th Field Artillery at Isle-la-Hesse. Earlier that day, they had been told to fire no more than 27 rounds with their 155mm howitzers – one-sixth the number of rounds they had expended each day at the start of the battle. At the same time, a P-38 of the 31st Photo Squadron came in low in another attempt to drop the most recent aerial photos of German positions. This time, however, flak caused the Lightning to crash, killing the pilot and copilot and leaving the vital photos buried in the wreckage near German-held Chenogne.[39]

Skytrains were now also towing Waco gliders, loaded with a very special cargo. In a particularly hazardous mission, a number of gliders managed to touch down safely inside the narrow perimeter with some 3,000 gallons of precious gasoline on board. But there was one glider that McAuliffe and his staff were expecting more impatiently than any other.

Earlier in the day, this particular glider, piloted by Lieutenant Charleton Corwin, had been towed out of Orléans. Captain Raymond Ottoman, a Skytrain pilot, safely put the glider down on the fighter strip at Étain in France. There four P-47 pilots from the experienced 362nd Fighter Group were selected to escort the Skytrain and glider, which were to fly in an entire team of highly skilled medical volunteers. The team was made up of five surgeons and four enlisted surgical assistants. Their commander was Lamar Soutter, a 35-year-old surgeon from a well-connected family in Boston. Major Soutter's horn-rimmed glasses formed a striking contrast with his head of sandy, curly hair. The men liked Major Soutter, never failing to be impressed by his "patient voice, resonant with the authority conferred by 300 years of Harvard."[40]

As soon as the medical equipment was on board, there was one last briefing. Then Captain Ottoman pulled away from Étain and headed for Bastogne with the packed Waco glider in tow. The atmosphere grew tense as the aircraft began to approach the Belgian town. On the way into Bastogne, Lieutenant Corwin suddenly heard a noise on his wing. "I looked out," the glider pilot said, "and there was a fighter next to me for an instant. The pilot waved at me and smiled, and I waved back." Shortly after 1500, Lieutenant Corwin brought his glider down safely in a snowy field inside the narrow perimeter. Vehicles instantly whisked Major Soutter and his team away. In the Heintz barracks and the Seminary alone, close to a thousand American casualties and more than a hundred German wounded were in dire need of treatment.[41]

Impressed as he was by the daring of airmen and surgical personnel, as dusk approached once again, McAuliffe realized that the situation for his men had become untenable. Only the arrival of Patton's Third Army would bring sufficient reinforcements, supplies, and medical aid to withstand another onslaught. The sound of the 4th Armored Division clashing with the Germans south of Bastogne now seemed even closer than it had that morning. But Patton's men had cruelly dashed the hopes of Bastogne's defenders more than once in the past few days. That Tuesday, December 26, Colonel Kohls, for one, was not convinced that Patton's men would bring relief any time soon. The division's supply officer had his men pay a visit to the house of Louis Grandjean in the center of Bastogne. They signed a requisition form for Monsieur Grandjean to hang onto until after the battle, loaded up 200 pounds of potatoes, and hauled the provisions off to the 101st Airborne's command post. Whatever might follow next, General McAuliffe and his staff in their underground shelter would at least have something to eat.[42]

CHAPTER 6

TO THE RESCUE

Throughout the siege, Bastogne's hard-pressed defenders never stopped wondering why Patton, with his formidable army and legendary reputation, was finding it so hard to break through to them. The flurry of activity immediately following the Verdun conference on Tuesday, December 19, had been vintage Patton: fast, furious, and unfailingly confident. Patton understood like no other that the relief of Bastogne was just the first step, and that the capture of this key crossroads in the southern part of the German salient would eventually allow his troops to catapult themselves towards Allied forces slugging their way down from the northern flank of the bulge. As soon as these troops shook hands, Patton believed, the massive trap that the Germans were creating for themselves might be closed shut with a clang that would reverberate all the way to Berlin.

Patton sensed an opportunity so momentous that he refused to be fazed by the fact that his entire Third Army stood poised for a major offensive in northeastern France that was to blast its way through the Saar region and crack the West Wall. As early as Wednesday, December 20, Middleton in Neufchâteau had been happy to inform McAuliffe that three of Patton's divisions had already departed Lorraine and were on their way to the Ardennes. That, however, was just the beginning of a breathtaking maneuver that involved pulling two-thirds of Patton's massive army out of pre-attack positions, wheeling troops 90 degrees to the north, and moving them across more than a hundred miles of icy roads in record time. The logistics of the entire operation were so complex that only a highly efficient staff could pull it off. "I worked," recalled Colonel Paul Harkins, one of Patton's aides, "30 hours a day for the next ten-day week." But only one man was able to provide the inspiration necessary to keep staff and troops going throughout this giant undertaking. "His generalship during this difficult maneuver was magnificent," Omar Bradley later said of Patton. "One of the most brilliant performances by any commander on either side in World War II."[1]

"As usual on the verge of action," Patton noted, as the spectacular maneuver unfolded, "everyone felt full of doubt except myself. It has always been my unfortunate role to be the ray of sunshine and the backslapper before action, both for those under me and also those over me." Such hyperbole, however, did not prevent Patton from remaining keenly aware of the realistic constraints and threats that stood to slow the advance on the long and hazardous route to Bastogne. At Verdun, the flamboyant general had insisted that he could launch the attack towards Bastogne as early as December 21. But at the urging of Eisenhower, and after talking with those commanding the spearhead troops in the assembly zone near Arlon, an experienced Patton eventually agreed that it would be better to allow preparations for one more day.[2]

It came as quite a relief for III Corps commander General John Millikin, who was to lead the counterattack towards Bastogne with three divisions. The 56-year-old from Danville, Indiana, had been born the son of a barber. He had steadily climbed through the army ranks, as superiors judged him to be "level headed," "forceful," and "aggressive." But Millikin had been sent to the European theater of operations only recently and suffered from a total lack of combat experience. The abrupt change in plans that had redirected his corps from Lorraine to the Ardennes with mind-boggling speed had done nothing to increase his confidence. To add to Millikin's concerns, two of the three divisions that made up his corps had not yet fully recovered from previous combat with the Third Army. The 80th Infantry Division, which was to form the right flank, was in fairly good shape. But Millikin worried about the 26th Infantry Division. It constituted the middle division of his attacking force and had been assigned the crucial task of shielding the 4th Armored Division's right flank as it made the main thrust towards Bastogne. Nicknamed the "Yankee Division" because of its origins as a National Guard unit from New England, the 26th Infantry Division had suffered heavy losses during the Lorraine campaign. Early in December, General Willard Paul, the division's commander from Massachusetts, had been heartened to learn that his men were to be taken out of the line for some desperately needed rest at Metz. But now the German offensive had cut this short, and Patton himself estimated that the 26th Infantry Division was arriving in the Ardennes with "four thousand green replacements."[3]

The 4th Armored Division, the steel fist of Millikin's corps, had built up a reputation for speed and daring, and was General Patton's favorite. But five months of intense fighting across France had taken a heavy toll on this outfit, too. Just recently, the division's exhausted commander had been sent back to the United States to recover. Patton had made General Gaffey his replacement. Hugh Gaffey was not just any general, but the chief of staff of Patton's own Third Army. The fact remained, however, that he, like Millikin, was still getting used to his new combat command even as he set out for the Ardennes at breakneck speed. Gaffey knew, moreover, that he was more than 700 men and almost two dozen officers short. Some 20 damaged Shermans had not yet been replaced. Many of the other tanks were so battle-worn that, in the words of the executive officer of Combat Command A, they were "literally falling apart." On some tanks, the turret's electrical system had broken down, forcing exasperated crews to crank it round by hand.[4]

The hurried trip to the Ardennes took a further toll on men and *matériel*. Infantrymen made the long trek from Lorraine in open trucks and trailers, many of them without overcoats or blankets as they watched "frost hanging from the trees and power lines." "We ate our K rations while we moved," a lieutenant of the 26th Infantry Division noted, "and there were no stops for nature's calls." Tank crews gunned their motors, but had great difficulty keeping their vehicles steady on the icy roads. "Some," one tank crewman observed, "would actually skate to the bottom of a slope and come to a stop by smashing into buildings at the foot." The crews lacked detailed maps, and the strain was intensified at night, when they approached the front in blackout conditions, with only the dim light of cat's eyes visible on the vehicles in front of them. After more than a hundred miles of this, a tank commander of the 4th Armored Division confessed that he arrived in the Ardennes "bone-weary."[5]

1

The line of departure for Millikin's three divisions in the Ardennes stretched along some 30 miles from the Alzette River in Luxembourg to the east, to the Belgian town of Neufchâteau in the west. The terrain in front of Millikin's men was rugged country. Fields and clearings alternated with dense woods; streams cut deep into the rocky soil; and sturdy farmhouses built from locally quarried stone stood like fortresses. The land was most unforgiving east of the road from Arlon to Bastogne, where Millikin's infantry divisions were tasked with crossing the deep corridors through which ran the swift Sûre and Wiltz rivers.[6]

The challenge ahead was further complicated by the fact that on the left flank of Millikin's III Corps there was virtually no force present that could protect the 4th Armored Division against a German counterattack. In theory, this was, of course, where the VIII Corps was located. But in his talks with Middleton Patton had soon established that this force now consisted "of nothing but remnants." Although it was clear that several crack German armored divisions were streaming past Bastogne, a nervous Millikin was told to make do with nothing more than an engineer battalion for cover on his vulnerable west flank. Patton was well aware of the grave risks. That is probably why he abandoned his firm principle of not getting involved with the command at lower levels. In the days immediately preceding the attack, the three-star general was repeatedly seen meddling in the affairs of III Corps headquarters, and even prescribing tactics to the commander of the 4th Armored Division.[7]

The tense atmosphere was heightened by the fact that a lack of time and the presence of dense cloud cover left little opportunity for serious scouting to find out more about the strength and deployment of the enemy. On Thursday, December 21, the need for reconnaissance was so urgent that Captain Travis was ordered to risk an attempt, despite the menacing weather. Setting out on his mission without an escort, the pilot of the F-6 Mustang "Mazie, Me, and Monk" failed to detect a single hole in the overcast sky. The reconnaissance pilot finally decided that he would have to take his Mustang all the way down to below the dense cloud ceiling. By the time he saw the mist melt, Travis realized he was flying at tree-top level. The pilot whispered a prayer. This was hilly country, and he knew that a missed ridgeline or a sudden downdraft would be the end of him. Despite repeated efforts by the enemy on the ground to bring the aircraft down, "Mazie, Me, and Monk" eventually made it back to its home base. The information the photographic reconnaissance brought back remained sketchy, but it was valuable enough for Captain Travis to be awarded a Silver Star.[8]

That same day, Patton decided to delay his offensive no more. If the risks were significant, so were the potential rewards. The overall picture clearly demonstrated that elements of the Seventh Army, the German force that was to shield the salient's southern flank, were still on the move. By striking sooner rather than later, Patton hoped, he would throw the enemy off balance and prevent it from digging in too deep. Millikin's III Corps, the Third Army commander announced, was to move off at 0600 next day. Chester Hansen, one of Bradley's aides, observed Patton that Thursday as he strode through 12th Army Group's headquarters "in his tightly tailored shack suit with the shining copper buttons, his leather pistol belt and the bone-handled pistol." He looked, Hansen noted, "huge."[9]

2

As Millikin's men readied themselves for the attack in the predawn darkness of Friday, December 22, massive loads of ammunition continued to be brought up to their rear. III Corps could count on the support of 25 battalions of corps and divisional artillery, some 300 field pieces altogether. In addition to the usual high-explosive shells, Bradley had just informed Patton that his troops were now allowed to use proximity-fused ammunition in unlimited quantities. This new fuse made American artillery shells more lethal than ever, as it made them explode in the air rather than on impact. The new technology had been top secret for quite some time and its use strictly limited. But tests had shown conclusively that the sharply increased fragmentation was guaranteed to cause carnage among enemy troops. The steady shipment to Millikin's sector of thousands of gas shells from Third Army stocks made for an even more sinister mood.[10]

Poison gas was stockpiled in anticipation of a worst-case scenario only, and would, as it turned out, never be used in the Ardennes campaign. At 0600 on Friday, Millikin's men moved off without a preparatory barrage of any kind, leaving all the ammunition stockpiles untouched. One of the main reasons was that the exact positions of the German units remained unknown. Still, the terse field order of III Corps that morning was to make contact with the main line of resistance, roll it up, and destroy "any enemy encountered."[11]

It was still pitch dark when the soldiers of General Paul's 26th Infantry Division started moving in their sector east of the main road from Arlon to Bastogne. Patton had urged Paul the day before to "go day and night." That was easier said than done, however. Paul's men walked straight into forests and ravines, and there would be no main north–south road for them to follow until they reached Eschdorf, seven miles away as the crow flies. Thousands of new arrivals had scarcely completed their training, let alone been near a front line. The whirlwind trip to the Ardennes, restless sleep in freezing foxholes, and stubborn rumors of German atrocities had already done much to erode confidence. Some men in the rifle companies were reported to have shot themselves in the foot during the night to escape a much worse fate in the looming battle.[12]

Having pushed northwards across three miles of slushy secondary roads and trails, it was the 104th Infantry Regiment on the division's right that first made contact with elements of Brandenberger's Seventh Army. In the vicinity of Grosbous, the Americans ran into Grenadier Regiment 914, the leading element of the 352nd Volksgrenadier Division. This enemy division was 13,000 men strong, but had been rebuilt from scratch after having suffered heavy losses in Normandy. The Volksgrenadiers varied in combat training and experience, but their commander, Erich Otto Schmidt, judged Grenadier Regiment 914 to possess a "good fighting spirit." This spirit immediately revealed itself that Friday morning, as leading elements of Paul's 104th Infantry were pushed back at least half a mile. Only the determined intervention of several battalions of artillery eventually managed to stabilize the situation.[13]

On Paul's left flank, and closest to the 4th Armored Division, the 328th Infantry Regiment made better progress. Perhaps to allay the fears of the many newcomers, its orders were that "no SS troops or paratroopers will be taken prisoners, but will be shot on sight." But the Americans managed to keep going for at least six miles with virtually no opposition. As they slogged on through snow and mud, Sergeant Bruce Egger from Idaho worried about his men in G Company. He had himself arrived as a replacement early in November, but combat in Lorraine had soon left him harder and wiser. Now Egger watched helplessly as about a third of the men in his company, mostly new arrivals, showed themselves unable to keep up with the pace. The stragglers were discarding overshoes and overcoats to lighten their loads, even as the cold turned their breath into vapor. Then suddenly, in mid-afternoon, the exhausting march abruptly came to a halt. Just south of Arsdorf, the 1st Platoon of the 26th Cavalry Reconnaissance Troop clashed with an unidentified German outfit that responded with brutal force. Although outnumbered ten to one, the platoon leader, Sergeant Lawrence Hatfield, managed to hold his men together long enough to fight a skilful delaying action and inflict heavy losses. Though the rest of the regiment was warned of serious trouble ahead, the question of the foe's identity remained unanswered. Intelligence had established that the 104th Infantry was blocking the 352nd Volksgrenadier Division as it tried to move in from the east, and that the 5th Fallschirmjäger Division was situated further to the west.[14]

For Colonel Hans-Joachim Kahler of the Führer Grenadier Brigade, the mystery surrounding his unit could only be to his advantage. He and his nearly 6,300 men had recently been released from the strategic reserve and had just arrived on the scene to help shore up defenses south of the Sûre River. With some 40 Mark IV and Panther tanks at its disposal, as well as 35 assault guns and tank destroyers, Kahler's brigade was more than capable of answering the call. The GIs of the 328th Infantry did not know it yet, but they had just had a brush with a "miniature panzer division."[15]

The American tanks of the 4th Armored Division had started rolling at the same time as Paul's infantrymen set off to their right. Gaffey's armor covered a sector that ran from Neufchâteau in the west to Bigonville just east of the Arlon–Bastogne highway. The hard-surfaced road was to serve as the main axis of their advance, with Combat Command A clinging to the highway itself and Combat Command B making its way along the secondary roads to the left. Since the armor was directly responsible for the relief of Bastogne, Patton had told Gaffey to be "ruthless." Shortly before noon, Patton further increased the pressure when, in a call to Millikin's headquarters, he spurred them on to "drive like hell." That was exactly what they were doing. By noon, Combat Command A had reached Martelange virtually unopposed. The town overlooked the Sûre River at a distance of 12 miles from Bastogne. At about the same time, Combat Command B came in sight of Burnon, only seven miles from Bastogne.[16]

In peacetime, Gaffey's Sherman tanks could have covered the distance in less than half an hour. But this was war, and the German paratroopers who stood between Patton's armor and Bastogne were getting ready to delay the Americans for what would turn out to be five long days. Ludwig Heilmann's division was, in fact, no longer one of elite paratroopers. With the exception of a small cadre of old-timers who had survived the onslaught in Normandy, his unit was made up of replacements from Luftwaffe and Navy service units. They had barely had sufficient combat training, let alone jump training. Heilmann himself was new to the division, having taken command barely a month earlier. But he had gained extensive combat experience on Crete and in Russia. More importantly, he had been a regimental commander at Monte Cassino, where he had learned invaluable lessons about defensive warfare. Heilmann was keenly aware that the training of many of his men was limited, and that they lacked much equipment, from radio sets to heavy mortars and artillery pieces. But he also knew that most of his paratroopers were less than 20 years old. This convinced him that his soldiers possessed both the stamina and the fighting spirit to conduct an effective defense.[17]

Paul Maus was one of the men Heilmann was counting on. He belonged to the 15th Regiment, the most capable in the eyes of the division commander, and the one given the task of pushing the shield as far west and south of Bastogne as possible. The previous day, Maus had participated in the battle for Sibret and had helped cut the road from Neufchâteau to Bastogne. The battle had cost the life of his trusted sergeant and friend, Karl Stiller, whose body had fallen on top of him as he dived for cover in a roadside ditch. Now, as he pushed southwest along the road to Neufchâteau, Paul Maus could not erase the memory of how he had lain in that ditch for more than an hour, afraid to move, all the while sensing the weight of his friend's bloodied corpse as it shielded him from enemy eyes. Suddenly, as Maus neared the hamlet of Rosière-la-Petite, about halfway between Bastogne and Neufchâteau, sniper fire called the German paratrooper to attention. By the time he reached a pile of sugar beets, several of his comrades lay dead. As Maus rose from behind the beets to catch a glimpse of the American sniper, there was a sharp zing and a burning sensation in his shoulder.[18]

Paul Maus's battle for Bastogne ended just as he and his comrades came to establish the westernmost position of Heilmann's division. That Friday, Brandenberger ordered his Seventh Army to halt "any further westward push," as intelligence was making it clear that the Third Army juggernaut was now rolling towards them at full steam. All elements of the 5th Fallschirmjäger Division now dug in and braced themselves for the clash with Patton's armor.[19]

That same afternoon, however, Gaffey's armor, despite Patton's exhortations, came to a halt as well. Engineers of Combat Command A discovered that the blown bridge over the Sûre River in Martelange would take a long time to replace because of the width and depth of the gorge, and because of the relentless harrying by Fallschirmjäger holed up in nearby buildings. Blown bridges and a small enemy rearguard at Burnon were also delaying Combat Command B. But it was only when this force crossed the Sûre and approached the village of Chaumont that fierce resistance brought it to a dead stop. There would be no more progress that day for either of Gaffey's combat commands.[20]

3

On the morning of Saturday, December 23, Patton was not happy with the loss of momentum among his spearheads. There was, however, one positive development. A sudden change in weather brought with it a blindingly blue sky. "Lovely weather," Patton observed dryly, "for killing Germans." As fighter-bombers from Weyland's XIX Tactical Air Command concentrated on Bastogne's perimeter, others roamed further south to pounce on troops and vehicles of Brandenberger's Seventh Army. In a German field hospital in Tarchamps, the medical staff was soon finding it impossible to treat all the wounded. The Luxembourg village sat wedged between the 26th Volksgrenadier Division besieging Bastogne to the north and the 5th Fallschirmjäger Division facing southward in the direction of Patton's Third

Army. Several homes, a café, the presbytery and school, and even the butcher's shop were turned into aid stations with Red Cross flags laid out on the roofs. More than a hundred horribly wounded soldiers were brought to the home of the Nanquettes that Saturday. The operating tables were drenched with blood, while corpses and amputated arms and legs were piled up outside. "The house," a villager noted, "was filled with a sickening odor."[21]

Air support did not suffice, however, to propel Millikin's corps forward. A serious worry on Saturday was that, while the 80th Infantry Division continued to make slow progress on the corps' extreme right, the 26th Infantry Division remained virtually stalled in the center. This in turn left the right flank of Gaffey's armor, already vulnerable on its left, dangerously exposed along the Arlon–Bastogne highway. More and more artillery was brought up to help Paul's infantrymen push their way forward, and the previous night, in a serious blow to the Führer Grenadier Brigade, the shelling had badly wounded the commander, Colonel Kahler. Now Lieutenant Colonel Kinney crawled close to the enemy lines. The commander of the American 102nd Field Artillery was determined to help direct fire onto enemy targets in person. Silhouetted against the snow and exposed to direct fire, Richard Kinney's leadership and bravery earned him the Distinguished Service Cross. Even then, however, Paul's men, and the many replacements in particular, remained "very timid." They avoided marching out ahead of tanks and were all too happy to have anti-aircraft artillery blast wood lines, hedges, and buildings in preparation for what proved to be no more than cautious advances.[22]

Even before noon, an impatient Patton was on the phone to III Corps headquarters. "There is," he rebuked Millikin's staff, "too much piddling around." Patton was particularly displeased about the delay of his armor. Throughout the previous night and all that morning, Gaffey's Combat Command B had been feeling its way around Chaumont, a tiny village on a secondary road just west of the highway from Arlon to Bastogne. Although artillery and fighter-bombers were blasting Chaumont, tanks and armored infantry were still preparing to move in. Told to make haste, Brigadier General Holmes Dager's Combat Command B set off on a coordinated attack at 1330.[23]

The Fallschirmjäger in Chaumont had arrived two days earlier. They were, the villagers observed, "boys between seventeen and twenty" who had smugly announced that they were "going to push the Americans back to America." Riding on tanks, American infantrymen now smashed into the village. More soldiers of the 10th Armored Infantry Battalion followed on foot. About half of the GIs were replacements. One of them was Charles Wilson, who had joined the unit only days earlier. A devout Christian with firm plans to become a pastor, the Chicagoan had asked to serve as a chaplain's assistant. Instead, he had been made part of a machine-gun squad and now found himself heading into his first battle.

When the GIs muscled their way into the village, an appalled Charles Wilson instantly had his first close-up experience of the carnage of war, in the form of a dead German: "His face is featureless, an indistinguishable red blob out of which protrudes a tuft of blond hair." The Chicagoan leaned hard against a tree. Then he retched and vomited on the snow.[24]

But Wilson had no time to be sick. No sooner had he and his comrades begun to think they were in control of the village than a ferocious counterattack rolled down from the hills and ridges surrounding it. A wave of fresh paratroopers stormed Chaumont, supported by some 15 mechanized assault guns from Sturmgeschütz Brigade 11 and a handful of Ferdinand Panzerjäger, armed with the dreaded 88mm gun.

Shermans of the 8th Tank Battalion maneuvered wildly so that they could get round to face the attackers. Gunners and loaders were "working furiously," observed Major Albin Irzyk, the 27-year-old battalion commander, "pouring out a volume of fire." But the sun had thawed much of the snow and frozen earth, causing many of the tanks to get bogged down in what one sergeant described as "a fathomless quicksand." Several Shermans had to be abandoned, while those still resisting proved easy pickings for the Germans. A shell hit the tank that carried the forward artillery observer, making it impossible for the field guns to lend close support. Another round smashed into Irzyk's Sherman, as the commander and his crew tried to back out of Chaumont as fast as they could. "There was a low, loud, deafening, earsplitting sound," the major noted, "followed by a terrible, horrible, powerful, frightening blow." Irzyk's tank was "shoved violently forward" and the crew "were tossed and bounced like rag dolls."[25]

By mid-afternoon, the battle had reached fever pitch. Terrified by the racket outside, Maria Gustin watched Jean Manderscheid stumble into their cellar, his arm mangled by a shell burst as he tried to escape the fighting. More villagers descended the basement stairs holding a dying woman. A deafening explosion rocked the cellar, and through the blinding dust Maria was horrified to hear the cries and pleas of an aunt and uncle who had arrived badly wounded.[26]

With barely more combat experience than Maria Gustin, Charles Wilson moved about in the fog of war as if trapped in a nightmare. He was hugging a tank in one of Chaumont's narrow streets as shells plowed the village to pave the way for the advancing Germans. "With every physical movement," the Chicagoan noted, "I am a squirt gun filling my pants." For a moment the GI panicked as the tank suddenly lurched forward, leaving him alone and unprotected. But then "a thunderous crash" knocked him off his feet. As Wilson looked up, he saw a tank crewman stand in the turret, his hands outstretched but his head missing. The mutilated corpse was propelled upwards and out onto the pavement. Another blood-soaked crewman appeared, stumbled out of the Sherman, and fell to the ground. As the tank swiveled wildly, the face of yet another American appeared in the turret. He waved at Wilson and his comrades. "We mount the blood-stained tank," a dazed Wilson noted. "We return to the woods."[27]

The day ended, one of Combat Command B's sergeants commented, in a "rout." Eleven of the 22 tanks that had entered Chaumont that afternoon failed to return to the ridge overlooking the village from the south. Shaken and wounded, Major Irzyk and his crew made it back to the ridge at dusk, surprised to be still alive after their turret was split open by a high-velocity round. A Company, the infantry unit that had spearheaded the entry into Chaumont, was all but annihilated. Charles Gniot, an A Company lieutenant from Milwaukee, Wisconsin, stayed behind to cover the withdrawal in the face of withering fire. He was one of 65 men that his company lost that day.[28]

Combat Command A in Martelange did not manage to cross the Sûre River until shortly after the start of the battle for Chaumont. Tanks and half-tracks rumbled across the 90-foot Bailey bridge and then accelerated as best they could on the slippery main road to Bastogne. It was growing dark when the spearheading light tanks came under heavy fire from paratroopers holed up in Warnach, a small village just east of the highway.

Armored infantry were ordered forward to flush out the Germans with the support of light and medium tanks. Howard Peterson was one of many replacements who had arrived in the assembly zone at Arlon just days earlier. The private was sickened to see inexperience claim casualties even before the Americans reached the enemy lines. As the scared replacements hugged the tanks, the unbuttoned overcoat of one of them "caught in the tracks and sucked his legs into the bogie wheels." Another tank broke through a fence at great speed, violently whipping a strand of barbed wire against a GI's head, "turning his face into raw hamburger."

The paratroopers were waiting for the Americans, and with their anti-tank guns snuffed out the attack in no time. One moment Howard Peterson was feeling the heat from the exhaust of the tank in front of him; the next he had "this funny sensation in my ears and the sky turned red." A hidden German self-propelled gun hit the Sherman a second time, and when a bazooka team in a ditch failed to silence the enemy gun, Peterson and his comrades beat a hasty retreat. More survivors filtered back from the woods. A wounded tank crewman called out for help. His right hand, Peterson recalled, "had been almost severed and was only hanging by some skin." Taking only a few steps at a time because the man kept passing out, Peterson and a comrade finally managed to reach safety at the end of their first day in battle.[29]

While Combat Command A became delayed at Warnach, Gaffey fretted about the gap that was developing between this task force and the 26th Infantry Division on its right. There were signs of an enemy build-up near Bigonville, a village some two miles southeast of Warnach. Gaffey could not afford to have more German troops threaten Combat Command A. He therefore decided he had no choice but to send in his reserve force. Although supported by massive shelling from the 94th Armored Field Artillery, neither the armored infantry nor the Shermans of the 37th Tank Battalion managed to break through to Bigonville that evening. Holding the Americans at bay from the woods just south of Bigonville, Heilmann's Fallschirmjäger were once again showing themselves tenacious fighters, highly skilled in defensive operations. The attackers, the American artillery commander observed, ran into "a hornet's nest."[30]

A combination of mines, anti-tank guns, and Panzerfausts stopped B Company of the 37th Tank Battalion in its tracks. Captain Charles Trover, the commander of C Company, was killed by sniper fire while providing directions from the turret. Lieutenant John Whitehill's Sherman hit a mine, which caused the tank to lose a track and made the bottom of the tank cave in. Whitehill, in command of A Company, jumped out and rushed to the Sherman behind him. He had barely taken over from the tank's sergeant when three shells tore into the armor in rapid succession. The driver and loader were wounded, but Whitehill again escaped without suffering much harm. He continued the fight on foot now, leading the assault with hand and arm signals, and on occasion grabbing hold of a nearby tank radio to yell urgent instructions amidst the deafening roar.[31]

Neither Whitehill nor his comrades from the proud 4th Armored Division at Chaumont and Warnach had been making much headway that day. "I am unhappy about it," an angry Patton had fulminated on the phone to Millikin's chief of staff at noon. He was even more upset that Saturday night.[32]

4

On Sunday, December 24, daybreak revealed clear skies again, and that at least promised continued Allied air superiority. At the close of Saturday, Heilmann had sketched a dismal picture of the consequences for the German troops. "At night," he reported, "one could see from Bastogne back to the West Wall, a single torchlight procession of burning vehicles." Events on Christmas Eve, however, were to make it increasingly clear that on the ground American superiority could not be taken for granted, as dogged German defense was turning Patton's northward advance into a grueling slog.[33]

This was most obvious in the sector east of the Arlon road to Bastogne, where Millikin's infantry divisions were inching their way to the Sûre River. On Sunday morning, advance companies of the 80th Infantry Division, III Corps' easternmost division, had reached the river, but only after a very bitter and costly fight for the key town of Ettelbruck. In the corps' center, however, Paul's 26th Infantry Division, responsible for the right flank of Gaffey's armor, continued to lag behind, with its lead elements at dawn still three and a half miles from the Sûre.

Paul's troops closest to the 4th Armored Division, those belonging to the 328th Infantry, eventually managed to shake loose during the day, so that by evening they, too, came in sight of the Sûre. Under cover of darkness, however, they were immediately challenged in villages just northeast of Bigonville. A large enemy force struck an engineer company on reconnaissance near Bilsdorf, and it was only because the American commander, Captain Cissna, chose to fight to the death to delay the Germans that some of his men lived to tell the tale. In Arsdorf, the GIs stumbled across a rearguard force of the Führer Grenadier Brigade, and it took two infantry battalions to dislodge them. The battle lasted throughout the night, as the grenadiers, holed up in cellars and attics, made the Americans fight for each of the Luxembourg village's streets and houses.[34]

But the main focus of the 26th Infantry Division was on Eschdorf, and here progress was being measured in yards. The town, several miles northeast of Arsdorf, was crucial to the Americans because it gave access to the main road to the Sûre. It fell to the Führer Grenadier Brigade to deny the 2nd Battalion of the 328th Infantry access to Eschdorf. In the course of Sunday afternoon, the Germans set about their task with grim determination in the woods south of the town. American mortar teams blasted furiously away at the enemy, but to no avail. Thunderbolts were called in to help, but a first mission failed when a dozen Focke-Wulfs – a rare sight in the skies over the Ardennes – took the American pilots completely by surprise. It was close to sundown when Major Kent Geyer successfully led P-47s of the 362nd Fighter Group low over the woods to bomb and strafe the grenadiers.[35]

Major Geyer's mission helped the 2nd Battalion break out of the woods and onto the open ground in view of Eschdorf. For the infantrymen, this was only the beginning of their ordeal, as they were ordered to continue the attack through the night. Many of the men had not slept much or eaten hot food since leaving Metz five days earlier. Eschdorf was situated on high ground, the frosty night was clear, and the Germans lay waiting. Several hours after midnight, two badly mauled companies finally managed to battle their way into Eschdorf. In response, an alert and experienced enemy sealed off the town, instantly blocking the way to reinforcements. Frustrated soldiers could hear the sound of the American weapons inside Eschdorf grow fainter with each passing hour.[36]

In Gaffey's sector, meanwhile, Combat Command B was being refitted after the carnage in Chaumont just west of the Arlon–Bastogne road. But Heilmann's Fallschirmjäger refused to let the tank crews get on with the job in peace. They used artillery and heavy mortars to harass them on the ridge south of Chaumont, and attempted to slip in small groups armed with Panzerfausts. Shortly after noon, 19-year-old John Di Battista and his comrades from Troop B came under even more pressure. Although they belonged to a lightly armed reconnaissance squadron, they had been told to protect the command's flank just east of the road into Chaumont. But from the forest nearby, German mortar teams were creating havoc in the American lines. The 2nd Platoon on Di Battista's right was given the order to charge the woods and clear them. Di Battista had arrived in August as a replacement with the squadron in Brittany. He had gained sufficient experience to know that his comrades would stand little chance. He saw the Fallschirmjäger repulse their first attack. Then he watched the Germans drive them back a second time. Angry at the platoon's failure, Captain Fred Sklar stormed onto the scene, drew his pistol, and took command of the third charge, only to be swallowed up by the German-held woods, never to return.[37]

Infuriated by the ceaseless harrying on a day when most of the surviving armor was forced to sit idle, Combat Command B took steps to obliterate the enemy in the forest. Artillery battalions rained down proximity-fused shells, causing the trees to explode and shred the Germans hiding beneath them. Eight P-47s added to the carnage as they dove onto the forest and dumped their lethal loads. Their nerves frayed by the violent noise all around them, Maria Gustin and some 30 fellow villagers in their cellar in Chaumont pledged to erect a chapel to the Holy Virgin and to live more piously if only their lives were spared.[38]

Charles Wilson sensed that the war was severely testing his own faith. It had forced him to leave behind his wife Loretta and his two-year-old daughter Beverly. Loretta herself had driven him to the induction center at Des Plaines, Illinois, and he often thought of how she had stayed behind in the car sobbing. He knew from her letters that they had now moved in with her parents on the farm in Greeley, Colorado. Colorado seemed awfully far removed from their old, snug lives in Chicago. As he readied himself for a fresh attack on Chaumont, to take place the following day, Charles Wilson seriously doubted that he would ever see his wife and child again.[39]

On the other side of the Arlon highway, Charles Hunsinger and Davis Ralston had the feeling of being "lost sheep" as they anxiously peered down on Warnach from the foxholes they had dug on a hill. Both men were from Anderson, Indiana, where Hunsinger had worked as a switchman for the New York Central Railroad. They had gone through basic training together, and the previous night had been trucked in straight from the replacement depot. They now belonged to the armored infantry of Gaffey's Combat Command A and were getting ready to launch the attack that was to dislodge the Germans from Warnach once and for all. "We were green troops," recalled Private Hunsinger, "and didn't know what to do, so we didn't do anything, but wait for someone to tell us something." When the signal was given, the men rose stiffly from their icy foxholes and hitched a ride on tanks that were soon roaring down the hill.

The battle that followed was vicious. As soon as the GIs had fought their way into the village, they found themselves staving off attack after attack rolling in from the nearby forest. American artillery and heavy mortars blasted the woods, joined by Shermans raking the trees with their .30 machine guns. But the paratroopers kept coming, backed up by two Panther tanks and several tank destroyers. Charles Hunsinger was told to grab a bazooka. And Davis Ralston joined him as his ammunition carrier. The men crawled forward, their hearts in their mouths. They had fired a bazooka just once, during basic training in the States. They knew that their lives, and those of many others, depended on getting this right. Then, suddenly, American armor blasted away over their heads and finished the job for them. There was no time even for a sigh of relief. Thick smoke drifted in and some GIs panicked as they took it to be poison gas. Charles Hunsinger was struck with terror when he realized he had left his gas mask behind on a half-track in the rear.

The smoke turned out to be coming from houses and barns ablaze in Warnach. But the incoming waves of German paratroopers from the woods were real enough, and the battle dragged on until dusk. By that time, the little village had cost the Americans nearly 70 dead and wounded. Charles Hunsinger and his comrades had killed some 160 Germans. The battle was "cruel and brutal," the private noted, "especially when we would capture them with our uniforms on or parts of our uniforms on."[40]

The battle for Bigonville was just as cruel and brutal. On Saturday night, the Fallschirmjäger had withdrawn from the woods to the town itself. There were no tanks to back them up, and they could expect little support from their artillery, as shells were now being rationed. But Heilmann's men zeroed in their mortars, set up machine-gun positions in key locations, and had snipers and Panzerfaust teams fan out across town. A brief but intense barrage heralded the start of the American attack. Horst Lange, a paratrooper from Hamburg, heard a soldier scream in agony: shrapnel had horribly mutilated his face, taking away most of his nose. But Lange and his comrades refused to be intimidated, determined to make the Americans pay a heavy price for Bigonville.

Tank commanders of Gaffey's Combat Command R entered the Luxembourg town to find resistance so stiff that they were soon having a hard time convincing infantrymen to let go of the armor's protection. Increasingly, however, the tank commanders themselves were falling victim to the Germans. As Lieutenant Whitehill peered out of the open hatch, a sniper's bullets ricocheted off the turret, close enough for paint flakes to sting his eyes. John Whitehill reached for a submachine gun. As the commander of A Company rose to spray the building he suspected of housing the assassin, a bullet caught his hand. The wounded lieutenant angrily yelled to the crew below deck, and within seconds a 75mm shell pulverized the sniper's hiding place. Captain Leach, B Company's commander, slumped in the turret as a sniper's bullet penetrated the side of his helmet and grazed his head. He had barely regained consciousness when another bullet ripped into his right arm. Despite his wounds, Jimmy Leach continued to coordinate the attack until the combined teams of tanks and infantry closed the noose around the Germans. His actions earned the Texan a Distinguished Service Cross.

As soon as the noise died down, Sophie Lutgen emerged from her cellar to greet the American liberators. But she was shocked to find that these were very different men from the soldiers who had liberated them in the autumn. They "looked wild," the girl observed, "with unshaven faces and a frightening glow in their eyes." They pointed their weapons at her and told her to go back inside. She was allowed back in the street only when they were done searching the house. Countless corpses of soldiers could be seen strewn about among the dead cattle. The scenes, the girl said, were "horrifying."

With the American trap firmly closed, German paratroopers all over Bigonville began to emerge with their hands over their heads. Before long, there were between 300 and 400 POWs, and the infuriated Americans had little patience with them. They told Horst Lange to remove his cap and jacket. Then they proceeded to frisk him thoroughly. They took his money and official papers and tossed away family letters and pictures. "Within minutes," Lange said, "I had nothing left but a dirty handkerchief and my life."

Lange soon had cause to fear even for his life: during his interrogation, an American punched him in the face a couple of times because he was not fast enough answering questions put to him in English. Josef Schröder, a Fallschirmjäger from Frankfurt, was even more scared. After having been stripped of all his belongings in a farmhouse courtyard, two GIs ordered him to face a wall. As soon as he had done so, his captors fired wildly into the air, leaving Schröder "beset by fear and terror." A lieutenant rushed to the scene and barked at the GIs to halt their cruel game. Then the officer asked the paratrooper to follow him. They entered the farmhouse and the American asked the German to translate what it was the woman inside wanted from him. Schröder immediately understood that she was in desperate need of food for her baby, but was afraid to step outside. The American and the German made for the nearest stable, milked a cow, and returned with a bowl, from which both the baby and the mother drank greedily.

The German prisoners were made to form a column for the march back to Arlon. But not before those who turned out to be sporting American footwear were told to take it off. Many of Heilmann's paratroopers had arrived in the Ardennes with holes in the soles of their boots. In Wiltz they had discovered large abandoned stocks of American footwear and had helped themselves. Now, as he stood in the snow in his stocking feet, Horst Lange bitterly regretted that decision. He had already lost his jacket, and now he had no choice but to take off his sweater, too. This he tore into strips to wrap around his freezing feet. As the column moved off, Horst Lange took comfort from the fact that all he needed to do now to survive the war was survive the cold.[41]

The unexpected delays at places like Chaumont, Warnach, and Bigonville were creating anxiety at higher levels, as it became clear that McAuliffe's men would not be able to hold out much longer. "Although the fourth armored continues to attack fiercely," Bradley's aide at 12th Army Group headquarters noted with an air of surprise, "they seem unable to get through." "This has been," a deeply annoyed Patton concurred in his diary at the end of the day, "a very bad Christmas Eve."[42]

That same evening, however, measures were taken to bolster the offensive the next day. Patton blamed himself for having ordered attacks to continue day and night in bad weather, as he now realized his troops were exhausted. Millikin told his divisional commanders to stabilize the lines for the evening and to have the men rest and prepare for a renewed push in the morning. It was also agreed that more needed to be done to enable the 4th Armored Division to punch a hole in the stubborn German defenses. That meant that some of Millikin's men were unlucky enough not to be allowed any rest. With Bigonville now in American hands, Combat Command R was told to abandon its positions east of the highway and to hurry up and execute a maneuver that would take it all the way to the division's extreme western flank. The dangerous gap that this left between the 4th Armored Division and the 26th Infantry Division was to be plugged by the newly arrived 6th Cavalry Group, some elements of which were simultaneously split off from the main body to strengthen the shield on the far west side of Gaffey's armor.

An equally important change involved the reinforcement of Gaffey's armor on and just west of the highway with an extra artillery battalion and two more battalions of infantry. The previous days had shown time and again that too few infantrymen were available to help tank crews clean out villages and woods. Since the 80th Infantry Division had already pushed up to the Sûre ahead of Paul's men, the units to be transported all the way from the eastern to the western flank of III Corps were the 318th Infantry's 1st and 2nd Battalions. Exhausted, their ranks depleted as a result of the bloody fight for Ettelbruck, the men from the 80th Division heaved themselves onto trucks and headed out into the night in search of yet another battle.[43]

5

As dawn broke on Christmas Day, the tension at III Corps was running high. Patton placed a phone call to Millikin's chief of staff to stress that he would be keeping a close eye on progress. Millikin was especially concerned about the 26th Infantry Division. He had urged General Paul to "get going," but early-morning reports were already showing that the 328th Infantry was again making little progress against the Führer Grenadier Brigade at Eschdorf.[44]

Although corps and division artillery hammered the northern approaches to prevent German reinforcements from arriving, the two American companies trapped inside the town were being devastated. Braving fierce fire, Captain Vaughn Swift, E Company's commander, somehow managed to break out of Eschdorf and reach 2nd Battalion lines. Guided by the desperate captain, Shermans and the men from G Company moved in to help rescue their comrades. But the relief effort quickly ran into trouble. As soon as the task force reached the town, two tanks received direct hits. Swift was clinging to the left side of one of them when a shell slammed into the other side, killing the entire crew and hurling the captain some 20 feet from the vehicle. The shaken company commander managed to get back to his men inside the town just in time to help stave off another German assault. Captain Swift killed at least a dozen of the attackers, before making his way to a radio and frantically calling for artillery support.[45]

Swift realized that artillery fire was crucial now to enable his men to survive the onslaught, because heavy German machine-gun fire was preventing infantry reinforcements from reaching them. Lieutenant Lee Otts was dismayed that morning by the inexperience of some of his men in G Company, as they tried to push into Eschdorf. The Alabaman officer yelled at a man who was "standing up firing" to get down, but before anyone could pull him to safety a bullet hit him "right in the forehead." Some newcomers were firing wildly at the skies, mistaking P-47s for enemy aircraft. Sergeant Bruce Egger was even more stunned by the loss of many of the company's old-timers, whose dark overcoats now made them easy targets against the bright snow.

German fire wrought havoc also among unarmed medics wearing red-cross armbands. George Jetzke was the first to go down, as bullets tore into his leg. Louis Potts continued to dress a soldier's wounds, only to be cut down when he rose to sprint to the next casualty. As one of the wounded GIs struggled to rise, he kept crying, "Mother, Mother! Help me!" "That beseeching plea," the sergeant from Idaho later wrote, "on that clear, cold Christmas morning will remain with me for the rest of my life."[46]

As tanks and infantry struggled to reach E and F Companies inside Eschdorf, F Company's Captain Seely watched more and more of his men become casualties, too. One of them, a forward artillery observer, spent Christmas Day in a roadside ditch. He was badly wounded and intense small-arms fire made any attempt to carry him back on a stretcher impossible. Private Paul Hauck, the company runner, found it too hard to bear. On several occasions, he crawled to the ditch from a nearby house, stayed close to the sergeant for a while, whispering encouragement and even lighting cigarettes for the hapless man. It was late afternoon when an entire battalion of the 104th Infantry was ordered to come to the aid of the 328th in Eschdorf.[47]

Middleton in his VIII Corps command center in Florenville, beyond the Semois River, was aghast at the continued slow progress of Millikin's III Corps. Reports were showing that even before dawn the Germans had launched a potentially decisive offensive against McAuliffe and his men in Bastogne. Middleton's staff thought it time to raise the spirits of the affable southerner with a Christmas gift. They presented the general with a quality Belgian Browning shotgun that had his name engraved on the walnut stock. The men feebly joked that they thought it an appropriate gesture, given that only a handful of troops remained to protect VIII Corps headquarters.[48]

Yet even as Middleton caressed his new gun, things slowly began looking up in the 4th Armored Division sector. As a result of the changes Millikin had made the previous evening, the 5th Fallschirmjäger Division almost immediately sensed (so Seventh Army commander Erich Brandenberger noted) the "greater strength" of the opposing armor. This had much to do with the arrival of the two infantry battalions from the distant 80th Division. Although the men from the 318th Infantry's 2nd Battalion had slumped to the ground from cold and exhaustion as soon as they got down from the trucks at Chaumont during the night, Major Albin Irzyk had been elated to see them.[49]

Shortly after dawn, the commander of the 8th Tank Battalion assigned them the crucial task of capturing the woods south and east of Chaumont. Infested with paratroopers, the woods had to be cleared before a combined force of tanks and infantry could plunge into the village. The fighting that ensued was savage and lasted most of the day. Major Irzyk's Shermans gave the 2nd Battalion all the backing they possibly could, one tank company alone firing 180,000 rounds of .30 ammunition into the forest on Christmas Day. But it was up to the foot soldiers to ferret the paratroopers out of their foxholes and log-covered dugouts. The GIs used grenades and bayonets to do this, but they relied on pure courage, too.[50]

By noon, the lead platoon of G Company had come to a dead stop, as it reached an open stretch that led from one patch of forest to the next. From behind a small ridge, Private Paul Wiedorfer sized up the situation. The newlywed 23-year-old from Baltimore, Maryland, had left behind his sweetheart Alice and a secure job at the city's gas and electric company. But it all seemed of little importance right now. Two machine-gun nests were dug in on the opposite side, and their rapid fire made it impossible for his comrades to advance. Without much thought for his own safety, Wiedorfer jumped to his feet and charged the enemy positions. There was no cover whatsoever and his comrades gasped as he slipped on a sheet of ice. Although the Fallschirmjäger trained all their fire on the lone American, somehow Wiedorfer managed to get close enough to lob a grenade at the first machine-gun nest. The private stormed through the acrid smoke and, with no more than a rifle, immediately assaulted the second position, forcing the surviving Germans to surrender. Private Wiedorfer's courage that day helped the 2nd Battalion regain its momentum and finish the job in the woods surrounding Chaumont. For his action, the private received the prestigious Medal of Honor, the highest American award for military gallantry. It was the first Medal of Honor to be awarded during the battle for Bastogne. But it would not be the last.[51]

Late in the afternoon, American tanks and infantry charged the village itself. By now, Maria Gustin and her fellow Belgians were sharing their cellar with wounded Fallschirmjäger. A medic and a chaplain were taking care of the casualties. Maria watched both Germans abandon their work and join the Belgians in prayer as the din of battle inched closer. They could hear a German firing away at the approaching Americans from a window in the kitchen above their heads. Then things suddenly fell deadly silent in the building. Seconds later, Americans burst into the cellar and hustled the Germans out of the cramped space. By the time Maria was allowed to come up to the kitchen, the GIs had put rations on the table. They asked her to boil water for coffee and heat up the food. As soon as she had the meal ready, the Americans began to wolf it down. At their feet lay the paratrooper who had been firing at them from the kitchen window. His body lay in a pool of blood. Gray brain matter streaked the ceiling.[52]

While Combat Command B pushed the Germans out of Chaumont on a secondary road just to the west, Combat Command A was slowly making headway along the highway itself, supported by its own armored infantry. But the newly arrived 1st Battalion of the 318th Infantry was assigned the urgent task of capturing Tintange. This village, about a mile and a half northeast of Warnach, was yet another potential assembly area for an enemy attack

1. A rare photo of African-American gunners of the 969th Field Artillery Battalion readying their heavy 155mm pieces just west of Bastogne as the Germans approach from the east.

2. A drawing by Horst Helmus, a soldier from Kokott's 26th Volksgrenadier Division, depicts a German anti-tank team in action at Assenois, just south of Bastogne, during the siege on December 21.

3. A blurred image of medics of the 101st Airborne at work inside Bastogne as winter tightens its grip.

4. The wreckage of an L-4 Grasshopper near Sibret. The light and agile spotter aircraft played a crucial role in bringing down American artillery barrages on enemy targets all around Bastogne.

5. Pathfinders of the 101st Airborne set up their equipment on a pile of bricks on December 23. They have just been parachuted into town and will guide C-47s loaded with urgently needed medical supplies and ammunition to the drop zones inside the besieged town's perimeter.

6. A crashed P-47 Thunderbolt near Marvie. German troops feared the powerful fighter-bomber, which they called the *Jabo*, more than anything else.

7. Another drawing from the hand of Volksgrenadier Horst Helmus shows Germans scanning the horizon at Assenois, the village through which Patton's 4th Armored Division would force its way into Bastogne from the south on December 26.

8. A 4th Armored Division half-track passes German POWs on a road south of Bastogne.

9. Belgian civilians stream out of Bastogne with few belongings. The photo appears to have been taken at the end of December, not long after the arrival of Patton's spearheads.

10. In Bastogne at the end of December, General Maxwell Taylor, commander of the 101st Airborne, congratulates Colonel William Roberts on receiving the Silver Star. The commander of the 10th Armored Division's Combat Command B played a vital role in helping the paratroopers withstand the German siege.

11. Another Silver Star from the hands of General Taylor in the same ceremony. Here the recipient is Colonel Clifford Templeton, commander of the 705th Tank Destroyer Battalion, an outfit that proved equally crucial in the Belgian town's defense.

12. American anti-aircraft artillery in position on Bastogne's perimeter. Although the Luftwaffe proved very weak in the Ardennes, several bombing raids caused massive destruction and much mayhem in and around the town.

13. American radar equipment joins anti-aircraft artillery on Bastogne's outskirts to help stave off more air attacks against the devastated town.

14. Troops and vehicles of Kilburn's 11th Armored Division mass southwest of Bastogne. These soldiers belong to the 63rd Armored Infantry Battalion.

15. GIs of the 345th Infantry on a road in Moircy. Culin's 87th Infantry Division played a key role in cutting the road to Marche and in helping American troops swing around Bastogne from the west.

16. Green troops of the 17th Airborne Division march towards the front line west of Bastogne in blizzard conditions in early January. Miley's men were to suffer heavy losses at Dead Man's Ridge.

17. A machine-gun team of the 35th Infantry Division in a frozen foxhole on the edge of the Harlange pocket, southeast of Bastogne.

18. Tanks and troops of Grow's 6th Armored Division go on the attack east of Bastogne on the last day of 1944. The medic and infantrymen are part of the 44th Armored Infantry Battalion.

19. "Führer command us and we will follow you!" A Waffen SS slogan on a wall in Moinet, a hamlet northeast of the Bastogne perimeter.

20. Two disabled German tanks on a road in the village of Neffe after renewed and bitter fighting at Bastogne's eastern gates in early January.

21. German soldiers surrender and are frisked by men of the 6th Armored Division.

22. A team of American litter bearers from the 64th Medical Group in action at a clearing station near the Neufchâteau highway, southwest of Bastogne.

23. Heavy casualties in the battle for Bastogne forced American commanders to rush in large numbers of inexperienced replacements. Here, newcomers on January 4 are hurriedly instructed in how to handle bazookas in a training area at Hompré, not far from the Arlon highway.

24. Men of Van Fleet's 90th Infantry Division march past a shrine to the Virgin Mary after the collapse of German forces in the Harlange pocket.

25. GIs of the 90th Infantry Division march captured Germans to prison pens in the rear.

26. On January 16, exactly one month after the start of the German counteroffensive, Patton's Third Army links up with Hodges' First Army at Houffalize, cutting off the bulge. Here, reconnaissance troops of the 11th Armored Division pose with patrols of the 84th Infantry Division. The infantrymen had pushed down from the north side by side with the 2nd Armored Division.

against the highway. The battle for Ettelbruck had left the ranks of the 1st Battalion severely depleted. Led by a new battalion commander and several replacement company commanders, the worn men first battled their way across a creek in a deep gorge and into the dense woods around Tintange. On Christmas Eve, Thunderbolts of the 362nd Fighter Group had spotted an enemy concentration in the patch of forest and had doused it with napalm. They had launched a second strike that day, felling trees and paratroopers alike with bombs, rockets, and more incendiaries. Now, though, on Christmas Day, it appeared that during the night the Germans had returned to the charred and splintered forest.[53]

Edgar Bredbenner had barely entered the deep gorge when a burst from a "burp gun" shredded the towel wrapped around his head for warmth, took off his helmet, and grazed his neck and ear. A medic quickly patched him up and Bredbenner pushed on into the woods. Mortar shells were dropping all around him, cutting down GIs left and right. Shortly after noon, Bredbenner's luck finally ran out when a tree burst tore open his thigh and lacerated much of his leg. A medic sprinkled some sulfa powder into the wounds and administered a shot of morphine. He told Bredbenner to head back and make his way to an aid station near the highway. Bredbenner was joined by a soldier who had had his heel shot away and by another who had been hit in the back. The wounded men were without overcoats, and the medics had not been able to find them blankets. It was close to dark when the shivering threesome finally struggled into the aid station.[54]

During the torturous hours it took Bredbenner and his comrades to get to the rear for treatment, the remaining men of the 1st Battalion battled their way into Tintange, but only after more P-47s had swooped down on the Fallschirmjäger blocking their way. During that time, tanks and armored infantry on the highway managed to push as far northward as Hollange, still seven miles from Bastogne. They, too, had much help from the air, as Thunderbolts systematically worked over targets in front of the spearheads. One of these targets was a German tank in Sainlez, a village just east of the highway. The steel prey sat under a bare tree between the Grégoire forge and stable. Sainlez had already been a target for Allied aircraft the previous day, and the Didiers' house had been among those set ablaze. Monsieur Didier and his seven children, their mouths and noses covered with wet rags, had sought shelter in the vaulted Grégoire stable, bringing the total number of people hiding there to 30. Now three American bombs instantly pulverized the tank and everything surrounding it. The blasts were so powerful that the turret was catapulted onto the roof of a neighboring house. When the

Germans came to the rescue, they found only one severely burnt woman alive on the bottom of a gaping crater. Of the 29 other people in the Grégoire stable there remained only body parts and shredded clothing. Despite her pain and shock, the survivor, a refugee from the fighting in Marvie, kept inquiring about her two children. It took people a long time to find the courage to tell her that they were among the dozen children incinerated that Christmas Day together with the enemy tank.[55]

German aircraft were no match for the American Thunderbolts and Mustangs over the area. But they came close enough in the course of the day to force General Patton's staff vehicle off the road during a visit to Combat Command A – the only time during the campaign in Western Europe that the Third Army commander came under direct attack from enemy planes. They proved much more of a nuisance to Edgar Bredbenner. A warm ambulance had taken him and other wounded Americans from the aid station to an airstrip further south for a flight out to a hospital in England. But the hospital transport had barely taken off than three German fighters pounced on it. Ablaze and with one engine out, the plane made it back to the airstrip with several of the crew and nurses now also casualties. "We were back mobile again," a shaken and dazed Bredbenner recalled, "and helped remove the dead and wounded." Ten minutes later, the plane exploded.[56]

On Christmas Day, on Gaffey's far left flank, Combat Command R started rolling towards Bastogne much later than the other two combat commands. Tanks and half-tracks had been negotiating treacherous roads throughout the night in response to the sudden order to move from Bigonville all the way west to the Neufchâteau–Bastogne highway. They had assembled at Bercheux before dawn and used much of the morning to rest, refuel, and get organized. It was almost noon when the troops of Combat Command R pushed off on the Neufchâteau road. Although under orders to probe in the direction of Bastogne, Combat Command R's role was essentially seen as supporting Combat Command B to its right. It was expected that, once Chaumont was taken, Combat Command B would make the main effort in the direction of McAuliffe's men. That is certainly also what General Maxwell Taylor believed. Taylor, the commander of the 101st Airborne Division, had been in the United States when his men were rushed to Bastogne. He had hurried back to Europe and was now impatiently waiting to reunite with his troops. He had latched on to Combat Command B's headquarters, convinced that it was their armored force that would take him to Bastogne along the fastest route.

Quite unexpectedly, however, Combat Command R on Christmas afternoon began slicing through the German defenses at the kind of speed that Patton had been hoping for from day one. Its troops raced through Vaux-lez-Rosières, where they cut off a small German engineer force, and overran Rosière-la-Petite, where they captured more than 60 paratroopers. Then they abandoned the highway and tried their luck along a secondary road just to the east. Their luck held for another few miles, until they encountered the first serious resistance at Remoiville. Little time was wasted in preparing the attack and, after only a brief artillery barrage, tanks and troops in half-tracks smashed their way into the village center. With Shermans blasting the houses at close range and infantry hurriedly fanning out across Remoiville, the enemy paratroopers barely had time to aim their Panzerfausts. By dusk, the village had been taken at a cost to the Germans of 35–50 dead, 42 wounded, and a stunning 327 prisoners. When a huge crater turned out to be blocking the road to Remichampagne, a halt had to be called for the day. Still, as dusk gave way to the first chill of night, the maps showed that in a single afternoon Combat Command R had come abreast with Combat Command B.[57]

<h2 style="text-align:center">6</h2>

After four days of heavy fighting, six long miles still separated even the most forward tanks of 4th Armored Division from Bastogne. Millikin had been under relentless pressure from Patton day after day. But on Tuesday, December 26, the Third Army commander also began to feel the heat when Major General Harold Bull, Eisenhower's operations officer, called him to say that the Supreme Commander was getting "anxious" about the delay in linking up with the besieged troops. Bull therefore urged Patton to "put every effort on securing Bastogne." The intervention made Patton fume. "What the hell," he jotted in his diary, "does he think I've been doing for the last week?"[58]

But while tempers flared at American headquarters, the mood among German commanders south of Bastogne was turning dark. With Chaumont, Tintange, and Remoiville lost the previous day, and large numbers of paratroopers captured, Heilmann considered Christmas Day to have been "the critical point" of the battle. He was convinced that his soldiers now realized "that the war had been lost." For several days, Seventh Army commander Brandenberger had been trying to shore up Heilmann's division with whatever firepower could be diverted to his sector. But that was not proving to be much. A lack of fuel and prime movers, slippery roads, and "the air situation" prevented artillery pieces in particular from reaching the front lines. One corps let it be known that an artillery battalion that existed on paper could not be sent up because it consisted of 122mm howitzers captured from the Russians on the Eastern Front for which there was no ammunition.[59]

This was all the more demoralizing because American firepower appeared to know no limits. Millikin's III Corps fired more than 55,000 rounds of artillery – some 4,387,746 pounds of explosives – to get to Bastogne. But it was "the air situation" more than anything else that left the Germans desperate. With the skies clear again on Tuesday, American fighter-bombers pummeled the front line south of Bastogne almost incessantly – and virtually unchallenged. The 362nd Fighter Group called it its "biggest mission in quite a while" and even then was receiving massive support from two other fighter groups. As Patton told his wife with relish in a letter that Tuesday, "They do scare the Huns."[60]

As the Germans were finally cleared from Eschdorf before dawn on Tuesday and the 26th Infantry Division began crossing the Sûre River, all eyes turned to the 4th Armored Division. Crawling northward along the Arlon highway, Combat Command A remained farthest removed from Bastogne. Shortly after daybreak, new threats emerged on both sides of the main axis. Tanks and armored infantry were forced to spend most of the day rooting out paratroopers in the village of Hollange, just west of the highway. For Major George Connaughton's 1st Battalion, the going was at least as tough east of the highway, where the men of the 318th Infantry tried to make their way from Tintange to Honville. Backed up by at least one of the dreaded 88mm guns, a strong enemy concentration sat dug in and ready to exact as heavy a price as possible.

American fighter-bombers were called in. They pounded the Germans in Honville and then went in search of the enemy north of the village. As had happened the day before, targets were spotted in ill-fated Sainlez. Thunderbolts doused the village with incendiaries, and within minutes cellars and stables were spewing smoke. Some 70 civilians dashed from the cellar of the Bihain farm. Carrying neither food nor blankets, panicked adults and screaming children stumbled southward to where they hoped the forest would make them invisible.[61]

The refugees from the Bihain farm drifted closer to Honville just as the battle for that village exploded in full force. So fierce was the fighting that in the space of an afternoon two Americans earned the Distinguished Service Cross for extraordinary heroism. When the advance of his company was halted by intense machine-gun fire, Private Augustus Means rose to his feet and blazed away at the enemy with his rifle. Although severely wounded before finishing his fourth clip of ammunition, Private Means slowly crawled forward into the raking fire and finally silenced his tormentors with a grenade. Meanwhile, in his tank Lieutenant Frederick Rau clenched his teeth, grimly determined to provide the suffering infantrymen with as much support as possible. A forward observer with the 274th Armored Field Artillery, Lieutenant Rau held his ground despite heavy fire, and continued to relay coordinates. As soon as the most dangerous guns appeared to be silenced, Rau and his crew plunged their tank into enemy lines, inflicting heavy casualties among the paratroopers.

But there were no medals on offer that day for the courage displayed by parents trying to find a safe haven for their children in the midst of battle. Caught in the artillery duel for Honville, the Bihain farm refugees were crossing a small forest stream when a series of explosions shook the earth and splintered the spruces around them. Madame Rollus temporarily lost her sight. When she recovered it, she found herself gazing at a scene of horror. Shrapnel had mangled her husband's knee and her daughter Gisèle's foot. Her two-year-old daughter Ghislaine was badly injured, too. The unearthly stillness and strangely contorted bodies of her two other children, aged six and eleven, instantly told her they were dead. It was too dangerous to stay put, and so the villagers, many of them wounded, continued to drag themselves through the icy stream. Monsieur and Madame Rollus had no choice but to follow and leave their dead children behind in the smudged snow. As the haggard group groped its way toward Honville, villagers took turns carrying the wounded Rollus children. It was night when they arrived in the American-held village. By that time, Ghislaine Rollus had bled to death. By that time, too, Major Connaughton had been relieved of his 1st Battalion command for not having acted more forcefully against the Germans on a day when Bastogne's besieged were desperate for aid.[62]

On Tuesday, the 2nd Battalion of the 318th Infantry managed to inch much closer to Bastogne than did the 1st Battalion. Working in tandem with Combat Command B and its armored infantry, the infantrymen of the 318th moved forward along the right flank as they pushed north of Chaumont. The next village, Grandrue, lay nestled amidst dense woods. There were clear signs now that Heilmann's men had become fatigued and discouraged. On several occasions, substantial numbers of paratroopers allowed themselves to be captured in Gaffey's sector. On just as many occasions, however, officers managed to rally their men and have them inflict heavy casualties on the Americans with no more than small arms. This was certainly the case in and around Grandrue, where, according to a regimental report, the Fallschirmjäger "fought viciously from their foxholes." The destruction of the enemy's positions in the woods required "constant use of the bayonet and hand grenade." So many acts of individual bravery were recorded in such a short period that it was later decided to award the entire 2nd Battalion a citation in honor of the "aggressiveness of the heroic infantrymen."[63]

Some soldiers of the 318th that Tuesday displayed the kind of courage that bordered on madness. Private Clifford Timberlake, a gunner in a heavy machine-gun squad, was advancing in support of a rifle platoon. As the riflemen neared the enemy objective, Timberlake spotted a paratrooper preparing to lob a grenade. In alarm, the private shouted to the riflemen and then stormed the enemy foxhole with complete disregard for his own life. Timberlake hurled himself at the German, engaged in hand-to-hand combat, and finally bludgeoned the soldier into submission with the machine-gun tripod he was carrying. The private from Kentucky received a Silver Star for his action. Still others would later be honored for the care and compassion they showed for the casualties strewn across the Grandrue forest. Badly wounded by shrapnel from an enemy artillery concentration, Private Arthur Kuhn from G Company refused all treatment until he had dragged two severely injured comrades to safety across open terrain and under ceaseless fire from a machine-gun position.[64]

By the end of the day, the GIs of the 2nd Battalion were close enough to Bastogne to witness C-47 transports fly in low to drop cargo amidst the flak. The men of G Company were horrified to see one of the aircraft suddenly burst into flames. Several of the crew managed to jump out just in time. With parachutes that barely had time to open, they crashed to earth somewhere between G Company and the enemy lines. Lieutenant Gabriel Martinez did not hesitate for a moment. He organized a rescue party and pushed into no man's land. Although German fire intensified as the infantrymen came closer, Martinez and his men refused to give up until all four injured airmen were brought back to American lines. When dusk fell shortly after, Gabriel Martinez and the men from 2nd Battalion were no more than 4,000 yards away from McAuliffe's troops in Bastogne.[65]

It was not, however, the progress of 2nd Battalion and Combat Command B that was causing excitement at higher headquarters. As soon as day broke on Tuesday, Combat Command R on Gaffey's far left had instantly resumed the daring and speed of the previous day. The driving force behind it all was the 37th Tank Battalion and its 30-year-old commander, Lieutenant Colonel Creighton Abrams. Born in Springfield, Massachusetts, Abrams had become noted for his aggressive leadership traits even while playing football for the champion high-school team. The eldest of three children and the only son of a railroad mechanic, the family's modest means had turned into hardship during the Great Depression. When West Point admitted Abrams as a cadet, his parents were unable to raise the deposit for his uniform and other expenses. The high-school superintendent had to call upon a wealthy family in the Abramses' hometown to persuade them to lend the promising young man the money.[66]

Poverty had made Abrams even more driven, and this showed when he was assigned responsibility for the 37th Tank Battalion. The men admired their stubby, cigar-chomping commander, but the training Abrams put them through at home and in England had been relentless. That degree of training, however, had helped make the battalion a successful part of the 4th Armored Division that Patton had come to like so much during the campaign in France. Now, at dawn on Tuesday, as the battalion plunged north of Remoiville, Colonel Abrams was an inspiration to his men once again. The previous day, the jeep their commander was in while reconnoitering ahead of his tanks had hit a mine. The explosion had catapulted Abrams into a ditch and seriously injured his driver. Abrams had been unharmed, and he already seemed to have forgotten about the incident as he pored over maps and spewed orders laced with profanity. "He looks and sounds," one soldier noted, "like a fire-eating dragon."[67]

Abrams was organizing the attack against the next village on the map, Remichampagne, as if it were a textbook combined-arms exercise. Four batteries of artillery were hammering enemy targets just ahead of Abrams' Shermans and Hellcat tank destroyers as they approached the village. Sixteen P-47 Thunderbolts joined the fray, unleashing their bombs and rockets. Much of Remichampagne was ablaze by the time the armor and infantry began sweeping its streets and farms.[68]

The Americans were tense and impatient. They tried to free cattle from the burning stables of the Zabus farm, and when that failed they mowed the animals down with their submachine guns. Although most Germans appeared stunned and demoralized, some refused to accept defeat. Ten-year-old Guy Zabus saw GIs flush two Germans from the Léonard farm. One of the soldiers remained defiant and refused to raise his hands above his head. The Americans beat him with the butts of their rifles until he obeyed.

The Belgian boy watched as the Americans next turned their attention to the Delhaisse farm. One German surrendered straight away, but another maintained a desperate fight. When he finally gave himself up, the young paratrooper turned out to be wearing parts of an American uniform. Enraged, a handful of GIs dragged the German across the courtyard, tied him to a pole with a cable, and shot him on the spot. Guy Zabus witnessed the execution without any particular feeling of shock or disbelief – "As if all that," he later recalled, "belonged to the logical order of things."[69]

By mid-afternoon, Abrams and the commander of the armored infantry were overlooking Clochimont from the hills just southwest of the village. A little more than two miles now separated Combat Command R from Bastogne. Plans called for Abrams to push on to Sibret along a secondary road leading northwest. But that would take him away from Bastogne and into a village known to be harboring a large German troop concentration. Abrams had lost seven Shermans and was now down to just 20 medium tanks; the armored infantry was already 230 men short. Another secondary road headed slightly northeast from Clochimont to Assenois, and from there straight into Bastogne. As Abrams and his infantry commander weighed their options, Skytrains and gliders appeared overhead. The desperate relief operation, and particularly the heart-wrenching sight of flaming transports spiraling down from the skies, led the commanders to agree that they should take a risk and head straight for Bastogne.[70]

It would soon be dark, however, and there was not a minute to lose. Abrams was already barking orders over the radio, rounding up 13 artillery batteries from Combat Commands R and B to ensure that a massive barrage would precede his spearheads into Assenois. Next Abrams called Lieutenant Charles Boggess to his command tank. Boggess had been put in charge of C Company just a few days previously, when the original commander was killed. C Company had nine tanks left and was to form the advance element of the final push. The tank crews were to receive the support of a company of armored infantry, some 45 men in half-tracks. The 32-year-old lieutenant from Vermilion County, Illinois, followed Abrams' finger as it traced the secondary road on the worn map. "Get to those men in Bastogne," Abrams concluded the hasty briefing.

At 1615 Lieutenant Boggess moved off in the lead tank. He was proud of his tight-knit crew. His driver had learned invaluable skills on a tractor in Georgia. The 76mm gunner had worked in a defense plant in New Jersey before the war. The loader came from a small farm near Bryan, Texas. And the bow gunner was from Arlington, Washington, and had just graduated from high school the previous year. They were "all battle-proven veterans," and Boggess knew that he could rely on them during the tough ride ahead. Nicknamed "Cobra King," their tank was a Sherman Jumbo, one of a limited number of medium tanks fitted with sloped and much heavier armor that could better withstand the impact of enemy shells.[71]

As Assenois came into sight, Lieutenant Boggess radioed Abrams and asked for the planned artillery concentration to be brought down on the village and surrounding woods. "The town," Boggess observed, "seemed to erupt." The Germans in Assenois were numerous, as Fallschirmjäger and Volksgrenadiers literally stood back to back. Heilmann's men had their guns trained on Patton's troops to the south, while Kokott's soldiers were eyeing McAuliffe's force to the north. More than 400 rounds pounded the area, while aircraft of the 402nd Fighter Group doused it with napalm and strafed anything that moved. Denyse de Coune pressed her body against the forest floor. On Christmas Day the Germans had chased her and 25 other civilians from Assenois and taken over their cellars. Of the people in their group, 17 were children, one of them no older than seven months. As explosions shook the trees and dirt and branches rained down on them, the villagers just lay there, their blankets frozen stiff like cardboard, their limbs too numb to allow them to get up and run. "We feel," a helpless Madame de Coune noted, "like we are in God's hands, and we resign ourselves to it."[72]

Lieutenant Boggess asked the barrage to be lifted only moments before his men reached the edge of Assenois. By that time, an American shell had already hit the jeep of the forward artillery observer, forcing the pilot in the spotter plane overhead to take over his duties. With the air still thick with smoke and dust, the armored spearhead took the dazed Germans by surprise as it raced through Assenois, guns blazing. Boggess's New Jersey gunner recalled using the 76mm cannon "like a machine gun," firing "twenty-one rounds in a few minutes." The small column that emerged from the village's northern edge was made up of Boggess's Sherman Jumbo, two standard Shermans, a half-track with armored infantry, and two more tanks bringing up the rear. Moments later, the half-track hit a mine. The explosion killed several of the infantrymen on board and forced the tanks behind the damaged vehicle to screech to a halt.[73]

Patton's spearhead to Bastogne was now reduced to just three tanks. All that remained between them and the besieged town was a small stretch of road wedged between dense forests. Lieutenant Boggess ordered the gunners in his crew to aim straight ahead. The second tank covered the woods to the left. The last tank's machine guns were raking the tree line to the right. A pillbox became visible up ahead. Boggess's cannon sent three rounds crashing into the concrete obstacle in rapid succession. German soldiers spilled out onto the road and the machine guns opened up. "They fell like dominoes," recalled Boggess. The lieutenant now motioned his driver to have the tank creep forward slowly. Colored parachutes were strewn about in a nearby field, and Boggess knew that this meant they were close to the American lines. Then, in the dusk, he spotted a line of foxholes. The helmeted figures in them held their fire. "Come on out," Boggess yelled, "this is the Fourth Armored." He had to repeat the call a couple of times before a shadow cut loose from one of the foxholes and slid towards the "Cobra King." The man stretched his arm up to the turret to shake hands. "I'm Lieutenant Webster of the 326th Engineers, 101st Airborne Division," said the paratrooper with a smile. "Glad to see you."[74]

With only three of Patton's tanks inside Bastogne's perimeter, the hand-shake between lieutenants Charles Boggess and Duane Webster at 1650 on Tuesday, December 26, was no more than a symbolic end to the siege. Slowly, however, more and more vehicles and troops of the 37th Tank Battalion trickled in, despite continued German harassment from the woods along the road from Assenois. Not long after the first handshake, a tank named "Thunderbolt" rolled into the paratroopers' lines. A painted cloud pierced by three jagged bolts of red lightning adorned the hull. Colonel Creighton Abrams clambered from his command tank. He and his crew had fought hard against a resurgent enemy at Assenois and had taken out an 88mm gun along the way. The tank commander was soon shaking hands with General McAuliffe, who had bolted from his underground headquarters and rushed to the southern perimeter to greet Patton's men in person. One of the "vaga-bonds" – the young Belgian men who had assisted the Americans during the siege – watched as a sentry in the middle of Bastogne's market square raised his arm to stop Patton's first Shermans, solemnly saluted the crews, and then directed them to the Grand'rue. Abrams and his staff were taken to the cramped space of the Heintz command post, where they received a raucous welcome. "They were happy to see us," noted Major Edward Bautz, Abrams' executive officer. "Real happy."[75]

But there was no time to relax. The secondary road that the 37th Tank Battalion had opened was far from a firm corridor. McAuliffe's men needed supplies of all kinds, from food to ammunition, and they needed them fast. Many of the severely injured had been languishing for days and required evacuation even faster. But the road from Assenois to Bastogne was no more than a slender umbilical cord, and Kokott was determined to see it cut by his Volksgrenadiers. "It was a daring thing and well done," wrote Patton in his diary that Tuesday, when he learned of Abrams' breakthrough. "Of course," he reflected, "they may be cut off, but I doubt it."[76]

Shaking off the effects of the shelling and bombing, the Germans struck hard at the Americans who tried to move through Assenois behind Abrams' spearheads. As dusk turned to dark, their main target was Combat Command R's 53rd Armored Infantry. James Hendrix stumbled from his half-track when C Company came under attack from two 88mm guns. He observed the murderous artillery from behind a hedgerow, clutching no more than an M1 carbine. Hendrix's home was a tin-roofed sharecropper's shack on farmland not far from Lepanto in Arkansas. His parents had had a hard time raising him and his ten brothers and sisters, and he had dropped out of school after the fourth grade. But the 19-year-old had hunted all his life and did not see much difference between handling a rifle in peacetime Arkansas and wartime Assenois. He took aim at a soldier near the 88mm gun closest to him and shot the German through the neck as soon as he popped up from his foxhole. In the melee that followed, Hendrix charged the foxholes, cracked one soldier's skull with his rifle butt, and forced both gun crews to surrender.

The small stretch of road beyond Assenois demanded even more courage from the armored infantry. Volksgrenadiers poured into the woods on both sides and began picking off vehicles loaded with GIs. Private Hendrix, who was later awarded the Medal of Honor for his actions that evening, had the driver of his half-track slam on the brakes. He had heard a wounded man cry out for help from a shot-up half-track. He climbed down from his vehicle and watched as it raced out of sight. Ammunition began exploding in the burning half-track, and with his rifle Hendrix kept returning German fire as he attempted to pull the GI from the wreckage. The soldier's clothes were smoldering, and Hendrix tried to put out the fire by rolling his own body over the man's. The GI died despite Hendrix's frantic efforts. Hendrix dragged the body into a ditch and jumped onto a fast-moving half-track. He had killed six Germans trying to save the life of one American. Somewhat further up the road, he passed the half-track he had been traveling in before the failed rescue: it had hit a Teller mine, and all his buddies lay dead in the twisted metal. Minutes later, Hendrix and another soldier were in a ditch beside the road trying to save the lives of two wounded members of a tank crew. They bandaged the men while trying to stave off more of Kokott's Volksgrenadiers. "My gun was so hot," recalled James Hendrix, "that resin was running out."[77]

As Hendrix and the others from C Company haltingly made their way to Bastogne, light tanks and more armored infantry were sent into Assenois to help hold the village. Meanwhile, A Company was ordered to push the Germans as far away from the road as possible. Though wounded in both legs, Captain Frank Kutak refused to be evacuated. From a jeep on the road, Kutak kept commanding his company, as the bitter fight for the woods went on deep into the night. German bombers made the situation still more chaotic when, once again, they began targeting Bastogne after nightfall. The first attack came in the middle of the evening. It destroyed a building not far from Colonel Roberts's command post in Hôtel Lebrun, blowing up one of the armored force's three main ammunition dumps and an SCR-399 radio truck for long-range communication. Another attack on the town followed shortly after midnight. Abrams' artillery commander estimated that they suffered at least 15 casualties in the bombardments.[78]

As they listened to the bombing and to small-arms fire to the west, a patrol led by Lieutenant Carr slowly felt its way northward, through fields and woods. The men belonged to the 318th Infantry's 2nd Battalion that was teamed up with Gaffey's Combat Command B. They, too, were now trying to make contact with McAuliffe's men on the southern perimeter. Several patrols had already gone out before them and failed to come back. But Lieutenant Carr's men were dressed in snow camouflage, made from the white parachutes of the downed airmen that Lieutenant Martinez had rescued in the afternoon. That, and a good dose of luck, allowed the patrol to reach the perimeter at about the same time as Captain Kutak's men completed their job on the Assenois road and handed over more than 400 German prisoners. Lieutenant Carr briefed the staff at McAuliffe's headquarters, pocketed a detailed overlay of the positions of Bastogne's defenders, and then began the dangerous trek back to the lines of his battalion, just north of Hompré.[79]

That night, McAuliffe and Abrams decided that they could no longer delay using the hazardous road through Assenois for supply and evacuation. More than 40 trucks moved up with some of the most urgently needed ammunition and equipment. Light tanks were dispatched to help protect 22 ambulances and 10 trucks as they whisked some 260 of the most critical patients out of Bastogne.[80]

The siege of Bastogne had cost the 101st Airborne Division 1,641 casualties, and the 10th Armored Division's Combat Command B another 503. The exact number of dead and wounded among the miscellaneous other troops, from the 9th Armored Division's Combat Command R to Team SNAFU and the separate artillery units, cannot be calculated, but there were many. At 1,400 casualties, the price the 4th Armored Division paid for the relief of Bastogne was high, too.[81]

But Patton was convinced that it had been worth paying that price. "The relief of Bastogne," the Third Army commander wrote to his wife, Beatrice, "is the most brilliant operation we have thus far performed and is in my opinion the outstanding achievement of this war." Stubborn American resistance in the northern shoulder of the German salient had earlier caused the *Schwerpunkt* of Hitler's Ardennes offensive to shift to von Manteuffel's Fifth Panzer Army further south. Middleton's decision to have American troops hold onto Bastogne had, significantly, cost this massive Panzer army much of its momentum. On the very day that Patton's troops reached McAuliffe's men, the 2nd Panzer Division, von Manteuffel's most forward spearhead, was being bludgeoned in the Celles pocket, not far from the Meuse River. Tuesday, December 26, was the moment when the initiative in the Ardennes shifted from the Germans to the Americans. "Now," a gleeful Patton told his wife, "the enemy must dance to our tune, not we to his." Patton knew that soon Allied armies would begin squeezing the salient from the north and the south, in the hope of eliminating as many of the enemy as possible. And he was convinced that Bastogne's roads would prove particularly invaluable when the signal came for his mighty Third Army to deliver the deathblow from the south.[82]

As the darkness deepened on Tuesday, grand strategy and military glory were the last things on Harry Sherrard's mind. A private in A Company of the 326th Engineer Battalion, the paratrooper had been among those shaking hands with Lieutenant Boggess's tank crew at dusk. "That night," the soldier noted, "we ate their C rations, drank some of their wine, had a bonfire, and I thought that maybe I should write home so my mom wouldn't have to worry about me."[83]

CHAPTER 7

A CLASH OF WILLS

Harry Sherrard's mother would have worried a great deal had she known what was being decided about Bastogne at Allied and German headquarters as her son put pen to paper. It was crystal clear to both sides that those who held Bastogne would control the situation in the salient's southern part. For the Allies, the immediate concern was to ensure continued access to the Belgian town, now that Patton's armor had at last punctured the besieging forces from the south. To do so, it was urgent to widen the breach by having American troops seize the Arlon highway east of the small Assenois road, as well as the Neufchâteau highway west of that narrow corridor.

It was obvious also, however, that any momentum building around Bastogne would have to be channeled into the much more massive effort of cutting off the bulge as soon as possible. Ultimately, this would happen only when Patton's Third Army managed to link up with General Hodges' First Army pushing down from the north. But the main effort of the German Ardennes offensive had initially been in the north of the salient, so the troops there needed more time to regain their balance. During a Christmas Day meeting with Montgomery in Zonhoven, a Flemish town just north of the salient, General Bradley had found the British field marshal, who was now General Hodges' new superior, very cautious and quite unwilling to switch to the offensive immediately. In part, this was because Montgomery wanted his forces to recover from the "bloody nose" he said the Germans had given them, and because he insisted on making sure that "the enemy had exhausted himself" before he went on the attack. To some extent, however, it may also have been because Montgomery continued to regard the Ardennes as a secondary theater of operations, while he kept his eye on what he had long pursued as the primary objective further north: a deep thrust into the German industrial heartland of the Ruhr and beyond.[1]

Whatever Montgomery's reasoning, Bradley had returned from the meeting in Zonhoven "exasperated" and "enraged." The American 12th Army Group commander was convinced that the British 21st Army Group commander was squandering a unique opportunity to "inflict a devastating defeat on the enemy" now that the Germans had unexpectedly stuck out their necks in the Ardennes salient. Patton wholeheartedly agreed with his superior's blistering assessment. "Monty," he fumed in his diary, "is a tired old fart. War requires the taking of risks and he won't take them." As soon as Bastogne was relieved on December 26, Bradley ordered a willing Patton to "inflict maximum damage" on the Germans inside the bulge. There would be no time lost waiting for Montgomery. This meant that there would be no rest and much risk for the tens of thousands of Americans in and around Bastogne who were to bear the brunt of the fighting in the Ardennes in the week ahead.[2]

While Bradley and Patton were hurriedly drawing up plans for offensive action to be launched from Bastogne, German commanders were frantically organizing a renewed attack on the Belgian crossroads. It had become clear to the German high command around Christmas that the attempt to cross the Meuse River was going nowhere. In the most optimistic scenario, German forces in the bulge might continue more limited offensives, such as an attack in the direction of Liège. In the worst case, corridors would have to be kept open to allow German troops to withdraw from the west to the east and prevent them from being caught in a massive trap. In both situations, however, it was crucial for German troops to gain firm control of Bastogne.[3]

Just as the German *Schwerpunkt* had earlier gravitated from Dietrich's Waffen SS in the north to von Manteuffel's Fifth Panzer Army in the center, so it now shifted from the drive on the Meuse to the capture of Bastogne. "The more likely it became that Bastogne would not capitulate," Seventh Army commander Erich Brandenberger summed up the situation, "the more dearly did the Army comprehend that this area would finally become the main point of the Battle of the Ardennes." On the very day that Patton's troops reached the 101st Airborne Division, Hitler was already directing Waffen SS troops from the salient's north towards Bastogne and releasing fresh troops from the strategic reserve. Paratrooper Harry Sherrard was about to be caught up in a ferocious collision between two armies equally determined to call Bastogne theirs.[4]

1

On the morning of Wednesday, December 27, Bastogne's exhausted airborne staff scarcely knew any more of the bigger picture than Harry Sherrard in his foxhole. Colonel Paul Danahy, the division's intelligence officer, sat slumped at a small table in the cramped Operations Room of the cellar command post. His heavy jaw "seemed to sag with weariness." Outside, General McAuliffe, "red-eyed" and "physically beat from loss of sleep," approvingly inspected a column of 4th Armored Division six-by-six supply trucks, lined up in the Heintz barracks courtyard.[5]

All eyes were on the slender corridor leading into Bastogne from Assenois that now was a hive of nervous activity. The main priority continued to be the evacuation of the estimated 1,500 wounded soldiers crammed into aid stations all over town. Protected by light tanks, a growing fleet of ambulances sped back and forth between Bastogne and corps hospitals. The casualties' hair was gray with dust, wrote newspaperman Jimmy Cannon of *Stars and Stripes*, "but it did not look strange because their faces were old with suffering and fatigue."[6]

Eight-year-old André Meurisse was one of the few civilian casualties to be given a place in an ambulance on Wednesday. Shrapnel had lodged in his arm during an American fighter-bomber attack against Mande-Saint-Étienne four days earlier and, despite treatment in the Seminary aid station, the limb had become severely infected. It had taken pleas from one of the town's priests to convince American medical personnel to make room for the suffering boy. Meanwhile, civilians who had remained unharmed during the siege also began squeezing through the Assenois corridor. In small groups, pushing bicycles and wheelbarrows loaded with suitcases, they picked their way south among shell craters, burnt-out vehicles, dead cattle, and the corpses of soldiers. "Don't look, don't look! Look straight ahead!" Victor Bouvy's mother kept insisting, as she tried to shield her petrified 11-year-old son from the horrors of war. "But we looked anyway," recalled Victor more than half a century later. "The corpses were frozen into unusual positions," remembered Paul Remiche, ten years old at the time of the escape from Bastogne, "hands and arms raised to the sky, as if imploring or in prayer."[7]

The small corridor continued to be rife with danger. Not far from Sûre, a battery of heavy American artillery opened up just as fleeing civilians passed by. In a matter of seconds, dozens of salvos were fired at the enemy in a deafening fury. "Each time," a refugee observed, "we felt as if our lungs would burst open." German bullets riddled the ambulance that was carrying André

Meurisse, miraculously sparing the Belgian boy and his father by his side. Monsieur Mutschen was not so lucky. Instead of fleeing Bastogne on Wednesday, he was determined to make his way into town to check on his 85-year-old father, who had been trapped during the siege. He was close to Assenois when a shell exploded and jagged shrapnel ripped into his arm and stomach. Monsieur Mutschen stumbled around in pain until two GIs in a jeep noticed him and took him to a hospital in Martelange.[8]

Amidst the wreckage and refugees, traffic jams formed as more and more trucks tried to reach Bastogne with critical supplies. Captain George Horn of the 426th Airborne Quartermaster Company was in command of one such convoy. It was made up of more than 50 supply vehicles, most of them loaded with ammunition, and the others with rations and 4,500 gallons of gasoline. Six tanks of the 4th Armored Division led the convoy. Each fifth truck was trailed by another armored vehicle. At one point, however, the convoy took a wrong turn, causing Captain Horn to lose six trucks and a tank, before he managed to get his men out of a German trap.[9]

There was chaos overhead, too. Another mammoth formation of close to 160 Douglas C-47 cargo planes and dozens of towed gliders from the 439th and 440th Troop Carrier Groups descended on Bastogne in several waves along the same flight path as in previous days. They were escorted by swarms of P-47s. But by now the Germans had their anti-aircraft batteries carefully zeroed in. "The flak," one glider pilot noted, "looked like a large black cloud."

Lieutenant Joe Fry and his crew were violently thrown about when an explosion slammed into the belly of their Skytrain. Fire spread rapidly from the belly to the tail, and then all the way to the line towing their glider. Fry ordered his crew to bail out, but he stubbornly kept his plane on course. Sighting his target at last, the pilot cut loose the glider plane and then hurriedly jettisoned six parapacks of ammunition. When he tried to get out, Fry found the cabin a sea of flames. He returned to the cockpit, dislodged the top hatch, and jumped out, praying the propellers would not chop him to pieces. He slammed into the frozen soil not far from Hemroulle, just west of Bastogne. American paratroopers came running towards the pilot and dragged him, his head badly burnt and his right leg mangled, into their rifle pit. They finally managed to revive him with some of their cache of cognac.[10]

Fry's Skytrain was just one of 19 that went down in flames over Bastogne that Wednesday. Stung by the heavy losses, Thunderbolt pilots pounced on German targets all around the corridor. Horst Helmus, the young Volksgrenadier from Kokott's division who had just left his home near Cologne for his first battle, took cover as *Jabos* attacked his 75mm anti-tank gun "again and again." At the end of one strafing raid, Helmus found the fellow 18-year-old who had become his friend dead in a pool of blood that had spurted from a severed artery.[11]

Meanwhile, trucks emptied of their supplies inside Bastogne were immediately filled again with glider pilots and wounded airmen who had been patched up. They were made to guard the nearly 700 German prisoners who were now whisked out of town on the same trucks. Enraged civilians yelled insults at the prisoners, as they slowly made their way south through the narrow corridor. Some Belgians threw rocks. One of the projectiles hit Charles Sutton on the eyebrow. Sutton had piloted a glider into Bastogne the previous day. A boy on the side of the road was horrified when he realized his mistake and saw blood trickling down the American's cheek. He made a sheepish gesture indicating he was sorry.[12]

Even as Combat Command R was rushing trucks to Bastogne and providing protection for the airborne trains, the rest of the 4th Armored Division was desperately trying to widen the breach east of the Assenois corridor. But German Volksgrenadiers and paratroopers put up fierce resistance with whatever weapons they still had at their disposal. Although a patrol of the supporting battalion of the 80th Infantry Division had reached Bastogne the previous night, it took extremely heavy fighting in the woods between Hompré and Bastogne for Combat Command B at last to establish firm contact with the airborne men on Wednesday evening. The men were rewarded with a belated Christmas Dinner of turkey and trimmings.[13]

Combat Command B's success in filling the gap between the Assenois road and the Arlon highway was not being matched, however, by Combat Command A on the highway itself. Part of the problem was that as the armor moved up the main road, a gap began to develop between it and the 26th Infantry Division on its right. This led to very tense and brutal combat between German paratroopers and Combat Command A in Sainlez and Livarchamps, two villages just east of the highway and still more than four miles from Bastogne. The ranks of the armored infantry were becoming so depleted as a result of wounds and trench foot that some 30 MPs had to be pressed into service as combat soldiers. Artillery barrages and P-47 strikes against Sainlez were followed by savage house-to-house fighting. On Wednesday alone, the 51st Armored Infantry suffered 47 casualties. Their comrades from the 35th Tank Battalion that day were down to 9 tanks out of the 35 they had set out with on December 22. Belgian villagers now found the GIs a far cry from the boyish liberators of September. The Americans who entered Livarchamps were said to be in "a foul mood." Gruff and irascible GIs in Sainlez wanted to know only one thing: were there any damned "Boches" left in the smoldering village?[14]

On Wednesday afternoon, General Maxwell Taylor, encouraged by Combat Command B's progress, told his long-time chauffeur, Sergeant Charles Kartus, to take him to Assenois. There they hid in a house where American and British correspondents like Walter Cronkite and Cornelius Ryan were weighing up the chances of making it into Bastogne alive. A 4th Armored Division officer warned them the corridor was still "so narrow you can spit across it." But Taylor, recalled to Washington D.C. early in December to discuss future airborne operations, had flown into Paris only the day before and was impatient to be reunited with his suffering troops. Wearing a helmet and a service-dress uniform, Taylor told Sergeant Kartus to gun the engine and make a dash for Bastogne. It was, the commander's chauffeur later admitted, "my own scariest hour of the war."[15]

The general and the sergeant arrived in Bastogne unscathed. The 43-year-old Taylor immediately made his way to the cellar command in the town's north. He congratulated McAuliffe on a job well done, toasted him with a glass of cognac, and then formally took over command. Having reviewed troop strengths and supplies, General Taylor reported to his superiors that his battered troops were ready for offensive action. That same Wednesday evening, Hitler ordered the corridor to be cut and Bastogne to be taken, come what may. Even as the order went out, five more German divisions were heading for the Belgian town. Earlier in the day, American soldiers in Madame Greindl's château in Isle-la-Hesse had invited the baroness to share a cigarette with them to celebrate the news of the arrival of Patton's men. Little did the defenders know, but it would be several more weeks before they could say goodbye to Bastogne. Many would never be given the chance to bid farewell at all.[16]

2

The good news on Wednesday was that Patton had arranged for the arrival of a new division on the corridor's right flank. Early in the morning, the 35th Infantry Division began crossing the Sûre River east of the Arlon highway. Its objectives were to fill the gap between the 4th Armored and 26th Infantry Divisions and aid Gaffey's Combat Command A in the push towards Bastogne.

The 35th Infantry Division was far from being a green outfit: led by General Paul Baade, a World War I veteran and, at 55, one of the oldest

American division commanders in Europe, the infantrymen had skillfully fought their way out of Normandy and engaged in bitter battles in Lorraine. At the same time, however, it was a battered and exhausted unit. Pulled out of Lorraine for refitting at Metz only days earlier, Baade had received the order to rush to Bastogne on Christmas Day, just as some 2,200 newly arrived replacements were being absorbed. Classes familiarizing the newcomers with the realities of battle had been abruptly cancelled. Troops had hastily been loaded onto trucks, which proceeded to cover the 80 miles in freezing temperatures and snow flurries with scarcely a break.[17]

Baade's men at first made good progress on Wednesday. Artillery and aircraft paved the way, raining down terrible punishment on Germans seeking cover in the area's small villages. Most of the 65 inhabitants of Villers-la-Bonne-Eau had gathered in the cellars of two farms. In the course of the day, however, three families decided they would be better off in the nearby forest. They had barely set out on their journey than a barrage struck down eight of them. The fate of the Garcia family was particularly cruel. Shrapnel shattered Monsieur Garcia's jaw and all but sheared off his wife's arm. Her lungs punctured, daughter Marie breathed heavily as she watched her youngest brother writhe in agony with part of his arm gone. Forced to leave the crumpled, lifeless body of 15-year-old Flore Garcia behind in the snow, the survivors held on to each other as they staggered back to Villers.[18]

By the afternoon, casualties among Baade's infantrymen were on the rise, too, as rugged terrain, several inches of snow, and furious artillery ripostes slowed them to a crawl. There was a shortage of galoshes and winter boots, and at night blankets froze so hard they resembled plywood. Vehicles had a hard time making their way through dense forests and ravines, forcing troops to carry supplies and the wounded, or transport them on makeshift sleds. The situation rapidly grew worse the next day. The tank battalion that usually supported the 35th Division had still not been brought up. Dark cloud cover moved in, heralding an end to five days of perfect flying weather.[19]

Faced with an increasingly determined opponent in adverse terrain and climate, inexperienced replacements began to show the strain. Eighteen-year-old rifleman Bob Hagel had sailed from New York City to southern France early in December. On December 23, he had joined L Company of the 320th Infantry Regiment at Metz. Now he was in the thick of battle east of the Arlon highway, with no clear idea of what was expected of him. Although he had never fired a bazooka in basic training because of "a bad right eye," he was told to carry the weapon after one of the regular bazookamen was killed. Bob Hagel estimated that at least one in three men in his company was a green replacement. "I'm sure," he said, looking back on the ordeal, "the veterans worried about us as much as the enemy."[20]

It took the 320th Infantry, Hagel's regiment, all of Thursday to advance less than half a mile. Its sister regiment, the 137th, spent much of that same day battling for control of a single German pillbox in one of the area's many treacherous ravines. To make matters worse, on Thursday evening Baade's reserve regiment, the 134th Infantry, was siphoned off to provide urgent support for Combat Command A on the Arlon highway. The armored command had managed to reach the airborne lines at Bastogne under the cover of darkness. This meant that it had at last come abreast with Gaffey's other two combat commands. The breakthrough resulted in control of the highway on the far right of what was now a much expanded corridor. But Combat Command A's hold on the main road from Arlon remained extremely tenuous. Losses among the armor's supporting infantry had been particularly high. Replacements, a private in the 51st Armored Infantry lamented, "come and go so fast that it is hard to keep track of who is with us and their names."[21]

The help of Baade's 134th Infantry Regiment became even more urgent for Gaffey when news arrived that the two infantry battalions from the 80th Division were now to return to their parent outfit without delay. The battalions had provided crucial support for Combat Commands A and B. In a week's fighting south and southeast of Bastogne, both these units had been whittled down from more than 800 men to fewer than 200. That Thursday evening, in his headquarters, Major Albin Irzyk, commander of the 8th Tank Battalion, toasted its supporting infantry battalion for having been "instrumental in tipping the scales." The mood was emotional. "The bonding that develops in combat," the 27-year-old major later tried to explain, "is absolutely peerless. There is nothing in life to which it can be compared."[22]

On Friday, the strong bonds between the German paratroopers facing Baade's men served them well in stiffening their resistance. Although the commander of the German Seventh Army knew that their line of defense had been prepared "with the most modest of means," he insisted it was "to be held at all costs." This the depleted ranks of the 5th Fallschirmjäger Division did. At dawn, civilians in a basement in Losange listened to the howling of an American preparatory barrage. The sound mixed weirdly with German typewriters rattling away in a nearby command post.[23]

The highly efficient German defense could not prevent the newly inserted 134th Infantry on Baade's left from seizing Lutrebois and slogging its way to Marvie, just southeast of Bastogne. But in the 35th Infantry Division's center, the 137th was having a much harder time. Sergeant Gerrit Scott was just one of many in his regiment that Friday who showed exceptional courage in the vicinity of Villers. When half a dozen tanks attacked his platoon, the soldier from Fremont, Michigan, grabbed a bazooka, used it to bring two tanks to a halt, and then continued to delay the others until he was taken prisoner. On the division's right, the 320th Infantry was fighting just as fiercely south of Harlange. Sergeant Harry Luther earned himself a Distinguished Service Cross in K Company, when he single-handedly silenced a machine-gun crew with a rifle and some hand grenades, and then went on to storm two more positions, capturing close to a dozen Fallschirmjäger in the process.[24]

Yet none of the countless acts of heroism on Friday sufficed to have the 35th Infantry Division push back the German line of defense stretching east of the Arlon highway from Lutrebois to Bavigne. The 654th Tank Destroyer Battalion was brought up to help the foot soldiers take out armor, artillery pieces, and machine-gun nests. But, highlighted against the snow, the destroyers, too, were soon proving to be excellent targets for the skilled Fallschirmjäger. Under a hail of machine-gun fire, Alvin Snead rescued a soldier from one burning destroyer, and then rushed to another that was spewing smoke. The vehicle blew up in his face, seriously wounding the medic from California who was later awarded a Silver Star for his actions. Sergeant Bill Brock and Corporal Edward Brannon had just left their destroyer to reconnoiter the area, when a concealed German tank took it out. Two of the crew managed to crawl out of the vehicle as the ammunition inside began to explode. There was no sign, however, of the driver. Twenty-six-year-old Bill Brock had reluctantly left behind a farm, his wife Nellie, and two children. Still, ignoring the fire from a nearby German tank, the Alabaman, accompanied by Corporal Brannon, dashed to the destroyer to save the driver, who could be heard screaming in agony. The men managed to get their wounded comrade out, but came under heavy fire when they tried to drag him away. Both Corporal Brannon and the driver were killed before reaching safety. Bill Brock was hit in the wrist, legs, and hip. The sergeant hid in a ditch until men from his unit came to rescue him.[25]

There were Silver Stars for Brock and Brannon, too. But no number of decorations could conceal the fact that the 35th Infantry Division was in serious trouble. Ironically, as the 134th Regiment reached Marvie on the extreme left, the 26th Infantry Division on the right began to make better progress than in previous days. This now caused Baade's 137th and 320th

Regiments to lag behind, giving rise to the dangerous formation of a German salient around the village of Harlange. The Harlange pocket was shaping up to be a threat to the Arlon highway east of the Bastogne corridor for many days to come.

At the same time, however, the flank on the opposite side of the corridor, along the Neufchâteau highway, was giving General Millikin at least as much of a headache. Aware of the concentrations of German armor that had formed west of Bastogne during the enemy's race to the Meuse, right from the outset of Patton's relief effort III Corps staff had fretted about the wide-open flank on its left. With only limited screening from engineer units and the 6th Cavalry Group, fears about its vulnerability to counterattack had refused to go away. It was with a sigh of relief, therefore, that Millikin's staff welcomed the arrival of the 9th Armored Division's Combat Command A in an assembly area 11 miles southwest of Bastogne.

Having covered 55 miles in 24 hours, on Thursday morning the armored force began to push northward along the Neufchâteau highway. To keep this vital artery open, as well as to expand the corridor, it was particularly crucial that Sibret be taken, a village a mile west of the highway and about as close to Bastogne as Assenois. Until noon, an unforgiving artillery barrage pounded Kokott's Volksgrenadiers, Heilmann's paratroopers, and petrified civilians. "In the cellars," one of the numbed villagers wrote, "we pray, we beg, we forget to eat."[26]

The battle in and around Sibret's ruins raged all afternoon. German resistance was unexpectedly strong because the troops of Heilmann and Kokott were now receiving support from a formidable armored force: von Manteuffel had ordered the fairly unscathed Führer Begleit Brigade to extricate itself from the offensive near Hotton on the Ourthe River. The outfit had just wound its way down from the northern part of the salient to help sever Bastogne's corridor from the west. Colonel Otto Remer was in command of an elite force of 7,000 men. They came from Hitler's headquarters guard and from the renowned Panzergrenadier Division "Grossdeutschland" that was still active on the Eastern Front. But it was the brigade's enormous firepower that was most welcome: an entire battalion of high-quality tanks, reinforced with large numbers of assault guns, 105mm pieces, and the "eighty-eights" that every American soldier dreaded.[27]

A severe fuel shortage had forced half the brigade's vehicles to tow the other half all the way from Hotton. Allied fighter-bombers had made the trip even more troublesome. But on Thursday, Remer's tank crews refused to waste any more time and hastily took on the armor of the 9th Armored Division near Sibret. A vulnerable gasoline engine had earned the American Sherman tank the unenviable nickname "Ronson Lighter" – a reference to the advertising slogan: "Lights up the first time, every time!" The American tank's tendency to catch fire when hit by a high-velocity round was all too obvious in the clash with Remer's long-barreled Mark IVs. As his Sherman was hit somewhere between Sibret and Chenogne, Thomas Dawson hurriedly slipped from the burning vehicle. Despite intense fire from tanks and small arms, the sergeant tried to fight the blaze. When that failed, he crawled to the Sherman's front hatch and managed to extricate two of his crew. Still ignoring the relentless shelling and machine-gunning, Dawson next clambered onto the turret to help rescue his other comrades. Just as he was lowering himself into the steel cauldron, enemy guns scored two direct hits. The sergeant from the 19th Tank Battalion vanished in the blaze.[28]

The battle for Sibret lasted into the night. Then the German survivors, camouflaged in bulging bed sheets, vanished into the woods, stealing back in the direction of Chenogne. The carnage wrought by Remer's force on Thursday could not stop Combat Command A from attempting to capture Chenogne the next day. Consisting of a church, a school, a grocery store, and 32 homes, the farm village counted a population of no more than 150. As the weather worsened and a Scandinavian cold front moved in with snow-laden skies, American artillery and aircraft worked the village over with high explosives and incendiaries for several hours. By the time they were done, the village was erased from the map. In the rock-solid cellars of the Ardennes, most villagers survived the explosions. It was the seeping napalm and white phosphorus that drove them from the burning rubble. Most of the civilians resettled in three farm shelters that remained safe. "As we trudged past the church and saw Christ suspended from the cross," recalled Marie-Josée Willot, then aged 19, "we said a prayer to ask for His help."[29]

There was no help that day for families that decided to flee the devastated village. In the afternoon, a group of 15 Belgians emerged from the forest near the hamlet of Mande-Sainte-Marie, about half a mile from Chenogne. As they traversed the windswept fields, a machine gun opened up and mowed down the suspicious line of dark shapes. For a long time, Monsieur Zabus lay still in the snow, afraid of drawing more fire. He watched blood ooze from his shoulder and melt a hole in the ice. When he finally found the courage to lift his head, he saw that his wife and teenage daughters were among the dead. He could not immediately tell if his eight-year-old son René was still alive, but the boy's chalk-white face and the mauled leg stump that had pumped out a giant pool of blood soon left him in little doubt. With the help of three other survivors, the wounded Monsieur Zabus made it to a nearby farm, where more civilians sat huddled together. All were forced to watch helplessly as the husband and father rocked back and forth, tormented by pain and grief.[30]

The machine gunner who killed Antoine Zabus's family that Friday was almost certainly a nervous soldier from the American force that desperately tried to take Chenogne all through the afternoon and evening. At one point, the men from Combat Command A managed to claw their way onto the southern fringe of the village, only to be thrown back by the Germans during the night. In the fight for the village thus far, Colonel Remer had lost 200 men and a dozen tanks. Some 300 American infantrymen and 29 Sherman tanks had fallen casualty to the Germans.[31]

Further to the rear, the Germans proved to be equally edgy now that the Americans were increasing the pressure west of Bastogne. In Flamierge on Friday they arrested eight Belgian villagers and refugees. The Germans accused them of being *"franc-tireurs"* and "partisans," and they herded the frightened men into the local forge. Guards trained a heavy machine gun on them. Worried wives and mothers were allowed to bring the prisoners some food and hot drinks. In the evening, the men were marched to a farm and subjected to intense interrogation. They were finally released unharmed, to a collective sigh from the community.[32]

That same Friday, knowing they would incur the wrath of Remer's troops if found out, the inhabitants of a farm in Mande-Sainte-Marie crouched low as they made their way to a nearby field, where two GIs lay gravely wounded. One soldier had lost a leg and was bleeding profusely. The other's face was so badly burnt that his features could scarcely be made out. The farmers hid the suffering Americans in their bedrooms and took care of them until medics from Combat Command A finally managed to come to their comrades' aid.[33]

Despite battles raging to the west and east, traffic pulsed through the corridor unabated. By noon on Thursday, a medical collecting company had evacuated the last stretcher case from Bastogne. On Friday morning, trucks arrived to pick up stragglers from the 28th Infantry Division. The men had helped defend the town with Team SNAFU, and were now being returned to what remained of their parent outfit. So many vehicles were moving in and out of town that a unit of more than 30 MPs had to be sent in to help prevent bottlenecks. Supply trucks, in particular, were clogging the roads in growing numbers. Airborne convoys stretched all the way to base camp at Mourmelon, loaded down with everything from ammunition and winter clothing to cigarettes and candy. The African-American gunners of the 969th Field Artillery hailed the arrival of plentiful stocks of shells armed with the deadly new proximity fuse for their 155mm howitzers.[34]

There was, however, no better boost for morale among Bastogne's defenders than the long-awaited arrival of mail from home that had been piling up in Mourmelon. Mike Heyman, the corporal in 10th Armored Division's Team Cherry who was billeted in the acting mayor's home, flashed a gleeful smile when he unwrapped a Christmas package stuffed with toys and trinkets. Mike's parents wanted him to distribute the presents among Europe's liberated children. "The littlest tykes went wild!" the corporal reported from Bastogne. "I was soundly and sincerely kissed by a multitude of grimy little faces."[35]

There was an even better Christmas present for two pupils in the Institute of Notre Dame's cellar labyrinth. On Thursday, a tall American officer barged in. He showed the girls a note from their father in Florenville, the town that hosted Middleton's VIII Corps headquarters. The note explained that their families were fine and that the officer had come to take the girls home in his jeep. They were the first boarding-school girls to be reunited with their parents since the start of the siege. The others had to be satisfied with vague promises that trucks would arrive the next day for their evacuation.[36]

Meanwhile, however, it was becoming clear to the men of the 101st Airborne that they were not going anywhere. On Thursday afternoon, a final airlift brought ten more tons of medical supplies into town. Even more ominous was the arrival of graves registration units. The newly arrived General Taylor went out of his way to be seen inspecting the front lines. He also made sure to distribute a message congratulating troops in the foxholes. But the paratroopers craved rest more than praise. Men of the 501st Parachute Infantry in Bizory were so cold they smashed not only the furniture of surrounding farms to have wood to burn, but even the pews of the village chapel. At the end of their tether, some could barely take the strain when Volksgrenadiers on the other side of Bizory had loudspeakers blare annoying music at them for what seemed like an eternity.[37]

During the first days following the arrival of Patton's armor, the paratroopers remained on the defensive. Even then, however, the situation proved constantly dangerous. The 26th Volksgrenadier Division had suffered more than a thousand casualties during the siege. But Colonel Kokott was still in command of 9,000 soldiers, and they continued to tighten the vice around Bastogne. The effects of artillery and snipers and of constant probing and patrolling added up in the units' casualty lists. By Friday, December 29, another 250 airborne men had been killed or wounded, or had gone missing – all during three days' fighting that barely merited mention in after-action reports.[38]

As early as Wednesday, 400 green airborne replacements had been dropped off to help plug the holes in Bastogne's front lines. Quartermaster trucks also kept reinforcing the ranks with veterans who had been left behind on December 18 while on leave in Paris and other French cities. For the paratroopers who had been with their units in Normandy and Holland, the anguish of each additional loss that followed the lifting of Bastogne's siege was hard to bear. On Friday, a retrieval party went out in search of two privates who were part of the 501st Parachute Infantry's intelligence reconnaissance team. The previous evening their patrol had run up against a German machine-gun position and the fighting had continued into the night. The men found the bodies of the lead scouts on a small trail. Arthur Teichman of Philadelphia lay on the right side of the path, and Norman Blanchette of New Bedford, Massachusetts, on the left side. Of the 24 men of the recon team that had jumped over Normandy, 11 were now left. "This was," confessed a grieving comrade, "a sad, sad day."[39]

The threats from the air continued as well. Additional anti-aircraft artillery batteries arrived and took up positions all over town. To avoid a bomb from taking out the 101st Airborne's staff all at once, on Friday it was decided to have the headquarters split up in three sections. Although one section remained in the underground cellars of the Heintz barracks north of town, another group settled down in Sibret, just southwest of Bastogne. General Taylor and Tony McAuliffe decided to move to the château in Isle-la-Hesse. Madame Greindl had just bid farewell to the artillery officers who had stayed there during some of the worst days of the siege. The baroness was more than happy to host the generals, as their stay was accompanied by the arrival of more and better food, as well as generators to provide electricity.[40]

The move had scarcely been completed when, early in the evening, the Germans unleashed one of the most punishing air raids of the Ardennes offensive. For some 20 minutes, more than 70 Junkers Ju 88s and 188s of *Kampfgeschwader* 66 pounded Bastogne with heavy loads of explosives, including cluster bombs. A direct hit caused the command post of the 796th Anti-Aircraft Artillery Battalion to collapse, burying half a dozen men in the rubble and blowing up three ammunition trailers. A blaze in adjoining buildings forced the 10th Armored Division's Combat Command B to evacuate its headquarters from Hôtel Lebrun.[41]

Maria Gillet watched the pupils in the Institute of Notre Dame bury their heads in their laps once again. The trucks that had been promised the previous day had failed to arrive, and the girls were exhausted. Many were running a high fever. The shocks of the explosions ran through the walls and squeezed the air from people's lungs. "One more night of this," thought Maria, "and we will go insane."[42]

The air raid caused mayhem, just as frantic activity at Allied higher headquarters was setting in motion a decisive counterattack for the next day. On Thursday afternoon, Eisenhower had met with Montgomery on a train in the railroad station of Hasselt, not far from the British commander's Zonhoven headquarters. Montgomery continued to worry about a renewed German push in the north of the salient. But, pressed by the Supreme Commander, he did concede that the First Army would be ready for offensive action at the start of January. This sufficed for Eisenhower to order the release of the only two divisions in strategic reserve in Western Europe at that time. The 11th Armored and 87th Infantry Divisions were instantly to become part of Patton's Third Army. Middleton was to add them to his depleted VIII Corps, so that on Saturday, December 30, he could commence the attack from the southwest of Bastogne. He was to swing around the town and then head northwards in the direction of Houffalize. This, a key town in the center of the bulge that Allied bombers had reduced to rubble in raids on December 26 and 27, was to be the meeting point for the Third Army from the south and the First Army from the north. The German troops caught between hammer and anvil would be smashed to pieces. Those still west of the pincer would be hopelessly trapped.[43]

But the bombardment on Friday evening was showing that the Germans had ambitions of their own involving Bastogne. These had firmed up at about the same time as Allied hopes were rising. On the day that Eisenhower met with Montgomery in Hasselt, Field Marshal von Rundstedt, commander in chief of the western front, ordained the destruction of the Bastogne corridor to be "of decisive importance." By Friday, an estimated 100,000 German troops had converged on Bastogne and another 30,000 were on the way. Their most urgent task was to attack the corridor from the west and the east, "for the purpose," noted Seventh Army commander Erich Brandenberger, "of rewelding our broken ring." But at a conference on Friday afternoon, Fifth Panzer Army commander von Manteuffel reminded his division commanders that, since Bastogne had now become the "central problem," the next step would be a final assault to capture the town once and for all.[44]

3

On Friday evening, troops from the 87th Infantry and 11th Armored Divisions could clearly hear the explosions of the bombs in Bastogne, as more and more of their vehicles pulled into the assigned assembly areas southwest of the town.

General Frank Culin's infantrymen had only the slightest of battle experience. They had arrived in France earlier in the month, had taken part in some brief engagements with the Third Army in the Saar region, and had then gone into reserve at Rheims just before Christmas. It had taken trucks the whole day to negotiate the congested hundred miles to the Ardennes. And they had not bothered to halt for anything. "We pissed in the gas cans and shit in a pile of straw," a soldier recalled. One of the battalion surgeons during the trip felt his stomach churn. "Maybe," he ventured, "the thought of going back into combat had something to do with it." It was so cold, remembered a sergeant from Hoosick Falls, New York, "that every breath felt as if our lungs were full of ground glass." When the GIs arrived, they looked "like sides of beef hanging in the meat locker."[45]

The men of the 11th Armored Division had no battle experience whatsoever. They had sailed from New York to Liverpool in September and, after a stormy crossing of the English Channel, had arrived in Cherbourg on December 17. General Charles Kilburn, a native of New Mexico, had found himself shepherding his troops through bitter cold and sleet, first to a holding position on the Meuse River, and then to the Ardennes bulge. During their brief stay at the Meuse, soldiers had been rushed through classes on everything from scouting and patrolling to mine detection. Jack Misener from Seattle, Washington, swallowed hard when his truck drove through the battlefield northeast of Paris where his father had sustained a severe stomach wound during World War I. But Kilburn's men soon realized that neither family stories nor army classes had prepared them for the real war. In their bivouac near Neufchâteau, John Fague and his comrades found themselves drawn to the mutilated corpses of German airmen that lay gray and rigid next to a crashed plane. "The sight of dead bodies," remarked the sergeant, "was something new to a nineteen-year-old boy from Shippensburg, Pennsylvania. I walked away with a hollow, sickening feeling in my stomach."[46]

German bombers pounded Bastogne two more times during the night, and again just before dawn on Saturday, December 30. When daybreak came the town was a shambles and fires were raging everywhere. The 4th Armored Division had already ordered all ammunition and gasoline trucks out of town to a more secure spot near Remoiville, on the road south from Assenois. Colonel Roberts now thought it safer to have part of the staff of his 10th Armored Division's Combat Command B established in Rosière-la-Petite, further down the Neufchâteau highway. Although most of the civilians in their cellars had survived the latest bombardment, a wave of panic spread across town. By mid-morning, an estimated 1,500 Belgians were clogging the vital artery coming in from Neufchâteau. Some had fled on bicycles or in horse-drawn carts. Most were on foot and had not even bothered to pack a suitcase. Several civilians collapsed from exhaustion and had to be picked up by American ambulances.[47]

Against the backdrop of mass confusion on the highway that morning, Middleton ordered the 87th Infantry and 11th Armored Divisions to attack from the area just west of it. In a phone call the previous day, the general from Mississippi had made it clear to Third Army headquarters that, because of their late arrival and exhausted state, he did not think these troops were ready. But Patton, eager to take the fight to the enemy, refused to brook any delay. "I insisted that they attack," he commented stonily, even "if it was only with their advance guards."[48]

The 87th Infantry Division formed the left prong of Middleton's attack. Its first objective was to sever the main road that connected Bastogne with Saint-Hubert in the west. That placed the brunt of the battle that morning on the men from the 345th Regiment. At the village of Moircy, they clashed with elements of the battle-hardened Panzer Lehr Division that had started falling back to the east. The fight raged all afternoon. Mitchell Kaidy, a 19-year-old New Yorker from the 1st Battalion, saw "a shudder" run through the unit when an enemy machine gun cut down the much-admired Captain Kromer, a "tall, handsome West Pointer who commanded A Company." Despite heavy losses among officers and men, the 1st Battalion finally succeeded in capturing Moircy. Late in the evening, however, Bayerlein's men launched a ferocious counterattack. The surgeon from the 3rd Battalion was ordered to send all his litter bearers forward to help carry the wounded. The carnage was beyond belief. "Strips of skin," recalled Private Kaidy much later, "were left hanging from bare trees."[49]

To the right of the 87th Infantry Division, closest to Bastogne, Kilburn's armor was to make the main effort. Troops moved off at exactly 0730, in darkness and dense fog. The 11th Armored Division's rearguard had continued to arrive throughout the night. There had been little time for reconnaissance and detailed planning. Artillery coordinates were sketchy, and air liaison teams had not yet arrived. As the GIs approached the front, Chaplain Regis Galvin solemnly drove past the entire length of his battalion's column. Wearing a helmet and a stole, the Franciscan friar from Virginia gave general absolution to the Catholic soldiers. He also had plenty of kind words for the scared men of other faiths.[50]

Kilburn's Combat Commands A and B moved forward abreast of each other, but separated by a large forest, the Bois des Haies de Magery. This further reduced the striking power of the woefully inexperienced division. West of the forest, Combat Command A aimed to reach Remagne, a village on a secondary road leading north. But as the men of the 63rd Armored Infantry crossed a ridge near the hamlet of Rondu, they fell foul of yet another Panzer Lehr force. German firepower tore the infantry to pieces. The American outfit took a hundred casualties in less than half an hour. New Yorker Clinton Barnard watched helplessly as his ten-man squad disintegrated before his eyes. J.B. Nance went down, and so did Sergeants Calvin and Cassidy. Then a shell blew up Lawrence Kushmider. Barnard was a close friend of the 24-year-old farmer from Asbury, New Jersey. Kushmider had told stories of his skating antics on the Broadway Roller Rink. He had let Barnard share in news from letters written by his parents, his sisters Josephine and Sally, and a brother who was serving in the China–Burma–India Theater. In between long weeks of training in England, they had gone away on passes together in London, Bristol, and Bath. Now, after one brief stretch of brutal combat, nothing much remained of Kushmider, the squad, or B Company.[51]

East of the Bois des Haies, Combat Command B was assigned the 11th Armored Division's most important objective of the day: Chenogne. The previous night, troops of the 9th Armored Division had been devastated in an attempt to take the village from Remer's Führer Begleit Brigade. Kilburn's men on Saturday were soon running into even more trouble. A first unforeseen circumstance was that they collided head on with the XLVII Panzer Corps, just as it hurled itself against the Bastogne corridor at exactly the same time that morning. This was a particularly nasty surprise, as it meant that there were more troops in the area than reports had indicated. Intelligence had identified Remer's brigade. It had also pointed to the presence of elements of the 15th Panzergrenadier Division, the outfit that had taken part in the failed Christmas attack west of Bastogne. But somehow it had completely missed the arrival of the 3rd Panzergrenadier Division, which had just come down from the northern salient. Walter Denkert's troops had suffered losses at the Elsenborn Ridge earlier in the offensive, and Allied fighter-bombers had attacked the division's panzer battalion at least 17 times en route to Bastogne. Still, Denkert, a general with combat experience in France and Poland, remained in command of more than 11,000 men.[52]

Ted Hartman was experiencing a strange mixture of dread and excitement. Last year, he had just started as a pre-medical student at a college near his hometown of Ames, Iowa, when the army sent him his draft papers. Now, aged 19, he was peering through a periscope and finding it hard to believe that he was driving an M4 Sherman into battle. All the tank's hatches were closed, and his view of the area ahead was severely restricted. But the deafening noise on the battlefield told him more than he wanted to know: the powerful enemy force on the other side was hammering them mercilessly. His company was part of Task Force Poker. It was to arc west of Chenogne with Combat Command B and push as far as Houmont. Due to delays and poor communication, there had been no artillery barrage to soften up the target and help pave the way. The losses in Hartman's company mounted rapidly. A first Sherman was taken out, then a second. More than a dozen tank crew members were dead before the target was reached. One of them was Captain Ameno, the company commander who served as the "anchor for 140 men."

Hartman and his comrades fought back, furiously blazing away at anything that appeared to be a threat. At the edge of Houmont, a line of shadows flitted through the billowing smoke of a barn. A machine gunner in one of the Shermans cut them down. There was only one survivor among the fleeing civilians. The previous day, Joseph Châlon, his three daughters, and three granddaughters had managed to escape the wrath of American aircraft in Chenogne. Now the 70-year-old Monsieur Châlon and his entire family had fallen victim to an American tank. Task Force Poker's armored infantry stormed forward and began clearing the village. The GIs were in a vicious mood. They burst into the underground shelters, shone torches on frightened Belgian faces, and brusquely checked and rechecked identities.[53]

To the east of Hartman, Task Force Pat, assigned the direct assault on Chenogne, failed to capture the key objective of the day. Things went wrong for the green troops from the very beginning. Within the first hour, Sergeant Fague and his fellow armored infantrymen lost touch with the tanks they were supposed to follow into battle from Jodenville. By the time the inexperienced officers had sorted out the situation, the tank crews already stood poised on a ridge for the attack. Fague and his comrades were still dismounting from their half-tracks when the platoon commander yelled at them to fix bayonets and charge a nearby forest. The order, Fague noted, caused an almost "hysterical feeling of fear." But before the infantrymen had a chance to launch the assault, the order was rescinded. Meanwhile, the Germans were causing carnage among B Company's tanks. One Sherman after another was set ablaze. Two men could be seen stumbling from their tank, burning like torches. The tanks began to pull back. First the order was given for the infantry to return to the half-tracks. Then they were told to dismount again and withdraw. What followed was "a mad scramble" in the direction of where the men had come from at dawn.[54]

Ten battalions of artillery from Middleton's VIII Corps joined the guns of the 4th Armored Division to help subdue the strong enemy southwest of Bastogne. Despite the deteriorating weather, Allied aircraft continued to break through the clouds to get at German vehicles and troops concentrated in and around Chenogne. They bombed and strafed the village's smoking ruins relentlessly. In the collective underground shelters, those civilians who could still stomach food nibbled at some dry crusts. "I so clenched my teeth in response to each new attack from the air," recalled one young woman, "that my jaw became locked and I could no longer move my mouth."[55]

German flak managed to destroy at least two Thunderbolts of the 362nd Fighter Group. Lieutenant Joseph Mancini bailed out, but his parachute failed to open in time. Robert Daw tried to land his damaged fighter-bomber, nicknamed "Spunky," but it slammed into a tree killing the lieutenant. Their comrades refused to be intimidated and continued to pursue targets great and small. In Chenogne's Burnotte farm, civilians saw more and more horribly wounded soldiers file into their shelter, part of which the Germans had turned into an aid station. One of the casualties was a courier. A projectile had caused the gas tank of his motorcycle to explode, and the German was covered in deep burns. The Belgian villagers were forced to listen to his shrieks and cries until he died.[56]

On that first combat day west of Bastogne's corridor, John Fague witnessed how several of his comrades "lost control of their nerves and broke down." Mac McCarty was one of them. Somehow the wounded soldier had made his way from the battlefield to an American aid station near Jodenville. When he came to and opened his eyes, the first person to appear in his field of vision was a captured German. McCarty's reaction was instantly violent. He thrashed about and yelled abuse. Medics could not get the GI to calm down until a chaplain quietly shepherded the enemy soldier out of the room.[57]

On the evening of Saturday, December 30, General Middleton decided that Combat Command B was in desperate need of more support in front of Chenogne. Combat Command R, the 11th Armored Division's reserve force, was hurriedly sent over. Even Combat Command A was now told to transfer from the area west of the Bois des Haies to that east of the forest. Culin's 345th Infantry Regiment spread itself thinner to fill the void.

The 4th Armored Division's artillery barrels were red hot that Saturday. Not only were they spewing shells in support of Middleton's hard-pressed men, but at the same time they were helping to stave off what the 35th Infantry Division described as "an extremely heavy counterattack" on the other side of the Bastogne corridor.[58]

The force that had slammed into Baade's infantry before dawn on Saturday was the formidable XXXIX Panzer Corps. The 167th Volksgrenadier Division formed the northern prong of the attack. This outfit had been hurriedly rebuilt after its destruction on the Eastern Front, and General Höcker's men lacked training and heavy mechanized weapons. For transport they relied on some 1,100 horse-drawn wagons and a number of beat-up Italian trucks. But the 11,000 Volksgrenadiers had only just arrived from east of the Rhine, so they were still fresh and morale was high.[59]

Höcker's troops soon overwhelmed the Americans south of Marvie on Bastogne's southeastern edge. Before noon, they cut the highway from Arlon and reached a forest just southeast of the equally vital Assenois road. But an alert Gaffey was quick to respond. He rushed troops from his 51st Armored Infantry to the area and called in all the firepower that was available. Each attempt by the Volksgrenadiers to break away from the forest was met with furious barrages. Fighter-bombers and the advanced technology of proximity-fused shells caused mayhem in the lead battalion. They were, an appalled Höcker noted, "cut to pieces."[60]

As Baade's men were being overrun by the Volksgrenadiers, one of the most battle-hardened and ruthless divisions in the German military was also hammering away at their positions just to the southeast. The elite 1st SS Panzer Division, known also as the "Leibstandarte Adolf Hitler," had come down from the north of the salient to help cut the corridor and capture Bastogne. As one of the initial spearheads of the Ardennes offensive, the division had lost dozens of tanks and had suffered more than 2,000 casualties. The move to the south had been a nightmare of blocked roads and fuel shortages caused by ceaseless Allied bombing of supply trucks and depots deep into the German hinterland. The tanks, "packed on the road, lined up two abreast," had been easy prey for the Thunderbolts. American pilots had reported crews "boiling out of the turrets." Yet, despite all that, Wilhelm Mohnke's outfit remained a powerful one, with some 16,000 men and a fearsome steel fist. Brutal warfare on the Eastern Front had forged a fierce esprit de corps among the men. It had also forced them through a process of barbarization. During the first week of the Ardennes offensive, Mohnke's men had massacred scores of American POWs at Baugnez and scores more Belgian civilians near Stavelot and Trois-Ponts.[61]

At Villers-la-Bonne-Eau, *Kampfgruppe* Hansen took two infantry companies of Baade's 137th Regiment by surprise and had them surrounded inside the tiny village. SS Panzergrenadiers tried to flush them out with the support of more than half a dozen tanks, but the Americans continued to hold on. Flamethrowers were brought forward. More tanks arrived, among them the dreaded *Königstiger* or King Tigers, 70-ton monsters fitted with long-barreled 88mm guns. After a couple of hours, radio messages came out of Villers pleading for a supporting barrage of smoke and high explosives. Then the radio suddenly went dead. Only one of the 169 GIs in Villers managed to get out.[62]

A concerted effort by the other men of the 137th, the 4th Armored Division's Combat Command A, and numerous artillery battalions finally managed to bring *Kampfgruppe* Hansen to a halt, just before it reached the Arlon highway. Meanwhile, an even more determined combined-arms response was organized to stop *Kampfgruppe* Pötschke in the Lutrebois sector of Baade's 134th Infantry. Pötschke's outfit was more powerful than Hansen's and jumped off closer to the highway.[63]

The 3rd Battalion was the first to feel the full brunt of the Waffen SS. Almost immediately, L Company found itself trapped inside Lutrebois. E Company of the 2nd Battalion tried to come to its rescue, but quickly became cut off, too. With the company commander and most platoon leaders among the casualties, Lieutenant John Davis quickly took control of the mauled unit. He helped E Company fight its way back to the 2nd Battalion, killing 40 Germans and capturing 7 in the process.[64]

The action earned the junior officer from Nebraska a Silver Star. But it did nothing to slow Pötschke's advance. Mark IVs and Panthers silenced L Company as soon as the GIs had fired their last bazooka rounds. Having captured Lutrebois, the *Kampfgruppe* pushed past the Château Losange. More American companies began to fall back from the forest. The arrival of men from Gaffey's 51st Armored Infantry did nothing to stem the tide. By mid-afternoon, the situation had turned critical, with dozens of enemy tanks heading for open terrain just east of Remoifosse, a village on the Arlon highway less than two miles from Assenois. But pilots in the 4th Armored Division's spotter planes showed exceptional daring. The light Piper Cubs came so close, a German tank crewman observed, that we "could have hit them with rocks." In frantic conversations the American airmen relayed information on the rapidly moving targets. Within minutes, B Company of the 35th Tank Battalion arrived on the scene, as did some tank destroyers.

Rolf Ehrhardt, a tank driver in Pötschke's 7th Panzerkompanie, heard an earsplitting sound when a round slammed into his turret. He hit the brakes and killed the motor. A quick inspection revealed that the 75mm cannon had been ripped off. The tank commander had suffered shrapnel wounds to his chest and burns to his face. Another comrade was wounded in the head. Spurred on by machine-gun fire, all five of the crew abandoned the now useless vehicle and stumbled back in the direction of the forest.

Fighter-bombers from Weyland's XIX Tactical Air Command joined the fray. Their bombs and rockets plowed the area, together with shells from Gaffey's 94th Armored Field Artillery. Manfred Thorn, the driver of another Mark IV tank, estimated that in less than ten minutes, eight of the 7th Panzerkompanie's tanks were destroyed. He turned his vehicle around, raced back to the edge of the woods, and sought cover behind a haystack. By dusk, the Americans had put a total of 15 German tanks and assault guns out of action and had prevented the *Kampfgruppe* from reaching the highway. Even commander Werner Pötschke was forced to abandon his tank when it, too, was badly damaged. In Russia in 1943, the SS Sturmbannführer had earned the Knight's Cross, one of the nation's highest decorations for bravery. Now, on December 30, 1944, he could be seen staggering amidst exploding shells, in desperate search of the security of another tank.[65]

Baade's troops and the men from the 51st Armored Infantry immediately went in pursuit of the decimated Waffen SS. The mopping-up resulted in fierce forest fighting. Mohnke's men proved exceedingly dangerous to all who came into contact with them. Auguste Forman was one of many civilians hiding out in the woods to escape being killed by artillery or air raids. On Saturday he made the mistake of slipping back to his home in Lutremange, most probably in search of food. He ran into some SS Panzergrenadiers, who took him for a spy and demanded to see his papers. But the young man had left them with his mother in the forest. He was shot on the spot.[66]

Patton shrugged off the danger that threatened to engulf the corridor that Saturday. He decided the time had come to risk a quick dash to Bastogne, as he personally wanted to decorate the most outstanding airborne commanders of the siege. McAuliffe was dumbstruck to see the commander of the Third Army climb out of his vehicle in the midst of the cauldron. "When Patton arrived," he recalled several decades later, "I embraced him. I dragged him to my jeep and made a tour of the town. I guess I wasn't thinking clearly anymore." At the Château Rolley, Patton rewarded both General McAuliffe and Colonel Chappuis with the Distinguished Service Cross. Steve Chappuis, commander of the 502nd Parachute Infantry in Bastogne's west, had been responsible for halting the most dangerous enemy attack on Christmas Day. A gloating Patton made a quick inspection of the blackened hulks of some of the German tanks that had come worryingly close on December 25. Then he caught a quick nap at the château and had his chauffeur gun their vehicle through the rumbling corridor again.[67]

Third Army headquarters called December 30 "a critical day." Patton characterized the enemy operations south of Bastogne that Saturday as "the biggest coordinated counterattack that troops under my command have ever experienced." The results were a mixed bag. Middleton's attack had clashed head on with a simultaneous attack by the XLVII Panzer Corps. This "lucky meeting," as Patton phrased it, had prevented the Germans from smashing into the corridor from the west. But it had cost Middleton's men dearly and had halted the first push away from the American access routes to Bastogne. Baade's infantry, Gaffey's armor, and massive firepower had kept the Volksgrenadiers and Waffen SS from cutting the corridor from the east. But the 35th Infantry Division was now left with an even more pronounced dent in its line. Also, in hurrying to its rescue, the battered 4th Armored Division had stretched itself to breaking point. And there was worse to come.[68]

4

Despite increasingly ominous skies and the loss of a dozen aircraft to flak, daring Allied pilots had continued to strike at German targets all around Bastogne on Friday and Saturday. But on Sunday, the last day of 1944, cloud cover became so impenetrable that, for the first time in a week, most flights in support of ground troops had to be cancelled. Patton remained determined, however, to hold the initiative and build momentum. He stubbornly refused to have the weather dictate his plans. Middleton's VIII Corps was under instructions to renew, in near-arctic conditions, the cumbersome attack west of the corridor even before the first glimmers of daylight on December 31.[69]

West of the Bois des Haies de Magery, the 345th Infantry fought hard to succeed where Kilburn's Combat Command A had earlier failed. Despite heavy losses sustained at Moircy and a dangerous extension of its front line, the troops from General Culin's 87th Infantry Division finally managed to wrest Remagne from Bayerlein's crack troops. The victory came at such a high price, however, that what was left of the unfortunate 345th Infantry had to be withdrawn and replaced by the reserve 347th.[70]

As Kilburn now threw his entire 11th Armored Division against the enemy in the gap east of the gloomy forest, the attrition rate there became even more worrisome. Combat Command R was rushed in from the division's reserve to form a blocking position on the left wing. Tanks skidded along the glistening ice on the secondary road from Morhet to Magerotte. Around mid-morning, the inhabitants of Magery, a hamlet near the northeastern tip of the forest, became embroiled in a vicious clash between American armor and Remer's Führer Begleit Brigade. Gérard Callay saw bullets ricochet from the façade of the vaulted stable where he had sought refuge with his mother and two sisters. An explosion blew a gaping hole in one of the walls, allowing Gérard a front-seat view of hand-to-hand combat and the death of a German wielding a Panzerfaust. As more and more Shermans pushed their way into Magery, the Callays' hiding place was set ablaze. Gérard and his family fled into the street, their arms raised, white handkerchiefs limp in their hands. An American tank crewman motioned them to make haste and hide in a small canal next to the road. The Callays scrambled to the other side, clawing their way through electric cables, cutting their arms on glass and debris. Fortunately, the canal, designed to carry water to the local mills that ground flour and sawed wood, was dry. But tanks in search of prey drove over it and caused its walls to crack. Some GIs caught sight of the frightened civilians and tossed cigarettes, chewing gum, and cans of food to them. Then, suddenly, the main canal higher up gave way, and a torrent of freezing water forced the Callays into the open again. They ran past the sawmill. There were corpses everywhere. Two young Germans stood next to a pile of wood, unarmed and ready to surrender. But the frenetic GIs paid them no attention. The Callays stumbled headlong into another barn. Inside, a fellow villager lay mortally wounded. A shell had shredded the octogenarian's leg and it was soaked in blood. By the time the battle calmed down, the old man, too, was quiet.[71]

Troops of the 55th Armored Infantry threaded their way through the Bois des Haies in an attempt to extend Combat Command R's shield. German snipers slowed their advance and eight GIs fell victim to mines. The

Americans had barely emerged from the forest's northern edge when they came under fire from Remer's elite force in the hamlet of Acul. It was the battalion's baptism of fire, and in the two-hour battle that followed, courage and confusion alternated in quick flashes. A lieutenant and deputy commander of A Company "created a panic, and almost everyone ran for his life, abandoning bazookas and boxes of machine-gun ammunition." But two sergeants, "looking absolutely cool," rounded up their squads and led them back to the front. A private earned a Silver Star when he zigzagged to the rear amid explosions and had artillery batteries lift the supporting fire that was tearing into their own positions.[72]

C Company's Joe Waddle tried to calm down as soon as Acul was in American hands. But it was not easy. The soldier from Columbia, Tennessee, had just killed for the first time. His victim had been a mere boy, about Joe's age. And, although the German had worn a helmet, the American "could not help imagining him having blonde hair." As Waddle was trying to come to terms with how, in a split second, "his animal instinct" had overruled "his religious principles" of many years, the Führer Begleit Brigade suddenly returned to take Acul back. Surprised and inexperienced, the armored infantry hurriedly stumbled back to where it had come from that afternoon. "We left everything behind in Acul," remembered Joe Waddle. "I myself came back with no more than my clothes and my rifle; others didn't even have their helmets anymore."[73]

On their first day of battle, the 55th Armored Infantry suffered 113 casualties. In the aid station, Richard Drebus considered himself one of the lucky men of his battalion. To protect himself against the onslaught of German tanks, the Wisconsin private had affixed a grenade launcher to the barrel of his M1 rifle. He had attempted to steady his nerves by doing "calculus problems" and "reciting the 23rd Psalm." Then, as he had tried to take aim, a shell fragment had torn into his cheek, leaving his head "totally numb." More rounds had exploded all around him as he had again tried to fire the grenade. Shrapnel had burrowed into his chest, back, arms, and legs. A big chunk of his heel had been lopped off. Yet somehow he had managed to crawl back to the rear. It was instantly clear to the medics that this had been Private Drebus's first and last day in combat. The way back would be long: ambulance to Neufchâteau, air evacuation to Paris, hospital train to Cherbourg, hospital ship to Southampton, another train to another hospital (this time in Wales), a series of operations, whirlpool therapy and interminable physical training, then the final trip to the United States. But Richard Drebus was happy to celebrate his twenty-first birthday somewhere on the vast Atlantic

Ocean. He knew that many of the comrades he had left behind near Bastogne would never reach that age.[74]

As Kilburn's armored division was being slowed down expertly for a second day in a row, Patton's patience began to wear thin. The outfit's command was not "what it should have been," he judged sternly, whereas the troops "fought well but stupidly and lost too many tanks." The green troops, Patton noted disapprovingly, were showing themselves "particularly inept at fighting in the woods."[75]

At Rechrival, just west of the Bois des Valets, Ivan Goldstein from Task Force Poker was amazed to be still alive at noon on Sunday. The previous day, he and his crew had been taken prisoner when their Sherman, the "Barracuda," had lost its way in an attack north of Houmont and they had stumbled into an enemy trap. Private Goldstein, the bow gunner, and Andrew Urda, the driver, had become separated from their severely injured comrades. During the interrogation on Saturday evening, the mood had turned nasty when a German officer from the Führer Begleit Brigade came to realize that Goldstein was a Jew. The two GIs had been locked up and told they would be executed at daylight. Goldstein had asked the Germans to spare the life of Urda, who was a Catholic Slovak-American, but the plea had failed to make any impression. The dawn execution on Sunday had been abandoned, however, when Kilburn's Combat Command A arrived in front of Rechrival to take over from Task Force Poker with more firepower.[76]

But the Germans were also bringing up reinforcements. Elements from the 3rd and 15th Panzergrenadier Divisions moved forward to help shield Rechrival from the Americans. Packed into a half-track, Private Harold Brandt, a 19-year-old college student from Pennsylvania, instantly felt the impact as A Company of the 63rd Armored Infantry passed Pinsamont. First, a Sherman ahead of him was hit and men could be seen "crawling out of the bottom of the tank." Then an 88mm shell exploded in the back of a nearby half-track, leaving four men dead in the twisted wreckage and four others badly maimed. Their nerves frayed, Brandt and the other newcomers panicked, turned their vehicles around, and sped back to Pinsamont. The company commander quickly sorted them out, ordering his men back without delay. "The second time down that road," Brandt recalled, "was far worse than the first time." As soon as they reached one of Rechrival's outlying barns, Brandt and his comrades jumped from the half-track and began digging foxholes. Mortar rounds, Nebelwerfer rockets, and 88mm shells plowed the fields. During brief lulls, a German loudspeaker system could be heard broadcasting "a hideous laugh," followed by a taunting "MEEEDIIC,

MEEEDIIC!" Harold Brandt had nurtured the superstition that if he could survive 1944, he would survive the war. The Pennsylvanian checked the watch his parents had given him for his high-school graduation. It had been smashed, leaving him with no way to count down the year's final agonizing hours.[77]

In the German lines, civilians in Flamierge, many of them refugees from Mande-Saint-Étienne, were praying for their liberation. Identity papers were brusquely being checked. Men had been arrested and ordered to bury the German dead. Most villagers were suffering from dysentery. On Sunday morning, General Kilburn had boasted to the airborne troops in Bastogne that his tanks would take Mande-Saint-Étienne that same day. In order to get there, however, they had to capture Chenogne first. And Remer's shock troops, reinforced by soldiers of the 3rd Panzergrenadier Division, kept throwing the men from Combat Command B back, just as they had done the previous day.[78]

In B Company of the 21st Armored Infantry, Sergeant John Fague saw the attitude of his men harden with each passing hour. As they neared the ridge for yet another jump-off to Chenogne, they passed casualties from the 9th Armored Division. The dead sat slumped in old foxholes, their frozen features covered with ice. Before Fague's platoon even had time to cross the ridge, an enemy machine gun opened up, leaving five boys they all knew well "kicking and writhing in the snow." Then, suddenly, Germans who had been putting up stubborn resistance from a house inside Chenogne ran out of ammunition and, from one moment to the next, decided to surrender with their hands in the air. As if in a daze, Sergeant Fague watched as one of his comrades from Missouri shot one of them. A fellow sergeant from Philadelphia followed suit, killing two others "with his .45 pistol." It was not just Patton's patience that was wearing thin on the last day of 1944.[79]

While lambasting the 11th Armored Division for its slowness southwest of the vital Belgian town, a hard-driving Patton that same Sunday had Millikin's III Corps go on the offensive east of the Arlon highway. The immediate goal was to keep an aggressive enemy off balance and to broaden the corridor. The ultimate objective was to advance towards Saint-Vith in a northeasterly direction, in order to add significant momentum to the Third Army's push into the salient from the launching pad that was Bastogne.

At first, the 4th Armored Division had been considered for the new operation. With no more than 42 tanks left, however, and with its armored infantry depleted, Gaffey had advised against it. Instead, on December 29,

General Robert Grow's 6th Armored Division had been ordered to commence the trip to Bastogne from Sarreguemines in northeastern France. Grow and his outfit came close to enjoying the same confidence that Patton had in the 4th Armored Division. Counting close to 12,000 men and a full complement of around 150 tanks and 130 tank destroyers and assault guns, the Super Sixth made an impression on all who watched its columns rumble past. Gaffey's battered troops were all too happy to make way for them and get some rest as a reserve force. "I have," wrote Private Charles Wilson to his wife Loretta in Colorado, "not had a good bath since December 10th. I have not shaved for the last month. I doubt that you would recognize me now by any combination of your five senses."[80]

But by dawn on Sunday, the Super Sixth was in a precarious situation. On paper, Millikin's offensive looked impressive, as three divisions were slated to jump off and push ahead abreast of each other. In reality, however, the massive blow from the XXXIX Panzer Corps the previous day had left the 35th Infantry Division licking its wounds. The objective of Baade's infantry on Sunday was to be the less ambitious one of regaining lost ground in the Harlange pocket. That meant that they were going to be unable to provide support for Grow's armor. At the same time, so long as there was a sizeable pocket between Baade's men and the 26th Infantry Division on their right, the latter division could take part in the offensive only disjointedly. There was more bad news. The previous day and night, several of the 6th Armored Division's own convoys had run into trouble. First they had been delayed by blizzards. Then they had become stuck among vehicles from the 11th Armored Division on the Neufchâteau highway. It was, Grow grumbled, "the worst traffic jam I ever saw."[81]

For Grow, the bottom line on the morning of December 31 was that the planned three-division offensive had now been whittled down to an attack using just one of his own three combat commands. During the night, Combat Command A had settled down behind paratroop lines in Bastogne's southeastern sector. The airborne cooks had been kind enough to fix the men a pancake breakfast. It was the last thing that went well for Grow's men that Sunday.[82]

They were still readying themselves for an attack in the direction of Neffe when artillery from Kokott's men and from forces in the pocket in the 35th Division's sector zeroed in on the assembly area. The 44th Armored Infantry Battalion was hit particularly hard. The unit descended into chaos in no time. An explosion blew up a water-supply truck, peppering the area with pierced jerry-cans. Another shell struck down the commander of C Company before he even had time to bellow instructions. In blast after blast, shrapnel claimed up to 40 casualties. The bloodied infantry hastily reorganized. Shortly after noon, they went on the attack with the support of the 69th Tank Battalion. As they approached Neffe, snow squalls slowed them down and Volksgrenadiers fought them to a halt. The GIs called in air support, but the fighter-bombers did not find their way through the menacing clouds. Lacking protection on both flanks, Grow's men now stuck out like a sore thumb. The order came for the troops to dig in and for the artillery to provide them with protection throughout the frigid night.[83]

"This has been a very long day for me," Patton confided to his diary late on December 31. West and east of the Bastogne corridor, his attempts at Blitzkrieg had now failed. The battle, Patton admitted in a letter to his wife, Beatrice, had now become "a slugging match." The Third Army commander reluctantly accepted that, for the time being, grinding down the enemy was to be more important than capturing terrain. The past two days had certainly been a success in that regard, as the Germans were thought to have suffered no fewer than 1,500 casualties.

But the war of attrition came at a high price for the Americans, too. So badly mauled was General Culin's 345th Infantry southwest of Bastogne that the regiment had to be pulled out of the line. In the same sector, the 11th Armored Division had lost some 350 men, most of them wounded. On the other side of the corridor, battle losses for the 35th Infantry Division during the last two days of 1944 came close to 600. Most of these had been incurred in the fighting for Lutrebois, a village with a peacetime population of no more than 150.[84]

Meanwhile, Kokott's Volksgrenadiers continued to chip away at the American defenses all around Bastogne's perimeter. On New Year's Eve, several companies with the strong support of artillery actually managed to get a foothold in Champs again. It took a combat team of paratroopers and tanks from the 10th Armored Division two hours to dislodge them. Such attacks, as well as the ceaseless patrolling and the constant threat of snipers and mortar and machine-gun fire, slowly made the casualties add up. During the last two days of 1944, Bastogne's airborne defenders suffered another 17 killed, 121 wounded, and 19 captured or missing. One of the dead was a veteran and a good friend of Ed Pieniak. Sergeant Pieniak, an exceptionally strong and tall man, was a hardened old-timer himself. But the sight of his lifeless comrade was one blow too many and it caused him to break down. "I remember blubbering and sobbing," the sergeant admitted unashamedly, "with tears flooding my eyes and snot flying out of my nose, as I stood over his body in the midst of a blizzard."[85]

Higher echelons worried just as much about the toll the weather was taking. Non-battle casualties were rising fast. Trench foot, in particular, had become endemic. Ed O'Brien, a medic in the regimental aid station of the 501st Parachute Infantry, gladly made use of the services of a platoon medic who had been sent to him to recover from battle fatigue. The man was told to heat large tubs of water, wash the paratroopers' feet, dry them thoroughly, and massage the blackened extremities vigorously. "The treatment," O'Brien was happy to note, "returned excellent results and a man was saved from a possible psychiatric ward."[86]

As the veterans of the siege were being patched up, still more reinforcements filtered in. On Saturday afternoon, close to 500 new men arrived for the 327th Glider Infantry. Before the year was out, more than 30 gunners had replaced casualties in the 969th Field Artillery, the all-black battalion that had kept up support for the airborne troops while also letting loose on the enemy in front of the 11th Armored Division. Paratrooper Gerald Johnston jumped from a truck and asked where he could find his old company in the sector of the 502nd Parachute Infantry. He had been severely wounded during the first hours of the campaign in Holland in September and had still been convalescing when the division hurriedly pulled out of Mourmelon on December 18. Private Johnston gathered his gear and headed for the company's foxholes west of Bastogne. He was assigned a dugout near a hedge. "We dragged the German body away, and there I was, back in the war again."[87]

There was no more patching up or reinforcing the 9th Armored Division's Combat Command R. It had been mauled during the desperate delaying actions east of Bastogne, and the siege had further cut its ranks down to skeleton size. Its 2nd Tank Battalion had lost 200 men and most of its Shermans. In ten days of fighting, nearly 70 percent of its 52nd Armored Infantry Battalion had ended up casualties. As New Year loomed, trucks lined up and took away what remained of the battered combat command.[88]

There was much commotion in the cellars of the Institute of Notre Dame that same day, when trucks pulled up and rumors started circulating about the imminent departure of the boarding-school girls. Many were crestfallen when it was announced that there were no more than two vehicles, and that the American drivers would accept only those girls who lived in and around Neufchâteau. Charlotte Foret's parents lived in Fauvillers, about as far away from Bastogne as Neufchâteau, but on the side of the Arlon highway. Together with many other saddened pupils, she watched some 30 fortunate girls pack their bags and climb onto the trucks. Charlotte had barely settled down for another long night in Bastogne than two GIs arrived to see her. Richard Bowman and Lawrence Bennett, both medics with the 704th Tank Destroyer Battalion, had their billet with the Forets in Fauvillers. The despairing parents had told the GIs that their daughter was trapped in Bastogne and that she was probably no longer alive. At dusk on New Year's Eve, the two Americans had downed a few cocktails of ethyl alcohol and lemon juice and slipped away without their commander's permission. They had made the dangerous trip along the Arlon highway in a jeep with painted red crosses named "Vitamin B." Nuns and teachers were reluctant to let the soldiers take off with the girl, but they finally relented when the GIs produced a hand-written note from the girl's father. An elated Charlotte asked if she could take a friend who was also from Fauvillers. There was, the GIs beamed, "plenty of room."[89]

As traffic and troops multiplied in the Bastogne corridor, American Civil Affairs teams arrived to provide assistance to the Belgians who had been left to fend for themselves in the heat of battle. In the château in Assenois, Gaffey's tank crews had struck Madame de Coune as surly and rough-hewn. On Wednesday they had taken over the premises from cellar to attic. To make more room, they had thrown the furniture out of the windows. Seeing that Madame de Coune and her children were running high fevers, and fearing an epidemic, Civil Affairs took a more caring attitude. On Sunday, a truck arrived to take them to safety further south. All along the corridor, army ambulances were now picking up civilian patients, from casualties with gangrened limbs to people in a diabetic coma. More evacuations followed, often allowing only a handful of farmers to remain behind to take care of the precious surviving cattle. In bombed-out Sainlez, farmers worked hand in hand with GIs to clean up corpses and carcasses that dogs were already tearing apart. Charred cattle lay strewn across the roads. Dead Germans, frozen solid, had been piled up like cordwood against a wall near the church. Amidst the stench of white phosphorus, bulldozers scraped away ice and earth to form mass graves.[90]

That Sunday evening, Madame Greindl was trying desperately to make the effects of the war disappear. To her extreme horror, she had just been invited to pay a visit to the airborne commanders who were enjoying a New Year's Eve dinner in her living room. For much of the battle, she had lived in the damp cellar of her château in Isle-la-Hesse, without access to water or fresh clothes. Her hair was a tangled mess, wrapped in a turban of beige linen. As she walked into the living room, Maxwell Taylor and Tony

McAuliffe introduced themselves to the Belgian woman. The baroness was struck by how young Taylor looked and by McAuliffe's friendly smile. The generals offered her a glass of champagne and some coffee. They chatted for about a quarter of an hour, Taylor trying his best to say some words in French. "I thank heaven," Madame Greindl thought to herself as she left the room, "for not having been near a mirror this evening."[91]

The men in the foxholes and dugouts of Bastogne's perimeter could not have cared less about appearances that night. Their commanders knew well enough what it was they were most interested in. A quiet cheer went up when news spread that hard liquor from the town's VIII Corps stocks would be distributed to celebrate the approaching New Year. Colonel Sink personally made the rounds of his airborne regiment to hand out bottles from his jeep. At midnight, a few bells could be heard heralding the dawn of 1945. After two weeks of ceaseless fighting, those who held Bastogne were in need of a stiff drink. A few hours later, more than 50 bombers from *Lehrgeschwader* 1 would again pound Bastogne, leaving fires burning everywhere.[92]

CHAPTER 8

NEW YEAR'S WOES

On New Year's Day, Patton refused to be cowed. At one minute after midnight, to mark the arrival of 1945, the massed artillery of his colossal Third Army spewed a fiery barrage at the enemy for 20 uninterrupted minutes, inflicting heavy casualties. In his General Orders for January 1, the three-star general acknowledged that the Germans had shown themselves to be "a cunning and ruthless enemy." But he told his troops that together they would make certain to have "our dead comrades avenged." Patton put on a particularly brave face during a press conference in Luxembourg City later that Monday. The famous commander emphasized that in the Ardennes, Bastogne had proved to be "just as important as the Battle of Gettysburg was to the Civil War." His Third Army, he assured the gathering, was now maneuvering to "hit this son-of-a-bitch – pardon me – in the flank." "We'll find him," Patton snarled to the delight of the reporters, "and kick his teeth in."[1]

Looking at the big picture, there was good reason for Patton to be brash and brazen. The bulk of his Third Army was now concentrated on the Bastogne corridor. Overall combat power was in good shape, with close to 350,000 men at his disposal and almost 2.8 million gallons of gasoline in forward depots. Even more encouraging was the news that Montgomery had at last indicated that in the next few days his troops would begin to relieve the pressure in the south by having the First Army attack towards Houffalize.[2]

At the same time, however, enemy pressure on the Western Front refused to abate. In the opening hours of the New Year, German aircraft in Operation Bodenplatte attacked 16 airfields in Belgium, Holland, and France in a surprise attempt to cripple Allied airpower. The day before, the enemy had launched Operation Nordwind, an all-out offensive against Allied troops in Alsace whose lines had become stretched when Third Army forces were siphoned off to the Ardennes. Hitler's counteroffensive in Belgium had created a serious Allied manpower crisis in the European theater. It was now feared that the situation in Alsace might force some of Patton's troops to be diverted to the French trouble area. Such an outcome, Hitler reasoned, might enable a renewed push to the Meuse River. But for that to happen, the Führer emphasized, "Above all, we must have Bastogne!" In the early hours of 1945, two more Waffen SS divisions of Dietrich's Sixth Panzer Army began heading south to Bastogne. There would be no quick end to the battle of attrition for what Patton had called Belgium's Gettysburg.[3]

1

West of the Bastogne corridor and on the 11th Armored Division's left, the 347th Infantry struggled to make headway on New Year's Day. Part of Culin's 87th Infantry Division, the fresh regiment had arrived to replace the mauled 345th and continue the push towards the road that ran west from Bastogne to Saint-Hubert. The snow was a foot deep in places, and more flakes were swirling down from menacing skies, whipped up into drifts by a stinging wind. Bayerlein's Panzer Lehr used its vast experience to slow down the American infantry and protect the vital road for as long as possible. Sent into combat without overshoes or overcoats, Culin's men dug in for the night, finding it "too cold to sleep." The following day, the GIs rose from their foxholes shivering and red-eyed. It took the 3rd Battalion until dark to capture Bonnerue, cutting one of the German lifelines to the west at great cost to Americans and Belgians alike. "It was like the apocalypse," one villager observed. "There were no more trees left, no more buildings, no more homes."[4]

The 11th Armored Division was being slowed down even more. Around noon on Monday, January 1, Remer's Führer Begleit Brigade lashed out at Combat Command A near Rechrival. The battle did not let up for several hours, leaving troops on both sides exhausted and furious. American soldiers lined Belgians up against walls, searched rooms, smashed furniture, and looted wine. They "roughed up" German prisoners, one Belgian noted, and "stripped them of their clothing until they were almost naked." Villagers watched a Sherman get hit and three of its crew hide in a farmhouse. The Germans chased after them, captured the GIs, and executed them on the spot. When Middleton checked on the division's commander later that day, he found Kilburn beginning to crack. "He was very nervous," said Middleton, "and kept most of those around him nervous."[5]

Meanwhile, all eyes were on Kilburn's Combat Command B on the division's right. Once again tanks and infantry jumped from the brow of the hill in front of Chenogne to capture the key village. Again the attack threatened to get stalled, as Denkert's Panzergrenadiers tore into the American ranks. Allen Cramer of the 21st Armored Infantry hurled himself over the side of his half-track. He stumbled towards a shallow depression in the earth to seek cover. Private Robert Yost beat him to it. Cramer ran a few more yards, flopped down, and burrowed into the snow. As he stole a glance at Yost, he saw a shell land right on top of him. "A huge explosion and smoke and debris rose from the site," recalled Cramer, "and there was no human being left where Yost had been a moment before."[6]

But tank crews and infantrymen pushed on, helped by massive amounts of firepower paving the way. The 575th Anti-Aircraft Artillery Battalion moved in close, emptying its heavy-barreled quad .50 Browning machine guns, the dreaded "meat choppers," straight into Denkert's positions. Fighter-bombers, very active again on Monday, swooped down on anything that moved. Artillery from three divisions and the airborne force inside Bastogne fired 6,000 rounds on targets in and around Chenogne. B Company's infantrymen were close to the village when a machine gun in a house near the road started rattling away. Sergeant Fague's ears were still ringing with the awful cries of "Medic! Medic!" that had rolled down the hill with him. Now he watched the German machine gun "knocking out boys all along the road." Shermans blew gaping holes in the big stone house, and some of Fague's comrades crept forward to hurl grenades into the openings. A single burst from the heavy enemy machine gun hit Lieutenant Wilbur Jones in the chest and Private Jim Cust in the forehead, killing both men instantly.[7]

The farmhouse was ablaze. In its spacious cellar, the Germans had set up an aid station, and muffled cries rose from those trapped inside. Machine gunners, medics, and patients were all trying to get out. But GIs were waiting for them with their guns ready. They mowed down the Germans, one after another. There was, confessed Fague, "no mercy in our hearts." A ring of bodies had already formed around the doorway when the GIs realized there were civilians inside, too. Crazed with fear, the Belgians burst from the burning building. The GIs held their fire and tried to calm them down. But the villagers dragged their children along and headed for the woods, ignoring warnings from the soldiers that they would not be safe there from the American artillery.[8]

It was not uncommon for soldiers who tried to surrender in the heat of battle to be shot. But John Fague claimed to have witnessed something even more sinister: the killing of perhaps as many as 60 German prisoners later in the afternoon, when the battle had been decided and Chenogne was in American hands. "After the killing and confusion of that morning," the sergeant admitted, "the idea of killing some more Krauts didn't particularly bother me." "My chief worry," he noted, "was that Germans hiding in the woods would see this massacre and we would receive similar treatment if we were captured." GIs later claimed that high-ranking officers in Combat Command B had spread word that matters would be made easier if no prisoners were taken. A few days after the battle, news of serious irregularities at Chenogne had climbed all the way to the top chain of command in the Third Army. Commenting on the poor performance of the 11th Armored Division at the start of the year, an annoyed Patton noted in his diary: "There were also some unfortunate incidents in the shooting of prisoners (I hope we can conceal this)."[9]

There was not much time that Monday to reflect on what war was doing to men's minds and morals. More than 120 GIs had become casualties in the battle for Chenogne. All but one of the village's 32 buildings had been razed to the ground, and 23 civilians had lost their lives. More than 300 head of cattle lay strewn amidst the rubble. The fight for Chenogne had lasted too long to allow any of the momentum to dissipate now. Supported by no fewer than 13 artillery battalions, Combat Command B pushed north and fought its way through the Bois des Valets. Then the men dug in for the night. They would try to get some rest before the capture of the next village on the map.[10]

For Combat Command B on Tuesday, January 2, that village was Mande-Saint-Étienne. The small farming community lay just north of the western highway to Marche, where the airborne troops had arrived in their trucks two weeks earlier. Some 3,800 rounds of artillery were brought down on the tiny objective. As they awaited the signal for yet another attack, Sergeant Fague and Paul Gentile warmed their hands around a tank's exhaust pipe. They did not hear the mortar round until it exploded. When Fague rolled Gentile's body over, he found that "blood was spurting from a gaping wound in his chest." He helped medics lift his comrade onto the hood of a jeep, crawled on top of Gentile to keep him from rolling off, and bounced to the rear over the frozen soil. "From the gray color of Paul's face, I knew it was all over for Paul," Sergeant Fague said. "But I couldn't give up."[11]

None of Fague's comrades could give up, as Denkert's Panzergrenadiers made them fight for each of Mande's streets and cellars until darkness fell. Shortly before midnight, the Panzergrenadiers returned. They shelled

Mande, just as the famished GIs were heating C rations over their Coleman stoves. "A picture of Christ and His Disciples at the Last Supper," Fague observed as he hugged a farm floor, "danced on the wall." The end of the preparatory shelling heralded the imminent arrival of enemy troops. John Fague grabbed his carbine and stormed out of the house. "A tanker yelled from the turret that he needed a bow gunner." Although he had never seen the inside of a tank, Fague volunteered. He squeezed himself into the steel monster with his carbine, cartridge belt, canteen, and entrenching tools. He had just dropped down behind the machine gun when a deafening explosion rocked the tank. The commander yelled that they had been hit and had to get out before the tank caught fire. By the time Sergeant Fague had wriggled to safety, the force of the German attack was petering out. The Americans hung on to Mande that night. But fear of another counterattack prevented them from catching the sleep they so badly craved.[12]

That Tuesday night, Kilburn's men were at last firmly in control of Chenogne. And the capture of Mande-Saint-Étienne meant that they had now also leaped across the key Bastogne highway to Marche. But the advance of six miles in four days had come at a very steep cost: more than 600 casualties, as well as the loss of 42 Sherman tanks and 12 light tanks. Nowhere was the human cost felt more starkly than in the newly erected aid stations of the division's 81st Medical Battalion. "I can still smell," said one of the staff a quarter century later, "the ether, the bitter coffee, cigarette smoke, and the persistent stench of putrefying flesh from the small heap of amputated arms and legs that had been tossed carelessly into a corner." "No one," he noted, "had the time or opportunity to dispose of the pitiful mound." When General Kilburn visited the aid station at Jodenville and asked head doctor Tony Mazzacano if there was anything he needed, the captain replied: "Some good whiskey for the men in Combat Command B." Shortly after, a visibly shaken Kilburn had 17 cases of bourbon delivered to the hospital.[13]

Of the GIs who were reported missing, some had been taken prisoner after less than a week on Europe's battlefields. In her château in Roumont, several miles northwest of Bastogne, Marie du Bus de Warnaffe had seen General von Lüttwitz take charge of operations against the crossroads town on Christmas Eve. Now, at the start of 1945, she watched close to a hundred American prisoners shuffle towards her home. "I am going to do you a favor," a German officer whispered maliciously, "and let you feed these men." All of the château's pantries had long since been picked clean. But determined to do something for the Allies, the viscountess ordered kitchen staff to boil water, add linden blossom, and scoop in some of the little sugar that was left. Then she and the servants rushed outside, lined up, and began pouring herbal tea into the canteens of the bedraggled Americans.[14]

By that time, Ivan Goldstein and Andrew Urda, the captured soldiers from Combat Command B's "Barracuda" who had escaped execution on December 31, had already walked all the way to Prüm in Germany. There, Private Goldstein was put to work on a railroad that Allied bombers had destroyed. American aircraft returned to complete the job in broad daylight. They injured Ivan Goldstein and killed 12 POWs working at his side.[15]

On the afternoon of Tuesday, January 2, Ed O'Brien of the 501st Parachute Infantry was heading south in an ambulance on the Neufchâteau highway. He was holding a unit of plasma over his head, as he accompanied one of the worst stretcher cases he had encountered thus far in Bastogne. A shell explosion had severed one of the officer's legs about eight inches above the knee, and the other leg a few inches below the knee. The driver increased his speed as the officer's ashen face told them he needed to get expert treatment soon. The medics dropped their critical patient off at a field hospital and then hurried back to Bastogne. They brought their vehicle to a screeching halt when they noticed large columns of fresh troops on the highway wearing the distinctive helmet of the paratrooper. Ed O'Brien was most surprised to learn that they belonged to another American airborne division. The men of the 17th Airborne Division were on their way to take over from an 11th Armored Division that the Germans at Bastogne had torn to shreds in just four days.[16]

2

If progress for the Americans west of the Bastogne corridor was slow and costly, on the other side of it the men of the 35th Infantry Division were getting absolutely nowhere in the first two days of 1945. Their push to the north had come to a halt as a result of Saturday's fierce counterattack by the XXXIX Panzer Corps. Although General Baade's troops had managed to drive the enemy away from the crucial Arlon highway, a salient had formed in their ranks that would have to be erased if they were to regain the offensive. But the Germans, well aware of how important this pocket of resistance had become, now dug in with grim determination, switching to what one of Baade's divisional reports described as a "stonewall type of opposition." Here too, blizzard-like conditions were making things more miserable for the soldiers, who lacked appropriate winter clothing. "Heavy snow and bitter cold," the 35th Division staff admitted, "took its toll of men through exposure and frostbite."[17]

Baade's infantry could ill afford to lose men to trench foot, as every soldier was needed in the desperate attempt to dislodge the enemy from the villages and forests of what became known as the Harlange pocket. Stumbling through deep snow and dense woods, the 137th Infantry tried to take Villers-la-Bonne-Eau, a hamlet of no more than 17 homes and 65 inhabitants. But the survivors of the 5th Fallschirmjäger Division were now fighting side by side with the men of the XXXIX Panzer Corps. And their commander's invaluable experience in defensive warfare again paid off, as the paratroopers halted the GIs with fierce fire from machine guns, mortars, and artillery. From their solid dugouts, Heilmann's men launched counterattack after counterattack, blocking progress with, in the words of a regimental after-action report, "the toughest opposition it had yet met in its combat experience." Just to the east, at the village of Harlange, the 320th Infantry repeatedly flung itself against the Fallschirmjäger on January 1 and 2. Despite the support of some 2,000 rounds of artillery each day, the regiment made no more gains than the 137th.[18]

The 134th Infantry's battle for Lutrebois was even more vicious. The small village was where the V-shaped Harlange salient came closest to the Arlon highway. On New Year's Eve, the 2nd Battalion had attacked eastward down a slope, in an attempt to capture the village from the Waffen SS. From a wooded crest on the other side of the valley, troops of the "Leibstandarte Adolf Hitler" had engaged in mass carnage, causing the battalion to take 90 casualties in a matter of minutes. Even in retreat, there had been displays of courage. Joseph Mack, a lieutenant from Atkinson, Nebraska, had stayed calm enough to have his anti-tank platoon kill 12 Germans and disperse an entire enemy column. The junior officer had then personally helped four wounded GIs make it back to the rear. Later in the day, Mack had been killed trying to rescue a trapped squad.[19]

Inspired and infuriated by the fate of men like Joseph Mack, on New Year's Day the 134th again rose from its foxholes for an attack across the bloody valley. Mohnke's 1st SS Panzer Division was now pulling back, although some elements lingered to cover the rear. In Lutrebois, a Waffen SS squad burst into the house of Ernest Zévenne. Without making clear what it was they wanted, the Germans told the 35-year-old and his friend, Marcel Colson, to step outside. As they were being marched to a nearby pasture, Ernest glimpsed the SS officer readying his rifle. The Belgian bolted as he heard the Mauser shot that killed his friend. Neighbors then risked their lives hiding the young man until the last of the Waffen SS had disappeared from Lutrebois. It was the Volksgrenadiers of the 167th Division who relieved the SS troopers, and it was this division that the 134th Infantry came up against on Monday. Although General Höcker's men were young and raw compared with Mohnke's seasoned troops, they, too, denied Baade's infantry access to Lutrebois. When, late in the afternoon, E and G Companies of the 2nd Battalion finally reached the woods east of the valley, a swift counterattack by the Volksgrenadiers instantly cut them off.[20]

Although the remnants of both companies would manage to filter back to their lines only the following morning, later that Tuesday the 3rd Battalion made some headway at last when K Company reached the outskirts of Lutrebois. But fire from a heavy machine gun, hidden away in a nearby farmhouse, made it impossible for the men to continue the advance. Sergeant David Cunningham grabbed a couple of phosphorus grenades. He slipped in behind the building, climbed onto the roof, and dropped his incendiaries down the chimney. The GI from Virginia was later awarded a Silver Star for the courageous action that enabled his company and the entire battalion to move forward and capture Lutrebois, a rare American victory in the Harlange pocket at the start of the year.[21]

More even than individual courage, it was industrial-scale shelling that allowed Baade's men to inch forward. To help the 134th Infantry cross the valley and seize Lutrebois, Millikin's III Corps coordinated colossal barrages. The 161st Field Artillery was just one of many battalions that took part in these. On the first day of 1945, it alone expended 2,692 rounds of ammunition. Harassment and interdiction fire continued uninterruptedly throughout the night. The following day, the battalion sent another 2,344 rounds over at the Volksgrenadiers. Forward artillery observers of the 161st crawled so close to the German lines that three of them were killed when they brought shells down on themselves. There were countless casualties among Höcker's men, and captured Volksgrenadiers readily confessed to American interrogation teams that the barrages were "worse than anything they have ever encountered." A Belgian woman on a farm just north of Lutrebois eyed one of the German POWs. The Volksgrenadier had an injured foot and appeared no older than 16. "But he is just a child!" she exclaimed to one of the American infantrymen. "Yes, ma'm," the GI replied laconically, "but he is a child that kills."[22]

The war for Bastogne cared nothing for the age of its victims. Nor did it distinguish between soldiers and civilians. German artillery in the Harlange pocket was strong, too. It retaliated with fierce barrages of its own, made even more intimidating by the hellish sound of Nebelwerfer rocket launchers. On January 2, Victorien Lefebvre was making his way back from Bastogne to Remoifosse, a village on the Arlon highway just northwest of Lutrebois. His sister had asked him to collect some urgently needed clothing and fresh linen from her home in Bastogne for her newborn baby. From a distance, Victorien suddenly sensed that something awful had happened while he was away. They had all been hiding in a stable of reinforced concrete in Remoifosse. But now he could see his brother-in-law and his sister, the baby in her arms, stumbling towards him through drifts of snow. A German shell had just smashed into their shelter. It had pulverized even the ceiling's steel girders. Six adults and children inside were dead, among them their father and their sister Juliette. Several others had sustained ghastly wounds, and an American ambulance had already arrived to take them away.[23]

The offensive against the Harlange pocket during the first two days of 1945 cost the 35th Infantry Division 260 casualties in return for gains that could be measured in yards. The Germans remained in control of the pocket, but at a price that was even higher: Heilmann's outfit and the Waffen SS lost 360 men. In just three days of battle east of the corridor, casualties in the 167th Volksgrenadier Division exceeded 530. As the Germans braced them-selves for more carnage in the Harlange pocket, they were impatient to get rid of the civilian population. Some 200 Belgians had lived in Lutremange in peacetime. Most of them had gone into hiding in the snow-covered forests that ran northward to Lutrebois. The Germans swept the woods and rounded them up. One group was told to make its way to Villers-la-Bonne-Eau with the help of no more than a pencil sketch vaguely outlining the location of minefields. The others were given escorts and taken eastward to Luxembourg in several groups. The marches were so grueling that villagers searched the pockets of dead soldiers for food, and drank from streams that stank of white phosphorus.[24]

The Harlange pocket was giving Millikin's III Corps much to worry about. To the east, it had created a solid wedge between Baade's men and the 26th Infantry Division. General Paul's foot soldiers had been having a very rough time from the moment they had jumped off with Patton's troops, before dawn on December 22. At the end of the year, Sergeant Bruce Egger from G Company had sensed that the worst was still to come. "I am afraid this war is far from being over," he had written to his parents in Idaho on December 27. "It's going to be a long tough grind and I know I'll need your prayers to see it through." Now, at the start of 1945, General Paul's troops were desperately trying to reach Wiltz, with an eye to severing the main road that kept feeding the German build-up east of Bastogne. But the fiery German defense facing them was made worse by the constant need to keep an eye on the dangerous thorn pointed at their left flank from Harlange. Sergeant Egger's ominous prediction was borne out all too soon. On New Year's Day, the 26th Infantry Division made no significant progress whatsoever. The following day, even with the help of the reserve regiment, the advance amounted to less than a mile.[25]

To the north, the predicament of the 35th Infantry Division left the 6th Armored Division even more in the lurch. Grow's troops were now completely on their own as they pushed away from Bastogne's eastern gates. Their immediate objective was to sever the various secondary roads that fed into the Harlange pocket from the north. At dawn on January 1, Major Burgess and his driver were under arrest and being held at gunpoint in Bastogne. They had been found hiding in the ruins of a building after a German bombardment. The officer finally managed to convince the paratroopers that he was indeed an American, and in fact the intelligence officer of Grow's Combat Command A. At airborne headquarters Burgess explained that his men had gone on the attack the previous day without adequate maps. He persuaded headquarters to part with some of the valuable aerial photos of Bastogne's eastern sector, so that the tank crews would be better prepared next time.[26]

The 44th Armored Infantry bore the brunt of Combat Command A's battle on January 1, as the battalion attacked due east towards Neffe and Wardin. The bitter cold caused rifles to malfunction, making it necessary for the men "to use hand grenades to knock rods loose and piss on them." White camouflage capes were rare and reserved for patrols only. Hurried attempts to daub the tanks white failed "because the paint would not stick to frozen surfaces." Kokott's Volksgrenadiers, expertly camouflaged and dug in deep, resisted ferociously, despite massive and incessant pounding from division and corps batteries. Although American reports stated that many of the German guns were "horse drawn," they spoke of "extremely heavy enemy fire" that was proving "responsible for a large number of casualties."[27]

In the early morning of January 2, more pressure was heaped upon the 44th Armored Infantry when a battalion of the 167th Volksgrenadier Division slipped in from the pocket to the south and struck at Wardin. It took the combined efforts of nine artillery battalions to beat them off. Grow now decided to send in Combat Command R. The 15th Tank and 9th Armored Infantry Battalions were soon making their way through the lines of the 44th. But heavy mortar fire struck A Company's assembly area, throwing the 9th Armored Infantry into disarray before they even had a chance to launch their attack against the woods surrounding Wardin. More confusion followed when B Company made contact with soldiers from Baade's 134th Infantry and mistook them for Germans in American uniform. By the time the firefight subsided, several of Baade's men had been killed or wounded.

Meanwhile, the 15th Tank Battalion tried to take Wardin without infantry support. The tiny village had turned into a graveyard for McAuliffe's paratroopers on December 19. It was no different for Grow's tank crews on January 2. Seven Shermans were lost in Wardin's streets. The Americans got as far as the church and were then repulsed. It was the signal for the Volksgrenadiers to storm out of the woods and hurl back the infantry, too. "The Germans," one report said, "attacked screaming across the draw." When it was all over, 104 men of the 9th Armored Infantry were missing in action, either dead or captured.[28]

The misfortunes of Combat Command A were being matched on its left, where Combat Command B had at last arrived to join the attack. At first, the 68th Tank and 50th Armored Infantry Battalions made good progress in a northeasterly direction, taking Bizory from Kokott's Volksgrenadiers with relative ease. But things quickly went awry when Grow's troops hit the main line of resistance at Arloncourt, around noon on January 1. A lightning German counterattack was stemmed only with the help of a field artillery battalion firing 500 rounds in just 20 minutes. Shortly after midnight, the Luftwaffe suddenly swooped down on Combat Command B's sector. The GIs had scarcely recovered from the surprise night attack when they were hit by advance elements of yet another new force. Tolsdorff's 340th Volksgrenadier Division had been rushed in to help put pressure on Bastogne from the northeast. Although the outfit had been much weakened in the battle for Aachen, more than 7,000 additional German troops were now arriving in the 6th Armored Division's area. It took the massed fire of nine field artillery battalions to bring Tolsdorff's spearheads to a halt in the dead of night.[29]

At dawn on January 2, Captain Winters' battalion of the 506th Parachute Infantry was called on to clear Kokott's Volksgrenadiers from the Bois Jacques. This dense wood was located north of Bizory and on the left flank of Grow's Combat Command B. As the skirmish lines pushed through the heavy snow that had piled up in the brush, men of E Company were startled to see an unsuspecting German soldier galloping on horseback down a logging road. By the time the Volksgrenadier caught sight of the Americans it was too late. A corporal from Ohio put three bullets in the back of the gray-clad rider as he tried to make his escape. The forest, one paratrooper noted, was "like something out of *The Legend of Sleepy Hollow*." The gloomy spot at the start of the year claimed the lives of almost a hundred men from the 101st Airborne. One of them was John Julian. He had been shot through the throat during a patrol. Babe Heffron had repeatedly tried to reach the body of his good friend, but each time the Germans had stopped him cold with bursts from a machine gun. Now, with the enemy pushed back and Julian's body at last retrieved, all that was left for Heffron to do was honor the pact they had concluded at jump school. The Philadelphian dutifully collected Julian's class ring, wallet, and wristwatch. He vowed to see to it that they safely reached his family.[30]

As Captain Winters' paratroopers pushed out the shield to its left, Combat Command B renewed its attack against Arloncourt with two tank battalions and a battalion of armored infantry. B Company of the 68th Tank Battalion spearheaded the attack. The enemy guns were camouflaged so well that the tank crews only noticed them in the snow when they opened fire from up close. In a matter of minutes, smoke was seen billowing from eight Shermans. "It was a massacre," observed Private Gerard Rossignol. "Some of the tankers were half way out of the tanks when they were machine-gunned before they were able to escape." Rossignol's tank was one of only a few that remained unscathed. His crew tried to ford a stream, but their vehicle got bogged down. As the icy water rose to Rossignol's navel, a German assault gun zeroed in on the trapped tank. The shell hit the Sherman's front center, ripped open the armor, and exploded inside. The searing heat made water and transmission oil hiss and evaporate. Rossignol felt a wrenching pain in his jaw and legs. The soldier from Maine groped his way to the hatch in the dense smoke, and his comrades outside rushed to his aid. They gave him a morphine shot and lifted him onto the deck of B Company's last remaining tank. That Sherman had not traveled more than five feet when a shell smashed into its turret, instantly killing everyone inside. Those on the deck were left unharmed. They flagged down a half-track just in time to escape from Arloncourt with their badly wounded comrade.[31]

The 50th Armored Infantry was making better progress, capturing Oubourcy fairly quickly, and finally also claiming victory at Michamps with the help of no fewer than 12 artillery battalions. Artillery support for Grow's men was massive and relentless. Colonel Lowell Riley, Grow's artillery commander, ordered the 6th Armored Division's two attached truck companies to haul nothing but ammunition. His gunners laid down smoke screens for the attackers, spewed high explosives at the enemy, and set hiding places ablaze with incendiaries. All in all, they expended more than 6,400 rounds on January 1 and more than 7,100 the day after. So heavy was the American shelling of Horitine that villagers were forced to abandon the solid cellars of their Ardennes farms for the even sturdier basement of the local tannery. In Michamps, men, women, and children formed bucket chains as they desperately tried to save some cattle from the soaring flames.[32]

By the second day of 1945, Kokott's Volksgrenadiers, too, were showing the strain caused by ceaseless battle. In Arloncourt they ran out of horses and commandeered villagers to help them pull carts piled high with ammunition. German ambulances were unloading so many dead soldiers at a collecting point in Benonchamps that the frozen corpses had to be stacked in the section of the train station where once lumber had been stored. Farmers in Oubourcy watched a German officer threaten seven soldiers with his pistol when they refused to leave the cellar and return to battle.[33]

Towards twilight on January 2, however, the atmosphere in the area changed abruptly with the arrival of a whole new caliber of German troops. They threw themselves against the American-held villages with huge energy and ferocity. These soldiers belonged to the 12th SS Panzer Division. The elite outfit (also known as the "Hitler Jugend" Division) had suffered more than 2,000 casualties in the northern salient. But that still left more than 16,000 men under the command of SS Standartenführer Hugo Kraas. And these men were part of a highly experienced fighting force that remained fanatically motivated. The division, one Waffen SS commander noted with trademark arrogance, was sent to von Manteuffel's Fifth Panzer Army "to clear up the situation at Bastogne." They certainly did that at Michamps and Oubourcy when, during the night of January 2, they threw the Americans back to where they had just come from.[34]

Little did Grow's tank crews know that what hit them late on Tuesday was only the spearhead of a much larger force. Kraas was under the command of Hermann Priess, who led the I SS Panzer Corps. Priess had just been ordered to contain the Americans northeast of Bastogne. To do so, he had also been given control of Kokott's Volksgrenadiers and of Tolsdorff's newly arrived 340th Volksgrenadier Division. Meanwhile, Priess was impatiently awaiting the arrival of yet another powerful force from the north – the 9th SS Panzer Division "Hohenstaufen."

Inside Bastogne, Ed O'Brien watched the 6th Armored Division set up an aid station at the Institute of Notre Dame. "They had everything," the medic from the 501st Parachute Infantry noted enviously. Grow's 76th Armored Medical Battalion brought in lumber to board up broken windows, and they installed generators to bring electric light to the cavernous rooms. Before long, they had turned the convent into a hospital that could hold up to 150 patients for treatment close to the front. The staff invited O'Brien to eat with them. "I walked by the kitchen truck and when my mess kit was filled," the paratrooper recalled, "I had roast beef, gravy, mashed potatoes, and all the bread I could eat." The combat medic topped off his meal with coffee and fresh-baked pie.[35]

It was a good thing the battalion had arrived well stocked. Demands on medical services rapidly multiplied as soon as Grow's troops pushed away from Bastogne: by the end of the second day, more than a hundred GIs were wounded. Several of the German casualties also ended up in the aid station of the 76th, and Belgian civilians added significantly to the division's burden. From Oubourcy to Wardin, Grow's Civil Affairs officers reported, there were "numerous problems of refugees, sick, wounded, dead people, and animals in the forward areas."[36]

After more than half a month of fear and hardship, inhabitants of the villages east of Bastogne scurried to the town as soon as the Americans had liberated them for a second time. As the Institute of Notre Dame again filled up with wounded soldiers and harried refugees, the situation for the pupils in the cellars became untenable. On New Year's Day, female nurses in Red Cross ambulances managed to reach Bastogne for the first time. The Belgian nurses set in motion the systematic evacuation of all the town's civilian patients. They also made sure to investigate the situation in the sisters' convent. On January 2, American trucks arrived to take the remaining pupils, their teachers, and some of the sisters to safety in Arlon. Maria Gillet and the others filed out of the pockmarked building. Their meager belongings were tied together in small bundles. The girls looked pallid and frail. They were chilled to the bone, but the trucks lacked tarpaulins. The Belgian girls drew blankets around their shoulders. They were told to lie on the vehicle floors face down. They stayed in that position until the trucks had whisked past Martelange and the sound of battle finally died away.[37]

Major Eugene Watts looked on with grim satisfaction as POWs were made to clear German cluster bombs that had failed to explode. He and the last of the headquarters personnel of the 9th Armored Division's Combat Command R were boarding trucks that would take them away from Bastogne, too. They were about to depart when one of the bombs went off close to the market square. "As the poor German fell groaning and screaming,"

Watts noted, "you could hear the laughter coming from the throats of our GIs in the trucks."[38]

3

On Wednesday, January 3, there was reason to cheer at Allied headquarters. At dawn, General Hodges' First Army launched its long-awaited attack from the north, as four divisions of the American VII Corps began their slogging match against the Germans in the bulge. They were joined by troops of the British XXX Corps, tasked with pushing in the nose of the enemy penetration. Any sense of optimism was tempered, however, by the obvious loss of momentum around Bastogne in the south. Patton looked on in frustration as maps told the story of the advance's snail's pace west of the corridor, deadlock in the Harlange pocket, and the brick wall in front of the 6th Armored Division northeast of Bastogne. Even Eisenhower, the Supreme Allied Commander, was expressing frustration, calling the Third Army's progress "slow and laborious."[39]

Things were about to get worse on Wednesday. During the night, the 12th SS Panzer Division had engaged in no more than piecemeal attacks to reclaim Michamps and Oubourcy. But now, with all its troops in position, the crack outfit teamed up with the 340th Volksgrenadier Division and stood poised to throw its full weight against the 6th Armored Division. At dawn in Michamps, "Hitler Jugend" soldiers in white capes arrogantly introduced themselves to gawking villagers as "those who never withdraw." They rounded up more than a dozen men in the village of Oubourcy. Ernest Charneux was led away with his granddaughter Nelly still in his arms. In one swift movement, the Belgian placed the child on the ground, broke free from his captors, and dashed away in the direction of Arloncourt. The Germans instantly opened fire, causing the villagers to flee in all directions. Monsieur Charneux never made it out of the village alive. Helped by the battering ram of a dozen 70-ton King Tigers, by nightfall Kraas's Waffen SS was in control of Arloncourt and tantalizingly close to gaining control over the two main roads leading into Bastogne from the east.[40]

On Thursday, the situation became critical for the 6th Armored Division. The entire outfit was on the front line, and there were no more reserves to commit. Temperatures kept dropping, and, even with woolen gloves on, GIs felt their fingers stiffen to the point where rounds could no longer be squeezed off fast enough. Still, Grow's men desperately pushed back against the combined pressure of Waffen SS and Volksgrenadiers. Sergeant Richard

Gard of the 44th Armored Infantry found his men disorganized in a patch of woods. Artillery and mortar fire had decimated his C Company platoon, and there were no more officers left. But the Ohioan impressed the survivors with his courage when he crawled forward under heavy fire and managed to drag back a wounded comrade. The platoon rallied around the sergeant and refused to give ground for much of the day. Private Henry Ebersole of the 50th Armored Infantry grabbed a machine gun and kept firing at infantry and tanks to protect the Headquarters Company. When all seemed lost, he abandoned his position under withering fire, only to return just in time with a couple of tank destroyers by his side.[41]

By mid-afternoon, however, none of the many acts of courage could ease the pressure. Elements of the 44th Armored Infantry panicked, broke, and fled all the way to Bastogne. Withdrawals began all along the line now. Grow had his troops abandon even Mageret and Wardin, the key villages on and near the roads to Bastogne from the east. All this happened, the division admitted, "with a great deal of confusion." Only the relentless effort by Grow's artillery stopped the withdrawal becoming a rout. So intense was the shelling, the artillery commander noted, that one of the division's field batteries "burned up their gun tubes."[42]

That night, all that remained of the hard-won gains made by the 6th Armored Division since December 31 was a narrow protrusion in the German lines, no deeper than two miles. Just to the north of it, the Belgians had seen their villages change hands several times in just a couple of days. In Arloncourt, the civilians were hungry, dirty, lice-ridden, and sick with diarrhea. That did not stop the Waffen SS from chasing the men from their cellars and ordering them to dig trenches in the freezing cold. Kraas's soldiers displayed their fanaticism with intense pride. On a wall in Moinet a slogan painted in black begged: "Führer command us and we will follow you!" A badly wounded German in Mageret pulled a photo from his pocket and showed villagers a portrait of Adolf Hitler. "If I die," he whispered to the Belgians, "I'll die for him."[43]

In two days, the 6th Armored Division suffered more than 300 casualties. Grow placed phone call after phone call to III Corps headquarters, pleading for reinforcements to be sent to his sector. The most likely source was the 35th Infantry Division to the south. But Baade's troops were being bled white in the Harlange pocket and could not spare any reserves. Artillery support for the 35th was stepped up with each new day. On January 3, the 161st Field Artillery alone expended close to 2,500 rounds. Even then, however, Baade's infantry was making little gain along the ten-mile front west of the pocket.[44]

It took the 320th Infantry until nightfall on January 4 to secure just four houses in Harlange, and German tanks and infantry immediately responded with an angry counterattack. The battle against the remnants of the 5th Fallschirmjäger Division was even tougher for the 137th Infantry. On the morning of January 4, the regiment tried to seize the road junction west of Villers-la-Bonne-Eau. They had been beaten back the previous day and now, despite heavy losses, refused to give up until they reached their objective. Medics dashed in and out of the front lines in brave attempts to evacuate the countless wounded. Four men from the division's medical battalion formed a particularly tight-knit litter team: Louis Beauchaine was from Warwick, Rhode Island; Ferdinand Bronzell from Chicago, Illinois; Gerald Fenner from Carthage, Missouri; and James Gollinger from Massena, New York. In the afternoon, the Germans launched a brutal counterattack against the captured road junction. The Americans managed to hold on, but at a terrible cost. Infantrymen entreated Bronzell and his comrades not to enter the heavy-shelled terrain in front of their foxholes, but the litter team ignored the warnings and sprinted towards the wounded. An explosion from a mortar round stopped them in their tracks. When the acrid smoke cleared, three of the litter bearers lay dead. Only the badly wounded Chicagoan, Bronzell, made it back to the rear. All four men were awarded a Silver Star for their selfless action in the Harlange cauldron.[45]

Although Lutrebois, the village closest to Bastogne and the Arlon highway, had been captured, the 134th Infantry was kept busy silencing the last defenders in cellars and attics. Under cover of darkness, GIs led the surviving villagers through the woods in groups of five, and loaded them onto trucks that whisked them off to safety. On January 4, the 134th went on the attack again, engaging the 167th Volksgrenadier Division in the forest east of Lutrebois. The Germans counterattacked as soon as they felt the pressure, and in no time at all the men of C Company discovered they were surrounded. They radioed battalion headquarters and were urged to give ground and filter back to Lutrebois. Sergeant Rex Storm and Private Dallas Viehe volunteered to stay behind to cover the evacuation of the walking wounded. Armed with no more than M1 rifles, they picked off dozens of Germans as they tried to close the net. Sergeant Mazzi hurried forward to lend a hand, setting up a machine gun to help stave off attacks against the column's rear. As dusk descended, Frank Mazzi and the other volunteers abandoned their positions and began to fall back, too. The more seriously wounded soldiers were to be left behind in the hope that the Germans would treat them humanely. But the injured men panicked and begged the volunteers to take them along. One casualty followed them on hands and knees until he was unable to keep up in the snow.

C Company's commander circulated among his men, instilling confidence in low whispers as they stumbled through the dense forest. Numb with cold, the GIs nibbled on D ration bars and swallowed melted snow. As darkness thickened, the column formed a human chain to maintain contact. It was past midnight when the company reached a road. The column had barely spread out on the slippery surface when a German machine gun opened up. In the melee that followed, the company commander was taken prisoner. Enraged by the ambush and its many casualties, Sergeant Solomon Plotsky searched for the machine gun's muzzle blast. As soon as he spotted it, he stormed forward. He grabbed the glowing barrel with his bare hands, wrestled the weapon from the German gunner, and knocked him out. Throughout the night, groups of men from C Company groped their way into friendly lines. Of the 120 men who had gone on the attack on Thursday morning, 37 made it back. Frank Mazzi was not among them. He had failed to make contact with the column after he had packed up his machine gun. But he had run into another straggler, Lawrence Eschelman, and together they had managed to slip into a village. As dawn broke on Friday, the sergeant from Pennsylvania and the lieutenant from Nebraska sat huddled in a cellar in Villers-la-Bonne-Eau, a village almost two miles southeast of Lutrebois and still firmly in German hands.[46]

There were no civilians in the cellars of Villers, because the Germans had thrown them out. On New Year's Day they had ordered all the able-bodied men to seek shelter elsewhere. Then, at dawn on January 3, they had barked at the 30 or so villagers who remained to assemble in the cold. The ragtag group was made up of women, children, and the elderly. Among them, too, were the members of the Garcia family who had survived the shelling tragedy a week earlier. Three Germans had ordered the Belgians at gunpoint to form a column. A woman had been placed at its head and made to carry a white flag. By the time Mazzi and Eschelman reached Villers, the unfortunate inhabitants were making their way through the snow in Luxembourg.

Nineteen-year-old Marie Garcia struggled to keep up with the rest. She had lost her shoes, and had no feeling in her frozen feet. Shrapnel had punctured her lungs, and blood seeped through the bandages each time she heaved her chest. Maria tried to hold on to her ten-year-old brother. Their parents, both severely wounded, endeavored to comfort a baby daughter and the youngest son, whose arm was horribly mangled. Each time the group slowed down, the Germans dealt out pitiless blows with the butts of their rifles. As the column wound its way out of the Harlange pocket in a north-easterly direction, the first food in two days presented itself in Tarchamps in the form of raw potatoes. The group was finally abandoned in Derenbach, where an Allied raid killed one of them. The villagers, disheveled and starving, begged some meat from soldiers who were cutting up a cow's carcass. The stony-faced Germans told them to get lost.[47]

The vicious nature of the battle in the Harlange pocket caused the 35th Infantry Division to lose close to 400 men on January 3 and 4 alone. This prevented Baade from sending any reinforcements north to Grow's sector. But the situation for the 6th Armored Division was getting more dire with each passing hour. After darkness on Thursday, January 4, elements of the 167th Volksgrenadier Division, supported by armor of the 1st SS Panzer Division, made a foray from the Harlange pocket in the direction of Wardin and the road from Wiltz to Bastogne. Only the intervention of mass artillery managed to blunt the attack. By midnight, Grow's divisional batteries had pounded the Germans with more than 13,000 shells.

From dawn to dusk on Friday, SS troopers and Volksgrenadiers kept hurling themselves at Bastogne from Wardin and Mageret, along the roads leading in from the east. Again Grow's artillery batteries saved the day. German guns destroyed five spotter planes on an airstrip close to Bastogne. But the surviving L-4 Grasshoppers instantly moved to Sibret and took off again, the pilots relentlessly observing and reporting targets from up close. Curtains of smoke were brought down to hide American positions and counterattacks. More than 11,600 rounds brought devastation to Kraas's Waffen SS and Tolsdorff's Volksgrenadiers.[48]

That Friday also, after two days of inclement weather, Grow's troops were fortunate to see the skies clear just enough to allow air raids again. A squadron of P-47s from the 362nd Fighter Group attacked German troop concentrations at Wardin with a vengeance. They released, so the after-action report stated, "500-lb GP bombs, M-76 incendiaries, and 150-gallon Napalms," leaving the small village "virtually destroyed."[49]

4

While the 6th Armored Division was being pushed to breaking point, para-troopers of the 101st faced the worst crisis on Bastogne's perimeter since the desperate Christmas days. At noon on January 3, two battalions of the 501st Parachute Infantry were sent into the Bois Jacques to help clear it and provide protection for Grow's left flank. They clashed head-on with two regiments of Tolsdorff's Volksgrenadiers that were about to jump off in coordination with the 12th SS Panzer Division on their left. German shells ripped the forest to shreds, and tree bursts mowed down paratroopers by the dozen. The battalions called on the 10th Armored Division's Combat Command B to come to their rescue. At dusk, however, a regiment of Kraas's Waffen SS also joined the battle. The situation now became untenable for the much smaller airborne force. "The sound," recalled a sergeant from E Company, "was deafening, and the ground was rocking and pitching like an earthquake." Frantic messages ordered the paratroopers to abandon their positions inside the forest and begin a precarious retreat in stygian darkness. In half a day's battle, Colonel Ewell's outfit suffered close to 150 casualties.[50]

In just three hours that same afternoon, a battalion of Colonel Chappuis's 502nd Parachute Infantry suffered equally devastating losses northwest of Bastogne. The newly arrived 9th SS Panzer Division was part of the coordinated attack that Hermann Priess unleashed with his I SS Panzer Corps on January 3. With massive force, the "Hohenstaufen" Division's 19th Panzergrenadier Regiment attacked west of the highway from Houffalize and Noville. Shortly after noon, an estimated 30 tanks and assault guns, followed by waves of infantrymen, tore into the 2nd Battalion's defensive line just north of Monaville and Longchamps. The paratroopers refused to give ground, absorbing the first shock virtually with their bare hands. Bazookas were unable to penetrate the thick skin of Panthers and King Tigers. But some men from D Company crept close enough to one tank to take aim with their bazooka at one of its tracks. Disabled, the tank kept resisting like a wounded animal, shelling and machine-gunning and killing one of the attackers. When suddenly the hatch was thrown open, a paratrooper leaped up on the tank. He tossed a phosphorus grenade down the turret, silencing the crew in a roar of flames. The battalion's losses piled up fast, as more German armor entered the fray. GIs struggled for breath as the enemy tanks crawled over their foxholes, gassing the men with carbon monoxide and causing their pits to collapse. D Company alone lost 48 men in no time. Warren Cobbett, one of the company's medics, jumped into a truck. Well aware that the vehicle lacked Red Cross markings, Cobbett braved enemy fire on the bald, snow-covered slope, careering from position to position to pick up badly wounded men.[51]

Lurching from crisis to crisis, General Maxwell Taylor now ordered all available reinforcements to be brought to bear against the Germans in Chappuis's sector. A company of the 326th Engineers hurried to the scene with mines and more bazookas. Elements of the 609th and 705th Tank Destroyer Battalions took up positions. All the division's artillery zeroed in on the approaching enemy, bringing down a punishing barrage. African-American gunners from the 969th Field Artillery took out a tank with a direct hit from one of their heavy 155mm rounds. But F Company, thrown into the battle as the regimental reserve, was not so lucky. Caught in the open as the tanks bore down on their objectives, the company was cut to pieces. As groups of survivors burrowed into hedges to escape the murderous fire, the company commander stepped forward with a piece of white cloth to announce their surrender.[52]

Surrender was not an option for 19-year-old Ed Peniche and his three comrades at Longchamps. They were part of the main line of resistance and manned one of C Battery's five 57mm guns in the 81st Anti-tank Battalion. The airborne gunners had watched the tanks lumber towards them on both sides of the road from Compogne. They had blown the gun off one of the monster Tigers and had damaged another one's turret. But now the Germans had pinpointed their position. The American gun was dug in deep and could not be moved. "The shells were so numerous," Peniche noted later, "that the ground shook." Private Peniche had been born Eduardo Alberto Peniche, in Mexico's Yucatán peninsula. He had joined his aunt and uncle in Kentucky as a teenager. Ed had fully embraced life in the United States, and after Pearl Harbor had volunteered for service in his adopted country's uniform, even though he was not legally a citizen. Now he was helpless as he watched his American comrades fall victim to shrapnel, one after the other. Darrell Garner, a private from South Carolina, was hit in the face and shoulder; Sergeant O'Toole from Indiana was bleeding profusely from the hip and leg and looked like he was going into shock. Ed Peniche crawled towards O'Toole to see if there was anything he could do. He slowed down when he sensed a wrenching pain in his knee. When he looked, he saw blood on his muddy trousers and he felt the leg go numb. As he tried to calm his breathing, he heard the moans of other men. "I remember praying," said Peniche, "both in English and Spanish."[53]

While Peniche and his comrades made it to the aid station, Corporal Edward Ford was lucky enough to survive the shelling of C Battery unscathed. He had his piece blast away until it had put out of action no fewer than seven tanks. Meanwhile, Sergeant William Carberry, a rifle squad leader, volunteered as a forward artillery observer. He moved from one exposed position to another, directing fire. His clothes torn by the blasts of enemy shelling, the sergeant deliberately shortened the American artillery's range until it came down on his own position, claiming his life as well as those of many of the enemy. Chappuis's 2nd Battalion earned three Distinguished Service Crosses in three hours. As daylight waned, Monaville and Longchamps remained in airborne hands through sheer courage and determination.[54]

That night, the 1st Battalion of the 327th Glider Infantry moved into the line at Champs to allow the 1st Battalion of the 502nd Parachute Infantry to go into reserve. Made up of troops that had been providing protection for the 101st headquarters at Madame Greindl's château in Isle-la-Hesse and of a large number of green replacements, the outfit's only anti-tank weapons were a handful of light 37mm guns. The glidermen had barely settled down when a regiment from the 15th Panzergrenadier Division again tried its luck where the perimeter's defenses had proved weakest on Christmas Day. The night attack with about a dozen tanks took the Americans completely by surprise and the front line on the crest in front of Champs disintegrated. Small pockets kept resisting against all the odds. A mortar squad from C Company was pinned down behind a deep embankment. "Our mortars," one soldier noted, "were firing without base plates – tube held by hands." Once again, General Taylor called on all available forces to help plug the breach. The battalion from the 502nd that had just gone into reserve had to be called out again. Destroyers were fighting duels with German tanks that were prowling the streets of Champs. Only at dawn on Thursday, when Bastogne's artillery threw its full weight against Deckert's Panzergrenadiers, did the threat subside.[55]

That evening, the 101st Airborne Division reported 34 tanks destroyed in its sector. These were heavy losses for the Germans. But, as was becoming the custom in Bastogne's battle of attrition, they had come at a very high cost for the Americans, too. In just two days, General Taylor had witnessed more than 530 of his paratroopers, seasoned veterans and green replacements alike, fall victim to the enemy's relentless pressure.[56]

5

Despite the vicious German attacks at the start of 1945, an impatient Patton remained adamant that those who held Bastogne should continue to develop their own pressure. With much of Millikin's III Corps stalled, all eyes were on General Middleton. His VIII Corps was expected to claw its way from the

area west of Bastogne, all the way to the Houffalize highway. But, with von
Lüttwitz's XLVII Panzer Corps blocking their path, Middleton's troops had
not even secured the highway running west from Bastogne to Marche. In just
three days, the Germans had inflicted more than 530 casualties on the newly
arrived 11th Armored Division, leaving the green outfit battered and dispirited, and desperate for reorganization in the rear. By now Middleton, too,
was physically and mentally exhausted.[57]

But Patton harangued and cajoled, instructing Middleton to throw into
battle the 17th Airborne Division as soon as it had taken over from the
11th Armored. Lacking armor and heavy artillery, Major General William
Miley's division appeared a most unlikely candidate for the role of battering
ram. But there were no other reserves left in the European theater, and so
Miley's men continued to pour into the front line just west of Bastogne. The
green troops had literally just stepped off the plane. Having been shipped to
Britain in August 1944, the paratroopers were still receiving training there
when, around Christmas, they had suddenly been airlifted across the
Channel to Rheims. From the French city they had been trucked all the way
to the Belgian town of Neufchâteau. So nervous were the untested troops
that at Mézières, not far from Sedan, one of the division's first casualties had
resulted from a clash with French gendarmes who had been mistaken for the
enemy.[58]

On Tuesday afternoon, Ed O'Brien, the paratrooper and medic from the
101st Airborne, had seen some of the first of Miley's men march northeast
along the Neufchâteau highway. The day after, on January 3, more columns
of the 14,000 paratroopers continued to trudge along that main road and the
smaller ones feeding into the battle zone to Bastogne's west. At the hamlet of
Monty, soldiers of the 513th Parachute Infantry found Kilburn's tank crews
itching to leave the war behind. When the 2nd Battalion commander asked
a tank commander for more information on what lay ahead, the answer was
curt: "Couldn't see anything, don't know anything, it's your baby." At Mande-
Saint-Étienne, John Fague's battered platoon assembled and climbed onto
half-tracks that were waiting to take them to the rear. The 19-year-old
sergeant from Pennsylvania watched animals stumble helplessly around in
streets and barnyards. Cows with "deep gashes in their sides" bellowed with
pain; one of the horses had "intestines protruding from its flank." Sergeant
John Paul from the 513th Parachute Infantry was trying to absorb the first
impressions of a village ruined by war. His eyes rested on smoldering debris,
wrecked American and German vehicles, cattle whose hooves pointed to the
somber sky. He noticed frantic movement in the belly of a dead horse. A dog

emerged from a jagged slit, all slimy with blood and grease. The newcomer jerked his head away and threw up in the street.[59]

Although troops from the 17th Airborne were still arriving after dark on Wednesday, VIII Corps was under strict orders to launch its attack shortly before dawn. All the mistakes that had been made with the 11th Armored Division on December 30 were about to be repeated on January 4. The paratroopers had arrived exhausted from the rushed trip in extreme cold. They had been given virtually no time to observe and reconnoiter the terrain in front of them. They had not even been able to set up reliable communications. Now they were expected to make the abrupt transition from a delicate relief operation to an all-out attack against concentrated armor. It was, General Miley pointed out meekly, "a large order for a new division."[60]

At least Kilburn's armored artillery had stayed put to provide support for the lightly armed paratroopers. At 0745, Lieutenant Samuel Calhoun watched a barrage rip apart a patch of forest 150 yards in front of his platoon. The 22-year-old Californian and three dozen men sat dug in on the northwestern edge of Mande-Saint-Étienne, just north of the Bastogne–Marche highway. The objective of their parent outfit, the 2nd Battalion of the 513th Parachute Infantry, was the village of Flamizoulle. To get there, Calhoun and his men would first have to cut through the woods. The snow-covered field sloped gently up to the tree line. It was completely devoid of cover.

At 0800, Calhoun had his platoon form a skirmish line and move forward, just moments before the barrage was lifted. Privates Gibbs and Herisek were just crossing the barbed wire fence 15 yards in front of the woods when the Germans opened fire. Both men were dead in seconds. Calhoun flopped down in the snow. Patrick Keller, his runner, lay at his side dead, bullets continuing to rip through his body. Crumpled men lay strewn all over the field. Calhoun could see tracers "ricocheting off their bodies." The lieutenant hugged the frozen ground. For at least half an hour he pretended to be dead, as machine guns kept up a steady bark. Then suddenly he jumped up and disappeared behind a pile of beets that he had spotted from the corner of his eye. Clifford Thompson, the platoon medic, lay dead some 35 yards to his left. A mortar squad began placing rounds of smoke in front of the woods. Slowly and deliberately, Calhoun and the other survivors crawled their way back to the line of departure.

The battalion commander ordered Calhoun to round up his men without delay and prepare to attack the woods again. Of the 37 soldiers that had attacked before dawn, 14 remained. The lieutenant led the remnants of his

F Company platoon behind an embankment to the left and told his men to
fix bayonets. To the right there would be support from a platoon of E
Company, led by Lieutenant Richard Manning. E Company, too, had been
mauled. Its commander had just been killed trying to silence a machine-gun
position with hand grenades. Calhoun took a deep breath and ordered his
men over the top of the embankment. This time, with platoons descending
on the objective from two sides, the paratroopers did reach the woods. They
engaged in ferocious hand-to-hand combat and gave no quarter. Lieutenant
Manning hurled himself against a log-covered trench and single-handedly
killed six Germans. He was leading his platoon in an attack against a
machine gun when a tree burst almost tore off his left leg. A sniper badly
wounded Samuel Calhoun, just as he was studying a map to locate the next
objective beyond the deadly forest.[61]

Both lieutenants were fortunate enough to be taken away on stretchers
before the start of the German counterattack. Elements of the 3rd
Panzergrenadier Division and Remer's elite Führer Begleit Brigade plowed
into Miley's paratroopers early in the afternoon. They continued to roll the
Americans back for the remainder of the day. Despite all the sacrifices of the
morning, Calhoun and Manning's 2nd Battalion was pushed all the way back
to its predawn line of departure. The same happened with the 1st Battalion
of the 513th, although at Cochelonval Sergeant Isadore Jachman grabbed a
bazooka from a dead comrade and chased away two tanks that were pinning
down his company. Jachman was a Jew from Berlin whose family had left
Germany when he was a child. His bravery on January 4 earned him a Medal
of Honor, but cost him his life.[62]

The predicament of the inexperienced airborne force was made worse by
the fact that west of Acul the 87th Infantry Division was making almost no
progress that Thursday. So treacherous were the German minefields in the
area that Belgian villagers had to be evacuated to the rear in single file,
walking behind GIs sweeping paths with detectors. Elements of Bayerlein's
Panzer Lehr finally stopped Culin's infantry cold at Pironpré. Their stonewalling, Miley noted wryly, left the western flank of his division "dangling in
the breeze." This proved to be particularly unfortunate for the 193rd Glider
Infantry when, in the afternoon, it became the target of Remer's and
Denkert's armored wrath. During the morning, supported by some
4,000 rounds fired by Kilburn's field artillery, the glidermen on the division's
left had managed to capture a string of villages from Rechrival to Renuamont.
This had brought them virtually in sight of Flamierge on the other side of the
Marche highway. Now, however, they too were suffering severe casualties

while being forced back to their line of departure. The day's dramatic reversals left General Miley aghast. "I don't know what is the matter with my men," he lamented. "We're just not getting anywhere."[63]

Before long, the soldiers of the 17th Airborne were referring to the elevated terrain along the Bastogne–Marche highway as "Dead Man's Ridge." In a single day, their baptism of fire claimed 275 casualties. Patton was very unhappy with General Miley's performance, and he traveled all the way to Bastogne to tell him so. The town was being shelled as the three-star general drove in. "I can never," he fumed after meeting Miley, "get over the stupidity of our green troops." But Patton was not just displeased. He was worried. "We can," he confided to his diary that Thursday, "still lose this war."[64]

All night long, ambulances and jeeps from regiments and medical companies worked overtime to get the wounded out. The 513th Parachute Infantry had to bring in GMC trucks to help with the evacuation. As Thursday went and Friday came, the paratroopers found themselves hiding behind a screen of artillery fire. It was Kilburn's gunners who continued to provide much of the vital protection. At dawn, the 490th Armored Field Artillery Battalion was preparing for another rough day in support of the 193rd Glider Infantry Regiment.[65]

Lieutenant John Cunningham, the artillery battalion's adjutant, had been appointed airborne liaison. The 36-year-old perfectly fit the mold of America's citizen soldier. A tall man with blue-green eyes and wavy brown hair, he had spent his youth in Louisiana catching turtles and garfish in the bayous. After her divorce, his mother had taken over the family's newspaper in Natchitoches. As soon as he obtained his college degree, John had become both manager and editor of the *Natchitoches Times*. He had married his college sweetheart, Famay Fournet, and driven her around in an old Ford. By the time he was shipped to war in Europe, John was the proud father of a daughter of nearly two and a son of just a couple of months. Now, as darkness slowly retreated on January 5, any thoughts of balmy Louisiana seemed unreal in the bitter cold of the Ardennes. Lieutenant Cunningham set out with a party of new forward observers in two jeeps. He had volunteered to guide the men to their frontline outposts. They pushed past Millomont, unaware that the glidermen had abandoned the area: Miley's airborne troops and Kilburn's armor were not on the same radio frequency, and, in the confusion of the past hours, no one had bothered to relay exact positions to the artillerymen any other way. As the jeeps came out of a bend on a path through a frozen field, Germans opened up from a farm on a slope. Machine guns riddled the jeeps, snuffing out the lives of John Cunningham and his companions in the blink of an eye.[66]

The loss of valuable men did little to slow the hellish fury of American artillery. Thousands upon thousands of shells were lobbed across the highway to Marche. The rounds failed to distinguish between the hated enemy and innocent civilians. The inhabitants of Flamierge knew full well that the sturdy farm cellars, built of Ardennes rock, offered the best chance for protection against barrages. But during an apparent lull, those hiding in the Bever farm risked going up to the kitchen. They were hungry and cold, and they got a fire going. They took off their shoes to rest their numb feet against the glowing stove. Just then, a shell came through the roof and exploded almost on top of the stove. Seven people were killed in a flash, while two others suffered horrific wounds. One of them was 38-year-old Marie Collard, a refugee from Mande-Saint-Étienne. The blast had torn off one of her feet. As the Germans kept Miley's men at bay, the woman slowly bled to death.[67]

However much the Americans pounded the villages in front of them, they made no more progress on Friday than they had on Thursday. The German opponent, Miley's chief of staff grudgingly admitted, was "a master in offensive-defensive delay and in organizing quick counter-attack." There was plenty of evidence of that on January 5. Regimental headquarters of the 513th reported that even their command post to the rear in Mande-Saint-Étienne was receiving direct hits from German artillery every five minutes. Snipers had moved in so close that they were picking off wiremen and taking aim at the command post's entry. The Germans had infested the area with booby traps and mines. In mid-morning, one such mine blew up a jeep from the 193rd Glider Infantry, killing a chief warrant officer and wounding the regimental adjutant. As he analyzed the stream of bad news, General Middleton decided that he had no other choice but to allow the 17th Airborne to reorganize. There would be no new attack for Miley's men until January 7. By now, Middleton was beginning to doubt whether his troops could even keep up a successful defense. A visitor to VIII Corps headquarters on Friday found the usually affable Mississippian "quite depressed."[68]

CHAPTER 9

THE LONGEST ROAD

Patton was gritting his teeth. "If you got a monkey in a jungle hanging by his tail," he had told reporters on the first day of 1945, "it is easier to get him by cutting his tail than kicking him in the face."[1]

As soon as he had wheeled around his Third Army to go to the rescue of Bastogne, Patton had started pleading for an even bolder strike against the base of the bulge. A simultaneous push from the south and the north at the shoulders, he was convinced, would force the Germans to withdraw quickly or face disastrous entrapment. It would, to use Patton's analogy, cut the monkey's tail. But the base of the bulge was almost 50 miles wide, and to slice through it with lightning speed would have required a good road network for mechanized units and fair weather for the air forces. Judging the conditions to be unfavorable, and fearing the consequences of such a dangerous gamble in the wake of the German surprise attack, Eisenhower, Bradley, and Montgomery had vetoed Patton's more ambitious plan. That is why, by the end of December, Patton had settled for a strike from Bastogne aimed at linking up with Hodges' First Army at Houffalize. But now, as the attrition worsened, Patton could not help bemoaning the decision to attack the salient's waist rather than its shoulders. As more reinforcements arrived, the Third Army commander was loath to see these, too, sucked into Bastogne's vortex. It was, he complained in his diary on January 4, "throwing good money after bad."[2]

The following day, however, Allied intelligence was suggesting that the enemy's large-scale, coordinated attack against Bastogne from the north had run out of steam. Even Hitler now had to concede that it would be impossible to capture Bastogne. Orders went out to the Waffen SS divisions to commence a gradual disengagement. But the remaining forces were told to continue to grind down the Americans and to fight the battle for Bastogne "to its conclusion." More attrition was to be expected around the Belgian town, because the Germans now also accelerated their retreat from the nose of the bulge. As the armored spearheads pulled back from the west, the density of troops facing Middleton's and Millikin's men, estimated on January 3 at 61,500 soldiers and 265 tanks and assault guns, was bound to increase further. To allow an orderly withdrawal through the Houffalize corridor, the Germans had to control the N15 that linked the town with Bastogne. To execute the vital linkup at Houffalize, Patton's men would have to wrest this key road from the Germans. With the initiative now in the hands of the Americans, the German soldier stood to remind his opponent why he was, as the 17th Airborne's chief of staff had already observed, "a master in offensive-defensive delay." Of all the Ardennes roads that the Americans spilled blood for at the Bastogne junction, the highway north to Houffalize would prove to be the longest.[3]

1

For the men of the 101st Airborne in and around Bastogne, the end of the massive German attack on January 4 signaled the start of four days of relative quiet. Mobile shower units were brought in and, for the first time in three weeks, paratroopers were able to wash away the dirt and grime. They peeled off their clothes and saw them sent off to laundry units in Rheims. There were rumors even of passes that would allow some to travel to Paris for much needed rest and recreation.[4]

More vehicles were plowing through the Bastogne corridor. Along the way, American trucks dropped off food and coal for Belgians determined to stick out the battle beside their cattle. Army medical teams fanned out, spraying all civilians in sight with DDT to prevent the spread of disease. The all-female Motor Corps of the Belgian Red Cross negotiated mined and cratered roads to collect civilians who were ill or wounded. On January 5, one such courageous ambulance driver picked up Madame Greindl's children at Isle-la-Hesse and took them to safety in Arlon. The following day, the baroness heated some water and spent most of the morning getting clean and coiffing her hair. Then she made her way to Bastogne's market square to report for duty at the local Red Cross office. But the building that had housed it was now a mere shell. Madame Greindl learned that volunteers were busy setting up a new space in the Institute of Notre Dame. She hurried to join them. She wanted to be ready for whatever fate still awaited her beloved town.[5]

The 101st Airborne was not granted much respite even while it was licking its wounds during the brief lull. On Friday morning, an earsplitting blast shook the town and a huge column of flame soared into the sky. Something had gone wrong near the Seminary while a truck was being loaded with mines for the 501st Parachute Infantry's front lines. When the smoke cleared, scarcely a trace remained of the 13 soldiers who had been at work on or near the vehicle. That same day, a shell in the rue Saint-Pierre killed a teenage girl who had volunteered to leave the safety of an underground shelter to try and find medicines for an elderly woman. Field guns continued to zero in on Bastogne from several sides. Now and then, a giant railroad gun joined in. From a tunnel seven miles to the southeast, it emerged just long enough each time to lob a couple more projectiles at the already devastated town.[6]

On January 7, shortly after General Middleton had been caught in a barrage during a visit to Bastogne, it was decided to move the last remaining section of the 101st Airborne headquarters from the Heintz barracks cellar to Isle-le-Pré, a hamlet a mile and a half southwest of town. The move no longer concerned Tony McAuliffe: his sangfroid at Bastogne had not gone unnoticed higher up, and earlier that day the airborne artillery general had learned that he had been given command of his own division. But the 103rd was an infantry division. There was much laughter and ribbing when, at a small party, the dyed-in-the-wool paratrooper received the canvas leggings of a foot soldier as a farewell gift.[7]

There was no respite whatsoever elsewhere in the bulge. Long before dawn on January 6, more than 90 British Lancaster bombers attacked Houffalize. Their objective was to "choke" the escape route for the Germans west of the Ourthe River. In just 12 minutes, a rolling thunder of 1,300 bombs wiped the small Ardennes town from the face of the map, taking the lives of some 120 inhabitants who sat huddled together in underground shelters.

Enemy armor, poor visibility, and heavy snow were slowing down the VII Corps of Hodges' First Army in the attack towards Houffalize from the north. In their push from the west against the nose of the bulge, the British XXX Corps found the going equally tough against Germans who, in the words of Bradley's top aide, "withdraw very stubbornly, die quite willingly."[8]

After the fiasco of Thursday and Friday, General Middleton had allowed Miley's paratroopers time to regroup and catch their breath on Saturday, January 6. But although Patton had agreed that the men of the 101st Airborne in Bastogne needed several days to recover, he refused to give the men of the newly arrived 17th Airborne more than a day's respite. They were to resume the northeasterly drive to the Bastogne–Houffalize road as soon as possible. "We have," the Third Army commander insisted, "to push people beyond endurance in order to bring this war to its end."[9]

Middleton was shaken by the massive losses that his VIII Corps had sustained in the past week. Patton admitted that he was forced "to use the whip" on the Mississippian to have him agree to attack at dawn on January 7. Even then, however, Middleton, fearing attacks against his left flank and rear, decided to keep the badly mauled 11th Armored Division in reserve. This fateful decision meant that the planned attack would go ahead with no more than the 17th Airborne just west of Bastogne and the 87th Infantry Division on its left. As the American foot soldiers readied themselves, German spearheads retreating from the nose of the bulge were forming a wall of armor in front of them.[10]

General Miley was edgy. He wanted to know more about the formidable enemy that was out there in the fog and snow. During their first clash, his green paratroopers had alternately been too frightened or too enraged to bother taking prisoners. Now Miley, in his orders for the next attack, urged his men to rush prisoners to the nearest regimental collecting points and not to allow them "to smoke, eat, drink, urinate or warm themselves until after interrogation."[11]

At 0800 on Sunday, January 7, the 194th Glider Infantry on the left wing and the 193rd Glider Infantry on the right were the first of Miley's regiments to jump off. Dense fog and swirling snow reduced visibility to about 75 yards. Artillery had doused the German lines with white phosphorus, and here and there paratroopers ran into groups of "badly burned Krauts." Deep snowdrifts, whipped up by a bone-chilling wind, quickly slowed the Americans down. Scouts wore snow capes and white helmet covers and had their weapons wrapped in strips of sheet. But all other troops lacked winter camouflage, and German snipers picked them off as soon as they loomed out of the fog. As the paratroopers pushed up against the main line of Denkert's 3rd Panzergrenadier Division, they were (in the words of one report) stopped by "a wall of defensive fire." The 194th failed to advance more than a mile, and came to an abrupt halt before Rechrival. Meanwhile, instead of taking Flamizoulle, the 193rd suffered 480 casualties along a stretch of some 500 yards, before being forced back to where its dawn line of departure had been.[12]

Matters were made worse that Sunday by the fact that elements of the Führer Begleit Brigade and Bayerlein's Panzer Lehr were preventing the 87th Infantry Division from moving forward abreast with Miley's paratroopers.

Unhampered by Allied fighter-bombers, the Germans fought fanatically to deny the division access to Tillet, a small village at the junction of two key secondary roads. Despite bravery that earned Culin's infantrymen numerous Bronze and Silver Stars, a Distinguished Service Cross, and even a Medal of Honor, they would fail to dislodge German armor from Tillet until January 9.[13]

The only good news of the day came from Miley's regiment in the sector's center. The 513th Parachute Infantry had joined the attack an hour after both glider regiments had pushed forward on the flanks. One of the regiment's paratroopers was 19-year-old Fred Glavan. The seventh of eight children, Fred was the son of immigrants from Slovenia who had settled in Minnesota's Iron Range. In his adopted hometown of Kinney, Fred's father scratched a living as a miner and school janitor. Three of Fred's brothers were also fighting in Europe; two others had been sent to the Pacific. All had remained safe thus far, and the siblings tried their best to write letters and stay in touch across the far-flung theaters of war. On New Year's Eve, Lud Glavan, an MP in Patton's Third Army, had managed to pay a visit to his younger brother. They had had a great time and had drunk too much. Now, a week later, at noon on Sunday, Fred Glavan and his comrades in the 3rd Battalion had just fought their way to a crest in front of Flamierge. With labored breathing they gazed down on what was to be their final objective of the day.[14]

When the signal came to continue the attack, the men soon found themselves descending into an inferno. There was virtually no cover on the downward slope, and the only supporting fire came from a couple of mortar teams. German tanks, artillery, and heavy machine guns had an easy time zeroing in on men in dark clothing, silhouetted against the bright snow. Experienced snipers proved selective, preferring to pick off American soldiers who carried radios, bazookas, and other vital equipment. Major Anderson had been in charge of the 3rd Battalion only since dawn, when shrapnel had wounded the regular commander even before the attack had commenced. But Morris Anderson rallied his men and radioed the regimental commander that he thought they could seize Flamierge with the help of artillery. The battalion had approached to within 150 yards of the village when a powerful barrage, brought down "by guess and by God," took the German defenders by surprise. The paratroopers stormed the village, hunting down Panzergrenadiers in the billowing smoke, "firing from the hip all the way." At 1515, the village was declared secure. Miley had scored at least one victory.

Or so it seemed. The Germans refused to have their main line of defense breached. A *Kampfgruppe* of the 9th Panzer Division, a veteran outfit that had just begun to arrive in the Bastogne sector, rushed in to help the Panzergrenadiers. From dawn to dusk on Monday, the combined force tried to dislodge the paratroopers with artillery, mortars, and flamethrowers. More than two dozen tanks stalked their prey, but bazooka teams thwarted each attempted breakthrough. Major Anderson had lost all communication with the outside world. Around midnight, however, a regimental radio operator managed to get close enough to Flamierge to reestablish contact with the lost battalion, and the order was given to withdraw that Monday night. The men were organized into groups of eight to ten, and they left at varying times and in different directions. Before slipping out, they mined and booby-trapped houses and barns. Two medics stayed behind to watch over the seriously wounded. It was almost dawn when Major Anderson left with the last party. They were barely 150 yards from Flamierge when a ferocious German artillery barrage blew the village into the sky.[15]

The Germans had successfully resealed their main line of defense just west of Bastogne. In doing so, they had once again prevented Middleton's troops from getting closer to the N15. On January 9, Major Anderson made it back to American lines with less than half of the 525 paratroopers he had set out with two days earlier. One of the many men he had lost was Fred Glavan. The 19-year-old Minnesotan had died from a sniper's bullet to the chest. A sister-in-law sent the sad news to Fred's five uniformed siblings in the distant theaters of World War II. "I never will be the same man," replied one anguished brother, a tank commander in the Philippines. "Why did it have to be him?"[16]

2

On January 5, even before the 17th Airborne launched its second ill-fated attack in the direction of the N15, Bradley and Patton had concluded that, in order for the Third Army to lend its full weight to the push towards Houffalize, the Harlange pocket would first have to be eliminated. The pocket southeast of Bastogne contained a dense concentration of German troops that continued to draw in and grind down not only the 26th and 35th Infantry Divisions, but also the 6th Armored Division. General Baade described the situation in the sector of his 35th Infantry Division as one of "pure attrition." Higher command concurred that an additional division was needed to help break the deadlock.[17]

A West Point classmate and football teammate of Bradley and Eisenhower, Major General James Van Fleet had a reputation as a superb division commander. Poverty had marked his boyhood in Florida, and the painful memory motivated him to excel in his career as a soldier. A veteran of World War I, the 52-year-old Van Fleet had already earned two Distinguished Service Crosses in World War II, one in Normandy and another during the drive to the Saar River. Now he was told to pull his 90th Infantry Division out of the Saar bridgehead and redirect it to the Ardennes. The plan was to bring the division in position south of the pocket and have it participate in a coordinated III Corps offensive on January 9. For the plan to succeed, however, the element of surprise was deemed crucial: the Germans were to remain in total darkness about the arrival of the veteran American division of 14,000 men. GIs were to cover their shoulder patches. All unit markings on vehicles had to be blotted out. There was to be strict radio silence during the division's 50-mile trip. III Corps was prohibited from making any mention of Van Fleet's ghost troops in telephone conversations and official reports.[18]

As Millikin eagerly awaited the arrival of the new force, orders came down for his other divisions to maintain the pressure on the pocket. Baade's men wearily obeyed without accomplishing anything, except to increase their casualties. By now Heilmann had lost more than 7,000 of his paratroopers, but still the battered outfit continued to resist the 35th Infantry Division every step of the way. Baade had massive supporting fire brought down on each village and road in his sector. On January 7, GIs from the 137th Infantry watched Villers-la-Bonne-Eau "being ripped apart by thundering artillery." Yet the following day, the eleventh day in a row, the regiment again failed to take the heavily defended hamlet of 17 homes. In the cellar of one of these, Sergeant Mazzi and Lieutenant Eschelman whispered to each other as Heilmann's men moved back and forth above their heads. It had now been more than two days since the Pennsylvanian and the Nebraskan had become separated from the 134th Infantry and ended up in Villers. Dust came down from the trembling cellar ceiling as they munched on raw potatoes to quell hunger and thirst.[19]

Grow was livid when he saw Millikin's orders to keep attacking. It was, he fumed, "the most absurd thing I ever read." For several days he had pleaded in vain with Millikin to send his hard-pressed armor some infantry reinforcements. His men had been without sleep for two nights, and he called III Corps to warn that in the next 24 hours battle fatigue would leave his 6th Armored Division "severely affected." It was true that Grow's interrogation teams were picking up signals from POWs that the 167th Volksgrenadier Division was in bad shape and weakening. German replacements were being thrown straight into battle after marches of more than 25 miles. Some said they had received "only one can of meat and a small loaf of bread in the past 3 days." Yet, like Heilmann's paratroopers, Höcker's Volksgrenadiers remained steadfast, their spirits lifted by the fanatical support of elements of the 1st and 12th SS Panzer Divisions.[20]

In the afternoon of January 6, Grow was told that he was to receive reinforcements from Baade's infantry, but that these would amount to no more than a single battalion from the 320th Infantry. Grow immediately understood that only superiority in artillery firepower could now save his division from an even worse fate than that of the previous days. On January 6 and 7, the 6th Armored Division's 105mm and 155mm howitzers pounded the enemy's positions with more than 17,000 rounds. Interrogation teams reported shell-shocked POWs filtering in "with blood coming out their mouths, ears, and noses." But the curtain of steel could not prevent the Americans from suffering more losses, too. On January 8, the Germans ambushed a detachment from Grow's 86th Reconnaissance Squadron. The unit's medic, Roosevelt DeCamilla, earned a Silver Star that day for carrying his comrade William Kirsch 300 yards through a heavy enemy barrage. Kirsch and DeCamilla were the only ones from the detachment's 30 soldiers to survive the massacre. That same day, the 6th Armored Division welcomed the arrival of 200 replacements, while Baade's outfit greedily absorbed close to 600.[21]

With their own numbers dwindling and no hope of reinforcements, the Germans in the Harlange pocket knew the Americans would launch a final offensive soon. On the evening of January 8, however, they were still totally oblivious to the arrival of the 90th Infantry Division. Open trucks had taken Van Fleet's men from the Saar to the southern flank of the pocket through blizzards and dense fog. On the eve of the attack, Patton insisted on meeting with Van Fleet in person at III Corps headquarters in Arlon. En route, Patton watched countless ambulances snake away from the front and trucks with men from Van Fleet's last arriving battalion creep towards battle. Patton waved at the men. Chilled to the bone, the men rose stiffly from their wooden benches to cheer as the jeep marked with three stars drove past. "It was," Patton noted, "the most moving experience of my life." In Arlon, Patton sat down with Van Fleet to go over the plan for the following day. He "patted me on the back," the awestruck division commander noted, "and said, 'Van Fleet, you've never failed me. I know you can do it.'"[22]

It was mid-morning on Tuesday when Millikin's men rose from their foxholes after a night of "disturbed, half-frozen sleep." The main axis of the III Corps attack was the Bastogne–Wiltz highway. The 6th Armored Division would attack along it in a southeasterly direction. Van Fleet's infantry was to move through the 26th Infantry Division near Nothum and push northwest on the key road. As soon as both forces managed to link up near Bras, a village halfway between Bastogne and Wiltz, all escape routes to the east would be cut off, leaving the enemy trapped in the Harlange pocket.[23]

Determined to inspire his men and monitor the situation with his own eyes, General Van Fleet moved so close to the front line when his first battalions jumped off that he barely escaped harm when a mortar shell killed several officers near him. His courage up front earned the commander an exceptional third Distinguished Service Cross. Forgoing preparatory shelling, Van Fleet's 357th Infantry on the left and his 359th regiment on the right took the Germans by surprise, overrunning several of their forward positions.[24]

Elsewhere in the pocket, however, there were no signs of similar momentum. The Waffen SS repulsed Grow's armor at Arloncourt. The 26th and 35th Infantry Divisions, tasked with applying pressure against the pocket from the east and west respectively, were measuring their advances in a few hundred yards at best. At corps headquarters, all eyes remained riveted on Van Fleet's outfit. But things were slowing down in his sector, too, as elements of the 9th Volksgrenadier Division came to the rescue of the Fallschirmjäger, who were now beginning to show the strain. The Volksgrenadiers were part of an outfit that, after having been destroyed in Romania in the autumn, had been refitted and trained in Denmark. It had arrived in the Ardennes just recently and now aimed its considerable firepower, including heavy 120mm mortars and wailing Nebelwerfers, at the 90th Infantry Division. But Van Fleet quickly adapted to the terrain's particular characteristics, forcing his men forward through ravines that blocked counterattacks against the flanks. By nightfall, his division had penetrated the pocket as deep as one mile. When Patton phoned III Corps that evening, Millikin reported, "I think old Van did pretty well."[25]

On Wednesday, January 10, the skies cleared just enough to allow a rare day of air activity over the Harlange pocket. Thunderbolts of the 406th Fighter Group roamed the skies like hawks in search of quarry. They pounced on Bras, strafing and bombing armor, troops, homes, and farms. The air raids on Tarchamps, a village in the center of the pocket, were so frightening that German soldiers hid among the civilians in the cellars, forcing furious officers to come down and chase them out. Just north of the pocket, fighter-bombers streaked past the roofs of Benonchamps, the noise unbearable as bombs tore at walls and foundations. The village church collapsed, leaving only the tower standing. "It was," a villager recalled, "like the end of the world." A single bomb pulverized the stable of the Guillaume farm. Of the 12 civilians who had sat packed together in the cramped space, nothing was ever found but bits of bone, skin, and clothing.[26]

For GIs on the ground, however, the feared fighter-bombers were a godsend, as they helped pave the way for victories long in coming. Having fought for Villers-la-Bonne-Eau for 13 days, on Wednesday Baade's infantrymen finally captured all the hamlet's 17 homes with the help of tanks, tank destroyers, and a company from a chemical battalion. Sergeant Mazzi and Lieutenant Eschelman could hardly believe that their five-day ordeal in one of the hamlet's cellars was now truly over. "We yelled like 2-year-olds," recalled the sergeant, "when we realized that Americans had taken the town."[27]

But the capture of hamlets like Villers came at a mounting cost. James Graff was one of hundreds of soldiers rushed in to replace the heavy losses in the 35th Infantry Division. They had sailed from Boston on December 22, with Scotland as their first destination. In Le Havre, on January 2, they had boarded a French train that had taken three nights and two days to reach Metz. On January 10, open trucks took the replacements right to the edge of the Harlange pocket. James Graff was assigned to C Company of the 134th Infantry. Sergeant Bob Landrum from Illinois showed the newcomer the way to his foxhole. Graff's numb mind registered "a knocked-out kraut chow wagon, a dead horse, a dead driver with the lines still in his hand." He caught sight of another lifeless German "lying on his back, his mouth filled with snow, with the bluest eyes you ever saw." That evening, like all evenings and mornings, Sergeant Landrum read a prayer for his platoon. "We all knelt in the snow," the scared replacement noted, "uncovered, with bowed heads."[28]

That same Wednesday, the 6th Armored Division was down so much in combat strength that Gaffey's battered 4th Armored Division was told to return to the front and attack through Grow's lines to provide more punch. By now, the 76th Medical Battalion was running a factory-style clearing station to deal with the rising number of casualties. The unit prided itself on the fact that on average no more than an hour and a half elapsed between a soldier getting wounded in Grow's sector and medics arriving at the Institute of Notre Dame with the casualty. All three floors of the convent and girls' school were being used for treatment. Countless soldiers suffered from frostbite and trench foot. Those who were brought in with symptoms of battle exhaustion received large doses of sedatives and some time to rest before being sent back to the front. Those who were brought in with similar symptoms a second time were taken to the evacuation hospital in Arlon. By the time the battle for Bastogne came to an end, the medical battalion had treated 3,000 patients.[29]

Keeping a close eye on progress and morale, on Wednesday Patton visited all three infantry divisions battling the Germans in the pocket. Even the 90th Infantry Division's headquarters was now describing progress as "torturously slow." Thunderbolts were pounding German positions in close coordination with Van Fleet's four field artillery battalions. The 343rd Battalion alone expended close to 1,500 shells on Wednesday. But the newly arrived Volksgrenadiers had dug in deep and proved determined and well equipped. Rough terrain, narrow roads, steep grades, and deep snow were also slowing down Van Fleet's troops. Many were falling victim to mines that detectors failed to find beneath snowdrifts. Engineers were working overtime, clearing landing strips for artillery liaison planes, and building sleds for the transport of ammunition and the evacuation of casualties. But the troops lacked winter camouflage, making them conspicuous targets in the bright white fields. By nightfall, losses for two days of battle had mounted to more than 260.[30]

But Van Fleet refused to have attrition eat up his crack division. Hatching another big surprise for the Germans, he decided to strike hard in stygian darkness at 0100 and to press the attack throughout the night without letup. In weather that had turned foul again, and with the heaviest artillery support yet, the ploy worked wonders. The 359th Infantry reported cutting through "sleep-confused Germans," overrunning three defensive positions, and capturing five 75mm guns. Resistance stiffened again as Van Fleet's troops approached three villages on the secondary road that fed into the Bastogne–Wiltz highway and formed a key escape route. Tank destroyers helped the 359th capture Bohey, taking out six tanks and annihilating a hundred infantry. The 357th Infantry fought for Doncols until dark and for Sonlez throughout the night. So much courage was needed to dislodge the Germans from the two villages that in both of them the 357th earned a Distinguished Service Cross.[31]

As the 90th Infantry Division closed in on the final objective of Bras from the southeast, the 6th Armored Division tried to do the same from the northwest. But the Germans continued to make a stand at Wardin, while Grow's battered outfit was on its own again: Gaffey's 4th Armored Division, which had come to its aid the previous day, had already been withdrawn. For in an atmosphere of intense nervousness since the surprise attacks in the Ardennes and the Alsace, American intelligence staffs mistakenly thought they had caught wind of another German strike, this time in the direction of Luxembourg City. With Eisenhower's approval, Bradley had ordered the Third Army to let go of one of its divisions at Bastogne to help screen the city. An angry Patton had halted Gaffey's armor in mid-attack and sent it southward.

Exhausted and freezing, Grow's decimated troops were now drawing on courage born of despair. In a field between dense woods just south of Wardin, troops of the 9th Armored Infantry came under fire from a German tank with a murderous 88mm gun. Sergeant Archer Gammon realized that his platoon was about to be hacked to pieces. The 26-year-old Virginian, a farmer from near Chatham, could think of nothing better to do than launch himself against the tank. Armed with a rifle and grenades, he killed six Germans who tried to protect the tank, as he rushed to within 25 yards of it. The tank backed up a short distance, stopped to fire a round, then backed away some more. The sergeant never stood a chance: the tank's next round scored a direct hit. By buying his men time to save their lives, Archer Gammon earned a posthumous Medal of Honor.[32]

The stonewalling of the 6th Armored Division at Wardin could not prevent the German pocket from collapsing. Grow's interrogation teams signaled that most of the prisoners from the 167th Volksgrenadier Division were deserters who blamed severe ammunition shortages on the fact that there were no longer enough horses to pull the wagon trains. Rations for the soldiers of the 340th Volksgrenadier Division were down to ten ounces of bread and one ounce of fat a day. There were reports of Volksgrenadiers who wore no winter clothing and moved about laboriously "because of bicycle trouble." The 1st SS Panzer Division was thrown into the breach at Doncols. Since the start of January, Mohnke's outfit had lost 60 tanks and more than 1,200 men, and there was now only so much that the "Leibstandarte Adolf Hitler" could still do. Meanwhile, the 5th Fallschirmjäger Division was so close to disintegrating that Heilmann began ordering withdrawals on his own authority. "For the first time in my military career," the veteran of Monte Cassino confessed, "I started to go my own way. I intended to save human lives." At the end of Thursday, January 11, 1,265 Germans were made prisoners in Van Fleet's sector alone. Patton heaved a sigh of relief in his diary: "The end of the Bastogne operation is in sight."[33]

The following day, Van Fleet also sent the 358th Infantry, his reserve regiment, into battle to help seal the pocket as quickly as possible. Even then, it took until evening for the 90th Reconnaissance Troop to make contact with the 6th Armored Division northwest of Bras and the 35th Infantry Division southwest of the village. Grow's men had now also captured Wardin. In the nearby hamlet of Harzy, Belgian civilians watched German officers feed documents to bonfires in front of their command post at the Brasseur farm. III Corps that Friday bagged more than a thousand prisoners. Helped by two wounded GIs who were bringing up the rear, Robert Catlin, one of Van Fleet's soldiers in the 359th, headed towards the prison pen with a bunch of German soldiers who were eager to get out of harm's way. They were almost there when a shell exploded among the prisoners. "One couldn't get up," Catlin remembered, "and one ran by me with his hand blown off." Although he did not feel any pain, Catlin saw blood running down his shredded pants. The American rifleman was on his way to an evacuation hospital in Luxembourg before the day was over.[34]

Robert Catlin was one of almost 1,100 casualties that Van Fleet's 90th Infantry Division suffered in the Ardennes in January 1945. Having taken more than 2,300 losses since late December, Baade's 35th Infantry Division was pulled out of the Harlange pocket as soon as it was sealed on January 12. The resistance in the pocket cost some seven different German outfits close to 8,000 men. More than 70 Belgian and Luxembourgian civilians paid with their lives for the second liberation of a handful of tiny villages in the border area. Some have estimated that about 100,000 shells plowed the densely forested triangle between Bras, Lutrebois, and Lutremange. In Benonchamps, just north of the pocket, one such shell on the first day of 1945 had horribly injured a 20-year-old girl called Marie. Shrapnel had torn the flesh from her shoulder, and shards sat lodged against her spine. By the time American medics were able to evacuate the village's wounded, Marie had been suffering unspeakable pain for almost two weeks. German doctors had not been able to spare any sedatives. They had barely had time to change her bandages. When Marie was carried away, the stench of rotting flesh was so sickening that the girl's grandmother begged God to take her life instead.[35]

3

Although III Corps set out to eliminate the Harlange pocket to allow the Third Army to shake loose in the direction of Houffalize, Patton wanted VIII Corps to simultaneously continue pressuring the enemy along the N15. Patton's insistence was bad news for the 101st Airborne. The reality was that on January 9 only Taylor's paratroopers were available for Middleton to build fresh momentum. The 87th Infantry Division was still busy mopping up in and around Tillet. Miley's dazed paratroopers were recovering from the second bloodletting along Dead Man's Ridge. And most importantly, a rattled Middleton insisted on holding back the 11th Armored Division, despite Patton's repeated exhortations.[36]

General Maxwell Taylor was to have his paratroopers strike in the direction of Foy, three miles north of Bastogne, and Noville, another two miles further north. Both villages on the N15 had played crucial roles in the defense of Bastogne. Both places were now just as vital for the push towards Houffalize. But Taylor's men would have to accomplish their task without the support of Kilburn's armor. There would be little assistance on their left from Miley's men, who were temporarily reduced to no more than patrolling activity. To make matters worse, on its right flank Taylor's outfit tied in with III Corps, a force too preoccupied with the Harlange pocket to be of any help. Colonel Harry Kinnard, the Texan operations officer and McAuliffe's right-hand man during the siege, had seen enough suffering in the past few weeks to haunt him for the rest of his life. Little did he realize, as he later acknowledged, that what lay ahead was "the toughest, most costly fighting at Bastogne."[37]

It took a battalion of Ewell's 501st Parachute Infantry from noon until dark on January 9 to advance 500 yards and capture Recogne just west of the N15. The hamlet cost the airborne troops some 40 casualties. Joseph McGregor was one of them. The lieutenant had suffered a bad head wound at Veghel during the first night of Operation Market Garden in September 1944. He had been through a long and painful recovery, only to return to his company in time to have a sniper in Recogne kill him with a shot to the head.[38]

Another of the casualties was Colonel Julian Ewell, the regimental commander himself. The Oklahoman had been the first to lead his regiment into battle with the Germans east of Bastogne on December 19. Now he was among the first to fall victim to the Germans north of Bastogne, when an artillery barrage took him and his chauffeur by surprise in their jeep. Medic Ed O'Brien, at work in the regimental aid station near the Seminary, was aghast to see his commander carried in with a lacerated leg. He had just helped the surgeon hold down a paratrooper who had a head wound "from which brain was oozing." Shrapnel in his back had also perforated his lungs. The patient was restless and was tearing at his bandages. General Taylor rushed in to check on Ewell just as O'Brien was helping the surgeon lift the colonel from the stretcher onto a table. Ewell's face was etched with pain and he was quickly given a shot of morphine. As they commenced treating the commander, the soldier with the head and lung wounds began praying. His voice gradually weakened. Ten minutes later he stopped breathing.[39]

Many more men were becoming casualties in Colonel Sink's 506th Parachute Infantry. The regiment had jumped off on Ewell's left with the Fazone woods as its objective. Donald Burgett, the 19-year-old private from Detroit, stormed across a field with his comrades, "yelling and screaming, running low and zigzagging through deep snow." On a nearby path, medic John Gibson saw a mine blow up a jeep and slam the dashboard and motor into the driver's chest. In the open field, a trooper sat holding his knee. The man had lost his lower leg. Gibson dropped down beside him, but the soldier refused all treatment. He asked the medic to light him a cigarette. He was pale and in shock and wanted Gibson to find him his boot. Gibson found it 20 feet away and put it at his side. "His foot," Gibson remembered, "and part of his leg were in the shoe."[40]

The paratroopers' agony had just begun. As soon as they entered the Fazone woods, the Germans threw massive mortar and artillery fire at them. A shell hit 1st Battalion headquarters, seriously injuring Robert Harwick, the major who had taken over the unit's command in Noville when Colonel LaPrade was killed on December 19. Medic John Gibson had served with the 3rd Battalion in Normandy and Holland, but nothing had prepared him for what was now happening just north of Bastogne. Barrages plowed into the forest throughout the afternoon and evening. Trees snapped and splinters tore into the men as they clawed into the snow and frozen earth. Gibson went to the rescue of a company commander who had had his foot almost severed at the ankle. The man was bleeding "like a stuck hog." As Gibson applied a pressure bandage, he saw an explosion strike down Robert Evans, a fellow medic. The next shell landed in a tree above Gibson. A fragment cut into his back, pierced his lung, and lodged against his liver. Now the medic was calling for a medic. The regiment had suffered 69 battle casualties, and Gibson waited for what seemed like an eternity for help to arrive. "I could hear," he noted, "the blood bubbles when I exhaled."[41]

At dawn on Wednesday, January 10, Donald Burgett stared at the corpse of a paratrooper that had been ground into the snow by vehicles in the deep of night. With his trench knife, the private fished a pack of Lucky Strikes from the human remains. He left the man's dog tags on the limb of a nearby tree. Insult was added to injury when, later that day, Burgett and his fellow paratroopers were suddenly told to give up their gains and fall back to the line of departure. The same imagined threat to the Third Army's right flank that forced the 4th Armored Division to depart the Harlange pocket had Patton decide that it was safer also to pull the 101st Airborne back inside Bastogne's perimeter. Patton made sure to visit Taylor's headquarters that Wednesday to explain the situation. The welcome news was that the paratroopers were to get a few days' rest. The worry was that soon they would be asked to retrace their steps along the deadly path to Noville.[42]

Patton's order to pull back the paratroopers on January 10 was made easier by the fact that the attack had not in any case been getting anywhere. One of the reasons was the lack of corps support; another was the concentration of German troops just north of Bastogne. The density there had been heavier than elsewhere in the salient ever since the *Schwerpunkt* of the offensive had shifted to the Fifth Panzer Army at the end of December. Now, however, as Hitler was allowing his troops to engage in phased withdrawals from the nose of the bulge, still more enemy troops were falling back on the N15. In Roumont, several miles northwest of Bastogne, Madame de Warnaffe had seen von Lüttwitz install his headquarters and American POWs beg for something to eat. Now the viscountess watched from her château as German troops headed back east. A soldier entered her kitchen. The German appeared far from young and in no hurry. He peeled some potatoes. When he had finished boiling them, he sat down at the table, placed a small bowl in front of him, and filled it with salt. Then he dipped a potato in the bowl and took a bite. He slowly repeated the procedure until he had eaten all the potatoes. Then he fell asleep on the chair.[43]

On January 11 and 12, American artillery kept battering the enemy lines west and north of Bastogne, in preparation for the decisive push towards Houffalize. A stable in Trois Monts, a village opposite the 17th Airborne sector, became a slaughterhouse when a shell exploded among two dozen civilians sitting huddled against the animals for warmth. Seven people, among them refugees from Bastogne, were left dead in the smoking debris. Nine others sustained horrific injuries. Fourteen-year-old Fernand Lambert sat staring at two bleeding stumps where once his legs had been.[44]

As it became clear that the Harlange pocket was collapsing, orders came for the push towards Houffalize to begin on January 13. This time, all the VIII Corps divisions were to participate in the attack. In Millikin's III Corps, Grow's 6th Armored Division would now turn its attention away from the pocket to cover the right flank of the 101st Airborne. Most importantly, Middleton at last ordered the 11th Armored Division back to the front line in support of the 17th and 101st Airborne Divisions. After the furious battle for Houmont, Ted Hartman, the Sherman tank driver from Iowa, had been able to rest and recover in a village several miles to the rear. He had been billeted in a home where one of the Belgian daughters had used fresh milk and D ration bars to ply the GIs with hot chocolate. Now, on Friday, January 12, Hartman and columns of whitewashed Sherman tanks were negotiating the slippery roads on the way back to a battle line "not far from where it had been when we were relieved nine days earlier."[45]

But on the morning of January 13, the battle line west of Bastogne suddenly began moving fast, as the Germans withdrew ever closer to the N15. The 87th Infantry Division encountered very little resistance that Saturday and came close to making contact with the red berets of the British 6th Airborne Division who were pushing in the bulge from the west. The 17th Airborne Division now took Dead Man's Ridge along the highway to Marche with equal ease. Closer to the highway leading north to Houffalize, however, resistance became increasingly savage. At Longchamps on Kilburn's right, the enemy launched fierce counterattacks against Combat Command A of the 11th Armored Division. An engineer battalion was rushed to the Nom de Falize wood to help get rid of a massive minefield hidden under deep snow. A single shell killed William and Henry Warcken, leaving the unit in shock as the good-natured twin brothers from North Dakota had been like a mascot to the men. A seesaw battle erupted for the Bois de Nom de Falize. In a single day, the patch of forest claimed 100 American and 150 German casualties.[46]

Despite a heavy morning barrage and skies clearing again for the fighter-bombers after two days of gray clouds, on Saturday an exhausted 101st Airborne Division found the going tough on both sides of the N15. East of the highway, elements of the 327th Glider Infantry attacked into the Bois Jacques, with Noville as their objective. Deckert's Panzergrenadiers had so thoroughly destroyed their ranks at Champs during the night of January 3 that cooks and supply personnel had been drafted in to serve as riflemen. One platoon sergeant took a long hard look at some photos in his billfold and then shot himself in the foot. Temperatures had dropped so low that Lieutenant Joe Carpenter died from his wounds in the forest because the plasma froze and would not flow. When the 502nd Parachute Infantry failed to keep pace on the glidermen's right, the Germans slipped in from behind. More than a hundred Americans now found themselves trapped in the gloomy Jacques forest.[47]

There were more wrenching scenes as Sink's 506th Parachute Infantry began its third battle for Foy, the key obstacle on the N15 before Noville and

Houffalize. In Richard Winters' 2nd Battalion, one company commander cracked during a charge, leaving the men in his company dangerously exposed. "Winters was going nuts on the radio," one paratrooper recalled. The commander was relieved in mid-battle and replaced by another junior officer. Donald Burgett saw an explosion kill three men near a machine-gun position. Gunner Paul Devitte survived, but only just. He had, Burgett noted, "his left arm torn off above the elbow, his right leg above the knee, and his left leg below the knee." Devitte begged his horrified comrades to look for his arm in the snow and to find him the watch that had been a graduation gift from his parents.[48]

Darkness had fallen by the time Foy was captured and cleared of Germans in house-to-house combat. It did not feel much like a victory to Captain Bernard Ryan, the 3rd Battalion surgeon. He lay on a mattress amidst the other wounded in a Belgian kitchen. German grenades and a Panzerfaust lay scattered about the room. Two bullets from a machine gun had drilled holes in Ryan's chest. The surgeon coughed up blood and said an act of contrition. Four captured Germans were brought up from the cellar. Curses flew and there were angry cries to have the men shot. Captain Ryan intervened and told the paratroopers to use the POWs as litter bearers. The wounded had to be evacuated without delay. There was bound to be a counterattack soon.[49]

The Germans hurled themselves against Foy in the deep of night, but failed to take the village. They returned at 0415 and were repulsed again. Two hours later, however, the bone-weary paratroopers were forced to withdraw when an entire battalion of infantry engaged them with the support of a dozen tanks. The enemy's fury had everything to do with Hitler's decision that Sunday to have the main line of resistance move further east and coincide exactly with the N15 from Houffalize to just north of Bastogne. Foy and Noville now became the anchor points of the German defense. Two hours after recapturing Foy, the Germans also struck hard at the 327th Glider Infantry just east of the highway. The glidermen battled desperately to stave off the attack. They finally managed to do so, but only at the cost of more than 50 casualties, including Lieutenant Colonel Hartford Salee, the 1st Battalion commander, who had his chin ripped away by German machine-gun fire.[50]

Richard Stokes, a reporter for the *St. Louis Post-Dispatch* who covered the battle east of the N15, said the Germans were fighting "with the desperation of men convinced that in their hands lies the salvation or downfall of their country for generations to come." Patton's assessment of the situation was less dramatic. He had visited Taylor's command post the previous day. The

101st Airborne had lost more than two hundred men that Saturday and Bastogne continued to be hit by shells. But Patton had made it clear that such bitter resistance north and northeast of Bastogne was "just what one would expect" as "the enemy must hold in order to extricate what he has left."[51]

"We will get them," the Third Army commander had promised himself in his diary on Saturday evening. As day dawned bright on Sunday, Patton's optimism appeared borne out by events on the ground. Three hours after the loss of Foy, paratroopers, supported by heavy artillery and tanks from the 11th Armored Division, reclaimed the crucial village within 30 minutes. It had taken VIII Corps two weeks to advance just three miles along the N15. Higher headquarters immediately understood the rapid victory at Foy to be "a tipping point."[52]

For troops in the chaos of battle, however, there was no discernible change. An hour after the recapture of Foy, just as its 3rd Battalion was moving through the lines of the 1st Battalion to keep up the pressure, the 502nd Parachute Infantry on the glidermen's right came under attack from its own air force east of the N15. Thunderbolts roared out of the cold blue sky, strafing and bombing American soldiers as they scurried for safety. When the attack was over, 12 men lay dead, including the 3rd Battalion commander. "Some of the men's faces," one corporal noted, "were blown out like toy balloons." More than two dozen paratroopers with hideous injuries were crying out for help amidst splintered pine trees and smoking craters. Medics rushed to the scene only to find that most of the morphine could not be used because it had frozen. "It was," one medic said, "the most horrifying experience I had from D-Day through all the 101st battles."[53]

There were other dark omens that Sunday. Five enemy aircraft screamed across the bright sky and attacked artillery concentrations around Bastogne so fast that dumbfounded troops on the ground scarcely had time to register their appearance. Without realizing it, the Americans had just witnessed in action the German Arado Ar 234, the world's first operational jet bomber.[54]

Meanwhile, an angry Captain Winters had other things to worry about. His 2nd Battalion, still smarting from the tough battle at Foy, had just been told to move out against Noville in deep snow, across an open field, and in broad daylight. Aware that the mission was exceedingly risky, Winters' men gathered outside Foy's damaged church. Stamping their feet, the paratroopers listened to an American chaplain's service through a hole in the wall. The men held hands and bowed their heads.[55]

Through a combination of good fortune, smart use of terrain, and support from an armored task force, by nightfall most of Winters' men had reached positions southeast of Noville unscathed. Fearing that their luck might run out during an attack the following morning, Winters ordered patrols to probe Noville's edges. Groping around in the dark, the men bumped up against Shermans. Frozen corpses lay strewn around them, buried in the snow since the retreat from Noville by the 506th Parachute Infantry and Team Desobry more than three weeks earlier.[56]

That same evening, Ted Hartman and the tank crews from B Company received orders to support an infantry battalion of the 11th Armored Division in an attempt to launch a surprise attack through Noville to capture the high ground just north of it. But the Germans were prepared. As the column of 12 tanks raced along Noville's main road, an 88mm shell struck the seventh Sherman. Gunner Wayne Van Dyke, a corporal from Havana, Illinois, dragged the wounded driver and bow gunner from the burning tank and into the shadow of a church wall. The five tanks behind the disabled Sherman instantly threw their gears into reverse, but one tank hit a mine and came to an abrupt halt, too. The six tanks in front of the burning tank, including Ted Hartman's, plunged forward. They regrouped in an apple orchard to form a semi-circular defense "much like the covered wagons of the old West." But the Germans inched closer and with Panzerfausts began to assault the Shermans one after the other.

Ted Hartman and a few other survivors of the ambush somehow made it back to their lines south of Noville on foot. They did it half-carrying and half-dragging a gunner whose eyes had been scorched by a Panzerfaust explosion. Wayne Van Dyke also managed to get out of Noville alive that night. He lifted his wounded comrades over the church wall, but the driver was too badly injured to take part in the escape. Van Dyke treated the man's wounds, made him comfortable behind the altar, and promised him they would be back. Then he left with the wounded bow gunner and, carrying the man on his back part of the way, finally made contact with paratroop outposts.[57]

In the early hours of Monday, January 15, the hundred and more glidermen in the Bois Jacques listened to the newest order in disbelief. They had just been reached by troops of the 502nd Parachute Infantry, after having been trapped in the forest for almost two days. They had hidden in abandoned German dugouts to escape the worst of the merciless shelling and had subsisted on raw potatoes left behind by the enemy. Now they had received some ammunition and a K ration each, and had been told to resume the attack at dawn. "I figured they wouldn't be satisfied," one of the rescued sergeants complained bitterly, "until we were all killed." Still, at the assigned hour, the glidermen obeyed the order and charged the enemy, "howling like Comanche Indians."[58]

All along Bastogne's front lines, Belgian civilians were now describing the battle as more savage than ever. Unshaven, grimy, their uniforms hung with bandoliers and grenades, American combat troops reminded locals of the *poilus* of the Great War. They were, a Belgian teenager noted, "more irascible, more afraid, stressed out." Ceaseless German counterattacks heightened the nervous atmosphere. The Führer Begleit Brigade launched a vicious strike against Oubourcy when a breach threatened the main line of resistance at the village east of the N15. The 603rd Tank Destroyer Battalion was called in to help when Remer's elite force dug in along a ridge north of Arloncourt, blocking all progress. Something snapped in Arthur Beyer that day when he saw his men held up by machine-gun positions. The corporal took out one position with the 76mm gun of his Hellcat. Then he abandoned the safety of his armored vehicle and, with nothing more than his carbine and grenades, began silencing the enemy along a quarter mile of the ridge. By the time the corporal from Iowa ran out of steam, he had killed eight Germans, captured 18 others, destroyed two machine-gun positions, and eliminated two Panzerfaust teams. The action earned the 25-year-old car mechanic from Mitchell County a Medal of Honor, the highest American decoration for military courage. It was the last of six such decorations bestowed on those who held Bastogne.[59]

In the course of the day, it became obvious that the enemy had begun pulling back even from the N15. West of the highway, elements of the 17th Airborne and 11th Armored Divisions moved against Compogne, a knot of secondary roads just above Noville. As they captured the village, the Americans bagged more than 400 POWs. "The Germans," Patton wrote to his wife that Sunday, "are definitely on the run." In fields and forests abandoned by the enemy, Americans found tiny hoops and nooses of twigs and cords, evidence that hunger was driving the Germans to catch and eat birds. Moving back and forth between positions, Warren Luft, a runner for the 11th Armored Division, saw two wounded Germans hold onto each other in the snow. They were older soldiers and they moaned with pain. Everything was moving so fast now that there was no time for medics to pick them up. As Luft returned to the spot a little later, he found that both men were dead. "Their heads were slouched over," he noticed, "and they were still holding and hugging each other."[60]

By noon, Noville, just five miles from Houffalize along the N15, had fallen to the Americans of the 506th Parachute Infantry without any significant resistance. Behind the altar in the village church, they found the tank driver from Van Dyke's crew. He was still alive. During the night, a German medic had changed his bandages a couple of times and assured him that it would not take the Americans long to make it back.[61]

On the extreme left flank of Middleton's VIII Corps, the 87th Infantry Division was taken out of the line on Tuesday, 16 January. At a cost of more than 1,100 men, Culin's force had now accomplished its task west of Bastogne. Tuesday was a relatively calm day also for the 17th Airborne Division on Culin's right flank. Miley's paratroopers had suffered a staggering 2,480 casualties. The survivors were all too happy to link up with Scottish troops of the 51st Infantry Division who were arriving from where the nose of the bulge had been.[62]

But the battle was not yet over for the 11th Armored Division, even though Kilburn's men had suffered more than 1,200 casualties in just ten days. They were told to cover the last miles to Houffalize and make contact with the Americans who were fighting their way towards them from the north. There was a sense of urgency now. Ted Hartman closed the turret of his new tank. The 19-year-old had just been made commander of the crew. Hartman's driver had never operated a tank except during training in America. They had named their new vehicle "Eloise," after the driver's girlfriend. Armored infantry clambered onto the tanks to hitch a ride. "Jockeying the tanks over those frozen hills of Belgium was a new experience for us," said one of the men. "The machines plunged and bucked through the snow drifts, necessitating a firm grip to stay on them."[63]

Major Michael Greene formed a task force and pushed ahead of the others. He had been told to keep moving and to leave any wounded behind for treatment by those who followed. His men had been issued morphine injection devices that they kept in their armpits to prevent the liquid from freezing. The lonely ride up front made the five-mile stretch look like the longest road in the world. "The men," one GI noted, "were tense and white-knuckled." Then suddenly, as the men rolled down a hill in sight of Houffalize, a sharp firefight erupted. The skirmish was brief and the German rearguard melted away.

By noon on Tuesday, and exactly one month after the start of the Battle of the Bulge, Greene's task force had established contact with elements of the 2nd Armored Division. Patton's Third Army had at last linked up with Hodges' First Army at Houffalize. The attempt to prevent the Americans from breaking out north of Bastogne had cost the Germans more than 7,000 casualties in January. Repeated Allied bombardments of the enemy escape route through Houffalize had left the town a moonscape of charred rubble. GIs kept their mouths covered to avoid inhaling the nauseating stench of burnt flesh from German and Belgian corpses.[64]

Late on Monday afternoon, a few more shells had rained down on Bastogne, causing further damage to the town's Franciscan church. But there had been no further explosions since then, and on Tuesday an eerie silence settled on the battered town. The 101st Airborne had lost 2,370 men during the siege of Bastogne in December. The battle for the town in January had claimed another 2,085 paratroopers. Somewhere between Foy and Noville, soldiers from an airborne artillery unit were detailed to collect frozen corpses for the graves registration units that would soon follow. "They were stacked 12 to a pile," one paratrooper noted, "with the Germans in separate groups from the Americans."[65]

Donald Burgett, the 19-year-old paratrooper from Detroit, helped round up a small group of POWs. In the haversack of one, they found "a piece of sausage and some black bread." A German sergeant begged them not to take the food. One of the paratroopers ignored the prisoner and "ground it under his heel into the snow." Burgett watched the defeated Germans stare at the ground. "I noticed," he said, "that they had tears in their eyes."[66]

Even on Tuesday, the men from the 101st Airborne continued to fight for villages north of Noville. Only in the afternoon did reports filter through of the linkup at Houffalize. Still better news was that the 11th Armored Division would be relieving the paratroopers the following day. At dawn on Wednesday, January 17, John Taylor stood in a barn door, smoking a cigarette butt he had found crumpled in one of his pockets. In September, the sergeant from the 506th Parachute Infantry had lost almost half his platoon in Holland. He had helped hold Bastogne for a month and had just fought his way into Foy and Noville. Now, as he drew deeply on the calming tobacco fumes, he looked back up the street into Rachamps, a tiny village a few miles northeast of Noville. Just as he began to relax, the sergeant heard a suspicious noise behind him inside the barn. He spun around. A door connecting the barn with the farmhouse was slowly being pushed open. A little old Belgian lady stepped into the barn and shuffled his way. She had some bread in her hands and a bowl of hot milk. She held the food out to the American. "I certainly welcomed that," the sergeant recalled decades later. "I've never forgotten."[67]

EPILOGUE

On the morning of Thursday, January 18, 1945, five hundred soldiers from the 101st Airborne Division stood to attention amidst the debris in Bastogne's marketplace. Swaddled in a warm coat, General Middleton, commander of the VIII Corps, climbed onto a makeshift platform. A biting wind whipped up snow and made the parachute that covered the podium bulge out. Middleton called out the names of a major, a lieutenant, a sergeant, and a private. As the men stepped forward, he handed each of them a Silver Star for courage shown at Bastogne. Then the corps commander thanked the representatives from all the 101st Airborne's units for their gallant perform-ance. "I think," he concluded his brief speech, "you're the best bunch of fighting men in the United States or any other army in the world." Acting mayor Léon Jacqmin presented General Taylor with the flag of Bastogne as a token of appreciation and affection from its people. Then, closing the ceremony on a lighter note, Maxwell Taylor demanded a receipt from his corps commander for the return of Bastogne. General Middleton produced a ready-made document affirming that his VIII Corps had been given back Bastogne and that they had found the Belgian town "Kraut disinfected."[1]

The defeat of the Germans at Bastogne had, of course, by no means been just the achievement of the 101st Airborne Division. Indeed, it is my hope that the reader of this book has come away with a much better under-standing, and greater appreciation, of the wide variety of American para-troopers, glidermen, infantry, tank crews, airmen, artillery gunners, engineers, and medical personnel who suffered and died during the long month it took to hold Bastogne and turn siege into offensive.

The victory at Bastogne, moreover, had come at a very high cost for each of the American divisions involved. When one adds up the numbers of those killed, wounded, captured, and missing in action in the battle for Bastogne, the losses for the American military stand at more than 20,000 men. That does not include air force personnel. It also does not take into account casualty figures for the 26th Infantry Division. This book has dealt only marginally with General Paul's men. But it should be kept in mind that, until the arrival of the 35th Infantry Division, it was Paul's outfit that provided vital flank protection for Patton's troops east of the Arlon highway. Also, Paul's infantry played an important role in the reduction of the Harlange pocket. These are points worth making, because the 26th Infantry Division alone suffered more than 2,600 casualties in the southern part of the salient between December 21, 1944 and January 16, 1945.[2]

Collateral damage – and friendly fire even more so – are never easy subjects to discuss. In 1997, for example, Stephen Ambrose in his best-selling book *Citizen Soldiers* let slip quite casually in his chapter on the Battle of the Bulge: "If a village had been or was the scene of a battle, its civilian population was usually gone." It is my hope also that this book has helped shine a light on the cruel fate of thousands of terrorized Belgians and Luxembourgers hidden away in dank collective shelters, dark cellars, and deathtrap barns while battle ebbed and flowed all around them for many weeks.[3]

Amazingly, inside the town of Bastogne, the number of noncombatant casualties remained quite limited, despite the incessant shelling and the many tons of aerial bombs: of the estimated 3,000 civilians surrounded in Bastogne, 21 were killed and 110 wounded. Most of the collateral damage, however, occurred on Bastogne's perimeter. Here people were caught in the crossfire of machine guns, mass shelling, and the merciless destruction wrought by fighter-bombers (almost all Allied aircraft). More than 400 Belgians and Luxembourgers died in dozens of small villages and tiny hamlets all around Bastogne. The number of wounded on the perimeter is virtually impossible to calculate, and many, especially the elderly, died of exhaustion and illness in the months following the battle.

The material damage was huge, even in a forested area that was sparsely populated. Of Bastogne's 1,250 homes, more than 200 were totally destroyed and some 450 were left uninhabitable; most others were at least partly damaged. Around the perimeter, some 700 homes were completely devastated and another 1,300 seriously damaged. For the region's small farmers, the loss of horses and livestock was made worse by the fact that some 1,500 stables and 1,400 barns had been razed to the ground.[4]

The high cost for American troops and Belgian civilians was made more painful still by the fact that the Battle of the Bulge did not end with the complete destruction of the massive armies that the Germans risked in their gamble to reach the Meuse and Antwerp and split open the Western Front. Total losses (killed, wounded, captured, and missing) for the 12 German divisions and two brigades involved in the battle for Bastogne amounted to some 25,000. This confirms that it was a battle of attrition more than anything else, especially after Patton's relief of Bastogne on December 26. It brings the combined losses for both opponents to more than 45,000 men in a battle fought for a small town with a peacetime population of 4,000 and a junction of seven roads.[5]

If one recalls, however, that at the start of January 1945 alone, some 62,000 German troops were concentrated in front of III and VIII Corps at Bastogne, the German losses in dead, wounded, and prisoners make clear that many more of the enemy managed to evade an Allied trap. This should not come as too much of a surprise, of course, given that Allied commanders had made a choice before the end of December to push in the bulge at the waist, rather than take a bold risk at the shoulder. By going for the tiger's jaws rather than his tail (to paraphrase a scornful Patton), they allowed the tiger to slip past the cage and into his lair. On January 28, 1945, when the Allies officially declared the entire salient erased, large numbers of the three German Ardennes armies had long since pulled out of the cauldron in carefully orchestrated phased withdrawals.[6]

The troops that escaped and the wounded that were patched up lived to fight another day. As early as the second week of January 1945, Hitler had ordered his elite SS panzer divisions to begin withdrawing from around Bastogne and to head towards the Soviet armies that were once again steam-rolling the Eastern Front. Waffen SS and Wehrmacht troops that made it back from the Ardennes would also be exacting a heavy toll on Allied troops as soon as they breached more of the West Wall and began crossing the mighty German rivers that held up the advance to Berlin.[7]

* * *

To the soldiers in the Ardennes – American and German – the bigger canvas of the war never made much sense, if they could see it at all. The men in the front lines fought their own private battles: with the enemy in dugouts just yards away, with fear and freezing temperatures, and with aching bones. They drew strength not from strategic purpose, but from the presence of comrades, fervent prayer, the photo of a wife or girlfriend, glowing thoughts of home. Immediately after the war, when job and family obligations took over, there was rarely occasion for veterans to revisit Bastogne. But, as time went by and veterans became older and began to retire, more and more of them started to return to the place that had defined who they were when they were young; the place also where many of their comrades had fallen, remaining young forever. Generally, American visits would go hand in hand with Belgian celebrations and official speeches. Meanwhile, Germans would slip quietly and mostly unnoticed into and out of the cemetery at Recogne, near the N15, where some 6,800 of their countrymen lie buried.

By the time of the fiftieth anniversary of the battle for Bastogne, so many American veterans were being drawn back to the area that the local authorities decided to create a special symbol to remember them by. A place was selected near Bizory to create a "Bois de la Paix" or "Wood of Peace." More than 4,000 birches, oaks, and beech trees were planted and dedicated to the civilians who suffered in the battle for Bastogne, and to the Americans who liberated them a second time. Bizory is where Americans of the 501st Parachute Infantry stopped Kokott's Volksgrenadiers in a brutal battle on December 20, 1944, bringing to a halt one of what would be many attacks on Bastogne's perimeter. In the years since the creation of the Bois de la Paix, the flood of veterans has slowed to a trickle and dried up. Today, visitors who enter the wood in winter, and listen to the swaying trees and shivering branches, can be forgiven for thinking that they hear also, carried on the bitter wind, the names of all those who once hoped they would hold Bastogne.

CAST OF CHARACTERS

Americans

Don Addor: private from Washington D.C. with Combat Command B, 10th Armored Division

George Allen: lieutenant from Philadelphia in charge of the 101st Airborne Division's POW compound in Bastogne

Lt. Col. Ray Allen: commander of the 3rd Battalion, 327th Glider Infantry Regiment, 101st Airborne Division

Maj. Gen. Paul Baade: commander of the 35th Infantry Division

Robert Bowen: sergeant from Maryland and member of the 327th Glider Infantry Regiment, 101st Airborne Division

Lt. Gen. Omar Bradley: commander of the 12th Army Group to the south of the salient

Lt. Col. Barry Browne: commander of a task force for the protection of the heavy artillery concentrated at Senonchamps; killed in action

Donald Burgett: private from Detroit with the 506th Parachute Infantry Regiment, 101st Airborne Division

Col. Steve Chappuis: commander of the 502nd Parachute Infantry Regiment, 101st Airborne Division

Brig. Gen. Frank Culin, Jr.: commander of the 87th Infantry Division

Maj. William Desobry: in charge of a force from Combat Command B, 10th Armored Division, blocking access to Noville, northeast of Bastogne

Bruce Egger: sergeant from Idaho in the 328th Infantry Regiment, 26th Infantry Division

Gen. Dwight D. Eisenhower: Supreme Commander of the Allied Expeditionary Forces in Europe

Col. Julian Ewell: commander of the 501st Parachute Infantry Regiment, 101st Airborne Division

John Fague: sergeant from Pennsylvania and infantryman in Combat Command B, 11th Armored Division

Maj. Gen. Hugh Gaffey: commander of the 4th Armored Division

Col. Joseph "Duke" Gilbreth: in charge of Combat Command R, 9th Armored Division

Maj. Gen. Robert Grow: commander of the 6th Armored Division

Ted Hartman: Iowan and Sherman tank driver in Combat Command B, 11th Armored Division

Lt. Gen. Courtney Hodges: commander of the First Army, tasked with pushing down from the northern salient and linking up with the Third Army at Houffalize

Maj. Albin Irzyk: commander of the 8th Tank Battalion, 4th Armored Division

Brig. Gen. Charles Kilburn: commander of the 11th Armored Division

Lt. Col. Harry Kinnard: 101st Airborne Division's operations officer and McAuliffe's right-hand man

Lt. Col. Carl Kohls: 101st Airborne Division's supply officer

Bill Korte: sergeant from Pennsylvania and member of the 110th Infantry Regiment, 28th Infantry Division

Lt. Col. James LaPrade: commander of the 1st Battalion, 506th Parachute Infantry Regiment, 101st Airborne Division, sent to help reinforce Team Desobry at Noville; killed in action

Fred MacKenzie: reporter for the *Buffalo Evening News* who spent the siege inside McAuliffe's command post

Brig. Gen. Anthony McAuliffe: 101st Airborne Division artillery commander, in charge of all American troops in Bastogne until the return of Maj. Gen. Maxwell Taylor on December 27, 1944

Maj. Gen. Troy Middleton: commander of the VIII Corps

Maj. Gen. William Miley: commander of the 17th Airborne Division

Maj. Gen. John Millikin: commander of the III Corps

Ed O'Brien: medic in the Seminary aid station of the 501st Parachute Infantry Regiment, 101st Airborne Division

James Parker: Californian captain and Ninth Air Force liaison inside Bastogne, responsible for coordination of air strikes around the perimeter

Lt. Gen. George S. Patton, Jr.: commander of the Third Army

Maj. Gen. Willard Paul: commander of the 26th Infantry Division

Jack Prior: captain fresh out of medical school at the University of Vermont and replacement for regular battalion surgeon in Combat Command B, 10th Armored Division

Col. William Roberts: commander of Combat Command B, 10th Armored Division

Francis Sampson: Catholic chaplain in the 101st Airborne Division

James Simms: private, Alabaman high-school teacher, and fresh replacement in the 506th Parachute Infantry Regiment, 101st Airborne Division

Col. Robert Sink: commander of the 506th Parachute Infantry Regiment, 101st Airborne Division

Maj. Gen. Maxwell Taylor: commander of the 101st Airborne Division who rushed back from the United States to take over from McAuliffe on December 27, 1944

Lt. Col. Clifford Templeton: commander of the 705th Tank Destroyer Battalion that was sent from Germany to help the Americans defend Bastogne

Charles Wilson: private from Chicago, married and father of a two-year-old daughter, who fought with a machine-gun squad in an infantry battalion of Combat Command B, 4th Armored Division

Richard "Dick" Winters: Pennsylvanian captain and executive officer of the 2nd Battalion, 506th Parachute Infantry Regiment, 101st Airborne Division

Paul Yearout: married, father of two small children, and lieutenant in the 110th Infantry Regiment, 28th Infantry Division

Britons

Field Marshal Sir Bernard Law Montgomery: commander of 21 Army Group to the north of the salient

Germans

Generalleutnant Fritz Bayerlein: commander of the Panzer Lehr Division

General Erich Brandenberger: commander of the Seventh Army, the southernmost of the three attacking armies

Generalmajor Hans-Joachim Deckert: commander of the 15th Panzergrenadier Division

Generalleutnant Walter Denkert: commander of the 3rd Panzergrenadier Division

SS-Oberstgruppenführer Josef "Sepp" Dietrich: commander of the Sixth Panzer Army, the northernmost of the three attacking armies

Generalmajor Ludwig Heilmann: commander of the 5th Fallschirmjäger Division

Horst Helmus: 18-year-old soldier from the vicinity of Cologne who was part of an anti-tank battalion in the 26th Volksgrenadier Division

Generalleutnant Hanskurt Höcker: commander of the 167th Volksgrenadier Division

Generalmajor Hans-Joachim Kahler: commander of the Führer Grenadier Brigade

Generalmajor Heinz Kokott: commander of the 26th Volksgrenadier Division

SS-Standartenführer Hugo Kraas: commander of the 12th SS Panzer Division "Hitler Jugend"

SS-Oberführer Wilhelm Mohnke: commander of the 1st SS Panzer Division "Leibstandarte Adolf Hitler"

SS-Gruppenführer Hermann Priess: commander of the I SS Panzer Corps

Generalmajor Otto Remer: commander of the Führer Begleit Brigade

Generalleutnant Theodor Tolsdorff: commander of the 340th Volksgrenadier Division

Generalmajor Meinrad von Lauchert: commander of the 2nd Panzer Division

General Heinrich von Lüttwitz: commander of the XLVII Panzer Corps

General Hasso Eccard von Manteuffel: commander of the Fifth Panzer Army, the army at the center of the attacking force, tasked with capturing Bastogne

Civilians

Madeleine Barthelemi: pregnant woman who fled the town center and hid in a cellar in the hamlet of Isle-le-Pré on Bastogne's southern perimeter

Denyse de Coune: inhabitant of Assenois who experienced the terrifying battle for the key village just south of Bastogne

The Garcia family: father, mother, and five children who suffered a cruel fate in Villers-la-Bonne-Eau, a village in the Harlange pocket, southeast of Bastogne

Maria Gillet: young woman training to be a teacher who sheltered in the underground corridors of Bastogne's Institute of Notre Dame

Baroness Greindl: mother of 12 children and proprietress of the château at Isle-la-Hesse whose husband had been sent to a Nazi concentration camp

Maria Gustin: woman who hid in a cellar and lived through the battle for Chaumont, south of Bastogne

Léon Jacqmin: veteran of the Great War and businessman who served as acting mayor of Bastogne during the month-long battle

André Meurisse: eight-year-old boy from Bastogne wounded during an Allied bombing raid on Mande-Saint-Étienne

Marie du Bus de Warnaffe: inhabitant of a château in Roumont, several miles northwest of Bastogne, where General von Lüttwitz had his command post

NOTES

A note on notes

The A, B, and ETHINT series references pertain to manuscripts produced by German military commanders on the performance of their units in the Ardennes. The series form part of the U.S. Army Foreign Military Studies Program (1945–54) and the originals are in the National Archives. Unless indicated otherwise, U.S. Army citations for the Distinguished Service Cross, the Silver Star, and the Bronze Star can be found at http://projects.military-times.com/citations-medals-awards/

Abbreviations in notes

BBC: Battle of the Bulge Historical Foundation Collection
CEGESOMA: Centre d'Études et de Documentation Guerre et Sociétés Contemporaines
CHC: Chester Hansen Collection
CMP: Charles MacDonald Papers
GHC: George Hofmann Collection
GKC: George Koskimaki Collection
HKP: Harry Kinnard Papers
JVP: James Van Fleet Papers
MDC: Maurice Delaval Collection
MHI: U.S. Army Military History Institute
PHC: Paul Harkins Collection
ROHA: Rutgers Oral History Archives World War II
RWC: Richard Winters Collection
SVG: Archives et Documentation du Service des Victimes de la Guerre
VSC: Veterans Survey Collection
WDP: William Duncan Papers
WMP: William Miley Papers

Introduction

1. Martin Blumenson, *The Patton Papers, 1940–1945*, Da Capo, Cambridge, Mass., 1996, 622.
2. Peter Mansoor, *The GI Offensive in Europe: The triumph of American infantry divisions, 1941–1945*, University Press of Kansas, Lawrence, Kans., 1999, 216; Harold Winton, *Corps Commanders of the Bulge: Six American generals and victory in the Ardennes*, University Press of Kansas, Lawrence, Kans., 2007, xv.
3. Quote is from Winton, *Corps Commanders*, 347.

4. John Nelson Rickard, *Advance and Destroy: Patton as commander in the Bulge*, University Press of Kentucky, Lexington, Ky., 2011, 15–18; Trevor Dupuy et al., *Hitler's Last Gamble: The Battle of the Bulge*, HarperCollins, New York, 1994, 9–12.
5. Dupuy et al., *Hitler's Last Gamble*, 35–40.
6. Hugh Cole, *The Ardennes: Battle of the Bulge*, Office of the Chief of Military History, Washington, D.C., 1965, 650–1; Dupuy et al., *Hitler's Last Gamble*, 18; Williamson Murray and Allan Millett, *A War To Be Won: Fighting the Second World War*, Belknap Press of Harvard University Press, Cambridge, Mass., and London, 2000, 468; and Rickard, *Advance*, 1.
7. On tanks and artillery, see Charles MacDonald, *A Time for Trumpets: The untold story of the Battle of the Bulge*, Quill William Morrow, New York, 1985, 618; Cole, *The Ardennes*, 659. Quotes are from Winton, *Corps Commanders*, 347, and Blumenson, *Patton Papers*, 613.
8. Rickard, *Advance*, 318–19; Winton, *Corps Commanders*, 337–8.
9. Such American actions, and the stubborn resistance at Bastogne in particular, constitute clear proof of strong small unit leadership. They also go some way to counterbalance a school of historiography that has emphasized the superiority of the German over the American military in World War II (see, for example, Martin van Creveld, *Fighting Power: German and United States Army performance, 1939–45*, Greenwood Press, Westport, Conn., 1982; Jörg Muth, *Command Culture: Officer education in the U.S. Army and the German armed forces, 1901–1940, and the consequences for World War II*, University of North Texas Press, Denton, Tex., 2011).
10. On the fate of Saint-Vith, see, for example, Raymund Graf, "Märtyrerstadt St. Vith," in Kurt Fagnoul (ed.), *Kriegsschicksale 1944–1945*, H. Doepgen-Beretz, St. Vith, 1969, 229–52.
11. Totals are calculated from personnel statistics in Appendix E of Dupuy et al., *Hitler's Last Gamble*. On artillery expenditure, see Rickard, *Advance*, 318.
12. Today the box with Bastogne's soil is preserved in the Harry S. Truman Library and Museum in Independence, Missouri. For the detailed history of the monument, see Michel Francard and Robert Moërynck, *Le mémorial du Mardasson à Bastogne*, Musée de la Parole en Ardenne, Marche-en-Famenne, 2005.

One: Lives for Time

1. Patricia Wharton, *Reading Between the Lines: A World War II correspondence, May 1944 – March 1945*, Privately published, Seal Cove, Maine, 1999, 70–3; Michael Weaver, *Guard Wars: The 28th Infantry Division in World War II*, Indiana University Press, Bloomington and Indianapolis, Ind., 2010, 188, 196, 209, 210.
2. Weaver, *Guard Wars*, 210; Frank Price, *Troy H. Middleton: A biography*, Louisiana State University Press, Baton Rouge, La., 1974, 4–13.
3. Robert Phillips, *To Save Bastogne*, Stein and Day, New York, 1983, 18.
4. John McManus, *Alamo in the Ardennes*, John Wiley, Hoboken, N.J., 2007, 1–3.
5. Phillips, *To Save Bastogne*, 20.
6. MacDonald, *A Time for Trumpets*, 101–2.
7. Kokott, B-040, 1, 2, 8, and "Füsilier-Regt 39," 1, Folder "26th Volksgrenadier Division," Box 10, CMP/MHI; Bayerlein, A-941, 6, 12, Folder "Panzer Lehr Division," Box 9, CMP/MHI.
8. E.T. Melchers, *Bombenangriffe auf Luxemburg in Zwei Weltkriegen*, Sankt-Paulus-Druckerei, Luxembourg, 1984, 431.
9. Dorothy Chernitsky, *Voices from the Foxholes: Men of the 110th Infantry during World War II*, Privately published, Uniontown, Pa., 1991, 26–8.
10. McManus, *Alamo in the Ardennes*, 20–8; Weaver, *Guard Wars*, 214–15.
11. Michael Green and James Brown, *War Stories of the Battle of the Bulge*, Zenith Press, Minneapolis, Minn., 2010, 40–1; and Chernitsky, *Voices from the Foxholes*, 41.

12. Phillips, *To Save Bastogne*, 52–3; MacDonald, *A Time for Trumpets*, 137–8; Helmus diary, December 16, 1944, Folder "German Diary and Sketches," Box 7, CMP/MHI; Kokott, B-040, 16, CMP/MHI.
13. McManus, *Alamo in the Ardennes*, 44; Cole, *The Ardennes*, 180–2.
14. Kokott, B-040, 16, CMP/MHI; von Lüttwitz, ETHINT-41, 2, Folder "XLVII Panzer Corps," Box "Correspondence German Historians and Veterans," CMP/MHI; Bayerlein, A-941, 17–18, CMP/MHI.
15. Helmus diary, December 16, 1944; "Füsilier-Regt 39," 1, CMP/MHI.
16. Phillips, *To Save Bastogne*, 49; McManus, *Alamo in the Ardennes*, 67–8, 75–6.
17. Kokott, B-040, 25, 27, CMP/MHI; Cole, *The Ardennes*, 186–7.
18. Cole, *The Ardennes*, 177–8; McManus, *Alamo in the Ardennes*, 64; Fritz Rasqué, *Das Oesling im Krieg*, Reprinted (originally published 1946), Éditions Emile Borschette, Christnach, 1991, 438–9.
19. McManus, *Alamo in the Ardennes*, 86; Weaver, *Guard Wars*, 216, 214.
20. Phillips, *To Save Bastogne*, 67–9; Cole, *The Ardennes*, 187.
21. Phillips, *To Save Bastogne*, 103–5, 159–60.
22. McManus, *Alamo in the Ardennes*, 88–91.
23. Gerald Astor, *A Blood-Dimmed Tide: The Battle of the Bulge by the men who fought it*, Dell, New York, 1994, 122–4.
24. McManus, *Alamo in the Ardennes*, 46–8.
25. Rasqué, *Das Oesling im Krieg*, 388–9.
26. Roland Gaul, "Brief historical survey," printed by author from www.luxembourg.co.uk/ NMMH/waryears.html (link no longer available); E.T. Melchers, *Luxemburg: Befreiung und Ardennen Offensive*, Sankt-Paulus-Druckerei, Luxembourg, 1982, 433–4.
27. McManus, *Alamo in the Ardennes*, 72, 89, 92–3; Rasqué, *Das Oesling im Krieg*, 142–4.
28. Phillips, *To Save Bastogne*, 25; McManus, *Alamo in the Ardennes*, 93–5, 106.
29. Johnson, "Battle of the Bulge," 4–5, 28th Infantry Division, Box 2, VSC/MHI; Joseph Maertz, *Luxemburg in der Ardennenoffensive 1944/45*, Sankt-Paulus-Druckerei, Luxembourg, 1981, 158–9, 164–71; MacDonald, *A Time for Trumpets*, 278–9; John Toland, *Battle: The story of the Battle of the Bulge*, University of Nebraska Press, Nebr., Lincoln and London, 1999, 91–2; Hohengarten, "Vor vierzig Jahren: Die Gestapo in der Ardennenoffensive," 7, Rap 429 – tr. 272 406, SVG.
30. Phillips, *To Save Bastogne*, 150, 160–1.
31. McManus, *Alamo in the Ardennes*, 136, 91–2, 138; Weaver, *Guard Wars*, 219.
32. Luc Rivet and Yvan Sevenans, *La bataille des Ardennes: Les civils dans la guerre*, Didier Hatier, Brussels, 1985, 150; Chernitsky, *Voices from the Foxholes*, 212.
33. Johnson, "Battle of the Bulge," 5–6, VSC/MHI.
34. Chernitsky, *Voices from the Foxholes*, 212; Johnson, "Battle of the Bulge," 5–6, VSC/MHI.
35. Chernitsky, *Voices from the Foxholes*, 42–3.
36. Ibid., 127–8.
37. McManus, *Alamo in the Ardennes*, 155–6.
38. Franz Legrand, "10 septembre 1944: La 1ère libération de Bastogne," *Pays de Bastogne*, 3 (September 1991), 2; Chernitsky, *Voices from the Foxholes*, 71–2; Rasqué, *Das Oesling im Krieg*, 428–9.
39. Maher, "Company C," 5, 28th Infantry Division, Box 2, VSC/MHI; Cole, *The Ardennes*, 192.
40. Chernitsky, *Voices from the Foxholes*, 339, 164–75.
41. "Questions Answered by Middleton," Folder "ETO Historian's File," Box 7, CMP/MHI; Cole, *The Ardennes*, 186; Weaver, *Guard Wars*, 240.

Two: Locking Shields

1. Winton, *Corps Commanders*, 156.
2. Dupuy et al., *Hitler's Last Gamble*, 178–9.

3. Ibid., 181.
4. Cole, *The Ardennes*, 295-6; Price, *Middleton*, 224-5.
5. Walter Reichelt, *Phantom Nine: The 9th Armored Division, 1942-1945*, Presidial Press, Austin, Tex., 1987, 135; McManus, *Alamo in the Ardennes*, 157-8.
6. Wharton, *Reading Between the Lines*, 77-8; Weaver, *Guard Wars*, 227; McManus, *Alamo in the Ardennes*, 157-60.
7. Chernitsky, *Voices from the Foxholes*, 339-43; Reichelt, *Phantom Nine*, 132; McManus, *Alamo in the Ardennes*, 160-1.
8. Shawn Umbrell, "First on the line: The 35th Engineer Battalion in World War Two and the evolution of a high-performance combat unit," Master's thesis, U.S. Army Command and General Staff College, Fort Leavenworth, KS, 2009, 4-5; Alfred Beck et al., *The Corps of Engineers: The war against Germany*, Center of Military History, Washington, D.C., 1985, 476-8.
9. Gillet journal, December 17, 1944, AA 1207, CEGESOMA; Lamotte letter, January 10, 1984, 4, AA 1207, CEGESOMA; André Drossart, "Bastogne en enfer," *Le Vif*, 157, December 22, 1983; Joss Heintz, *Dans le périmètre de Bastogne, décembre 1944 – janvier 1945*, Les Presses de l'Avenir, Arlon, n.d., 66; Cercle d'Histoire de Bastogne, *Bastogne – Hiver 44-45: Des civils témoignent*, Bastogne, 1994, 436-7, 444, 445, 462, 498.
10. Letter mayor Bastogne to mayor Longchamps, October 21, 1948, AA 145, CEGESOMA; Olivier Orianne, *Un mois en enfer: La bataille des Ardennes en province de Luxembourg*, Weyrich, Neufchâteau, 2005, 37.
11. Don Addor, *My Last Battle: Noville outpost to Bastogne*, Trafford, Victoria, BC, 2004, 5-10.
12. Laurence Critchell, *Four Stars of Hell*, Battery Press, Nashville, Tenn., 1982, 221-2; George Koskimaki, *The Battered Bastards of Bastogne: The 101st Airborne in the Battle of the Bulge*, Ballantine Books, New York, 2007, 9-10. Quote is from Stephen Ambrose, *Band of Brothers*, Simon & Schuster, New York, 2001, 170.
13. Koskimaki, *Battered Bastards of Bastogne*, 28, 29-30, 32-3, 38; William Guarnere and Edward Heffron, *Brothers in Battle, Best of Friends*, Berkley Caliber, New York, 2007, 154; Donald Burgett, *Seven Roads to Hell: A Screaming Eagle at Bastogne*, Dell, New York, 2000, 1-2; Ambrose, *Band of Brothers*, 165-8.
14. Col. William Roberts interview, January 12, 1945, Folder "10th Armored Division," Box 2, CMP/MHI; Price, *Middleton*, 230.
15. According to Colonel Ralph Mitchell's study, the 101st Airborne's strength at the time of the alert was 805 officers and 11,035 enlisted men. Ralph Mitchell, *The 101st Airborne Division's Defense of Bastogne*, Combat Studies Institute, Fort Leavenworth, Kans., 1986, 8.
16. Quote is from Fred MacKenzie, *The Men of Bastogne*, David McKay, New York, 1968, 6. McAuliffe was awarded the Silver Star for his action in Normandy.
17. Dupuy et al., *Hitler's Last Gamble*, 179-80.
18. McManus, *Alamo in the Ardennes*, 162.
19. Cole, *The Ardennes*, 307.
20. Kinnard interview, 40-3, HKP/MHI; MacKenzie, *The Men of Bastogne*, 3.
21. Burgett, *Seven Roads to Hell*, 48.
22. MacKenzie, *The Men of Bastogne*, 13-14.
23. Koskimaki, *Battered Bastards of Bastogne*, 47, 109; Critchell, *Four Stars of Hell*, 238-9.
24. Helena Smith, "A few men in soldier suits," *American Heritage*, VIII:5 (1957), 30; Beck et al., *Corps of Engineers*, 478.
25. Cercle d'Histoire de Bastogne, *Bastogne: Des civils témoignent*, 32-4; Rivet and Sevenans, *La bataille des Ardennes*, 192-3.
26. Koskimaki, *Battered Bastards of Bastogne*, 55-9.
27. ibid., 60-1.
28. Francis Sampson, *Look Out Below! A Story of the airborne by a paratrooper padre*, Catholic University of America Press, Washington, D.C., 1958, 105-6, 110.
29. CCR, "After Action Report, 1-31 December 1944," Folder "9th Armored Division," Box 1, CMP/MHI. Quote is from Chernitsky, *Voices from the Foxholes*, 343-4.

30. Cole, *The Ardennes*, 297; Charles Sklenar, "Mess on the front," February 27, 2010, at www.battleofthebulgememories.be
31. McManus, *Alamo in the Ardennes*, 189–90, 191–2.
32. Wickert, "My Experience," 1–5, Folder "10th Armored Division," Box 2, CMP/MHI.
33. Cole, *The Ardennes*, 303; Eugene Patterson, *Patton's Unsung Armor of the Ardennes: The Tenth Armored Division's secret dash to Bastogne*, Xlibris, Bloomington, IN, 2008, 66–7.
34. Cercle d'Histoire de Bastogne, *Bastogne: Des civils témoignent*, 53–4, 115–18; Heintz, *Périmètre*, 143.
35. Critchell, *Four Stars of Hell*, 240; Umbrell, "First on the Line," 95–7.
36. Sklenar, "Mess on the front."
37. O'Hara interview, 1–4, Folder "10th Armored Division," Box 2, CMP/MHI; Robert Houston, *D-Day to Bastogne: A paratrooper recalls World War II*, Exposition Press, Smithtown, NY, 1980, 93–8; Koskimaki, *Battered Bastards of Bastogne*, 64–76; McManus, *Alamo in the Ardennes*, 200–5; Cercle d'Histoire de Bastogne, *Bastogne: Des civils témoignent*, 64–6; Rasqué, *Das Oesling im Krieg*, 81–2, 394.
38. Bayerlein, A-941, 9, Folder "Panzer Lehr Division," Box 9, CMP/MHI.
39. McManus, *Alamo in the Ardennes*, 165, 178.
40. MacDonald, *A Time for Trumpets*, 489.
41. Watts to MacDonald, February 28, 1985, Folder "Major Eugene Watts," Box 1, CMP/MHI; McManus, *Alamo in the Ardennes*, 184–6.
42. Etters to his family, December 2, 1944, 10th Armored Division, Box 1, VSC/MHI.
43. MacDonald, *A Time for Trumpets*, 494–5; Koskimaki, *Battered Bastards of Bastogne*, 83; McManus, *Alamo in the Ardennes*, 196–7.
44. Astor, *A Blood-Dimmed Tide*, 223–4.
45. Orianne, *Un mois en enfer*, 37.
46. Burgett, *Seven Roads to Hell*, 53–5.
47. Ibid., 60–6.
48. James Simms, *A Soldier's Armageddon*, Sunflower University Press, Manhattan, Kans., 1999, 14–15.
49. Koskimaki, *Battered Bastards of Bastogne*, 94–5; Burgett, *Seven Roads to Hell*, 89.
50. Addor, *My Last Battle*, 30–5.
51. Desobry interview, August 7, 1983, Folder "10th Armored Division," Box 2, CMP/MHI; Astor, *A Blood-Dimmed Tide*, 226–7; MacDonald, *A Time for Trumpets*, 496–7.
52. Simms, *A Soldier's Armageddon*, 20.
53. MacKenzie, *The Men of Bastogne*, 64, 69–74.
54. Joss Heintz, *Dans le périmètre de Bastogne, décembre 1944 – janvier 1945* (updated and expanded edition), Musée en Piconrue, Bastogne, 2005, 6, 196–200.
55. "C'était leur Noël 44," *CRIBA-Estafette*, 227 (February 2004), 3.
56. Michael Collins and Martin King. *Voices of the Bulge: Untold stories from veterans of the Battle of the Bulge*, Zenith Press, Minneapolis, Minn., 2011, 113–15.
57. Peterson, "326th Medical Company," 1–3, Folder 31, Box 25, GKC/MHI; Koskimaki, *Battered Bastards of Bastogne*, 113.
58. Peterson, "326th Medical Company," 3, GKC/MHI; Mark Bando, *101st Airborne: The Screaming Eagles in World War II*, Zenith Press, St. Paul, Minn., 2007, 167–8; Koskimaki, *Battered Bastards of Bastogne*, 117.
59. McManus, *Alamo in the Ardennes*, 232.
60. Edward O'Brien, *With Geronimo across Europe: An account of a combat medic in the 501st Parachute Infantry Regiment during World War II*, 101st Airborne Division Association, Sweetwater, Tenn., 1990, 181–9.

Three: Locking Horns

1. "Summary Weather Conditions," Folder "ETO Historian's File," Box 7, CMP/MHI; Hansen, "Diaries," December 20, 1944, Folders 2–4, Box 5, CHC/MHI; Price, *Middleton*, 248.

2. "Recommendation Distinguished Unit Citation," 1–2, Tank Destroyer Battalions, Folder "Walsh, Francis," Box 3, VSC/MHI.
3. Cole, *The Ardennes*, 308–9.
4. Raymond Bell, "Black gunners in Bastogne," *Army*, 54:11 (2004), 50–2.
5. Dick Winters, *Beyond Band of Brothers: The war memoirs of Major Dick Winters*, Berkley Caliber, New York, 2008, 169–70.
6. S.L.A. Marshall, *Bastogne: The story of the first eight days*, Infantry Journal Press, Washington, D.C., 1946, 65; Dupuy et al., *Hitler's Last Gamble*, 187.
7. Burgett, *Seven Roads to Hell*, 108; McManus, *Alamo in the Ardennes*, 234.
8. Von Lüttwitz, ETHINT-41, 2, Folder "XLVII Panzer Corps," Box "Correspondence German Historians and Veterans," CMP/MIII; Burgett, *Seven Roads to Hell*, 103–4.
9. "Award of Bronze Star Medal," January 26, 1945, Folder "Donations Members 10th Armored Division," Box "Donations Members Armored Divisions," BBC/MHI.
10. Simms, *A Soldier's Armageddon*, 21–9.
11. MacKenzie, *The Men of Bastogne*, 93–7; McManus, *Alamo in the Ardennes*, 242, 245.
12. Dupuy et al., *Hitler's Last Gamble*, 187.
13. McManus, *Alamo in the Ardennes*, 245; Burgett, *Seven Roads to Hell*, 117.
14. Koskimaki, *Battered Bastards of Bastogne*, 132; Burgett, *Seven Roads to Hell*, 112; Simms, *A Soldier's Armageddon*, 30.
15. Leonard Rapport and Arthur Northwood, *Rendezvous with Destiny: A history of the 101st Airborne Division*, 101st Airborne Division Association, n.p., 1965, 488; Burgett, *Seven Roads to Hell*, 120.
16. Dupuy et al., *Hitler's Last Gamble*, 187; Simms, *A Soldier's Armageddon*, 40.
17. V-mail Etters to his family, no date, 10th Armored Division, Box 1, VSC/MHI; Addor, *My Last Battle*, 44.
18. Lester Nichols, *Impact: The battle story of the Tenth Armored Division*, Gateway Press, Louisville, Ky., 1983, 101, 104–5.
19. Addor, *My Last Battle*, 44–56.
20. Simms, *A Soldier's Armageddon*, 40–1.
21. Koskimaki, *Battered Bastards of Bastogne*, 142, 149; MacKenzie, *The Men of Bastogne*, 55.
22. MacDonald, *A Time for Trumpets*, 500; Dupuy et al., *Hitler's Last Gamble*, 188; Burgett, *Seven Roads to Hell*, 136.
23. Cole, *The Ardennes*, 454.
24. William Hayes, "Battle of the Bulge at Bastogne," April 20, 2002, at www.battleofthe bulgememories.be; Heintz, *Périmètre*, 143.
25. Marshall, *Bastogne*, 75; MacKenzie, *The Men of Bastogne*, 90–1.
26. Heintz, *Périmètre*, 143; MacKenzie, *The Men of Bastogne*, 90, 92.
27. "Leo LeBlanc, 1919–2004," *Pays de Bastogne*, 2 (April–June 2004), 2–4. For details of the first battle for Marvie, see Marshall, *Bastogne*, 100–7.
28. Koskimaki, *Battered Bastards of Bastogne*, 157–9; Heintz, *Périmètre*, 40, 43, 196.
29. Denison, "Soldiering On," 5, 10–11, 101st Airborne Division, Box 1, VSC/MHI.
30. Heintz, *Périmètre*, 43–4; Cercle d'Histoire de Bastogne, *Bastogne: Des civils témoignent*, 222.
31. Roberts interview, January 12, 1945, Folder "10th Armored Division," Box 2, CMP/ MHI; Robert Anderson, *A Soldier's Tale: 150th Signal Company, 10th Armored Division*, Privately published, Ransom Canyon, Tex., 2000, 26.
32. Koskimaki, *Battered Bastards of Bastogne*, 186; J.D. Morelock, *Generals of the Ardennes: American leadership in the Battle of the Bulge*, National Defense University Press, Washington, D.C., 1994, 121–5; Rickard, *Advance*, 89, 94–109, 121–2. For the reaction to Patton's announcement, see the handwritten recollection of his aide, Paul Harkins, album #2, 21–2, PHC/MHI. The Germans were, of course, also well aware of the importance of Bastogne for Patton's inevitable counteroffensive. See Bayerlein, A-941, 13, Folder "Panzer Lehr Division," Box 9, CMP/MHI.

33. Winton, *Corps Commanders*, 168; Rickard, *Advance*, 117–20, 129.
34. MacKenzie, *The Men of Bastogne*, 122–3, 127–8; Cole, *The Ardennes*, 456, 458.
35. "Recommendation Distinguished Unit Citation," 2, Tank Destroyer Battalions, Folder "Walsh, Francis," Box 3, VSC/MHI; Koskimaki, *Battered Bastards of Bastogne*, 179–80; Marshall, *Bastogne*, 77–9.
36. Rivet and Sevenans, *La bataille des Ardennes*, 192–3; Cercle d'Histoire de Bastogne *Bastogne: Des civils témoignent*, 32–5.
37. George Allen, *To Bastogne for the Christmas Holidays 1944*, n.p., 1994, 7–10.
38. Marshall, *Bastogne*, 79–85.
39. Koskimaki, *Battered Bastards of Bastogne*, 202–11; Marshall, *Bastogne*, 85.
40. McAuliffe quoted in Critchell, *Four Stars of Hell*, 227.
41. MacDonald, *A Time for Trumpets*, 508.
42. Bayerlein, A-941, 13, CMP/MHI.
43. Von Lüttwitz, ETHINT-41, 5, CMP/MHI; Kokott, B-040, 68, 72–3, Folder "26th Volksgrenadier Division," Box 10, CMP/MHI; Cole, *The Ardennes*, 177.
44. Cercle d'Histoire de Bastogne *Bastogne: Des civils témoignent*, 70–1; Bayerlein, A-941, 12, CMP/MHI.
45. Engelbert letter in *Pays de Bastogne*, 1 (January–March 2005), 11–12.
46. Chernitsky, *Voices from the Foxholes*, 345–7; Cole, *The Ardennes*, 323.
47. Florence Bastin, "Sibret: Journal de l'offensive," *Cahiers de la Haute-Sûre*, 3 (1985), 141–3; Heintz, *Périmètre*, 157–8, 200.
48. Cole, *The Ardennes*, 324–5, 462–3.
49. Roger Marquet, *Du sang, des ruines et des larmes: Chenogne, 1944–1945*, Weyrich, Neufchâteau, 2004, 27–8, 31; André Burnotte, "Noël 1944 à Chenogne," *Cahiers de la Haute-Sûre*, 3 (1985), 156–7; Orianne, *Un mois en enfer*, 90–1.
50. Danny Parker, "Order of battle" in Charles MacDonald, *A Time for Trumpets: The untold story of the Battle of the Bulge*, Quill William Morrow, New York, 1985, 654–5.
51. Orianne, *Un mois en enfer*, 91–2.
52. Dupuy et al., *Hitler's Last Gamble*, 190–1. Kokott later said that von Lauchert should have ignored these orders and "still have exploited this opportunity." Kokott, B-040, 77–8, CMP/MHI.
53. Jim Hatch, Box "502nd Parachute Infantry," GKC/MHI.
54. Cercle d'Histoire de Bastogne, *Bastogne: Des civils témoignent*, 192–3, 133.
55. Hohengarten, "Vor vierzig Jahren," 6–7, Rap 429 – tr. 272 406, SVG; Commission Crimes de Guerre, Ministère de la Justice, Royaume de Belgique. *Les crimes de guerre commis pendant la contre-offensive de von Rundstedt dans les Ardennes*, Georges Thone, Liège, 1948, 26–36; Heintz, *Périmètre*, 107–10; Rivet and Sevenans, *La bataille des Ardennes*, 196–8; Cercle d'Histoire de Bastogne, *Bastogne: Des civils témoignent*, 166–7; Matthieu Longue, *Massacres en Ardenne, hiver 1944–1945*, Racine, Brussels, 2006, 71–5.
56. Ministry of Justice, Kingdom of Belgium. *War Crimes Committed during von Rundstedt's Counter-Offensive in the Ardennes: Bande*, Georges Thone, Liège, 1945, 13–22.
57. MacKenzie, *The Men of Bastogne*, 108.
58. ibid., 107–8; Koskimaki, *Battered Bastards of Bastogne*, 182–4.
59. Koskimaki, *Battered Bastards of Bastogne*, 185.
60. Addor, *My Last Battle*, 186; Marshall, *Bastogne*, 69.
61. O'Brien, *With Geronimo across Europe*, 189–93; Sampson, *Look Out Below!*, 107–8.
62. Bernadette Dumont, *Bastogne, 1944*, Privately published, Jumet-Gohissart, 1974, 7–9; Rivet and Sevenans, *La bataille des Ardennes*, 182–3; Cercle d'Histoire de Bastogne, *Bastogne: Des civils témoignent*, 448–50.
63. Heintz, *Périmètre*, 156–7, 189.
64. Roberts interview, CMP/MHI; Patterson, *Patton's Unsung Armor*, 72–3.
65. Patterson, *Patton's Unsung Armor*, 68.
66. Wharton, *Reading Between the Lines*, 78, 81.
67. Addor, *My Last Battle*, 58–65, 179–80.

68. Allen, *To Bastogne*, 12; MacKenzie, *The Men of Bastogne*, 139–40, 149, 151, 155–8. On the engineer depot, see quote from after-action report in "Les combats de Marvie," *Pays de Bastogne*, 4 (December 1991), 6.
69. Cercle d'Histoire de Bastogne, *Bastogne: Des civils témoignent*, 451–2.

Four: Trapped

1. Michael Doubler, *Closing with the Enemy: How GIs fought the war in Europe, 1944–1945*, University Press of Kansas, Lawrence, Kans., 1994, 216–17; Cole, *The Ardennes*, 462.
2. Cole, *The Ardennes*, 465.
3. Cercle d'Histoire de Bastogne, *Bastogne: Des civils témoignent*, 253–5.
4. André Meurisse, *De croix noires en étoiles blanches: Un enfant du terroir bastognard se souvient des années 1940–1945*, Cercle d'Histoire de Bastogne, Bastogne, 1994, 36–41.
5. Cole, *The Ardennes*, 465; Robert Bowen, *Fighting with the Screaming Eagles: With the 101st Airborne from Normandy to Bastogne*, Casemate, Philadelphia, Pa., and Newbury, UK, 2010, 167–71; Koskimaki, *Battered Bastards of Bastogne*, 217–20.
6. Meurisse, *De croix noires en étoiles blanches*, 44–6; Koskimaki, *Battered Bastards of Bastogne*, 220.
7. Price, *Middleton*, 260; Winton, *Corps Commanders*, 168–9; Kinnard interview, 44, HKP/MHI.
8. MacDonald, *A Time for Trumpets*, 488.
9. MacKenzie, *The Men of Bastogne*, 83.
10. Roberts interview, January 12, 1945, Folder "10th Armored Division," Box 2; CCR, "After Action Report, 1–31 December 1944," Folder "9th Armored Division," Box 1, CMP/MHI; James Van Straten and Lynn Kaufman, "Lessons from Team SNAFU," *Military Review*, 57:5 (1987), 59–62.
11. Critchell, *Four Stars of Hell*, 259; Roberts, "Reflections and Impressions," 1, 3, Folder "10th Armored Division," Box 2, CMP/MHI.
12. Kinnard interview, 51–2, HKP/MHI; Roberts, "Reflections and Impressions," 3, CMP/MHI; Cole, *The Ardennes*, 307–8, 460, 462.
13. Letter, mayor Bastogne to mayor Longchamps, October 21, 1948, AA 145, CEGESOMA; "Civil Affairs/Military Government. 21 Army Group. Operations North West Europe, 1944/1945," 16, AA 4, CEGESOMA; Heintz, *Périmètre*, 66–7.
14. Cercle d'Histoire de Bastogne, *Bastogne: Des civils témoignent*, 433, 492–3, 542–4; Heintz, *Périmètre*, 68; Alain Colignon, "La 'grande bataille d'Ardenne', pour mémoire," *Segnia*, 24 (1999), 276; Harry Coles and Albert Weinberg, *Civil Affairs: Soldiers become governors*, Office of the Chief of Military History, Washington, D.C., 1964, 816.
15. Cercle d'Histoire de Bastogne, *Bastogne: Des civils témoignent*, 435–6; Heintz, *Périmètre* (updated edition), 53.
16. "Chronique des Pères Franciscains," *Pays de Bastogne*, 3 (September 1991), 6; Heintz, *Périmètre*, 67–68; Cercle d'Histoire de Bastogne, *Bastogne: Des civils témoignent*, 439, 487.
17. Gillet journal, December 21–22, 1944, AA 1207, CEGESOMA.
18. "Award of Silver Star," February 12, 1945, Folder 17, Box 24, GKC/MHI.
19. Cercle d'Histoire de Bastogne, *Bastogne: Des civils témoignent*, 499–503.
20. Ibid., 493–4.
21. Marshall Heyman, *Christmas in Bastogne*, Basyc Publications, Falls Church, Va., 1994, 307–8.
22. Captured German letter translated by S-2 Section 501 PIR, Cartledge, 101st Airborne Division, Box 1, VSC/MHI; Cole, *The Ardennes*, 464–5.
23. Henke, "Wir fordern Bastogne zur Übergabe auf," 45–53, Folder "Panzer Lehr Division," Box 9, CMP/MHI; MacKenzie, *The Men of Bastogne*, 165–6; MacDonald, *A Time for Trumpets*, 511–13; Kokott, B-040, 98, Folder "26th Volksgrenadier Division," Box 10, CMP/MHI.

24. Gillet journal, December 22, 1944, AA 1207, CEGESOMA.
25. Koskimaki, *Battered Bastards of Bastogne*, 233–4.
26. Watts to MacDonald, February 28, 1985, Folder "Major Eugene Watts," Box 1, CMP/MHI; Cole, *The Ardennes*, 473–4.
27. MacKenzie, *The Men of Bastogne*, 174–7, 180–1.
28. Hansen, "Diaries," December 23, 1944, Folders 2–4, Box 5, CHC/MHI; Burgett, *Seven Roads to Hell*, 191.
29. Winton, *Corps Commanders*, 209–10; MacKenzie, *The Men of Bastogne*, 173–4.
30. Richard Killblane, *The Filthy Thirteen*, Casemate, Havertown, Pa., 2003, 1–7, 160–6; Nigel de Lee, *Voices from the Battle of the Bulge*, David and Charles, Newton Abbot, UK, 2004, 146.
31. Marie du Bus de Warnaffe, *Journal des tristes jours, 1944–1945*, Cercle d'Histoire de Bastogne, Bastogne, 1994, 27–8.
32. Dupuy et al., *Hitler's Last Gamble*, 196.
33. Bowen, *Fighting with the Screaming Eagles*, 172–98; Koskimaki, *Battered Bastards of Bastogne*, 236–43; Marshall, *Bastogne*, 152–4.
34. Watts to MacDonald, CMP/MHI.
35. Ulysses Lee, *The Employment of Negro Troops*, Center of Military History, Washington, D.C., 1966, 644–50.
36. Baroness Greindl, *Noël 1944 à Isle la Hesse*, Desclée, De Brouwer, Bruges, 1945, 30–1, 41–4.
37. Heintz, *Périmètre*, 112–13.
38. "LTC William Parkhill – 441st Troop Carrier Gp," Folder 90, Box 31, GKC/MHI. On the supply operation that Saturday, see Danny Parker, *To Win the Winter Sky: The air war over the Ardennes, 1944–1945*, Combined Books, Conshohocken, Pa., 1994, 230.
39. Critchell, *Four Stars of Hell*, 266.
40. Koskimaki, *Battered Bastards of Bastogne*, 257–8.
41. Orianne, *Un mois en enfer*, 104; Don Malarkey, *Easy Company Soldier*, St. Martin's Press, New York, 2008, 167; Cercle d'Histoire de Bastogne, *Bastogne: Des civils témoignent*, 484.
42. Paul Remiche, "Un de Bastogne en hiver 44 et au printemps 45," *Pays de Bastogne*, 3 (July–September 2004), 9–10; Gillet journal, December 23, 1944, AA 1207, CEGESOMA.
43. Marshall, *Bastogne*, 133–4; Ambrose, *Band of Brothers*, 186.
44. Koskimaki, *Battered Bastards of Bastogne*, 279–80; Jack Prior, "Réveillon de Noël 1944 à Bastogne," *Pays de Bastogne*, 4 (October–December 2002), 20–2.
45. "Une médaille, 66 ans après," *CRIBA-Estafette*, 302 (January 2011), 3; MacDonald, *A Time for Trumpets*, 507; Martin King, *L'infirmière oubliée: L'histoire inconnue d'Augusta Chiwy*, Racine, Brussels, 2011, 17, 19, 53, 97.
46. O'Brien, *With Geronimo across Europe*, 193–6; Koskimaki, *Battered Bastards of Bastogne*, 280–1; Critchell, *Four Stars of Hell*, 258, 260.
47. Prior, "Réveillon de Noël 1944 à Bastogne," 22–3; Gillet journal, December 22–3, 1944, AA 1207, CEGESOMA.
48. CCB, "Summary of Operations," 13, Folder "10th Armored Division," Box 2, CMP/MHI; Woldt to MacDonald, July 16, 1982 and newspaper clippings, Folder "101st Airborne Division," Box 5, CMP/MHI; Jim Hatch, Box "502nd Parachute Infantry," GKC/MHI; Dan Gianneschi, *The 362nd Fighter Group History*, Aires Press, Chicago, Ill., 1981, 11.
49. Parker, *To Win the Winter Sky*, 222, 231. Claims of tank "kills" by those who flew the aircraft need to be taken with a grain of salt, however. See Ian Gooderson, "Allied fighter-bombers versus German armour in North-West Europe 1944–1945," *Journal of Strategic Studies*, 14:2 (1991), 210–31.
50. Parker, *To Win the Winter Sky*, 225–9; Jim Hatch, Box "502nd Parachute Infantry Regiment," GKC/MHI.
51. Marshall, *Bastogne*, 145; Meurisse, *De croix noires en étoiles blanches*, 41–6, 56–7.
52. Marshall, *Bastogne*, 123–4.
53. Loiacono memoir, 10th Armored Division, Box 1, VSC/MHI.

54. James McDonough and Richard Gardner, *Skyriders: History of the 327/401 Glider Infantry*, Battery Press, Nashville, TN, 1980, 104–5; Cole, *The Ardennes*, 472.
55. Marshall, *Bastogne*, 126–7; Cole, *The Ardennes*, 472.
56. Koskimaki, *Battered Bastards of Bastogne*, 267.
57. Ibid., 268.
58. Loiacono memoir, 10th Armored Division, Box 1, VSC/MHI.
59. Marshall, *Bastogne*, 196–9; Dupuy et al., *Hitler's Last Gamble*, 225.
60. MacKenzie, *The Men of Bastogne*, 205; Cole, *The Ardennes*, 472–3.
61. Reichelt, *Phantom Nine*, 154; Greindl, *Noël 1944*, 45, 47–9.
62. Cole, *The Ardennes*, 472–4.
63. Raymonde Havelange, "Bastogne," *La Cité*, December 23, 1984; André Drossart, "Bastogne en enfer," *Le Vif*, December 22, 1983, 155, 157; Heintz, *Périmètre*, 68; Dumont, *Bastogne, 1944*, 16; Rivet and Sevenans, *La bataille des Ardennes*, 181–2.
64. Lamotte letter, January 10, 1984, 6–10, AA 1207, CEGESOMA.
65. Gillet journal, December 21, 1944, AA 1207, CEGESOMA; Rivet and Sevenans, *La bataille des Ardennes*, 184.
66. Marcus Brotherton, *We Who are Alive and Remain*, Berkley Caliber, New York, 2009, 148; Burgett, *Seven Roads to Hell*, 177–8.
67. Captured German letter translated by S-2 Section 501 PIR, Cartledge, 101st Airborne Division, Box 1, VSC/MHI; Koskimaki, *Battered Bastards of Bastogne*, 222; Winters, *Beyond Band of Brothers*, 171–2.
68. Koskimaki, *Battered Bastards of Bastogne*, 224.
69. Folder "Winters Questionnaire," Box 2, RWC/MHI; Simms, *A Soldier's Armageddon*, 50, 52.
70. Winters, *Beyond Band of Brothers*, 172–5; Marcus Brotherton, *A Company of Heroes*, Berkley Caliber, New York, 2010, 117–18.
71. Cercle d'Histoire de Bastogne, *Bastogne: Des civils témoignent*, 414.
72. Lynn Compton, *Call of Duty: My life before, during, and after the band of brothers*, Berkley Caliber, New York, 2008, 137; MacKenzie, *The Men of Bastogne*, 71; Allen, *To Bastogne*, 9–17.
73. Cole, *The Ardennes*, 665–8.
74. Hansen, "Diaries," December 24, 1944, Folders 2–4, Box 5, CHC/MHI; Cole, *The Ardennes*, 661; David Remoel, "Battle of the Bulge" in Wesley Craven and James Cate (eds), *Europe: Argument to V-E Day, January 1944 to May 1945*, vol. III of *The Army Air Forces in World War II*, University of Chicago Press, Chicago, Ill., 1951, 693–5; MacKenzie, *The Men of Bastogne*, 239; Gooderson, "Allied fighter-bombers," 215–17.
75. Marshall, *Bastogne*, 130–1; Cole, *The Ardennes*, 474.
76. Heintz, *Périmètre*, 158–9.
77. Cercle d'Histoire de Bastogne, *Bastogne: Des civils témoignent*, 422, 343, 84.
78. Cole, *The Ardennes*, 468, 470; Parker, *To Win the Winter Sky*, 255; de Lee, *Voices from the Battle of the Bulge*, 144–6.
79. Roberts, "Reflections and Impressions," 2, CMP/MHI.
80. MacDonald, *A Time for Trumpets*, 511; Prior, "Réveillon de Noël 1944 à Bastogne," 23; Cole, *The Ardennes*, 472, 475.
81. Copy of Roberts's message in Elgin's letter to MacDonald, Folder "10th Armored Division," Box 2, CMP/MHI; Marshall, *Bastogne*, 155; MacKenzie, *The Men of Bastogne*, 211–12.
82. Koskimaki, *Battered Bastards of Bastogne*, 283.
83. Critchell, *Four Stars of Hell*, 274–5.
84. Warnaffe, *Journal*, 30.

Five: The Skin of Their Teeth

1. Parker, *To Win the Winter Sky*, 271; MacKenzie, *The Men of Bastogne*, 212–14.

2. Chernitsky, *Voices from the Foxholes*, 184–5; Orianne, *Un mois en enfer*, 113–14; Gillet journal, December 24, 1944, AA 1207, CEGESOMA.
3. King, *L'infirmière oubliée*, 147; Collins and King, *Voices of the Bulge*, 206, 215; MacKenzie, *The Men of Bastogne*, 214–15.
4. Koskimaki, *Battered Bastards of Bastogne*, 291.
5. Winton, *Corps Commanders*, 224.
6. Captured German letter translated by S-2 Section 501 PIR, Cartledge, 101st Airborne Division, Box 1, VSC/MHI.
7. MacKenzie, *The Men of Bastogne*, 218.
8. MacDonald, *A Time for Trumpets*, 527; Andrew Winfree, *The African American Artilleryman in World War II (ETO): A chronology*, Trafford, Victoria, BC, 2006, 121, 286, 288; Chernitsky, *Voices from the Foxholes*, 182–4.
9. Cercle d'Histoire de Bastogne, *Bastogne: Des civils témoignent*, 456–8.
10. Kokott, B-040, 126–7, Folder "26th Volksgrenadier Division," Box 10, CMP/MHI.
11. Koskimaki, *Battered Bastards of Bastogne*, 316–23.
12. Ibid., 298.
13. Kokott, B-040, 129, CMP/MHI.
14. MacKenzie, *The Men of Bastogne*, 23; Koskimaki, *Battered Bastards of Bastogne*, 325–7; Duncan, "Reflections," WDP/MHI; Leonard Swartz, Folder 5, Box 13, GKC/MHI.
15. Heintz, *Périmètre* (updated edition), 68–9; Cercle d'Histoire de Bastogne, *Bastogne: Des civils témoignent*, 392–3, 528; Koskimaki, *Battered Bastards of Bastogne*, 328–32.
16. MacKenzie, *The Men of Bastogne*, 234–5.
17. Ibid., 184; Dupuy et al., *Hitler's Last Gamble*, 227; Allen, *To Bastogne*, 20.
18. Von Lüttwitz, A-939, 14, Folder "XLVII Panzer Corps," Box "Correspondence German Historians and Veterans," CMP/MHI; Kokott, B-040, 129, CMP/MHI; Winfree, *African American Artilleryman*, 283; CCB, "Summary of Operations," 13–14, Folder "10th Armored Division," Box 2, CMP/MHI.
19. Merle McMorrow, *From Rome to Berlin via Bastogne*, BookSurge, Charleston, S.C., 2009, 194–200.
20. Koskimaki, *Battered Bastards of Bastogne*, 309–10, 312.
21. Von Lüttwitz, ETHINT-41, 5–6, Folder "XLVII Panzer Corps," Box "Correspondence German Historians and Veterans," CMP/MHI; Parker, *To Win the Winter Sky*, 289.
22. Green and Brown, *War Stories*, 162–6; Bowen, *Fighting with the Screaming Eagles*, 200–4.
23. Parker, *To Win the Winter Sky*, 291–2; Heintz, *Périmètre*, 87–8; Cercle d'Histoire de Bastogne, *Bastogne: Des civils témoignent*, 456–8.
24. Cole, *The Ardennes*, 479.
25. Koskimaki, *Battered Bastards of Bastogne*, 335–6 and www.101airborneww2.com/souvenirs3.html. For the photograph, see Bando, *101st Airborne*, 181.
26. Hansen, "Diaries," December 24, 1944, Folders 2–4, Box 5, CHC/MHI; "Personal Narrative Wilkey," 26, unnamed folder, Box 1, CMP/MHI; Marshall, *Bastogne*, 169.
27. Lamotte letter, January 10, 1984, AA 1207, CEGESOMA; Greindl, *Noël 1944*, 54–7; Gillet journal, December 25, 1944, AA 1207, CEGESOMA.
28. Rivet and Sevenans, *La bataille des Ardennes*, 177–9; Cercle d'Histoire de Bastogne, *Bastogne: Des civils témoignent*, 252–6; R.R., "Il y a trente ans – L'offensive des Ardennes: Cet Américain qui m'a sauvée," *La Libre Belgique*, December 18, 1974.
29. Heintz, *Périmètre* (updated edition), 222; Koskimaki, *Battered Bastards of Bastogne*, 339–40.
30. Hansen, "Diaries," December 24, 1944, Folders 2–4, Box 5, CHC/MHI; "Mercy Flight," Taflinger interview, January 29, 1945, Folder "1 Dec – 31 Dec 44," 80th Infantry Division, Box 17, VSC/MHI; www.ww2-airborne.us/units/326med/326med_report_bb.html
31. Christian Limbrée, *45 ans après: L'offensive von Rundstedt à Rochefort*, Cercle Culturel et Historique de Rochefort, Rochefort, [1989], 65. Artillery commander Richard Metz quoted in Remoel, "Battle of the Bulge," 695.

32. Cercle d'Histoire de Bastogne, *Bastogne: Des civils témoignent*, 558–9; Cole, *The Ardennes*, 480.
33. MacKenzie, *The Men of Bastogne*, 254–5.
34. Roberts, "Reflections and Impressions," Folder "10th Armored Division," Box 2, CMP/MHI; letter McAuliffe to General Hoyt Vandenberg of the Ninth Air Force, January 25, 1945, reproduced in Gianneschi, *The 362nd Fighter Group History*, 11.
35. De Lee, *Voices from the Battle of the Bulge*, 117–18; Parker, *To Win the Winter Sky*, 311.
36. Gianneschi, *The 362nd Fighter Group History*, 392.
37. Helmus diary, December 26, 1944, Folder "German Diary and Sketches," Box 7, CMP/MHI; MacKenzie, *The Men of Bastogne*, 255–6.
38. Gianneschi, *The 362nd Fighter Group History*, 392; Cercle d'Histoire de Bastogne, *Bastogne: Des civils témoignent*, 98, 100, 102; Heintz, *Périmètre*, 108.
39. Winton, *Corps Commanders*, 210; Cole, *The Ardennes*, 470; Parker, *To Win the Winter Sky*, 313; Heintz, *Périmètre* (updated edition), 222–3.
40. On the petrol run, see Cole, *The Ardennes*, 468.
41. For Lieutenant Corwin's story, see Folder 10, Box 31, GKC/MHI. On Major Soutter and his team, see www.med-dept.com/testimonies/james_sunshine.php and www.ww2-airborne.us/units/326med/326med_report_bb.html. See also, Gianneschi, *The 362nd Fighter Group History*, 131.
42. Requisition form, HQ 101st Airborne Division, Office of the Assistant Chief of Staff, G-4, December 26, 1944, AA 145, CEGESOMA.

Six: To the Rescue

1. Harkins, Album #2, 24, PHC/MHI. For the Bradley quote, see Carlo D'Este, *Patton: A genius for war*, HarperCollins, New York, 1995, 684. See also Paul Munch, "Patton's staff and the Battle of the Bulge," *Military Review*, 70:5 (1990), 51–4.
2. Rickard, *Advance*, 106–7, 122, 137, 157.
3. Winton, *Corps Commanders*, 44–8; Cole, *The Ardennes*, 511–12; George Patton, *War As I Knew It*, W.H. Allen, London, 1947, 190.
4. Cole, *The Ardennes*, 512–13; Pattison interview, "Relief of Bastogne," 21, Folder "318 Dec 44," 80th Infantry Division, Box 16, VSC/MHI.
5. Edgar Bredbenner, "We never got to England," November 26, 2011, at www.battleofthebulgememories.be; Bruce Egger and Lee MacMillan Otts, *G Company's War: Two personal accounts of the campaigns in Europe, 1944–1945*, University of Alabama Press, Tuscaloosa, Ala., and London, 1992, 99; Lewis Sorley, *Thunderbolt: General Creighton Abrams and the army of his times*, Simon & Schuster, New York, 1992, 70; and Albin Irzyk, *He Rode Up Front for Patton*, Pentland Press, Raleigh, N.C., 1996, 239–40.
6. Don Fox, *Patton's Vanguard: The United States Army Fourth Armored Division*, McFarland, Jefferson, N.C. and London, 2003, 307; Cole, *The Ardennes*, 510–11.
7. Rickard, *Advance*, 122; Cole, *The Ardennes*, 511, 515; Fox, *Patton's Vanguard*, 309–10.
8. Parker, *To Win the Winter Sky*, 206.
9. Rickard, *Advance*, 158; Hansen, "Diaries," December 21, 1944, Folders 2–4, Box 5, CHC/MHI.
10. Rickard, *Advance*, 126, 150; Kevin Allen, "The successful use of proximity fuses in the Battle of the Bulge," *Military Heritage*, 12:4 (2011), 14–18.
11. Rickard, *Advance*, 147, 150.
12. Cole, *The Ardennes*, 520–2; Rickard, *Advance*, 152; Egger and Otts, *G Company's War*, 101.
13. Roland Gaul, *The Germans*, vol. 1 of *The Battle of the Bulge in Luxembourg*, Schiffer, Atglen, Pa., 1995, 22, 35–6; Cole, *The Ardennes*, 520–2.
14. Egger and Otts, *G Company's War*, 102–3; Rickard, *Advance*, 167. Hatfield received the Distinguished Service Cross for this action.
15. Dupuy et al., *Hitler's Last Gamble*, 218.
16. Rickard, *Advance*, 154; Winton, *Corps Commanders*, 220.

17. Heilmann, B-023, 3–4, 18, Folder "5th Paratroop Division," Box 10, CMP/MHI.
18. Author interviews Maus, July 20, 1984, and July 25, 1986.
19. Brandenberger, A-876, 30, 68, Folder "Ardennes Offensive of Seventh Army," Box 12, MDC/MHI.
20. Cole, *The Ardennes*, 525–6.
21. Blumenson, *Patton Papers*, 606; Cercle d'Histoire de Bastogne, *Bastogne: Des civils témoignent*, 244.
22. Dupuy et al., *Hitler's Last Gamble*, 219; Rickard, *Advance*, 167; Cole, *The Ardennes*, 522–3.
23. Cole, *The Ardennes*, 526.
24. Maria Lozet-Gustin, "Journées tragiques de décembre 1944 à Chaumont," *Cahiers de la Haute-Sûre*, 3 (1985), 136; Charles Wilson, *Frail Children of Dust: From Bastogne to Bavaria with the Fourth Armored Division*, Austin and Winfield, San Francisco, Calif., 1993, 68–72.
25. Rickard, *Advance*, 160–1; Irzyk, *He Rode Up Front for Patton*, 250–3.
26. Pattison interview, 23, VSC/MHI; Lozet-Gustin, "Journées tragiques," 136–7.
27. Wilson, *Frail Children of Dust*, 77–9.
28. Rickard, *Advance*, 160; Irzyk, *He Rode Up Front for Patton*, 253–5; Cole, *The Ardennes*, 528–9. Gniot was posthumously awarded the Distinguished Service Cross.
29. Green and Brown, *War Stories*, 198–202.
30. Parker, "Recollections," 20, 4th Armored Division, Box 20, VSC/MHI.
31. www.bigonville.info/Bigonville_in_World_War_II/John-A-Whitehill.html
32. Winton, *Corps Commanders*, 221–2.
33. Parker, *To Win the Winter Sky*, 231.
34. Cole, *The Ardennes*, 543–4.
35. Parker, *To Win the Winter Sky*, 262; Cole, *The Ardennes*, 541.
36. "YD in Battle of the Bulge," 11–12. Undated copy of *Yankee Doings*. Folder "Donations Members 26th Infantry Division," Box "Donations Units, Army, Corps, Infantry Divisions," BBC/MHI.
37. Fox, *Patton's Vanguard*, 388; John Di Battista, "With CCB/4th Armored Division in the Bulge," December 2, 2002, at www.criba.be
38. Pattison interview, 24, VSC/MHI; Fox, *Patton's Vanguard*, 388; Lozet-Gustin, "Journées tragiques," 137.
39. Wilson, *Frail Children of Dust*, 82–3.
40. Hunsinger, untitled recollections, 1–4, Folder "Donations Members 4th Armored Division," Box "Donations Members Armored Divisions," BBC/MHI; Fox, *Patton's Vanguard*, 349–50; Cole, *The Ardennes*, 530.
41. For Schröder's story, see Astor, *A Blood-Dimmed Tide*, 303–4. For the testimonies of Lange, Lutgen, and Whitehill, see www.bigonville.info/Bigonville_in_World_War_II
42. Hansen, "Diaries," December 24, 1944, Folders 2–4, Box 5, CHC/MHI; Blumenson, *Patton Papers*, 605.
43. Winton, *Corps Commanders*, 222, 224.
44. Rickard, *Advance*, 174–5.
45. The action earned Swift the Distinguished Service Cross.
46. Egger and Otts, *G Company's War*, 106–10.
47. "YD in Battle of the Bulge," 12, BBC/MHI.
48. Price, *Middleton*, 260–1.
49. Brandenberger, A-876, 70, MDC/MHI; Irzyk, *He Rode Up Front for Patton*, 258–9.
50. Pattison interview, 24, VSC/MHI.
51. *The Congressional Medal of Honor Library: World War II*, Dell, New York, 1984, vol. II, 214–15.
52. Lozet-Gustin, "Journées tragiques," 137–8.
53. Fox, *Patton's Vanguard*, 350–3; Parker, *To Win the Winter Sky*, 262, 291.
54. Bredbenner, "We never got to England."

55. Linda Didier-Robert, *La mémoire de Sainlez: L'offensive von Rundstedt vécue au village*, Cercle d'Histoire de Bastogne, Bastogne, n.d., 44–9; Michel Marteau, "Nous ne fêterons plus jamais Noël!" *Le Soir Illustré*, December 20, 1984; Heintz, *Périmètre*, 91–3, 196, 198–9.

56. Fox, *Patton's Vanguard*, 355–6; Bredbenner, "We never got to England."

57. Fox, *Patton's Vanguard*, 397–401.

58. Rickard, *Advance*, 176.

59. Heilmann, B-023, 41–2, CMP/MHI; Brandenberger, A-876, 65–9, MDC/MHI.

60. Rickard, *Advance*, 178; Parker, *To Win the Winter Sky*, 311; Blumenson, *Patton Papers*, 607.

61. Didier-Robert, *La mémoire de Sainlez*, 61–2, 64, 66–7.

62. Ibid., 67–8; Heintz, *Périmètre*, 93; Fox, *Patton's Vanguard*, 431.

63. 318th Infantry report, "December, 1944," 21–3, Box 17, and unit citation, April 6, 1945, Folder "318 Dec 44," 80th Infantry Division, Box 16, VSC/MHI.

64. Kuhn was awarded a Silver Star.

65. Martinez was a recipient of the Distinguished Service Cross.

66. Sorley, *Thunderbolt*, 13–17.

67. Ibid., 39–43; Wilson, *Frail Children of Dust*, 89–90.

68. Fox, *Patton's Vanguard*, 403.

69. Roger Marquet, "La bataille pour Bastogne," in Christian Kraft de la Saulx (ed.), *Jours de Sursaut*, vol. 21 of *Jours de Guerre*, Dexia, Brussels, 2001, 193–5.

70. Fox, *Patton's Vanguard*, 403–5.

71. Richter, "Lieutenant Boggess," 4th Armored Division, Box 20, VSC/MHI.

72. Ibid.; Parker, *To Win the Winter Sky*, 311; Denyse de Coune, "Souvenirs de guerre: Assenois 1944–1945," *Cahiers de la Haute-Sûre*, 3 (1985), 124–6.

73. Fox, *Patton's Vanguard*, 407–8.

74. Richter, "Lieutenant Boggess," VSC/MHI.

75. Sorley, *Thunderbolt*, 52; Fox, *Patton's Vanguard*, 405; Cercle d'Histoire de Bastogne, *Bastogne: Des civils témoignent*, 497; interview Edward Bautz, ROHA. Abrams received the Distinguished Service Cross for his action at Assenois.

76. Blumenson, *Patton Papers*, 607.

77. Esther Bindursky, "Arkansas Pine Knot," *Saturday Evening Post*, October 20, 1945, 16–17, 126. For the private's citation, see *Congressional Medal of Honor Library*, vol. I, 165.

78. Cole, *The Ardennes*, 555; CCB, "Summary of Operations," 14, 18, Folder "10th Armored Division," Box 2, CMP/MHI; Parker, "Recollections," 21, VSC/MHI.

79. 318th Infantry report, "December, 1944," 24–5, VSC/MHI.

80. Cole, *The Ardennes*, 555; MacDonald, *A Time for Trumpets*, 532.

81. MacDonald, *A Time for Trumpets*, 532.

82. Blumenson, *Patton Papers*, 608.

83. Koskimaki, *Battered Bastards of Bastogne*, 356.

Seven: A Clash of Wills

1. MacDonald, *A Time for Trumpets*, 589–90; Russell Weigley, *Eisenhower's Lieutenants: The campaign of France and Germany, 1944–1945*, Indiana University Press, Bloomington, Ind., 1990, 544–5.

2. MacDonald, *A Time for Trumpets*, 589–90; Blumenson, *Patton Papers*, 608; Rickard, *Advance*, 198.

3. Winton, *Corps Commanders*, 203; Blumenson, *Patton Papers*, 608.

4. Winton, *Corps Commanders*, 208–9; Brandenberger, A-876, 64, Folder "Ardennes Offensive Seventh Army," Box 12, MDC/MHI.

5. MacKenzie, *The Men of Bastogne*, 260.

6. De Lee, *Voices from the Battle of the Bulge*, 261–2.

7. Meurisse, *De croix noires en étoiles blanches*, 46–7, 51–2; Orianne, *Un mois en enfer*, 154; Paul Remiche, "Un de Bastogne en hiver 44 et au printemps 45," *Pays de Bastogne*, 3 (July–September 2004), 12–13.

8. Heintz, *Périmètre* (updated edition), 216; Koskimaki, *Battered Bastards of Bastogne*, 373; Cercle d'Histoire de Bastogne, *Bastogne: Des civils témoignent*, 279–80.
9. Rapport and Northwood, *Rendezvous with Destiny*, 595-6.
10. Koskimaki, *Battered Bastards of Bastogne*, 361–4.
11. Parker, *To Win the Winter Sky*, 325; Helmus diary, December 27, 1944, Folder "German Diary and Sketches," Box 7, CMP/MHI.
12. MacKenzie, *The Men of Bastogne*, 262–5; Koskimaki, *Battered Bastards of Bastogne*, 375.
13. Fox, *Patton's Vanguard*, 421–3.
14. Fox, *Patton's Vanguard*, 432–4; Cercle d'Histoire de Bastogne, *Bastogne: Des civils témoignent*, 236; Didier-Robert, *La mémoire de Sainlez*, 71–3.
15. Rapport and Northwood, *Rendezvous with Destiny*, 591–2; Fox, *Patton's Vanguard*, 419–21.
16. Winton, *Corps Commanders*, 226; Rickard, *Advance*, 202, 207–8; Greindl, *Noël 1944*, 57.
17. Monthly After Action Report, December 1944, Folder "After Action Reports July through December 1944, 137th Infantry," 35th Infantry Division, Box 2, VSC/MHI; *Presenting . . . The 35th Infantry Division in World War II, 1941-1945*, Battery Press, Nashville, Tenn., 1988, 1, 138; Winton, *Corps Commanders*, 227.
18. François Bertin, *La ruée de von Rundstedt à travers nos Ardennes*, Musée de la Parole au Pays de Bastogne, Bastogne, 1988, 53; Heintz, *Périmètre*, 53–4.
19. Cole, *The Ardennes*, 609, 649–50.
20. Robert Hagel, "My Combat with the 320th Infantry Regiment," October 8, 2009, at www.criba.be
21. Calvert, "Battle of the Bulge," 12, Box 1, 4th Armored Division Papers, MHI; Dupuy et al., *Hitler's Last Gamble*, 293–4; Rickard, *Advance*, 210.
22. Pattison interview, "Relief of Bastogne," 110, Folder "318 Dec 44," 80th Infantry Division, Box 16, VSC/MHI; Irzyk, *He Rode Up Front for Patton*, 265–6.
23. Brandenberger, A-876, 75, MDC/MHI; Cercle d'Histoire de Bastogne, *Bastogne: Des civils témoignent*, 209–10.
24. Douglas Sterner, "World War II Awards to Members of 35th Infantry Division," 9, 173, at www.35thinfdivassoc.com, under Units, 134th Inf. Regt., Awards/Citations.
25. For the three Silver Star citations, see Sterner awards document, 32–3, 179, at www.35thinfdivassoc.com. See also www.tankdestroyer.net for information on Brock's background: "People" tab, then "Honorees."
26. Heintz, *Périmètre*, 200. Quote is from Bastin, "Sibret," 144–5.
27. Parker, "Order of Battle," 646; Dupuy et al., *Hitler's Last Gamble*, 474.
28. Rickard, *Advance*, 203; J. Ted Hartman, *Tank Driver: With the 11th Armored from the Battle of the Bulge to VE Day*, Indiana University Press, Bloomington and Indianapolis, Ind., 2003, xiii. Dawson was posthumously awarded the Distinguished Service Cross for his actions on December 28.
29. Marquet, *Du sang*, 40–52; Orianne, *Un mois en enfer*, 175.
30. Marquet, "La bataille pour Bastogne," 200–1; Rivet and Sevenans, *La bataille des Ardennes*, 189; Heintz, *Périmètre*, 115–16.
31. Dupuy et al., *Hitler's Last Gamble*, 291.
32. Heintz, *Périmètre*, 134–5; Cercle d'Histoire de Bastogne, *Bastogne: Des civils témoignent*, 379.
33. Marquet, *Du sang*, 43.
34. Cercle d'Histoire de Bastogne, *Bastogne: Des civils témoignent*, 433; Chernitsky, *Voices from the Foxholes*, 187; Burgett, *Seven Roads to Hell*, 216.
35. Heyman, *Christmas in Bastogne*, 318–20.
36. Gillet journal, December 28, 1944, AA 1207, CEGESOMA; Cercle d'Histoire de Bastogne, *Bastogne: Des civils témoignent*, 460.
37. Rapport and Northwood, *Rendezvous with Destiny*, 599–600; Gillet journal, December 28, 1944, AA 1207, CEGESOMA; Cercle d'Histoire de Bastogne, *Bastogne: Des civils témoignent*, 44.

38. Dupuy et al., *Hitler's Last Gamble*, 296, 475.

39. Rickard, *Advance*, 396; Koskimaki, *Battered Bastards of Bastogne*, 383–6.

40. Rapport and Northwood, *Rendezvous with Destiny*, 602; Koskimaki, *Battered Bastards of Bastogne*, 379–81; Greindl, *Noël 1944*, 58–64.

41. Parker, *To Win the Winter Sky*, 351; Cole, *The Ardennes*, 660; CCB, "Summary of Operations," 14, Folder "10th Armored Division," Box 2, CMP/MHI; Nichols, *Impact*, 114.

42. Gillet journal, December 28, 1944, AA 1207, CEGESOMA.

43. MacDonald, *A Time for Trumpets*, 594–5.

44. Rickard, *Advance*, 210; Dupuy et al., *Hitler's Last Gamble*, 296–7; Brandenberger, A-876, 75, MDC/MHI; Cole, *The Ardennes*, 618–19.

45. Dupuy et al., *Hitler's Last Gamble*, 295–6; Astor, *A Blood-Dimmed Tide*, 357; Caldwell, untitled recollections, December 29, 1944, and Coleton, "Battlefield Pledge," 20–1, 87th Infantry Division, VSC/MHI.

46. Hartman, *Tank Driver*, xv; Collins and King, *Voices of the Bulge*, 146; Berry Craig, *11th Armored Division Thunderbolts*, vol. II, Turner Publishing, Paducah, Ky., 1992, 114; Fague, "Bulge," 1, 11th Armored Division, Box 1, VSC/MHI.

47. CCB, "Summary of Operations," 15, Folder "10th Armored Division," Box 2, CMP/MHI; Fox, *Patton's Vanguard*, 424; Gérard Gerardy, "Six journées d'enfer pour Bastogne assiégée," *La Cité*, December 21, 1984; Heintz, *Périmètre* (updated edition), 62–3.

48. Rickard, *Advance*, 217; Blumenson, *Patton Papers*, 610.

49. Kaidy, "3rd Army," 3–4, and Caldwell, untitled recollections, December 29, 1944, 87th Infantry Division, VSC/MHI.

50. Rickard, *Advance*, 218–19; Patrick Kearney, "Our Bulge Chaplain," June 26, 2003, at www.criba.be on

51. Craig, *Thunderbolts*, 107.

52. Rickard, *Advance*, 223–4; Dupuy et al., *Hitler's Last Gamble*, 289–90; Parker, *To Win the Winter Sky*, 327–8.

53. Hartman, *Tank Driver*, 1–2, 54–6; Marquet, *Du sang*, 57–60.

54. Fague, "Bulge," 2–5, VSC/MHI.

55. Orianne, *Un mois en enfer*, 180.

56. Burnotte, "Noël 1944 à Chenogne," 162–3; Marquet, *Du sang*, 60–1, 73, 102.

57. Fague, "Bulge," 5, VSC/MHI; Marquet, *Du sang*, 67–8.

58. Monthly Operations Report, December 1944, Headquarters, 35th Infantry Division, Box 2, VSC/MHI.

59. Parker, "Order of Battle," 648.

60. Winton, *Corps Commanders*, 229; Dupuy et al., *Hitler's Last Gamble*, 476, 531; Rickard, *Advance*, 228.

61. Dupuy et al., *Hitler's Last Gamble*, 472; Parker, *To Win the Winter Sky*, 344.

62. Fox, *Patton's Vanguard*, 438–9; Cole, *The Ardennes*, 625.

63. Fox, *Patton's Vanguard*, 438–9.

64. See Davis's Silver Star citation in Sterner awards document, 51–2, at www.35thinfdivassoc.com

65. Fox, *Patton's Vanguard*, 440–5.

66. Longue, *Massacres en Ardenne*, 214–15; Heintz, *Périmètre* (updated edition), 43.

67. Heintz, *Périmètre* (updated edition), 83; Orianne, *Un mois en enfer*, 156–7.

68. "Notes," Headquarters Third Army, January 16, 1945, Folder "Thomas Gillis," 4th Armored Division, Box 20, VSC/MHI; Rickard, *Advance*, 232; Blumenson, *Patton Papers*, 609.

69. Parker, *To Win the Winter Sky*, 345, 353.

70. Cole, *The Ardennes*, 643.

71. Cercle d'Histoire de Bastogne, *Bastogne: Des civils témoignent*, 365–7.

72. William Fee questionnaire and George Reimer, "History of Company B," 4–5, 11th Armored Division, Box 1, VSC/MHI.

73. Marquet, "La bataille pour Bastogne," 205–8.

74. Reimer, "History of Company B," 5; Drebus questionnaire, 11th Armored Division, Box 1, VSC/MHI.
75. Patton, *War As I Knew It*, 211; Blumenson, *Patton Papers*, 612.
76. Degive et al., *La véritable histoire du Sherman de la place McAuliffe à Bastogne*, Cercle d'Histoire de Bastogne, Bastogne, 1999, 20–4, 28, 38, 52.
77. Brandt questionnaire, 11th Armored Division, Box 1, VSC/MHI.
78. Heintz, *Périmètre* (updated edition), 106; Cercle d'Histoire de Bastogne, *Bastogne: Des civils témoignent*, 379–80; Cole, *The Ardennes*, 644–5.
79. Fague, "Bulge," 5–10, VSC/MHI.
80. Cole, *The Ardennes*, 627; Wilson, *Frail Children of Dust*, 91.
81. Rickard, *Advance*, 235.
82. Koskimaki, *Battered Bastards of Bastogne*, 407.
83. Lieutenant Colonel Brown and Captain Fry interview, 1, February 1, 1945, Folder "After Action Reports 1944–1945," Box 9, GHC/MHI; George Hofmann, *The Super Sixth: History of the 6th Armored Division in World War II*, Sixth Armored Division Association, Louisville, Ky., 1975, 279.
84. Blumenson, *Patton Papers*, 610; Dupuy et al., *Hitler's Last Gamble*, 299, 301.
85. Rapport and Northwood, *Rendezvous with Destiny*, 609–10; Dupuy et al., *Hitler's Last Gamble*, 301; Bando, *101st Airborne*, 188.
86. O'Brien, *With Geronimo across Europe*, 203–7.
87. Rapport and Northwood, *Rendezvous with Destiny*, 609; Bell, "Black gunners in Bastogne," 53; Koskimaki, *Battered Bastards of Bastogne*, 406–7.
88. Reichelt, *Phantom Nine*, 157, 161–2.
89. Gillet journal, December 31, 1944, AA 1207, CEGESOMA; "La rescapée de Bastogne," 17–18, *Groupe d'études et de recherches sur la bataille du saillant* No. 6 (1991).
90. Denyse de Coune, " "Souvenirs de guerre," 128–9; Rivet and Sevenans, *La bataille des Ardennes*, 194; Didier-Robert, *La mémoire de Sainlez*, 76–80.
91. Greindl, *Noël 1944*, 63–5.
92. Rapport and Northwood, *Rendezvous with Destiny*, 609; Koskimaki, *Battered Bastards of Bastogne*, 408; Parker, *To Win the Winter Sky*, 361–2.

Eight: New Year's Woes

1. "Notes," HQ Third Army, January 16, 1945, Folder "Thomas Gillis," 4th Armored Division, Box 20, VSC/MHI; Blumenson, *Patton Papers*, 611–13.
2. Rickard, *Advance*, 238–9.
3. MacDonald, *A Time for Trumpets*, 588–9.
4. "History of Company B," 13, Folder "Wayne Aldinger," 11th Armored Division, Box 1, VSC/MHI; Orianne, *Un mois en enfer*, 201.
5. Cercle d'Histoire de Bastogne, *Bastogne: Des civils témoignent*, 355, 362–3; Price, *Middleton*, 267–8.
6. Collins and King, *Voices of the Bulge*, 251.
7. Craig, *Thunderbolts*, 53; CCB, "Summary of Operations," 15, Folder "10th Armored Division," Box 2, CMP/MHI; Rickard, *Advance*, 243; Fague, "Bulge," 11–13, 11th Armored Division, Box 1, VSC/MHI.
8. Fague, "Bulge," 14, VSC/MHI. An estimated 10 Germans lay dead in the doorway of the Burnotte farm when the civilians stormed out. According to a villager, 11 more Germans were lined up against the wall of the farm shortly after and executed in cold blood. See Longue, *Massacres en Ardenne*, 221–5.
9. Fague, "Bulge," 14–16, VSC/MHI; Marquet, *Du sang*, 81; Blumenson, *Patton Papers*, 615. On the killing of German POWs at Chenogne, see also Toland, *Battle*, 328–9.
10. Marquet, *Du sang*, 99–102.
11. Fague, "Bulge," 17–18, VSC/MHI; Cole, *The Ardennes*, 646–7.
12. Fague, "Bulge," 18–20, VSC/MHI.

13. Craig, *Thunderbolts*, 51; and Dupuy et al., *Hitler's Last Gamble*, 303.
14. Warnaffe, *Journal*, 45–6.
15. Degive et al., *Véritable histoire*, 29–30.
16. O'Brien, *With Geronimo across Europe*, 194.
17. Monthly Operations Report, January 1945, 1, Headquarters, 35th Infantry Division, Box 2, VSC/MHI.
18. Monthly After Action Report, January 1945, 1–2, 137th Infantry and 216th Field Artillery, 35th Infantry Division, Box 2, VSC/MHI.
19. Cole, *The Ardennes*, 635. Mack was posthumously awarded a Silver Star. See Douglas Sterner, "World War II Awards to Members of 35th Infantry Division," 119, at www.35thinfdivassoc.com, under Units, 134th Inf. Regt., Awards/Citations.
20. Heintz, *Périmètre* (updated edition), 43–4; Longue, *Massacres en Ardenne*, 214–15; Cole, *The Ardennes*, 635.
21. Sterner awards document, 48, at www.35thinfdivassoc.com
22. Monthly After Action Report, January 1945, 161st Field Artillery, 35th Infantry Division, Box 2, VSC/MHI; Cercle d'Histoire de Bastogne, *Bastogne: Des civils témoignent*, 216–17.
23. Cercle d'Histoire de Bastogne, *Bastogne: Des civils témoignent*, 212–13.
24. Dupuy et al., *Hitler's Last Gamble*, 306–7, 476; Cercle d'Histoire de Bastogne, *Bastogne: Des civils témoignent*, 226, 228, 244.
25. Egger and Otts, *G Company's War*, 113; Dupuy et al., *Hitler's Last Gamble*, 306.
26. Burgess, "Combat Command 'A' History," Folder "After Action Reports, Unit Histories, Accounts 1944–1945," Box 9, GHC/MHI.
27. After Action Report, Headquarters 44th Armored Infantry; Lieutenant Colonel Charles Brown and Captain George Fry interview, 1–2, February 1, 1945; "Task Force Kennedy" and "Miscellaneous Notes," Folder "After Action Reports 1944–1945," Box 9, GHC/MHI.
28. Captain Rice and Lieutenant Blundell interview, Folder "After Action Reports 1944–1945," Box 9, GHC/MHI; Cole, *The Ardennes*, 633–4; Heintz, *Périmètre* (updated edition), 40.
29. Cole, *The Ardennes*, 630, 632; Dupuy et al., *Hitler's Last Gamble*, 477.
30. Ambrose, *Band of Brothers*, 196–8; Malarkey, *Easy Company Soldier*, 174; Dupuy et al., *Hitler's Last Gamble*, 305; Guarnere and Heffron, *Brothers in Battle*, 180–1.
31. De Lee, *Voices from the Battle of the Bulge*, 208–12; Cole, *The Ardennes*, 632–3.
32. Goodin to Cavanagh, February 7, 1979, 3, Folder "6th Armored Division," Box 1, CMP/MHI; Riley interview, 2–3, Folder "After Action Reports 1944–1945," Box 9, GHC/MHI; Cercle d'Histoire de Bastogne, *Bastogne: Des civils témoignent*, 82–3, 89.
33. Cercle d'Histoire de Bastogne, *Bastogne: Des civils témoignent*, 66, 91, 99.
34. Dupuy et al., *Hitler's Last Gamble*, 473; Kraemer, A-924, Folder "Commitment Sixth Panzer Army," Box 13, MDC/MHI.
35. Letter, Volpe to Hofmann, 10, November 20, 1973, Folder "After Action Reports, Unit Histories, Accounts 1944–1945," Box 9, GHC/MHI; O'Brien, *With Geronimo across Europe*, 200–1.
36. "HQ 6th Armored Division, Civil Affairs Section, Historical Summary December 1944," Folder "After Action Reports 1944–1945," Box 9, GHC/MHI; and Dupuy et al., *Hitler's Last Gamble*, 305.
37. Gillet journal, AA 1207, CEGESOMA; Raymonde Havelange, "Bastogne," *La Cité*, December 23, 1984.
38. Watts to MacDonald, February 28, 1985, Folder "Major Eugene Watts," Box 1, CMP/MHI.
39. Rickard, *Advance*, 246.
40. Cercle d'Histoire de Bastogne, *Bastogne: Des civils témoignent*, 87, 92, 100; Heintz, *Périmètre*, 146–7; Dupuy et al., *Hitler's Last Gamble*, 308.
41. Gard was awarded a Silver Star, Ebersole a Distinguished Service Cross.
42. Winton, *Corps Commanders*, 232–3; Rickard, *Advance*, 258; Goodin to Cavanagh, CMP/MHI.

43. Cercle d'Histoire de Bastogne, *Bastogne: Des civils témoignent*, 51, 99; Heintz, *Périmètre* (updated edition), 243.
44. Dupuy et al., *Hitler's Last Gamble*, 309; Rickard, *Advance*, 257–8; Monthly After Action Report, January 1945, 1, 161st Field Artillery, 35th Infantry Division, Box 2, VSC/MHI.
45. Monthly After Action Report, January 1945, 2, 137th Infantry, 35th Infantry Division, Box 2, VSC/MHI. All four medics were awarded a Silver Star. See Sterner awards document, 24–5, 33, 65, 74, at www.35thinfdivassoc.com
46. On the civilians in Lutrebois, see Cercle d'Histoire de Bastogne, *Bastogne: Des civils témoignent*, 206. For C Company's experience, see Ardennes chapter in 134th's history by Butler Miltonberger and James Huston, at http://coulthart.com/134/chapter_9.htm. Silver Stars were awarded to Mazzi, Plotsky, Storm, and Viehe. See Sterner awards document, 123, 154, 184, 200, at www.35thinfdivassoc.com
47. Rivet and Sevenans, *La bataille des Ardennes*, 200–2; Heintz, *Périmètre*, 52–4, 201; Orianne, *Un mois en enfer*, 236–43. Both Madame Garcia and her daughter Marie eventually died of their wounds.
48. Dupuy et al., *Hitler's Last Gamble*, 310; Rickard, *Advance*, 258, 264; Riley interview, 3, Folder "After Action Reports 1944–1945," Box 9, GHC/MHI.
49. Gianneschi, *The 362nd Fighter Group History*, 132.
50. Koskimaki, *Battered Bastards of Bastogne*, 427; Rapport and Northwood, *Rendezvous with Destiny*, 622.
51. Dupuy et al., *Hitler's Last Gamble*, 307; Koskimaki, *Battered Bastards of Bastogne*, 416–17, 422. Cobbett earned a Distinguished Service Cross that day.
52. Rapport and Northwood, *Rendezvous with Destiny*, 625–6; Koskimaki, *Battered Bastards of Bastogne*, 418, 423.
53. Green and Brown, *War Stories*, 277–81.
54. Both Ford and Carberry were awarded a Distinguished Service Cross for bravery on January 3, 1945.
55. Rapport and Northwood, *Rendezvous with Destiny*, 627–30; Koskimaki, *Battered Bastards of Bastogne*, 445.
56. Rickard, *Advance*, 256; Dupuy et al., *Hitler's Last Gamble*, 309.
57. Dupuy et al., *Hitler's Last Gamble*, 466; Winton, *Corps Commanders*, 249.
58. Winton, *Corps Commanders*, 240–1; "Regimental History," Folder "193rd Glider Infantry," Box 1, WMP/MHI.
59. "513 Parachute Infantry Regiment," Folder "17th Airborne Division," Box 5, CMP/MHI; Fague, "Bulge," 20, VSC/MHI; and Marquet, *Du sang*, 111–12.
60. "17th Airborne in The Bulge," Folder "17th Airborne Division," Box 5, CMP/MHI.
61. Calhoun, "Bayonet Charge," 17th Airborne Division, Box 1, VSC/MHI. Manning received a Distinguished Service Cross for his action in the woods.
62. *Congressional Medal of Honor Library*, vol. I, 172–3.
63. Paula Fourny, *Hiver 1944–1945. Moircy-Jenneville-Bonnerue: Des civils confrontés aux horreurs de la guerre*, Privately published, Libramont, 1995, 10; "17th Airborne in The Bulge," Folder "17th Airborne Division," Box 5, CMP/MHI; Craig, *Thunderbolts*, 47; Rickard, *Advance*, 256.
64. Dupuy et al., *Hitler's Last Gamble*, 309; Blumenson, *Patton Papers*, 615.
65. "513 Parachute Infantry Regiment," Folder "17th Airborne Division," Box 5, CMP/MHI.
66. Cunningham received a Silver Star for volunteering for the dangerous job and paying with his life. See also http://familytreemaker.genealogy.com/users/m/e/t/Mildred-Methvin/WEBSITE-0001/UHP-0104.html
67. Heintz, *Périmètre* (updated edition), 108–9.
68. "17th Airborne in The Bulge" and "513 Parachute Infantry Regiment," Folder "17th Airborne Division," Box 5, CMP/MHI; "Regimental History," Folder "193rd Glider Infantry Regiment," Box 1, WMP/MHI. Winton, *Corps Commanders*, 429, note 145.

Nine: The Longest Road

1. Blumenson, *Patton Papers*, 612.
2. MacDonald, *A Time for Trumpets*, 599–600; Blumenson, *Patton Papers*, 615.
3. Rickard, *Advance*, 255, 257.
4. McMorrow, *Rome to Berlin*, 204.
5. Greindl, *Noël 1944*, 69–71.
6. O'Brien, *With Geronimo across Europe*, 208; Cercle d'Histoire de Bastogne, *Bastogne: Des civils témoignent*, 477, 479.
7. Rapport and Northwood, *Rendezvous with Destiny*, 633.
8. Alfred Dubru, "L'anéantissement de Houffalize par les bombardiers de la Royal Air Force," *Glain et Salm, Haute Ardenne*, 48 (1998), 25–6, 33–6; Hansen, "Diaries," January 6, 1945, Folders 2–4, Box 5, CHC/MHI.
9. Blumenson, *Patton Papers*, 616.
10. Ibid., 616, 619.
11. G-2 Periodic Report, January 5, 1945, Folder "G-2 Reports," Box 1, WMP/MHI.
12. "17th Airborne in The Bulge," Folder "17th Airborne Division," Box 5, CMP/MHI; "Regimental History," "193d Glider Infantry Regiment," and "193rd Regiment at the Bulge," Folder "193rd Glider Infantry," Box 1, WMP/MHI.
13. Dupuy et al., *Hitler's Last Gamble*, 330–2; Kaidy, "3rd Army," 8–9, 87th Infantry Division, VSC/MHI. The Medal of Honor was awarded posthumously to Curtis Shoup of the 346th Infantry. See *Congressional Medal of Honor Library*, vol. II, 154–5.
14. Larry Oakes, "A Family's Contribution," *The Star Tribune*, May 29, 2000, A1 and A8.
15. "513 Parachute Infantry Regiment," Folder "17th Airborne Division," Box 5, CMP/MHI; Don Pay, *Thunder from Heaven: Story of the 17th Airborne Division, 1943–1945*, Battery Press, Nashville, Tenn., 1980, 22, 67.
16. Oakes, "A Family's Contribution."
17. Blumenson, *Patton Papers*, 616; Rickard, *Advance*, 264.
18. Folder "Background Materials," Box 1, JVP/MHI; Winton, *Corps Commanders*, 322–3; Rickard, *Advance*, 266.
19. Dupuy et al., *Hitler's Last Gamble*, 475; Monthly After Action Report, January 1945, 3–4, 137th Infantry, 35th Infantry Division, Box 2, VSC/MHI. On Mazzi and Eschelman, see also http://articles.philly.com/1988-09-13/news/26231661
20. Rickard, *Advance*, 266; Periodic Reports January 1945, Box 4, GHC/MHI.
21. Rickard, *Advance*, 266–7, 273; Riley interview, attachment "Daily Ammunition Expenditure," Folder "After Action Reports 1944–1945," Box 9, GHC/MHI; Benjamin Goodin, "Le Bois Jacques," March 17, 2002, at www.battleofthebulgememories.be; "Award Silver Star DeCamilla," Folder "Donations Members 6th Armored Division," Box "Donations Members Armored Divisions," BBC/MHI.
22. Patton, *War As I Knew It*, 215–16; "Conversations," Vol. I, 69, Box 1, JVP/MHI.
23. After Action Report, January 1945, 6, Folder "Headquarters, Monthly After Action Reports for 1945," 90th Infantry Division, Box 3, VSC/MHI.
24. Patton, *War As I Knew It*, 216.
25. Rickard, *Advance*, 280.
26. Parker, *To Win the Winter Sky*, 462; Rasqué, *Das Oesling im Krieg*, 611; Cercle d'Histoire de Bastogne, *Bastogne: Des civils témoignent*, 60.
27. Monthly After Action Report, January 1945, 4–5, 137th Infantry, 35th Infantry Division, Box 2, VSC/MHI. On Mazzi and Eschelman, see http://articles.philly.com/1988-09-13/news/26231661
28. Green and Brown, *War Stories*, 286–94.
29. Letter Volpe to Hofmann, 11–12, November 20, 1973, Folder "After Action Reports, Unit Histories, Accounts 1944–1945," Box 9, GHC/MHI.
30. After Action Report, January 1945, 7–9, Folder "Headquarters, Monthly After Action Reports 1945," 90th Infantry Division, Box 3, VSC/MHI. See also the combat history of the 315th Engineer Combat Battalion and the January 1945 after action report for the

343rd Field Artillery Battalion, 90th Infantry Division, Box 4, VSC/MHI; Dupuy et al., *Hitler's Last Gamble*, 335.

31. After Action Report, January 1945, 9–10, Folder "Headquarters, Monthly After Action Reports 1945," 90th Infantry Division, Box 3, VSC/MHI. The decorations went to Private Everett Callaway and Sergeant Alfred Padilla.

32. Dupuy et al., *Hitler's Last Gamble*, 335–6; *Congressional Medal of Honor Library*, vol. I, 136.

33. Periodic Reports January 1945, Box 4, GHC/MHI; Voigt, "340. Volks-Grenadier-Division," 48, AA 484, CEGESOMA; Rickard, *Advance*, 284–5; Blumenson, *Patton Papers*, 622.

34. After Action Report, January 1945, 10–11, Folder "Headquarters, Monthly After Action Reports 1945," 90th Infantry Division, Box 3, VSC/MHI; Heintz, *Périmètre* (updated edition), 40. Catlin's story was posted on www.battleofthebulgememories.be on April 24, 2011.

35. Marie survived; the grandmother died four days after the girl's evacuation. Cercle d'Histoire de Bastogne, *Bastogne: Des civils témoignent*, 58–9, 62, 219. All American and German casualty figures are from the personnel statistics in Dupuy et al., *Hitler's Last Gamble*, Appendix E.

36. Rickard, *Advance*, 275.

37. Sampson, *Look Out Below!*, 228.

38. Bando, *101st Airborne*, 198–9.

39. Critchell, *Four Stars of Hell*, 306; O'Brien, *With Geronimo across Europe*, 208–10.

40. Burgett, *Seven Roads to Hell*, 239; Koskimaki, *Battered Bastards of Bastogne*, 458.

41. Rapport and Northwood, *Rendezvous with Destiny*, 637; Koskimaki, *Battered Bastards of Bastogne*, 456–9.

42. Burgett, *Seven Roads to Hell*, 242–3, 245; Rickard, *Advance*, 305.

43. Warnaffe, *Journal*, 49.

44. Heintz, *Périmètre*, 136–7. The boy died later that day in a German hospital.

45. Hartman, *Tank Driver*, 59, 61.

46. Reimer, "History of Company B," 6, 11th Armored Division, Box 1, VSC/MHI; Craig, *Thunderbolts*, 37, 132.

47. Koskimaki, *Battered Bastards of Bastogne*, 470–3.

48. Malarkey, *Easy Company Soldier*, 186–7; Burgett, *Seven Roads to Hell*, 248.

49. Koskimaki, *Battered Bastards of Bastogne*, 477–8.

50. Winton, *Corps Commanders*, 292, 318–19; McDonough and Gardner, *Skyriders*, 118.

51. Hofmann, *Super Sixth*, 301; Rapport and Northwood, *Rendezvous with Destiny*, 650; Blumenson, *Patton Papers*, 624.

52. Blumenson, *Patton Papers*, 624; Winton, *Corps Commanders*, 319.

53. Koskimaki, *Battered Bastards of Bastogne*, 493–7.

54. Parker, *To Win the Winter Sky*, 467.

55. Brotherton, *We Who are Alive and Remain*, 161.

56. Koskimaki, *Battered Bastards of Bastogne*, 488–90.

57. Hartman, *Tank Driver*, 64–8. Van Dyke received a Silver Star for rescuing his comrades at Noville.

58. Koskimaki, *Battered Bastards of Bastogne*, 473, 503.

59. Orianne, *Un mois en enfer*, 274–5; Rickard, *Advance*, 290; *Congressional Medal of Honor Library*, vol. I, 42–3.

60. Craig, *Thunderbolts*, 33; Blumenson, *Patton Papers*, 624; Burgett, *Seven Roads to Hell*, 256. Luft's story was posted on www.criba.be on December 25, 2009.

61. Hartman, *Tank Driver*, 68.

62. Dupuy et al., *Hitler's Last Gamble*, 341–2 and Appendix E.

63. Ibid., 466; Hartman, *Tank Driver*, 68–9; "History of Company B," 15, Folder "Wayne Aldinger," 11th Armored Division, Box 1, VSC/MHI.

64. Craig, *Thunderbolts*, 115–16. Casualty figures have been calculated from personnel statistics in Dupuy et al., *Hitler's Last Gamble*, Appendix E.

65. Dupuy et al., *Hitler's Last Gamble*, 466; "Chronique des Pères Franciscains," *Pays de Bastogne*, 1 (March 1993), 7; McMorrow, *Rome to Berlin*, 205.
66. Burgett, *Seven Roads to Hell*, 264.
67. Koskimaki, *Battered Bastards of Bastogne*, 9, 512.

Epilogue

1. Rapport and Northwood, *Rendezvous with Destiny*, 663–5.
2. American casualty figures are from Dupuy et al., *Hitler's Last Gamble*, Appendix E.
3. The Ambrose quote is from page 235 of the 1998 Touchstone edition. In an earlier book, *The Unknown Dead*, I looked through the eyes of the civilians to rewrite the history of the Battle of the Bulge. I did this, in part, to refute Stephen Ambrose's casual, and rather cavalier, observation in *Citizen Soldiers*.
4. Colignon, "Grande bataille," 266, note 7; Heintz, *Périmètre* (updated edition), 145–6, 149–57; Giovanni Hoyois, *L'Ardenne dans la tourmente*, J. Dupuis, Marcinelle-Charleroi, 1945, 86; Louis Lefèbvre, *La bataille de Bastogne*, Bastogne, n.d., 129.
5. German casualty figures have been taken from Dupuy et al., *Hitler's Last Gamble*, Appendix E, and from Rickard, *Advance*, 316–17.
6. MacDonald cites January 28, 1945 as the end date set by the U.S. Army. MacDonald, *A Time for Trumpets*, 617. As early as January 18, Eisenhower was predicting that the enemy "will probably manage to withdraw the bulk of his formations." See Rickard, *Advance*, 300–1.
7. Many of the American soldiers killed during the campaigns inside Germany rest at the Margraten cemetery in the Netherlands. The American military cemetery lies just across the border from the German city of Aachen because Eisenhower refused to have his men buried in enemy soil. Their story, and that of the Dutch adoption of the ten thousand graves and names on the Walls of the Missing, is told in my book *The Margraten Boys*. Most of the Americans who died in the Battle of the Bulge are buried in the cemeteries of Henri-Chapelle and Neuville-en-Condroz, Belgium, and Hamm, Luxembourg.

BIBLIOGRAPHY

Primary sources

Archival

Archives et Documentation du Service des Victimes de la Guerre
Brussels, Belgium

Croix-Rouge: Province de Luxembourg
B8/2: Blessés Civils – Fiches
Folder: Mahnen

B8/3: Blessés Civils – Listes
Folders: Bastogne, Généralités

B8/7: Lettres des bourgmestres – Constats de décès
Folders: Bastogne, Longchamps, Noville, Sibret, Villers-la-Bonne-Eau, Wardin

Rap 429 – tr. 272 406
Hohengarten, André. "Vor vierzig Jahren: Die Gestapo in der Ardennenoffensive."

Centre d'Études et de Documentation Guerre et Sociétés Contemporaines
Brussels, Belgium

AA 4
"Civil Affairs/Military Government. 21 Army Group. Operations North West Europe 1944/1945."

AA 16
"History of the Civil Affairs Division, War Department Special Staff, World War II to March 1946: Civil Affairs Division Activities with Respect to Belgium."

AA 145
Folder: Bastogne
Letter mayor Bastogne to mayor Longchamps. October 21, 1948.
Requisition form, HQ 101st Airborne Division, G-4. December 26, 1944.

AA 484
B-678: Voigt, Hans-Hubert. "Bericht über die Kämpfe der 340. Volks-Grenadier-Division seit Weihnachten 1944."

AA 1207
Box: VI-VIIIA
Folder: Bastogne
Gillet, Maria. "Siège de Bastogne: Souvenirs des jours d'angoissc ct des nuits interminables."
Lamotte, Louise. Letter. January 10, 1984.

AA 1230
SHAEF Mission to Belgium and Luxembourg. Fortnightly reports.

AA 1456
Survey French-speaking municipalities 50th anniversary of the liberation.

Croix-Rouge de Belgique
Brussels, Belgium

Executive Committee reports, General Board reports, and reports from provincial committees and local sections to Brussels headquarters, December 1944 – January 1945.

Rutgers Oral History Archives World War II
New Brunswick, New Jersey

Bautz, Edward. 37th Tank Battalion, 4th Armored Division.
Kneller, Franklin. 506th Parachute Infantry, 101st Airborne Division.

U.S. Army Military History Institute
Carlisle, Pennsylvania

4th Armored Division Papers
Box 1/Folder: Robert Calvert

Creighton Abrams Papers
Box B
Folder: DeWitt C. Smith
"Conversations Between Major General DeWitt C. Smith and Lieutenant Colonel Jack Bradshaw and Lieutenant Colonel Bill Sweet." Senior Officers Debriefing Program. Carlisle Barracks, PA: USAMHI, 1975.

Battle of the Bulge Historical Foundation Collection
Box: Donations Members Armored Divisions
Folder: Donations Members 4th Armored Division
Hunsinger, Charles. Untitled recollections.

Folder: Donations Members 6th Armored Division
DeCamilla, Roosevelt. Silver Star citation, January 8, 1945.
Box: Donations Units, Army, Corps, Infantry Divisions
Folder: Donations Members 26th Infantry Division
Clippings *Yankee Doings*

Box: 9th Armored Division, 89th Cavalry Reconnaissance Squadron
Folder: After Action Reports, 1–31 December 1944
B, C and E Troop Narratives
German documents translated by HQ 9th AD, December 18, 1944
Squadron Headquarters Narrative

Maurice Delaval Collection
Box 12
Folder: Ardennes Offensive Seventh Army
A-876: Brandenberger, Erich. "Ardennes Offensive of Seventh Army."

Box 13
Folder: Commitment Sixth Panzer Army
A-924: Kraemer, Fritz. "Commitment of Sixth Panzer Army in the Ardennes 1944/45."

William H. Duncan Papers
Manuscript of biography on Douglas T. Davidson: "Reflections on World War II."

Julian J. Ewell Papers
"Conversations Between Lieutenant General Julian J. Ewell and Mr. Robert Crowley and Lieutenant Colonel Norman M. Bissell." Senior Officers Debriefing Program. Carlisle Barracks, PA: USAMHI, 1979.

Chester B. Hansen Collection
Box 5
Folders 2–4: Official Papers – War Diaries, December 1944 – January 1945

Paul D. Harkins Photograph Collection
Album #2

George F. Hofmann Collection
Box 4: G-2 Reports 1944–1945
Folder: Periodic Reports December 1944 and January 1945

Box 9: After Action Reports 1944–1945
Folder: After Action Reports 1944–1945
"After Action Report, Hq 44th Armored Infantry, 1 February 1945."
"Hq 6th Armored Division, Civil Affairs Section, Historical Summary December 1944."
"Interview with Lt Col Charles E. Brown, Bn CO and Capt George W. Fry, Co C CO, 44th Armd Inf, 6th Armd Div. Bastogne Action."
"Interview with Capt John Rice and 1st Lt Ronald Blundell, 9th Armd Inf, 6th Armd Div."
"Interview with Col Lowell Riley, CO 6th Armd Div Arty."
"Miscellaneous Notes."
"Task Force Kennedy."

Folder: After Action Reports, Unit Histories, Accounts 1944–1945
Burgess, H. Higbee. "Combat Command 'A' History, 6th Armd Div."
Volpe, Peter. Letter to George Hofmann. November 20, 1973.

Harry W.O. Kinnard Papers
Kinnard interview by Jacob Couch. Senior Officer Oral History Program, Project 83-6.

George E. Koskimaki Collection
Box 13/Folder 5
Swartz, Leonard.

Box 25/Folder 31
Peterson. "326th Medical Company."

Box 31
Folder 10
Corwin, Charleton.

Folder 90
"LTC William Parkhill – 441st Troop Carrier Gp."

Box: 502nd Parachute Infantry
Hatch, Jim.

Charles B. MacDonald Papers
Box 1
Unnamed Folder
"The Ardennes 1944–45: Personal Narrative of Malcolm Richard Wilkey."

Folder: 6th Armored Division
Letter Ben Goodin (S-3), Div. Artillery, 6th Armored Division to Wm. C. C.
Cavanagh. February 7, 1979.

Folder: 9th Armored Division
HQ CCR, 9AD, "After Action Report 1 – 31 December 1944."

Folder: Major Eugene Watts
Letter Watts to Charles MacDonald. February 28, 1985.

Box 2
Folder: 10th Armored Division
CCB, 10 AD. "Summary of Operations Day by Day."
Desobry, William. Interview. August 7, 1983.
Elgin, William. Letter to Charles MacDonald. June 16, 1982.
O'Hara. Interview.
Roberts, William. Interview. January 12, 1945.
Roberts, William. "Reflections and Impressions of Bastogne."
Wickert, Wayne. "My Experience in the Battle of the Bulge."

Box 5
Folder: 17th Airborne Division
"17th Airborne in The Bulge." Interviews Major General Miley et al. January 19, 1945.
"513 Parachute Infantry Regiment, 2–13 January 1945." Interviews Colonel Coutts et al.
    January 14–16, 1945.

Folder: 101st Airborne Division
Letters George Woldt to Charles MacDonald and attached clippings. July 6 and 16, 1982.

Box 7
Folder: ETO Historian's File
"Questions Answered by Lieutenant General Troy Middleton in Letter to Theater Historian,
    30 July 1945."
"Summary Weather Conditions and Their Effects during the Ardennes Offensive." February
    4, 1945.

Folder: German Diary and Sketches – Horst Helmus

Box 9: German Army: Armored Formations
Folder: Panzer Lehr Division
A-941: Bayerlein, Fritz. "Panzer Lehr Division, 1 December 1944 – 26 January 1945."
Henke, Hellmuth. "Wir fordern Bastogne zur Übergabe auf: Ardennenoffensive Winter
    1944."

Box 10: German Army: Infantry and Paratroops
Folder: 5th Paratroop Division
B-023: Heilmann, Ludwig. "Ardennes Offensive: 5 Parachute Division."

Folder: 26th Volksgrenadier Division
B-040: Kokott, Heinz. "26th Volksgrenadier Division in the Ardennes Offensive."
"Füsilier-Regt 39 (26th VGD) in the Battle of the Bulge."

Box 12
Folder: Percy Ernst Schramm
A-858: Schramm, Percy Ernst. "The Course of Events in the German Offensive in the
    Ardennes."

Box: Correspondence German Historians and Veterans
Folder: XLVII Panzer Corps
A-939: Von Lüttwitz, Heinrich. "The Commitment of XLVII Panzer Corps in the Ardennes
    1944–1945,"
ETHINT-41: Von Lüttwitz, Heinrich. "XLVII Panzer Corps Investment of Bastogne."

Folder: 5th Panzer Army
ETHINT-46: Von Manteuffel, Hasso-Eccard. "An Interview with Gen Pz Hasso von
    Manteuffel."

Folder: I SS Panzer Corps
A-877: Priess, Hermann. "Commitment of I SS Panzer Corps during the Ardennes
    Offensive."
B-779: Lehmann, Rudolf. "Commitment of I SS Panzer Corps during the Ardennes
    Offensive."

William M. Miley Papers
Box 1
Folder: G-2 Reports

Folder: 193rd Glider Infantry
"193d Glider Infantry Regiment."
"193rd Regiment at the Bulge."
"Regimental History."
"Second Battalion 193d Infantry North of Mande St. Etienne."

James A. Van Fleet Papers
Box 1
"Background Materials for Oral Interviews."
"Conversations Between General James A. Van Fleet and Colonel Bruce H. Williams."
    Vol. I. Senior Officers Debriefing Program. Carlisle Barracks, PA: USAMHI, 1973.

Veterans Survey Collection
17th Airborne Division
Box 1
Calhoun, Samuel. "The Bayonet Charge Made at Mande St Etienne."

101st Airborne Division
Box 1
Cartledge, Carl. Translated German letters.
Denison, Frank. "Soldiering On."

4th Armored Division
Box 20
Boggess, Charles. Undated Illinois magazine article by Donald Richter, "Lieutenant Charles
    Perry Boggess: First to Bastogne."
Gillis, Thomas. Headquarters Third United States Army, "Notes on Bastogne." January 16,
    1945.
Parker, Robert. "Recollections of the Second World War."

10th Armored Division
Box 1
Etters, John. Letters to his family.
Loiacono, Elturino. Untitled memoir.

11th Armored Division
Box 1
Aldinger, Wayne. "History of Company B, 21st Armored Infantry."
Brandt, Harold. Questionnaire.
Drebus, Richard. Questionnaire.
Fague, John. "The Battle of the Bulge from My Small Corner."
Fee, William. Questionnaire; George Reimer's memoir, "A History of Company B of the
    55th AIB."
Shebs, Theodore. "Bastogne, And Other Great Events."

28th Infantry Division
Box 2
Johnson, Ralph. "Battle of the Bulge."
Maher, John. "Company C, 110th Infantry in the Ardennes."

35th Infantry Division
Box 2
Folders: After Action Reports July 1944 through May 1945, 134th Infantry
Folder: After Action Reports July through December 1944, 137th Infantry
Folders: Operations Reports July 1944 through May 1945, Headquarters
Folder: After Action Reports July through December 1944, 161st Field Artillery
Folder: After Action Reports July through December 1944, 216th Field Artillery

80th Infantry Division
Box 16
Folder: 318 Dec 44
Pattison, Hal. Interview "Relief of Bastogne."
Unit citation. April 6, 1945.

Box 17
Folder: 1 Dec – 31 Dec 44
318th Infantry report, "December, 1944."
"Mercy Flight into Bastogne on 25 December 1944." Interview with Lt. Taflinger. January
    29, 1945.

87th Infantry Division
Booth, Robert. "The Personal Experiences of Robert T. Booth Who Was a Prisoner of War
    in Belgium and Germany."
Caldwell, Jesse. Untitled recollections.
Coleton, John. "A Battlefield Pledge . . . Forty Years Later."
Kaidy, Mitchell. "The 3rd Army Strikes Back."

90th Infantry Division
Box 1
Robison, Eugene. "Following Orders in the Infantry."

Box 2
Meli, John. Questionnaire; "A Secret Trek to the Bulge."

Box 3
Folder: Headquarters, Monthly After Action Reports 1945

Box 4
Folder: 358th IR, Monthly After Action Reports January – February 1945
Folder: 315th Engineer Combat Battalion, Combat History May 1944 through May 1945
Folder: 343rd Field Artillery, After Action Reports, June 1944 – May 1945
Folder: 344th Field Artillery, After Action Reports, June 1944 – May 1945
Folder: 345th Field Artillery, After Action Reports, January 1945 – May 1945
Folder: 915th Field Artillery, After Action Reports, June 1944 – May 1945

Tank Destroyer Battalions
Box 3
Walsh, Francis. Questionnaire; Recommendation Distinguished Unit Citation; "History of
    the 705th Tank Destroyer Battalion."

Richard D. Winters Collection
Box 2: Winters Memories/Winters Personal
Folder: Bastogne
Folder: Winters Army Service Experience Questionnaire

Box 18: Band of Brothers Research Materials Part II
Folder 1: Critique #1 by Winters/Lipton
Folder 2: Critique #2 by Winters/Lipton

Box 20: Kingseed Research Materials Part II
Folder: Bastogne

Books and articles

Addor, Don. *My Last Battle: Noville outpost to Bastogne*, Trafford, Victoria, BC, 2004.
Allen, George. *To Bastogne for the Christmas Holidays 1944*, n.p., 1994.
Anderson, Robert. *A Soldier's Tale: 150th Signal Company, 10th Armored Division*, Privately published, Ransom Canyon, Tex., 2000.
Astor, Gerald. *A Blood-Dimmed Tide: The Battle of the Bulge by the men who fought it*, Dell, New York, 1994.
Bastin, Florence. "Sibret: Journal de l'offensive," *Cahiers de la Haute-Sûre*, 3 (1985), pp. 141–51.
Blumenson, Martin. *The Patton Papers, 1940–1945*, Da Capo, Cambridge, Mass., 1996.
Bowen, Robert. *Fighting with the Screaming Eagles: With the 101st Airborne from Normandy to Bastogne*, Casemate, Philadelphia, Pa., and Newbury, UK, 2010.
Brotherton, Marcus. *We Who are Alive and Remain*, Berkley Caliber, New York, 2009.
Brotherton, Marcus. *A Company of Heroes*, Berkley Caliber, New York, 2010.
Burgett, Donald. *Seven Roads to Hell: A Screaming Eagle at Bastogne*, Dell, New York, 2000.
Burnotte, André. "Noël 1944 à Chenogne," *Cahiers de la Haute-Sûre*, 3 (1985), pp. 153–65.
Cercle d'Histoire de Bastogne. *Bastogne – Hiver 44–45: Des civils témoignent*, Bastogne, 1994.
Chernitsky, Dorothy (ed.). *Voices from the Foxholes: Men of the 110th Infantry during World War II*, Privately published, Uniontown, Pa., 1991.
Collins, Michael and Martin King. *Voices of the Bulge: Untold stories from veterans of the Battle of the Bulge*, Zenith Press, Minneapolis, Minn., 2011.
Commission des Crimes de Guerre, Ministère de la Justice, Royaume de Belgique. *Les crimes de guerre commis pendant la contre-offensive de von Rundstedt dans les Ardennes*, Georges Thone, Liège, 1948.
Compton, Lynn. *Call of Duty: My life before, during, and after the band of brothers*, Berkley Caliber, New York, 2008.
The Congressional Medal of Honor Library: World War II, Dell, New York, 1984.
Critchell, Laurence. *Four Stars of Hell*, Battery Press, Nashville, Tenn., 1982.
De Coune, Denyse. "Souvenirs de guerre: Assenois 1944–1945," *Cahiers de la Haute-Sûre*, 3 (1985), pp. 111–33.
De Lee, Nigel. *Voices from the Battle of the Bulge*, David and Charles, Newton Abbot, UK, 2004.
Dubru, Alfred. "L'anéantissement de Houffalize par les bombardiers de la Royal Air Force," *Glain et Salm, Haute Ardenne*, 48 (1998), pp. 17–39.
Dumont, Bernadette. *Bastogne, 1944*, Privately published, Jumet-Gohissart, 1974.
Egger, Bruce and Lee MacMillan Otts. *G Company's War: Two personal accounts of the campaigns in Europe, 1944–1945*, University of Alabama Press, Tuscaloosa, Ala., and London, 1992.

Fourny, Paula. *Hiver 1944–1945. Moircy–Jenneville–Bonnerue: Des civils confrontés aux horreurs de la guerre*, Privately published, Libramont, 1995.

Green, Michael and James Brown. *War Stories of the Battle of the Bulge*, Zenith Press, Minneapolis, Minn., 2010.

Greindl, Baroness. *Noël 1944 à Isle la Hesse*, Desclée, De Brouwer, Bruges, 1945.

Guarnere, William and Edward Heffron. *Brothers in Battle, Best of Friends*, Berkley Caliber, New York, 2007.

Hartman, J. Ted. *Tank Driver: With the 11th Armored from the Battle of the Bulge to VE Day*, Indiana University Press, Bloomington and Indianapolis, Ind., 2003.

Heintz, Joss. *Dans le périmètre de Bastogne, décembre 1944 – janvier 1945*, Les Presses de l'Avenir, Arlon, n.d.

Heintz, Joss. *Dans le périmètre de Bastogne, décembre 1944 – janvier 1945* (updated and expanded edition), Musée en Piconrue, Bastogne, 2005.

Heyman, Marshall. *Christmas in Bastogne*, Basyc Publications, Falls Church, Va., 1994.

Houston, Robert. *D-Day to Bastogne: A paratrooper recalls World War II*, Exposition Press, Smithtown, N.Y., 1980.

Irzyk, Albin. *He Rode Up Front for Patton*, Pentland Press, Raleigh, N.C., 1996.

Killblane, Richard. *The Filthy Thirteen*, Casemate, Havertown, Pa., 2003.

Koskimaki, George. *The Battered Bastards of Bastogne: The 101st Airborne in the Battle of the Bulge*, Ballantine Books, New York, 2007.

Lozet-Gustin, Maria. "Journées tragiques de décembre 1944 à Chaumont," *Cahiers de la Haute-Sûre*, 3 (1985), pp. 135–39.

MacKenzie, Fred. *The Men of Bastogne*, David McKay, New York, 1968.

McMorrow, Merle. *From Rome to Berlin via Bastogne*, BookSurge, Charleston, S.C., 2009.

Malarkey, Don. *Easy Company Soldier*, St. Martin's Press, New York, 2008.

Meurisse, André. *De croix noires en étoiles blanches: Un enfant du terroir bastognard se souvient des années 1940–1945*, Cercle d'Histoire de Bastogne, Bastogne, 1994.

O'Brien, Edward. *With Geronimo across Europe: An account of a combat medic in the 501st Parachute Infantry Regiment during World War II*, 101st Airborne Division Association, Sweetwater, Tenn., 1990.

Orianne, Olivier et al. *Un mois en enfer: La bataille des Ardennes en province de Luxembourg*, Weyrich, Neufchâteau, 2005.

Patterson, Eugene. *Patton's Unsung Armor of the Ardennes: The Tenth Armored Division's secret dash to Bastogne*, Xlibris, Bloomington, Ind., 2008.

Patton, George. *War As I Knew It*, W.H. Allen, London, 1947.

Prior, Jack. "Réveillon de Noël 1944 à Bastogne," *Pays de Bastogne*, 4 (October–December 2002), 20–2.

Rivet, Luc and Yvan Sevenans. *La bataille des Ardennes: Les civils dans la guerre*, Didier Hatier, Brussels, 1985.

Sampson, Francis. *Look Out Below! A Story of the airborne by a paratrooper padre*, Catholic University of America Press, Washington, D.C., 1958.

Simms, James. *A Soldier's Armageddon*, Sunflower University Press, Manhattan, Kans., 1999.

True, William and Deryck Tufts True. *The Cow Spoke French: The story of Sgt. William True, American paratrooper in World War II*, Merriam Press, Bennington, Vt., 2002.

War Crimes Commission, Ministry of Justice, Kingdom of Belgium. *War Crimes Committed during von Rundstedt's Counter-Offensive in the Ardennes: Bande*, Georges Thone, Liège, 1945.

Warnaffe, Marie du Bus de. *Journal des tristes jours, 1944–1945*, Cercle d'Histoire de Bastogne, Bastogne, 1994.

Wharton, Patricia. *Reading Between the Lines: A World War II Correspondence, May 1944 – March 1945*, Privately published, Seal Cove, Maine, 1999.

Wilson, Charles. *Frail Children of Dust: From Bastogne to Bavaria with the Fourth Armored Division*, Austin and Winfield, San Francisco, Calif., 1993.

Winters, Dick. *Beyond Band of Brothers: The war memoirs of Major Dick Winters*, Berkley Caliber, New York, 2008.

Internet materials

Lange, Horst. "Auszug aus den Erinnerungen von Horst Lange, damals in der 5. Fallschirmjäger-Division." www.geocities.com/rguy.geo/lange_de.html
Lion-Lutgen, Sophie. "Erinnerungen an die folgenschweren Tage der Rundstedtoffensive: Aus meinem Tagebuch." www.geocities.com/rguy.geo/lutgen.html

Interviews

Author interviews with Paul Maus of the 5th Fallschirmjäger Division in Möderscheid, Belgium, July 20, 1984 and July 25, 1986.

Secondary sources

Allen, Kevin. "The successful use of proximity fuses in the Battle of the Bulge," *Military Heritage*, 12:4 (2011), pp. 14–18.
Ambrose, Stephen. *Band of Brothers*, Simon & Schuster, New York, 2001.
Bando, Mark. *101st Airborne: The Screaming Eagles in World War II*, Zenith Press, St. Paul, Minn., 2007.
Bartov, Omer. *The Eastern Front, 1941–45: German troops and the barbarisation of warfare*, Palgrave Macmillan, Houndmills, UK, 2001.
Beck, Alfred et al. *The Corps of Engineers: The war against Germany*, Center of Military History, Washington, D.C., 1985.
Bell, Raymond. "Black gunners in Bastogne," *Army*, 54:11 (2004), pp. 48–53.
Bertin, François. *La ruée de von Rundstedt à travers nos Ardennes*, Musée de la Parole au Pays de Bastogne, Bastogne, 1988.
Cole, Hugh. *The Ardennes: Battle of the Bulge*, Office of the Chief of Military History, Washington, D.C., 1965.
Coles, Harry and Albert Weinberg. *Civil Affairs: Soldiers become governors*, Office of the Chief of Military History, Washington, D.C., 1964.
Colignon, Alain. "La 'grande bataille d'Ardenne', pour mémoire," *Segnia*, 24 (1999), pp. 265–306.
Craig, Berry. *11th Armored Division Thunderbolts*, vol. II, Turner Publishing, Paducah, Ky., 1992.
Degive, Jacques et al. *La véritable histoire du Sherman de la place McAuliffe à Bastogne*, Cercle d'Histoire de Bastogne, Bastogne, 1999.
D'Este, Carlo. *Patton: A genius for war*, HarperCollins, New York, 1995.
Didier-Robert, Linda. *La mémoire de Sainlez: L'offensive von Rundstedt vécue au village*, Cercle d'Histoire de Bastogne, Bastogne, n.d.
Doubler, Michael. *Closing with the Enemy: How GIs fought the war in Europe, 1944–1945*, University Press of Kansas, Lawrence, Kans., 1994.
Dupuy, Trevor et al. *Hitler's Last Gamble: The Battle of the Bulge*, HarperCollins, New York, 1994.
Eisenhower, John. *The Bitter Woods: The Battle of the Bulge*, Da Capo, Cambridge, Mass., 1995.
Elstob, Peter. *Bastogne: The road block*, Macdonald, London, 1968.
Elstob, Peter. *Hitler's Last Offensive*, Secker and Warburg, London, 1971.
Fox, Don. *Patton's Vanguard: The United States Army Fourth Armored Division*, McFarland, Jefferson, N.C., and London, 2003.
Francard, Michel and Robert Moërynck. *Le mémorial du Mardasson à Bastogne*, Musée de la Parole en Ardenne, Marche-en-Famenne, 2005.

Gaul, Roland. *The Germans*, vol. 1 of *The Battle of the Bulge in Luxembourg*, Schiffer, Atglen, Pa., 1995.

Gianneschi, Dan. *The 362nd Fighter Group History*, Aires Press, Chicago, 1981.

Gooderson, Ian. "Allied fighter-bombers versus German armour in North-West Europe 1944–1945," *Journal of Strategic Studies*, 14:2 (1991), pp. 210–31.

Hofmann, George. *The Super Sixth: History of the 6th Armored Division in World War II*, Sixth Armored Division Association, Louisville, Ky., 1975.

Hoyois, Giovanni. *L'Ardenne dans la tourmente*, J. Dupuis, Marcinelle-Charleroi, 1945.

King, Martin. *L'infirmière oubliée: L'histoire inconnue d'Augusta Chiwy*, Racine, Brussels, 2011.

Lee, Ulysses. *The Employment of Negro Troops*, Center of Military History, Washington, D.C., 1966.

Lefèbvre, Louis. *La bataille de Bastogne*, Bastogne, n.d.

Longue, Matthieu. *Massacres en Ardenne, hiver 1944–1945*, Racine, Brussels, 2006.

MacDonald, Charles. *A Time for Trumpets: The untold story of the Battle of the Bulge*, Quill William Morrow, New York, 1985.

MacDonald, Charles. *The Last Offensive*, Center of Military History, Washington, D.C., 1990.

Maertz, Joseph. *Luxemburg in der Ardennenoffensive 1944/45*, Sankt-Paulus-Druckerei, Luxembourg, 1981.

Mansoor, Peter. *The GI Offensive in Europe: The triumph of American infantry divisions, 1941–1945*, University Press of Kansas, Lawrence, Kans., 1999.

Marquet, Roger. "La bataille pour Bastogne" in Christian Kraft de la Saulx (ed.), *Jours de Sursaut*, vol. 21 of *Jours de Guerre*, Dexia, Brussels, 2001.

Marquet, Roger. *Du sang, des ruines et des larmes: Chenogne, 1944–1945*, Weyrich, Neufchâteau, 2004.

Marshall, S.L.A. *Bastogne: The story of the first eight days*, Infantry Journal Press, Washington, D.C., 1946.

McDonough, James and Richard Gardner. *Skyriders: History of the 327/401 Glider Infantry*, Battery Press, Nashville, Tenn., 1980.

McManus, John. *Alamo in the Ardennes*, John Wiley, Hoboken, N.J., 2007.

Melchers, E.T. *Luxemburg: Befreiung und Ardennen Offensive*, Sankt-Paulus-Druckerei, Luxembourg, 1982.

Melchers, E.T. *Bombenangriffe auf Luxemburg in Zwei Weltkriegen*, Sankt-Paulus-Druckerei, Luxembourg, 1984.

Milmeister, Jean. "Zum Einsatz von Kommandos der deutschen Sicherheitspolizei in Luxemburg während der Ardennenoffensive," *The Bulge*, 2 (2002), pp. 3–9.

Mitchell, Ralph. *The 101st Airborne Division's Defense of Bastogne*, Combat Studies Institute, Fort Leavenworth, Kans., 1986.

Morelock, J.D. *Generals of the Ardennes: American leadership in the Battle of the Bulge*, National Defense University Press, Washington, D.C., 1994.

Munch, Paul. "Patton's staff and the Battle of the Bulge," *Military Review*, 70:5 (1990), pp. 46–54.

Murray, Williamson and Allan Millett. *A War To Be Won: Fighting the Second World War*, Belknap Press of Harvard University Press, Cambridge, Mass., and London, 2000.

Nichols, Lester. *Impact: The battle story of the Tenth Armored Division*, Gateway Press, Louisville, Ky., 1983.

Parker, Danny. "Order of battle" in Charles MacDonald, *A Time for Trumpets: The untold story of the Battle of the Bulge*, Quill William Morrow, New York, 1985.

Parker, Danny. *To Win the Winter Sky: The air war over the Ardennes, 1944–1945*, Combined Books, Conshohocken, Pa., 1994.

Parker, Danny. *Battle of the Bulge: Hitler's Ardennes offensive, 1944–1945*, Da Capo, Cambridge, Mass., 2004.

Pay, Don. *Thunder from Heaven: Story of the 17th Airborne Division, 1943–1945*, Battery Press, Nashville, Tenn., 1980.

Phillips, Robert. *To Save Bastogne*, Stein and Day, New York, 1983.

Presenting . . . The 35th Infantry Division in World War II, 1941–1945, Battery Press, Nashville, Tenn., 1988.

Price, Frank. *Troy H. Middleton: A biography*, Louisiana State University Press, Baton Rouge, La., 1974.

Rapport, Leonard and Arthur Northwood. *Rendezvous with Destiny: A history of the 101st Airborne Division*, 101st Airborne Division Association, n.p., 1965.

Rasqué, Fritz. *Das Oesling im Krieg*, Reprinted (originally published 1946), Éditions Emile Borschette, Christnach, 1991.

Reichelt, Walter. *Phantom Nine: The 9th Armored Division, 1942–1945*, Presidial Press, Austin, Tex., 1987.

Remoel, David. "Battle of the Bulge" in Wesley Craven and James Cate (eds), *Europe: Argument to V-E Day, January 1944 to May 1945*, vol. III of *The Army Air Forces in World War II*, University of Chicago Press, Chicago, 1951.

Rickard, John Nelson. *Advance and Destroy: Patton as commander in the Bulge*, University Press of Kentucky, Lexington, Ky., 2011.

Robert, Linda and Denise Raths. *La mémoire de Sibret*, Cercle Historique de Bastogne, Bastogne, 2003.

Schrijvers, Peter. *The Unknown Dead: Civilians in the Battle of the Bulge*, University Press of Kentucky, Lexington, Ky., 2005.

Senonchamps se souvient, Les Foyans, Senonchamps, 1994.

Smith, Helena. "A few men in soldier suits," *American Heritage*, VIII:5 (1957), pp. 28–31 and 104–05.

Sorley, Lewis. *Thunderbolt: General Creighton Abrams and the army of his times*, Simon & Schuster, New York, 1992.

Toland, John. *Battle: The story of the Battle of the Bulge*, University of Nebraska Press, Lincoln, Nebr., and London, 1999.

Tolhurst, Michael. *Bastogne*, Leo Cooper, Barnsley, UK, 2001.

Umbrell, Shawn. "First on the line: The 35th Engineer Battalion in World War Two and the evolution of a high-performance combat unit," Master's thesis, U.S. Army Command and General Staff College, Fort Leavenworth, Kans., 2009.

Van Straten, James and Lynn Kaufman. "Lessons from Team SNAFU," *Military Review*, 57:5 (1987), pp. 54–63.

Visart de Bocarmé, Anne-Marie. *Mourir à Buchenwald: Vie et mort du gouverneur résistant du Luxembourg René Greindl*, Omer Marchal, Villance-en-Ardenne, 1995.

Weaver, Michael. *Guard Wars: The 28th Infantry Division in World War II*, Indiana University Press, Bloomington and Indianapolis, Ind., 2010.

Weigley, Russell. *Eisenhower's Lieutenants: The campaign of France and Germany, 1944–1945*, Indiana University Press, Bloomington, Ind., 1990.

Winfree, Andrew. *The African American Artilleryman in World War II (ETO): A chronology*, Trafford, Victoria, BC, 2006.

Winton, Harold. *Corps Commanders of the Bulge: Six American generals and victory in the Ardennes*, University Press of Kansas, Lawrence, Kans., 2007.

ILLUSTRATION CREDITS

1, 8, 14, 15, 16 and 26 courtesy of World War II Signal Corps Collection, U.S. Army Military History Institute. 2 and 7 courtesy of Charles MacDonald Papers, U.S. Army Military History Institute. 3 courtesy of George Koskimaki Collection, U.S. Army Military History Institute. 4, 6, 12, 13, 18, 19, 20, 21, 22, 23, 24 and 25 courtesy of William Given Collection, U.S. Army Military History Institute. 5 and 9 courtesy of National Archives (photos 111-SC-222396 and 292623). 10 and 11 courtesy of S.L.A. Marshall Collection, U.S. Army Military History Institute. 17 courtesy of the U.S. Army Heritage and Education Center.

ACKNOWLEDGMENTS

I have been working on this book for a very long time. In fact, I think it would be no exaggeration to say that I have, on and off, been thinking about this brutal battle, paying visits to Bastogne and surroundings, and collecting relevant materials for almost 30 years. I would like to express heartfelt thanks to all who have contributed to this book one way or another in the course of three decades. I apologize for mentioning here only briefly those that stand out most conspicuously among the many others.

At the exemplary U.S. Army Military History Institute in Carlisle, Pennsylvania, extremely rich in American and German sources on the Battle of the Bulge, senior researcher Richard Sommers, now with a white beard after more than 40 years of service, was again exceedingly helpful, as were Melissa Wiford, Shannon Schwaller, and Clif Hyatt. Shaun Illingworth, director of the Rutgers Oral History Archives World War II, was kind enough to grant swift permission for the use of several of the collection's transcribed interviews with American veterans who suffered in the battle for Bastogne.

On the German side, I was fortunate enough to be able to interview, on several occasions and in great detail, Paul Maus, a veteran of the 5th Fallschirmjäger Division, the outfit that bore the brunt of Patton's massive effort to break through to Bastogne. It was Paul Maus who made it possible for me to participate in one of the division's reunions in the 1980s. I gratefully used that unique occasion to listen to the harrowing stories of veterans who would otherwise have been most reluctant to open up to an outsider.

In Belgium, I received significant and enthusiastic support in many different and sometimes unexpected places. The Centre d'Études et de Documentation Guerre et Sociétés Contemporaines in Brussels is exceptionally rich in Allied, German, and Belgian civilian material on the Battle of the Bulge. Director Rudi Van Doorslaer was instrumental in securing a half-year fellowship at the Center in 2012, which allowed me to mine many of the lesser-known sources, as well as take a giant leap forward in my publication schedule. At the Archives et Documentation du Service des Victimes de la Guerre, also in Brussels, Gert De Prins proved extremely efficient in ferreting out relevant sources on the Ardennes from the Belgian Red Cross archives. A word of gratitude also to Christian Kraft de la Saulx, president of the Centre de Recherches et d'Informations sur la Bataille des Ardennes, for his offer of assistance and to the kind people at Bastogne's Syndicat d'Initiative and at the Musée en Piconrue's wonderful exhibition "J'avais 20 ans en 1945 à Bastogne." Very special thanks to Vanessa de Callataÿ, granddaughter of Baroness Greindl, and her husband Stephan for the information they provided and for a charming stay at their castle in Isle-la-Hesse, which served as the headquarters of the 101st Airborne Division in the darkest hours of the battle.

International research is expensive – and even more so when it is conducted from remote Australia. The Faculty of Arts and Social Sciences of the University of New South

Wales in Sydney, where I have been teaching United States history for a decade, has made much of the travel for this book possible with financial help through the Special Studies Program and a Research Project Grant.

Heather McCallum, my superb editor at Yale University Press in London, instantly grasped the potential of a book on the Battle of the Bulge that would focus on the siege of Bastogne and weave into the story the plight of American and German soldiers, as well as Belgian civilians. She has stuck by me ever since, striking that rare balance between unrelenting perfectionism and warm empathy. Thanks also at Yale University Press to associate editor Rachael Lonsdale and to Anne Bihan for her expert management of translation rights. Clive Liddiard, my copy editor, made this a better book, and I thank him for his eagle eye and dry wit.

Much gratitude goes to Caroline Finch in Norfolk for once again agreeing to serve as a gentle and patient gatekeeper for the English language.

My final word of thanks goes to my wife Elle and to my family in Belgium and England. They serve to remind me time and again that in a world capable of extreme cruelty, there is always also much love.

GENERAL INDEX

Abrams, Lt. Col. Creighton 161–6
Acul 192–3, 225
Addor, Pvt. Don 34–5, 51, 63–4, 82
African-American soldiers 58, 98–9, 110, 116, 121, 125, 132, 180, 198, 221
air forces
    Allied 5, 56, 57, 95–6, 99–101, 103–5, 105–6, 114–15, 116, 126, 127, 130, 131–2, 146, 147, 158, 161, 171, 182, 186, 188, 188–9, 190, 201, 219, 230, 237, 238, 246, 250, 252, 268n49
    German 119–20, 121–2, 128, 130, 156, 166, 181–2, 184, 200, 214
alcohol 200, 205
Allen, Lt. George 70–1, 114, 124
Allen, Lt. Col. Ray 98, 124
Allerborn 29–30, 30–1
Allied coalition warfare 2, 68, 168–9
Alsace 201–2, 239
Alzette River 136
American military
    air superiority 5, 56, 57, 95, 99–101, 116, 127, 132, 146, 158, 171, 201
    artillery strength 203, 208, 211, 212–13
    casualties in battle for Bastogne (total) 251–2
    casualties in the Bulge (total) 4
    Civil Affairs 33, 34, 88, 90, 199, 214
    friendly fire 115, 211, 246, 252
    fuel stocks 3–4, 79–80, 132, 171, 201
    industrial strength 3
    inexperience of replacements 144, 174, 174–5, 183, 194
    intelligence failures 2–3, 14–15
    manpower situation 4, 202

    morale 35, 100, 105, 111, 112–13, 117, 173–4, 253–4
    performance comparison with German military 261n9
    relations with British forces 2
    treatment of civilians 186, 198–9, 202, 229
    troops in Bastogne area (total) 6
    troops in the Bulge (total) 3
Anderson, Maj. Morris 232–3
Antwerp 2, 4, 16, 129–30
Arado Ar 234 jet bomber 246
Ardennes
    geographical characteristics 2
    German invasions of 1914 and 1940 2
    width and depth of German breakthrough 3, 228
Arlon 68–9, 235
Arloncourt 131, 211, 212, 215, 216, 236
Arlon highway 81, 168, 188, 190, 206, 215, 252
Arsdorf 139, 146
Assenois 162–6, 199

B-26 Marauder 125–6
Baade, Maj. Gen. Paul 173–4, 233
Bailey bridge 144
Bande 78
Barnes, Lt. Col. Hubert 98–9
Barthelemi, Madeleine 84–5, 128
Bastogne
    aerial supply runs 95–6, 99–101, 116, 127, 132, 171
    air controllers 57, 104–5, 114–15
    American casualties (total) 251–2
    ammunition stocks 79, 101, 116, 171

INDEX OF MILITARY UNITS